Arlene Dahl's Lovescopes

OTHER BOOKS BY ARLENE DAHL

BEYOND BEAUTY

ARLENE DAHL'S SECRETS OF SKIN CARE

ARLENE DAHL'S SECRETS OF HAIR CARE

YOUR BEAUTY SCOPE
(a series of 12 astrological books on beauty)

ALWAYS ASK A MAN

The Astrological Key
to a More Exciting,
Fulfilling Love Life

The Bobbs-Merrill Company, Inc.
Indianapolis/New York

Published by The Bobbs-Merrill Co., Inc.
Indianapolis/New York

First Printing
Designed by Harry Chester Associates.

Library of Congress Cataloging in Publication Data

Dahl, Arlene.
Lovescopes.

1. Astrology. 2. Love—Miscellanea. I. Title.
BF1729.L6D33 1983 133.5'864677 83-6387
ISBN 0-672-52770-7

Manufactured in the United States of America

To my children:

Lorenzo, Carole Christine, and Sonny, who have taught me many lessons of love from their Aquarius, Leo, and Sagittarius love signs

and

to my inspiration:

Marc Rosen, a loving Libran, who gave balance, enthusiasm, and a home to this project.

ACKNOWLEDGMENTS

To Carol Tonsing, my creative Pisces friend, sounding board, astrological partner, and work force: I bow deeply with grateful thanks.

And to those others who have helped me compile my love notes throughout this book, I would like to express my gratitude for their invaluable assistance:

- *Taurean* Bill Adler, who took my dream and gave it substance;
- *Capricorn* Grace Shaw, who put this book into orbit;
- *Scorpio* Barbara Lagowski, who guided *Lovescopes* to completion;
- *Sagittarian* Leonard Franklin, who was the catalyst for this project;
- *Pisces* Diane and Leo Dillon, whose magnificent illustrations captured the spirit of the 12 astrological signs;
  and
- Last, but most important, *Aquarian* Carroll Righter, the master astrologer, my teacher and my friend, without whom this book could not have been written.

May the stars shine upon you!

P.S. — I would also like to thank:

- *Taurean* Lex Barker
- *Capricorn* Fernando Lamas
- *Aquarian* Christian R. Holmes III
- *Sagittarian* Alexis Lichine
- *Aries* Rounsevelle W. Schaum

. . . for their invaluable help in my research.

Contents

Preface

My interest in astrology began when I was in high school in Minneapolis and began to study astronomy. The patterns formed by the stars and the constellations in the heavens fascinated me. The natural offshoot of this interest was astrology.

One day my father brought home an astrology magazine and tossed it on the dining room table. (My father, a Sagittarian, was interested in all aspects of human behavior.) My innate curiosity got the better of me and I eagerly leafed through the pages. Since that day, I've been a student of astrology and have read as much as possible about it.

A few years later, in Hollywood, I met Carroll Righter, the foremost authority on the subject. He became a great friend, as well as my teacher, and advised me from time to time on my career. (He gave up counseling me on my romantic life when I disregarded all his good advice. You see, my heart never read a horoscope!)

Frequently, I consulted him on major career decisions — when I was offered roles in two major motion pictures at the same time and when I was undecided whether I could combine writing with my acting commitments. Then, too, there was the time when I wondered if I should disregard all professional advice and introduce a totally new line of sleepwear in the middle of July. His advice then, as always, was right on target.

Later, when I was interviewing famous personalities in the course of writing my syndicated beauty column, I discovered that there were many others who followed the stars and their astrological cycles.

Although I've always considered myself to be the "captain of my ship," I do consult these cycles whenever I want to launch a new design or undertake a new business venture. It's like crossing the street when the signal says "Go" instead of "Stop."

All three of my beautiful children were born under Sun signs compatible with mine and with other family members. My eldest, Lorenzo Lamas, is an Aquarian, with Cancer rising and Moon in Aquarius. My daughter, Carole Christine Holmes, is a Leo with Libra rising, Moon in Virgo; and my youngest son, Sonny Schaum, is a Sagittarian with Aquarius rising, Moon in Aries. Lorenzo was a natural happening, but I must confess that, with Sonny and Carole, I deliberately chose the date and the hour of their Caesarean births. The result has been a very close, harmonious and mutually supportive relationship among all in the family!

So many of my friends were students of astrology (we all like to know more about ourselves) that I thought it might be fun to include an article combining beauty and astrology in my thrice weekly syndicated column. I introduced this feature early in 1963 and called it "Your BeautyScope." The response was so enthusiastic that I decided to run "Your BeautyScope" on a weekly basis.

The following year, I added an astrological beauty-of-the-month feature, an in-depth portrait of a well-known celebrity — her personal tastes in colors, gems, flowers, perfumes, wardrobe, home furnishings, and *men*.

In 1965, I was asked to write a series of twelve books — one for each sign of the zodiac — based on these popular features. The series was titled *Your BeautyScope*, and the books became so successful that I was asked to revise them ten years later.

With background and accumulated information, I began another project, entitled "Lovescopes," combining *love* and astrology, for cable television. My theory was that, while most of us are fascinated by astrology, *everyone* is interested in love. By combining these two appealing subjects, we can learn more not only about ourselves and our loved ones, but also about those we hope to love. This television series was written, produced and launched successfully last year on the Hearst/ABC Daytime Cable network.

People often ask me if astrology has helped me create my roles on the screen, stage and television. Definitely! For the past two years, I've played the role of the scheming Lucinda on ABC's daytime drama, "One Life To Live." Imagining Lucinda as a Taurus with Scorpio rising, Moon in Leo certainly helped me characterize this flamboyant, materialistic and manipulative fascinator!

This book is a natural outcome of all that I have learned about astrology and love. It should:

- increase your knowledge of yourself as a love partner.
- show you how to bring out your lover's true potential.
- uncover your lover's secret desires and fantasies.
- indicate what makes your lover want you and what will make him or her want you more!

ENJOY!

Introduction

How the stars can help you find your true love and make your love life more exciting and fulfilling

This book centers on the two subjects with which every man and woman is deeply concerned: romance and sex. At the moment of your birth, the Sun, Moon, Venus, Mars, and other planets formed a unique pattern that set you apart from anyone else. The same is true of your love partner. This pattern is called a horoscope. Most astrologers work out a horoscope from your exact time and place of birth to locate the position of the stars, and thus to give you an insight into your true self and analyze your prospects for a happy and successful life. But very few of us live alone. We all act, re-act, and interact with others, happily or unhappily.

I want to help you find your ideal love partner or, if you already have one, to help you understand your mate better and bring out your full love potential together. To do this, you must know how Mars, the planet of active sexuality, and Venus, the key to your affectionate nature, are placed in relation to your respective birth signs, and whether your Sun-and-Moon combination is harnessing the proper emotional tides.

These basic influences cannot be denied. Astrology, when intelligently applied, can help you to recognize your most congenial partners, to develop your sexual skills, and to practice the emotional, psychological, and physical techniques most likely to give you and your partner the utmost satisfaction.

Earlier this year, when I was a part of ABC-TV's "Good Morning New York," many viewers called in with astrological questions like: "I'm a Libran married to an Aries. It was supposed to be wedded bliss, but now it's coming apart at the seams. What should I do?" Or "I'm a Cancer (Ooops, Moon Child) married very happily for thirty-five years to an Aquarian but, according to every astrology book, we're not supposed to get along!" Upon closer scrutiny, I found out that his Moon and Mars were placed in Cancer (her Sun sign) and her Venus was in the same sign as his Aquarius Sun, making their relationship compatible on many levels. (Aquarian President Ronald Reagan for example, gets along splendidly with his lovely Cancer wife, Nancy!)

THE SUN

The Sun is the center of existence. Around its flaming sphere all other planets revolve in perpetual orbits. This body is constantly sending out its beams of light and energy without which no life on earth would be possible. In astrology, it symbolizes everything we are trying to become, the center around which all of our activity in life will always revolve. It is the symbol of our basic nature and describes the natural and constant thread that runs through everything we do, from birth to death, on this planet.

Everything in the horoscope ultimately revolves around this singular body. Although other forces may be prominent in the charts of some individuals, the Sun is the nucleus of our being and symbolizes the complete potential of every living human being. Your essential self, your basic drives, your very nature, all spring from the position of the Sun at the time of your birth.

The possibility for all development is found in the Sun (yours and your partner's), and it marks the character of your personal aura. It symbolizes strength, vigor, ardor, generosity, and the ability to function effectively as a mature individual and a dynamic force in society. At its best, the Sun is the creative consciousness of the gift of life (the undeveloped solar nature is arrogant, pushy, undependable, and proud, and is constantly using force). Our true partner can bring out the best in us if our love complements — and compliments — us!

Your Sun may be the only planet in its particular zodiac sign.* Though you, for example, may have a Libra Sun, your Moon may be in Pisces, your Venus in Taurus, and so forth. Or your Sun could be reinforced in its significance by several other planets placed in the same sign. If a new acquaintance's Sun falls on your Sun sign, you will most likely feel very comfortable with this person, as though you've known each other for years. You should agree on many things and have much in common. You will also admire and understand many of the other person's opinions and qualities. The bonds between you are bound to be strong. This person can have a powerful effect on your life. Except for other aspects within each of your charts (which may be in opposition to your Sun sign), your relationship should be as warm as the Sun itself.

THE MOON

Your emotional reactions depend upon the position of the Moon at the time of your birth. If your Moon is in the same sign as your partner's Sun, this augurs well for a lasting relationship, as you will have a deep emotional bond between you.

The Moon also rules your subconscious. Since all of us make subconscious or emotional decisions in life, a partner's compatible Moon can make for a very strong tie. As a matter of fact, most people in India believe that our Moon sign is more important in charting romance and marriage than the Sun sign. Indian families still plan unions between their children based on this aspect.

*The word *planet* in astrology does not have the same scientific meaning as it does in astronomy. Although the Sun and the Moon are not technically planets, they are astrologically classified that way.

You will instinctively feel friendly and drawn to people whose Moon falls on your Sun. You will be interested and feel protective of each other for reasons you may not be able to explain. This aspect can often be found in the charts of happily married couples. (The Moon stands for the woman in a man's chart.) However, if other aspects in the chart (Sun, Mars, or Venus) are conflicting or opposed, the Moon person's moodiness and emotional demands may aggravate you even though you may understand and sympathize with the causes.

VENUS

Your love nature (your passionate reaction to lovemaking) is ruled by the position of your Venus at birth. Unless your charts are beset by every affliction in the zodiac, you and the person whose Venus falls on your Sun (or vice versa) are going to share a warm passion and love. If other aspects are favorable (Mars, Moon, and Sun), this placement should form the basis for a happy marriage. But even if a love relationship is not involved, someone's Venus on your Sun (or vice versa) still indicates a mutual understanding, warmth and affection.

MARS

The manner in which your energies function depends upon the position of your Mars at birth. This planetary placement indicates physical love. You will never be neutral toward anyone whose Mars falls on your Sun! You can count on a very strong sexual attraction. In all cases, the Mars-ruled tendencies of a friend or lover will have an energizing force on you, pushing you to try harder, do more, be better than you are. If the Mars aspects are afflicted, either squared or in opposition to yours (see Chapter 16), you and your partner could quarrel over this forcefulness, or their domination and interference in your life. If well aspected, you will find the Mars person a courageous inspiration.

THE OTHER PLANETS

The other planets are less important to your Lovescope and work this way:

The planet *Saturn* governs your future. Your ability to respond to change is ruled by *Uranus*. Your creative goals and visions are governed by *Neptune*, while your opinions and judgments are controlled by *Jupiter*. *Mercury* is the planet of practical reasoning (the written and spoken word), while *Pluto*, the latest planet to be discovered, rules the world of politics and ideologies. The history makers are the Big Five: Jupiter, Saturn, Uranus, Neptune, and Pluto — representing the powers of judgment, strategy, change, progress, and beliefs.

Each of these planets will be present in every chart in a different position and relationship (or aspect) to each other. And these variations from chart to chart explain the infinite variations in individuals (even those born under the same Sun sign). Another important influence in a person's chart is the rising sign (or Ascendant), which is the zodiacal sign that was passing over the eastern horizon at the moment of your birth. It is this sign that will modify your *physical* appearance (and approach to life), which may differ from your Sun sign ("Oh, but you don't *look* like a Leo!"). Only if you were born near sunrise would your basic Sun sign and Ascendant be the same — and that circumstance would emphasize the strong physical characteristics of your birth sign. (That's me!)

Following the general descriptions of each of the twelve Sun signs is a Sun-Cast, describing how your lover's birth sign reacts with yours. (There are clouds and sunshine!) Then turn to the chapters on the Moon, Venus, and Mars to learn their special and significant influence on your sign and that of your love partner. Some combinations of signs augur well for long-term love relationships, some should be kept as friendships and some should be avoided at all costs!

The chemistry* between two human beings can overcome nearly anything else, including our sense of reason. If it's strong enough, it can override or cancel out any good advice you may gain from these pages!

However, even if you choose to ignore the old adage, "Forewarned is forearmed," this book will give you the opportunity to discover *why* the relationship didn't work or *why* your action triggered an unwelcome response in your partner.

There are, of course, no two people of any signs who are exactly alike in their responses. Even two people of the same sign may not react the *same* way to a given situation (although the likelihood is good). There is not only the question of free will — which exists in all of us — but also the issue of the Moon, Venus, and Mars's placement in relation to your partner's. Then too, if either you or your partner were born on the cusp, we must also weigh (consider) the power of the approaching sign against how much influence the passing sign has on you (and, therefore, on your partner).

LOVE

Being in love and being loved in return is the most important "happening" in a person's life. Love — the fulfilling kind — is everyone's ideal. Perhaps that is why so many people look to astrology to find their "perfect partner."

But love can mean different things to different people: sex, romance, companionship, acceptance, security, good times. Before entering into a long-term relationship with *anyone,* it is essential to find out how your partner defines love. Hopefully it will be compatible with your definition.

This is why I have written this book . . . to give you an insight into your character and your emotions as well as those of your prospective lover, using the four planets — Sun, Moon, Mars, and Venus — that make up your "Lovescope." They're your key to a more fulfilling love relationship and a happier life.

With this in mind, read on!

*"Sometimes chemistry is just good timing, regardless of the elements!" Anon.

We begin with the element of Fire, which starts the cycle of the zodiac. Fire spreads light, energy, warmth, and drama . . . and so it follows that those born with their major planet, the Sun, in a Fire sign have these glowing characteristics in abundance. And the Fire sign vibrancy that ignites all those around them is only a reflection of their inner flame and deep passion for living.

The three Fire signs are Aries, Leo, and Sagittarius. These are the most dynamic, optimistic, and energetic signs of the zodiac. They are self-involved, volatile types — quick to anger, quick to forgive. They are adventurous, powerful people who act as a source of inspiration for everyone.

Aries (March 21-April 19) is the first Fire sign of the zodiac and ushers in the first day of Spring. It is ruled by the red planet Mars and symbolized by the Ram. Aries is the pioneer of the zodiac, and the courageous Ram likes to be first in everything. Unfortunately, impatient Aries often must learn to complete one task before starting another.

The Aries woman is exciting, enthusiastic, impetuous, and independent. The male Aries is pretty "hot stuff," as well. He's ardent, ambitious, adventurous and temperamental. Both males and females are eager to meet any challenge and want to control every situation. Both have a tendency to fall in love too easily and out of it just as quickly. Typical of the fiery Aries temperament are Warren Beatty and Diana Ross.

The second Fire sign, *Leo* (July 23-August 22), is ruled by the Sun and symbolized by the Lion. They're the royalty of the zodiac and their downfall is often too much pride. They must learn the true meaning of love . . . to tell the difference between love and flattery or they'll be duped and dumped!

The Leo woman loves the spotlight. She's glamorous, regal, affectionate, and a big spender. The Leo man is a great lover . . . generous, proud, possessive. He demands center stage, yet makes an attentive and energetic parent. Both love to be sincerely appreciated. Treat him like a King, her like a Queen — or they'll crown you! Two exemplary regal Leos are George Hamilton and Sally Struthers.

The third Fire sign is *Sagittarius* (November 22-December 21), ruled by Jupiter, the planet of good luck. They're the philosophers of the zodiac. But like their symbol, the Archer, they get right to the point and frank Sags must learn to cultivate diplomacy and tact. The Sagittarius woman is an adventuress, a good sport, and more intellectual than emotional. She'd rather fight for a good cause than cook for her spouse. The Sagittarius man adores beautiful women, especially those with shapely legs. He's daring, passionate, and honest to a fault. These great bachelors of the zodiac are hard to tie down, though. They'll bluntly inform you of their need for freedom, sometimes even on the first date. Both men and women have a great sense of humor, a lifelong case of wanderlust, and an affinity for animals. Typical Sagittarians are Jane Fonda, Frank Sinatra, and Phil Donahue.

A relationship between two people of the same element may be compatible but it is rarely dynamic. Since most of us look for an exciting and challenging mate, we are usually attracted to those whose elements contrast with ours. (This type of relationship will be anything but boring and could be constructive.)

For instance, the dynamic Fire signs, dedicated to keeping their flame alive, could be drawn to practical Earth signs to accomplish their goals (or a partner with an abundance of planets in Earth signs in his or her horoscope). Earth can keep their flame steady, add fuel to their fire . . . or, if essential aspects are incompatible, suffocate the flame. Fire signs must keep their options open and be ready for adventure and excitement. Possessiveness, an emphasis on material possessions, or rigidity of any kind can stifle them. The challenge is to use the strong yet flexible material base of Earth to make more interesting adventures possible, to cope with the details of everyday life, and insure that the projects of ingenious Fire signs run smoothly.

Fire uses Air to fan the flame of their ideas. Fire signs love to dramatize, to take the spotlight, to exaggerate. Air signs add logic, a balanced objective view. The danger here is too much "hot air" — a combination that sparks much enthusiastic sales talk but no action! (Fire signs are wonderful salesmen and communicators . . . making ideas come to radiant life, boldly rushing in where others fear to tread, sometimes with good reason!)

The emotions of Fire signs can be kindled by a partner who plays on their strong sense of fantasy. They often look for a mate of heroic stature, who cannot possibly exist. The creativity of the Water signs provides a wonderful stage setting for the drama of Fire; sensitive Water signs tune in to Fire's fantasy, stoke Fire's ego, and get the romance off to a steamy start. But too much water can douse the flame: there's a difference between emotional depth and a tidal wave!

We are both student and teacher to our lovers, in the ways we complement or conflict with each other's elements. Each sign must confront its need for balance with the other elements in order to grow and reach its full love potential.

1 HOT STUFF ARIES

March 21-April 19

Aries falls in love with a deafening crash, for better or worse. Since Rams don't develop good judgment until they've made a few mistakes, you can expect to have an on-again, off-again love life in your earlier years. Indeed, some elusive Aries prefer to play the game of love indefinitely (Hugh O'Brian and Marlon Brando come to mind) never enjoying the prize for long.

You Aries were born under the Fire sign ruled by Mars, the power house of the zodiac, the giver of sexual energy, and the most dynamic of planets. You're an action-packed dynamo, with great drive and enthusiasm. Your special lesson is to use that drive constructively. In love, you must learn to channel your great energy to give greater pleasure to everyone. (No one can charge others' sexual batteries like you!)

You love adventure and chancing the unknown. (Both heroes of the hit television series *Star Trek* were played by Arians — William Shatner as Captain Kirk and Leonard Nimoy as Mr. Spock.) Aries will leap into a love affair, rushing headlong into the experience, never fearing the consequences. Sometimes you get burned, especially when you fail to heed good advice. (Here's where astrology can serve as a roadmap to forecast the pleasures, or warn of treacherous terrain ahead.)

You're capable of meeting any challenge, especially when you've learned a bit of self-control, patience, and respect for the opinions of others. Any lover will appreciate your inventiveness (you do love to try new positions), your enthusiasm (you're *always* ready), and your sunny good humor!

Underneath that radiant self-confidence, however, there could be a tiny bit of insecurity. You might never admit it, but I'll bet you long for a loyal, devoted mate who's going to put YOU first in his or her life. Your ideal lover must also be a continual challenge (to earn your respect) and a safe harbor for your restless spirit. Sound impossible? Just ask Arians Gloria Steinem or Warren Beatty.

THE ARIES/PISCES CUSP
(March 18-23)

A steamy combination of Water and Fire, you're both a dreamer and a doer. The sensitivity of Pisces meets the dynamic energy of Aries in your cusp placement, endowing you with extra empathy and a double dose of charisma. Your magnetism draws people to you — but you don't *have* to let emotions take over every time! If you don't let your feelings muddle your goals, you can accomplish much. And with Pisces creativity and Aries inventiveness, you could be a fun playmate!

THE ARIES/TAURUS CUSP
(April 18-23)

One of the zodiac's true hedonists, you've got Aries drive plus Taurus determination and practicality, bringing lots of life's goodies your way! You're smoothly sensual and know how to give volcanic pleasure to your lover. The materialist in you will help you to collect and show off your treasures in the best of taste. Your anger can be your Achilles' heel, however. Though slower to be aroused than most Aries, once ignited, the explosion is atomic, sending everyone scurrying for shelter!

THE HOT STUFF ARIES MAN

He's a man with a temper, though a true romantic as well. He'll search for years for the ideal partner and when he finds her, he'll promptly put her on a pedestal. (She'll need very good balance to stay there.) He appreciates a beautiful woman with many talents and varied interests, one who is clever enough to match wits with him.

He's a stickler for doing the right thing at the right time. He detests lying or deception of any kind and will never forgive it in a woman. Although he's an exacting and demanding creature, he's the kind of man most women prefer as a lover or a husband . . . distinguished, proud, faithful (once caught), and very passionate.

HOW TO MAKE HIM NOTICE *YOU*

- Don't make his conquest too easy. The Aries man loves a challenge, so play a little hard to get.
- Fire-engine red is the Aries "turn-on" color. Always wear a touch of it somewhere interesting.
- Make him feel important. This is a man who needs a lot of ego stroking. Whatever you do, don't flirt with other men or talk about your past . . . he's the jealous type.
- Aries men have a lot of energy and love sports (indoor and outdoor). It

helps if you're good at both. But remember, SHARE his hobbies, don't compete with him!

- The Aries man is very honest and lays all cards on the table. It's best to be up front with him, too! He detests double dealing.
- Aries are animal lovers . . . so make sure that Fido and you become good friends . . . bring along some dog biscuits to make sure!
- Don't keep him waiting . . . Aries men are very impatient!
- Get interested in his career. This is good advice for impressing *any* man . . . but Aries will expect it. He'll also count on you to entertain his business friends graciously with little or no notice, and understand those long business trips.

HIS LESSONS TO LEARN

- Happy hunting! Aries is famous for loving the pursuit more than the conquest. Learn to savor your prize for a long time.
- Stoke her fires, too! "Me-first" Aries must learn to share, both in bed and out. Develop sensitivity and consideration and use your great inventive skills to help HER blossom. (Read her Sun sign's characteristics to help her reach her full love potential.) That way, you'll *both* have more pleasure!
- Cool that temper. (Learn to compromise — you can't have your own way *all* the time.)
- Court her friendship: respect her goals and ideas (but don't be patronizing).
- Fan the flame in bed. Your partner may not be as energetic as you are. Take time to explore her full potential. (Her planetary placements will give you important clues. Venus in Aries, for instance, would give you a sensational sparring contest. Moon or Mars in Scorpio will explore your kinkier side. Another Aries Sun sign will want to top you every time!)

THE ARIES WOMAN . . . COMING ON STRONG!

She's a take-charge woman who can stop traffic. She's as assertive as Bette Davis, sunny as Doris Day, energetic as Ann Miller, and as optimistic as Debbie Reynolds. She's born to give orders (but has to learn when to stop!).

She's clean-cut and straightforward. Although she loves to flirt (subtle maneuvers are not her style), she prefers a dramatic confrontation to get her way. She was the original liberated woman, in the person of Cleopatra. Her energetic personality makes friends and she acquires new beaus with considerable ease, but she's likely to discard them just as quickly — unless they are the Mark Antony type — super-strong-willed and masterful.

As magnetic as the female Aries is, she sometimes has difficulty sustaining her red-hot love affairs. She's more successful portraying the dynamic career woman (and often makes her home an office). In love, she plays the romantic heroine, surmounting great obstacles to win her man (though the obstacles sometimes are of her own making).

She loves to take the initiative, make the phone calls, decide where to dine and what play to see. Although she has a lot of charm, there are few men who will appreciate her taking the lead for any length of time. (The man who won't object, won't appeal to her for long!)

She needs a lover who can match her dynamic personality. They may have a marriage full of verbal (and physical) duels, but she enjoys this kind of sparring. The Aries woman thrives in an atmosphere of conflict, provided, of course, that love conquers all in the end.

She is intensely jealous and explodes if she feels someone is stealing her thunder (or her man). However, she is rarely as good an actress in bed as out of it. She is a receiver rather than a giver and would much prefer to be dramatically "taken" than made love to. She is never quite sure to what extent "the actress" conceals "the real woman." The man who strips away her disguise, overpowers and reveals her inner self, will dominate.

HOW TO "TURN ON" THE ARIES WOMAN

- Give her lots of affection, not criticism! The Aries woman comes on strong, but she needs moral support.
- Be romantic . . . she loves adventure. Think up some new never-before things to do!
- Take her to exotic places . . . she's just the one to share a jungle safari, an Alaskan fishing trip or a visit to the Seychelles Islands.
- Take her to a restaurant with exotic, spicy food. It's a great prelude to a spicy evening elsewhere.
- She's got energy to burn, so don't try to tie her down.
- She's not the ethereal type . . . so give her something solid to grab!
- Make her feel as if she's the first . . . and certainly the last love of your life!
- Treat her to a new hair-style, cut, and color.
- Give her something red . . . roses, rubies, your heart!

HER LESSONS TO LEARN

- Be a steady flame — not a flicker! (Aries women love change for its own sake.) There's a big difference between motion and action, so use your famous energy where it really counts!
- Don't always go for broke! Save your dollars (and *his*) for a rainy day.
- Learn to interact with your lover . . . instead of taking over.
- Curb your tongue. (Develop its *other* talents!) Learn to listen . . . you might hear something worthwhile.
- Develop patience. It's what you achieve in the long run that counts!
- Don't neglect your image. Always in a hurry, Aries sometimes forgets those finishing touches so important to good grooming.

YOUR ARIES SUN-CAST

With celebrity couples and romantic pairings . . . for better or for worse . . . from the screen, stage, television, and real life!

WITH AIR SIGNS: Your natural Aries charm and persuasiveness help you make warm friends easily. Associations with the Air signs — Libra, Gemini, and Aquarius — are particularly good for you. Like you, they overflow with enthusiasm and original ideas. An added benefit — they tend to think things over FIRST!

GEMINI-ARIES

Joan Collins and Warren Beatty

SMILING SUN: With scintillating Geminis, you'll never be bored. They're a constant challenge and love intrigue and fun even more than you do. You'll have a wonderful, inventive time in and out of bed.

CLOUDS: You might be Number One with Gemini, but the chances are you won't be the one and only! Geminis are fickle and not known for fidelity. They're the gay gadabouts! Their kicks are mental — and that means all kinds of games — some of them a bit kinky. Straight-arrow Arians may find traffic-directing in the bedroom not to their liking. Can be a bit hard on the ego.

LIBRA-ARIES

Yves Montand and Simone Signoret

SMILING SUN: You'll find the perfect playmate here. Loving Librans are sexy, as flirtatious as you are, good-looking, and so charming! You're both social animals who love a good time. Level-headed Librans are diplomatic; they take the edge off Aries's bluntness, make you more tolerant, yet let you do your own thing.

CLOUDS: Libras are butterflies who can't be pinned down. Aries's rudeness can turn them off fast, while a Libran lover's indecision and passiveness could drive Aries to distraction — elsewhere. You hate to be kept waiting. Fiery Aries likes a good battle, but Librans won't stand and fight. They avoid confrontations at all costs!

AQUARIUS-ARIES

Farrah Fawcett and Ryan O'Neal
Mia Farrow and André Previn

SMILING SUN: You can share exciting adventures with people born under this innovative, freedom-loving sign. And they'll give you plenty of space for your flights of fantasy. When you share the same cause, this is a sure winner.

CLOUDS: Aries needs lots of attention and Aquarius people are just too busy with yoga classes, political crusades, or graduate degrees to be there when you need them. They can be a bit detached in bed and sometimes might prefer their oddball friends to cuddling with YOU.

WITH OTHER FIRE SIGNS: As long as someone keeps adding the logs, you can keep the home fires burning!

ARIES-ARIES

Warren Beatty and Julie Christie
Clare Boothe Luce and her Henry

SMILING SUN: Here's someone who can really keep your hectic pace and play all the romantic roles you can dream up. This could be the soulmate you've been looking for! You'll both protect and defend each other . . . and be a constant challenge. You'll never be bored!

CLOUDS: This mixture is often too hot to handle. You're both jealous types who can't stand anyone to curb your freedom. And when you both want to be "first," someone (or something) has to give. Better decide who's going to be boss in the beginning!

LEO-ARIES

Eddie Fisher and Debbie Reynolds
Linda Ronstadt and Jerry Brown
Ginny and Henry Mancini

SMILING SUN: Together you explode with energy. You're both outgoing, magnetic, a real challenge to each other. Super-hot in bed. A fun couple!

CLOUDS: You both want center stage and when these two egos clash, the force is nuclear. Too much fire could burn this one out, unless you learn not to compete.

SAGITTARIUS-ARIES

My father and mother
Douglas Fairbanks, Jr., and Mary Pickford

SMILING SUN: Jovial Sag is a fellow hunter who loves to prowl with you. This could be your luckiest Fire-sign gamble. You're both impetuous, romantic idealists who love to travel. You positively ignite in bed, and usually give each other lots of space to develop individually.

CLOUDS: You may not like living on the edge ALL the time. Sags put their interests first, are blunt and have a temper. They will not provide you with too much financial or emotional security — after all, they've got adventures of their own to pursue. But it's still a great bet!

WITH WATER SIGNS: Whether Water signs are wet blankets or whether you generate a lot of steam together depends on your willingness to see *their* point of view!

CANCER-ARIES

Former President Gerald Ford
and his Betty

SMILING SUN: This intuitive sign knows just what you want in bed. Their business acumen could also provide the cash to finance your dreamier schemes. And you both make super parents.

CLOUDS: Cancers, both male and female, love to mother their lovers . . . and can often *smother* them in so doing. Cancer likes cozy evenings at home . . . Aries leaps out of the hearth. Cancers voice their complaints loudly . . . Aries *runs* from guilt trips.

SCORPIO-ARIES

Robert Kennedy and his Ethel
Rock Hudson and Doris Day in *Pillow Talk*

SMILING SUN: You two Mars-ruled signs hypnotize each other in bed. You generate cosmic power together, and deserve each other's genuine admiration for bravery, courage and stamina. A delicious challenge!

CLOUDS: The power play could become a real tug of war. Neither likes to surrender on any issue. Both of you are *possessive* of each other, demanding freedom for *yourself* . . . and both are overly jealous. Careful!

PISCES-ARIES

Ursula Andress and
Jean-Paul Belmondo

SMILING SUN: Languid Pisces loves your energy and knows just how to make you feel on top of the world. You happily feed each other's egos and instinctively complement each other.

CLOUDS: Pisces may be a bit too mysterious for you . . . you're never quite sure of what they *really* think and sometimes stomp on their tender feelings without even knowing it! Then they turn on the waterworks or take an impromptu sail, which dampens your spirit and makes you feel lonely.

WITH EARTH SIGNS: You shake up solid Earth signs and put some *fun* in their life! They give you some much-needed stability and organization!

TAURUS-ARIES

Anouk Aimee and Albert Finney
Constance Towers and John Gavin
Berry Berenson and Tony Perkins

SMILING SUN: Taurus could provide the stable launching pad for Aries's dreams. Their sensuality in bed is another plus. You shine a bright new light in Taurus's too predictable life.

CLOUDS: Taurus can't be bossed or pushed. You must learn *patience*. Don't play with the Taurus temper, either. Yours is a *flash-fire*. Though slow to start, theirs is an *earthquake* with enough power to bring about devastating damage.

VIRGO-ARIES

Ingrid Bergman and Gregory
Peck in *Spellbound*

SMILING SUN: Reserved Virgos are a challenge to Aries. They'll love to put your house in order. You'll help them live out some of their exotic fantasies. You're both idealists, honest and loyal.

CLOUDS: With cash . . . you're *open-handed*, while Virgos are *tight-fisted*! Their nagging criticism could spoil your spontaneous fun (they like to plan ahead). They also like to point out life's pitfalls. Your overconfidence could irritate them. So could your casual approach to fashion. (Virgo is the zodiac's neatnik.)

CAPRICORN-ARIES

Diane Keaton and Warren Beatty in *Reds*

SMILING SUN: You two hard-workers could climb a long way together. Capricorn works for *money* and status; Aries works for *glory*. You both improve with age. (Capricorn makes you grow up!) A lusty, sexy partnership.

CLOUDS: Capricorn may have a prudish side, which smothers your passionately inventive flame. You hate to be tied down, while Capricorn needs stability and pushes for solid results.

OTHER FAMOUS ARIES PERSONALITIES

WOMEN

Bette Davis
Joan Crawford
Billie Holiday
Ali McGraw
Sandra Day O'Connor
Diana Ross
Erica Jong
Pearl Bailey
Ethel Kennedy
Clare Boothe Luce
Mary Pickford
Gloria Swanson
Anita Bryant
Julie Christie
Aretha Franklin
Barbi Benton
Jane Powell
Simone Signoret
Ann Miller
Debbie Reynolds
Doris Day
Betty Ford
Marsha Mason
Virginia Knauer

MEN

Gregory Peck
Marlon Brando
James Caan
Richard Chamberlain
Francis Ford Coppola
Elton John
Wayne Newton
Harry Reasoner
Stephen Sondheim
David Frost
Peter Ustinov
Omar Sharif
Tennessee Williams
Alec Guinness
Merle Haggard
Henry Luce
Anthony Perkins
Rod Steiger
André Previn
James Garner
Hugh Hefner
Ryan O'Neal
Warren Beatty
William Shatner
Leonard Nimoy
Hans Christian Andersen
Otto von Bismarck
Jerry Brown
Wernher von Braun
Charlie Chaplin
Casanova
Clarence Darrow
Robert Frost
Vincent van Gogh
Harry Houdini
Henry James
Thomas Jefferson
Nikita Khrushchev
Steve McQueen
General George Patton
Paul Robeson
Leopold Stokowski
Spencer Tracy
Lowell Thomas
Arturo Toscanini
Henry Mancini
Wilbur Wright

CELEBRITY COUPLES AND ROMANTIC PAIRINGS

Betty Ford (Aries) and Gerald Ford (Cancer)
Marsha Mason (Aries) and Neil Simon (Cancer)
Clare Boothe Luce (Aries) and Henry Luce (Aries)
Simone Signoret (Aries) and Yves Montand (Libra)
Spencer Tracy (Aries) and Katharine Hepburn (Scorpio)
Gregory Peck (Aries) and Veronique Passani (Aquarius)
Steve McQueen (Aries) and Ali McGraw (Aries)
Ryan O'Neal (Aries) and Farrah Fawcett (Aquarius)
André Previn (Aries) and Mia Farrow (Aquarius)
Warren Beatty (Aries) and Julie Christie (Aries)
Anthony Perkins (Aries) and Berry Berenson (Taurus)
Omar Sharif (Aries) and Barbra Streisand (Taurus) in *Funny Girl*
Marlon Brando (Aries) and Vivian Leigh (Scorpio) in *Streetcar Named Desire*
Denise Hale (Aries) and Prentiss Hale (Leo)
William Shatner (Aries) and Leonard Nimoy (Aries) in *Star Trek*
Henry Mancini (Aries) and his Ginny (Leo)

LUCKY ARIES PLACES TO BE

Canada
Ireland
Denmark
Germany
England
Puerto Rico

2
LEO—THE ROYAL ROMANTIC

July 23-August 22

Leos are the actors and actresses of the zodiac, ruled by the Sun — the most powerful of all cosmic influences in astrology — and symbolized by the proud, courageous lion. If all the world's a stage, as Shakespeare said, you will always find a Leo playing a leading role with solar flair!

Leos revel in the spotlight and know almost instinctively what their "audience" wants and how to please them. They are creative and imaginative and can capture the public's imagination and hold it for years (like Mae West!).

The power of the Sun can burn or warm those it shines upon. Leos inspire fierce loyalty among their friends and envy among others. Wise Leos are careful to control their appearances, taking the spotlight only when they choose and maintaining a low profile at other times (often hiding behind huge "shades" like Jacqueline Onassis and Mick Jagger).

After too much public glare, Leos need to retreat, to be silent and alone, to revitalize . . . forsaking chic French restaurants for quiet coffee shops, or better yet, going off to a sunny retreat.

Although you Leos are creative, you also know how to use the talents of others . . . this gift makes you born leaders. You inspire others to achieve more than they ever dreamed possible (like John Derek with his Bo). This characteristic is particularly appreciated by your sexual partners! You rarely waste time . . . your methods are simple, straightforward, and to the point. ("Why don't you come up and see me sometime?")

Leos adore to be adored . . . and to be in *love*. They are greatly disappointed when things don't work out, often tolerating a less than ideal union because their great pride hates to admit defeat in anything.

Leos are productive and restless, with a curiosity and quest for knowledge that drives them on to greater accomplishments. Marriage is never enough for Leos at home — they are always looking for dramatic roles in the social sphere. You'll find them entertaining the town's leading citizens, shining at the local country club, or ensconced anywhere the elite gather. Even the Leo on a leash seems determined to carve out a special identity, a memorable image apart from his or her mate.

Leos love passion and intrigue and usually find it, or create enough drama to satisfy their theatrical style. But when they finally do give their hearts to someone, they're loyal, loving, and faithful.

What do Leos like most? Recognition and romance. But sometimes Lions get their manes tangled with a lot of flattery. (Leos love to be stroked in the right place at the right time . . . and sometimes at the wrong time!) Leos are very persuasive . . . they can sell anything to anybody if they *believe* in it. You can always tell a Leo — but you can't tell them much!

Leo is the most generous sign of the zodiac. Making others happy makes Leos happy, too. They hate anything petty in people or situations. Their regal tastes often carry quite a price tag. This could be a problem if a Leo's mate is a close-fisted Virgo or Capricorn. Leo wants the best of everything and usually gets it! Former First Lady Jacqueline Onassis indulged her taste for the finest in refurbishing the White House and her wardrobe. (The latter became a cause célèbre.)

THE LEO/CANCER CUSP
(July 21-26)

Your heart is on your sleeve! The intuitiveness and emotion of moon-ruled Cancer combines with Leo's solar flair . . . and the effects can be dazzling. Your sensitive Cancerian side picks up on just what your audience wants while your Leo magnetism attracts and keeps a following. You care passionately about everything you do, and therefore, accomplish your pet projects efficiently and with panache. You have an eye for power and excellent innate leadership abilities. Some of you may seem shy and retiring, but under the surface, you're waiting for the perfect chance to strut your stuff. I'll bet your home is spectacular . . . with Cancer's nesting instinct plus Leo's dramatic flair for decor.

THE LEO/VIRGO CUSP
(August 21-26)

When Virgo shrewdness tempers extravagant Leo ways, a winning business combination is the result. During off hours, you seek out only the best, but temper those regal tastes by buying at the best price. You look for a powerful mate who will help you up the social ladder; but be careful not to be too demanding of your partner. You're very communicative and a good writer — why not write it down while you're living it up for fun and profit in later years! And, with your erotic sense of fantasy, your sweetheart will wait by the mailbox for X-rated missives.

THE LEO MAN

Leo men are usually strong masculine types who do things in a *big* way. They're the high rollers . . . at home in Texas, Las Vegas, or Monte Carlo. The Leo man is generous to a fault (sometimes his magnanimous instincts wreak havoc with his paycheck). He wants the very best for himself and those he loves. He'll take you first class all the way (even when he can't afford it!).

The Leo man expects life to revolve around him and won't tolerate sharing the spotlight (a problem for career-minded lady executives). He has a great need to be king and to rule the roost. (Be sure there's a comfortable throne ready for him every night.) He has presence, confidence, and great style. His warm and sunny disposition makes him a joy to live with and love.

HOW TO CAPTURE A LEO KING OF HEARTS

- Keep him center stage in your life. And always give him good reviews.
- He's very generous and loves to entertain. (He also loves to pick up checks in restaurants, so keep some cash stashed away for a taxi ride home.)
- Look your most glamorous. Leos love a beautiful, elegant "quiet" leading lady. She mustn't be heard above his roar!
- Develop your hidden talents. He'll love to show you off.
- Make your bedroom sensuous with soft lights, fur throws, perfumed sheets and lots of mirrors.
- Plan a vacation in the sun together. Leo is ruled by the Sun and he loves to get a tan. Rome, Colorado, and Hawaii are super Leo-ruled places for that rendezvous.
- Sunny colors like yellow, gold, orange, and coral please him. And for evening drama, try gold lamé!
- Wear a subtle perfume with potent power . . . like a rose and jasmine blend.
- He likes a bit of mystery, too . . . the feeling that he's discovering you for the first time. Behave like a queen, gracious and regal, and you'll be treated royally.

HIS LESSONS TO LEARN

- Learn the difference between praise and flattery! You don't need to hear *every day* that you're the greatest, the best, the handsomest, the most charming!
- Listen to others occasionally. You don't have to make the major decisions all the time. (The Leo man must watch that he doesn't become too rigid and one-sided.)
- Learn to save and plan ahead financially. You make and lose money rapidly. Your extravagant nature can actually *resent* money in the bank (after all, it could be buying you and yours a few of the finer things in life).
- Learn to accept gifts graciously, as well as give them.
- Learn how to relax and refill. It's important to your health and well-being.

THE LEO WOMAN

A Leo woman stands out in the crowd. You can't mistake her because she has a flair for the dramatic and a regal bearing that sets her apart. Leos combine authority with elegance.

Since the Leo woman is gracious and warm, she revels in large crowds and is never happier than when dashing from party to party with a group of sparkling companions.

She's incurably romantic and idealistic, a dreamer who does her best to make her (and your) dreams come true. She is attracted to unusual, dynamic men, who are sometimes slightly eccentric (she loves a challenge). Sometimes there is a terrific clash of temperament in these alliances, a conflict of egos, ambitions, and goals. Stubbornly, she will try over and over again through many love affairs (and marriages) to find the one man who will bring her happiness and fulfillment (Leo hates to admit defeat). It takes time for her to know herself well enough to choose the kind of man who can make her happy and with whom she'll be in complete harmony.

When she has finally found "Mr. Right," her affectionate and passionate nature makes her a wonderful mate.

HOW TO MAKE YOUR LEO LADY SHINE WITH PLEASURE!

- Leos expect the best . . . so take them first class.
- They love yellow roses and tiger lilies for birthdays, anniversaries — or just any old day.
- Pay attention to your appearance. They love good-looking, well-dressed men.
- Give Leos lots of affection . . . they'll return it tenfold!
- Anything gold is sure to catch their eye.
- Enjoy Leo's wild side and don't try to tame them.
- The Lioness is not a domestic kitten, though she does purr when stroked in the right places. (She loves to make love on a fur rug.)
- Take her to the presidential suite of an elegant hotel for a lunchtime rendezvous.
- Canary diamonds and cabochon rubies are guaranteed to put a sparkle in her eyes.
- Meet her at the airport in a Rolls-Royce with a bottle of vintage champagne. (You may never make it home!)
- Leos love to delegate minor chores. Why not give her a maid or secretary once a week!
- When the Lioness roars, wait until the mood passes. She will never carry a grudge or seek revenge.
- And love them, love them, love them!

HER LESSONS TO LEARN

- Develop a sincere interest in others. You're a born leader and can bring out the best in others, but you must also appreciate THEIR feelings, desires, and aspirations.
- Let the sun shine through. Although you're basically an extrovert, the warmth of your personality doesn't always come through on first meeting. You may even appear cold and aloof, communicating a haughtiness that can be detrimental to your career and personal relationships.
- Give others space to live and operate. Do not try to impose your will on those you love.
- Guard against ostentation. With your penchant for posh things, you could be tempted to buy a sable on a beaver income. This could lead to financial disaster. It can also make a false impression on your friends and associates and drive your lover to distraction!

YOUR LEO SUN-CAST

With celebrity couples and romantic pairings . . . for better or for worse . . . from the stage, screen, television, and real life.

WITH OTHER FIRE SIGNS: You're both determined to get what you want. Just be sure you want the same things!

ARIES-LEO

Henry Mancini and his Ginny
Tony Mann and Rhonda Fleming
Debbie Reynolds and Eddie Fisher

SMILING SUN: A *red-hot* romance! Just be sure to bank the fire so it lasts. You're both energetic and confident, with real star-quality. If there's enough room on stage, you've got a hit!

CLOUDS: You're both self-centered and hate to take orders (though you love to give them). Your quarrels could be fierce and frequent. Aries always wants to be FIRST . . . and so do you. Both of you must learn to take turns.

LEO-LEO

Senator Robert Dole (Cancer/Leo cusp) and Elizabeth Hanford Dole, Secretary of Transportation

SMILING SUN: A powerful couple, the two of you can light up the skies together. You'll each rule over your own territory and glory in each other's success, having found a worthy mate to share your throne. In bed, you're the most joyous pair in the jungle.

CLOUDS: Here are two stars, but one stage! Each must learn when to play the lead. Remember, "There are no small parts, only small actors!" (Lee Strasberg).

SAGITTARIUS-LEO

Lillian Russell and "Diamond Jim" Brady

SMILING SUN: Most Leos are confident enough to handle this gregarious Fire sign who loves wine, women, and song. You're both high-rollers who love jet-set glitter. You're a warm-hearted companion to the jovial Sag, who joins in the fun and makes the party happen!

CLOUDS: Sag may not be around long enough to give you the attention you need (and deserve!). You are both *open-handed* and open-hearted, so you may have to count on lucky Jupiter to pull your Sag through his gambling sprees.

WITH AIR SIGNS: Your regal charisma draws sociable Air signs to you like moths to a flame. They'll bask if those sweet words are for your ears only . . . they'll burn if they don't curb those flirtatious ways. You've got to be Number One, *always!*

GEMINI-LEO John F. Kennedy and Jacqueline

SMILING SUN: Sparkling Gemini delights you with good humor and ready wit. They're never boring, in bed or out! You love their style and finesse (they know something about everything). They love to entertain (you could be the perfect co-stars).

CLOUDS: Mercurial Geminis go off on tangents; they find it difficult to concentrate on one thing at a time. They need you to give them direction. They're not known for fidelity, either. You'll have to curb your possessive nature and learn to live with their flirtations. Don't look for deep emotions, strong sustenance, or a peaceful co-existence in this pairing. Opt for variety and mental stimulation instead.

LIBRA-LEO Former President Jimmy Carter and his Rosalynn

SMILING SUN: As sociable as you are, Librans could *pair* with you as well as *party*. Their talent for peacemaking could keep the Lion tamed. They'll bring you the perfect gift, create a beautiful home, and provide you with a luxurious setting in which to radiate!

CLOUDS: You're both extravagant; someone has to watch the cash flow *carefully*. Libra loves to flirt and may not give you the total concentration you require (in fact, Librans could be a touch too critical at times). Since they are constantly weighing and balancing, you may have to make most of the decisions.

AQUARIUS-LEO Helen Gurley Brown and David Brown
Burt Reynolds and Loni Anderson
Baroness Sandra and Baron Enrique di Portanova

SMILING SUN: They're a bit *cool* emotionally, but you've got enough firepower for you both! You love Aquarius's brilliant mind (and famous friends). They're sure to get attention for their humanitarian causes or political rallies. And, they'll intrigue you with some sexy experiments in bed.

CLOUDS: Aquarius is everyone's pal . . . but their work is sure to take first place in their lives, not you! You may find it hard to get them *alone*. If you can be tolerant and push them ahead in their career (and handle the money), this could work. However, Aquarians tend to get so wrapped up in public causes that they forget the more personal things in life . . . remind them!

WITH EARTH SIGNS: Your radiant charm brightens the life of hard-working Earth signs. You're both lusty and ambitious . . . but watch how you spend your energies . . . so you'll both profit!

TAURUS-LEO Bianca and Mick Jagger
Alana and George Hamilton

SMILING SUN: Sensual Taureans can give you hours of delight in bed. They'll love the beautiful, luxurious home which you'll provide. Taurus will promote your grand schemes so that they'll bring in cash. You'll appreciate Taurus's loyalty and devotion.

CLOUDS: The Bull may be a bit slow or downright *stubborn* in reacting to your enthusiastic ideas (especially when it comes to parting with cash). You *love* to shine on the social scene, but Taurus is extremely possessive and will want you to shine for him or her alone. (They do love to show you off, though . . . but no touching, or the Bull will charge!) Don't rush Taureans . . . if you push them too hard, they'll trample everyone and everything in sight — including you.

VIRGO-LEO

Greta Garbo and Robert Taylor in *Camille*

SMILING SUN: You appreciate Virgo's attention to details (you hate to be bothered with them). And you sense that, under that cool exterior lies a *hot* fantasy life for you alone to uncover. Virgo gives you much attention and warm-hearted concern.

CLOUDS: Virgo's picky criticisms can cloud your sunny nature. And your luxury-loving side balks under Virgo's close scrutiny of the budget. Still, you could cash in on this combo!

CAPRICORN-LEO

George Burns (Capricorn/Aquarius cusp) and Gracie Allen

SMILING SUN: Ambitious and distinguished Capricorns make *impressive* partners for regal Leos. You're both lusty in bed (though Capricorn may hide this under a very proper surface). Capricorns love to move in the world of power . . . just like you! And their plans have such a solid basis that they're sure to succeed and gain recognition. A very appealing match.

CLOUDS: Capricorn's melancholy moods depress you, while your extravagant ways drive Caps crazy! Capricorn is so devoted to the pursuit of success that you may be overlooked or overshadowed. Still, it's worth a try.

WITH WATER SIGNS: They are sensitive to all your desires and know how to stroke you in just the right places! It could be purrrr-fect if you can deal with their torrents of tears and heavy emotional nature without getting drowned.

CANCER-LEO

Barbara Stanwyck and Robert Taylor
Josephine and Napoleon
Lynn Marshall and Prince Egon von Furstenburg

SMILING SUN: Sexy, perceptive Cancers know just how to touch your warm Leo heart. They make you feel so important to them. And they pamper you. You give them confidence. They have a talent for money — earning and saving it — *that* you need! This Sun- and Moon-ruled combination could make beautiful dreams come true.

CLOUDS: Moody Moon Children often dampen your sunny nature with sudden flash-floods of self-pity. (Leo hasn't time for petulant pouters or complainers.) Frugal Cancer may think you're too wasteful and extravagant (Weeeellllll?). The home-loving crab may want to warm the hearth, while you enjoy kicking up your heels, partying on a grand scale. May be a lot of water under your bridge.

SCORPIO-LEO Bo Derek/Linda Evans and John Derek

SMILING SUN: A powerful lover who commands your respect in and out of the boudoir, Scorpio is a creative achiever who matches your flair for drama with awesome imagination. Scorpio possessiveness can make you feel secure and valued (most of the time).

CLOUDS: Proud Leos may bridle when Scorpio tries to control their lives with subtle maneuvers (to you, they sometimes seem downright underhanded). You're open and aboveboard, while Scorpio almost never says what he or she *really* thinks (though they read *you* like a book). Scorpio will try to budget you (the nerve!) and greet your extravagances with cold stony stares. A steamy combination running *very* hot or *very* cold.

PISCES-LEO Lord Snowdon and Princess Margaret
Ursula Andress and John Derek
Ellen Terry and George Bernard Shaw

SMILING SUN: This partnership can be creative heaven, a mating of inner and outer strength. Leo gives Pisces confidence and Pisces gives Leo appreciation, a listening ear, and very sweet words (Pisces are the poets of the zodiac). Pisces are marvelously original and their artistic talents blossom under your warm encouragement.

CLOUDS: Pisces are often shaky under stress and definitely need to be pushed to achieve. (They procrastinate a lot!) Your roars could bring on cloudbursts and closed minds. These folks are hard to pin down. You're never quite sure when they'll swim away to calmer streams — not so good for Leo (you like to be *sure* of your mate). A will-o'-the-wisp combination.

OTHER FAMOUS LEO PERSONALITIES

WOMEN

Elizabeth Hanford Dole
Eugenia Sheppard
Mae West
Lucille Ball
Rosalynn Carter
Amelia Earhart
Valerie Harper
Jacqueline Kennedy Onassis
Princess Margaret
Princess Anne
Bobbie Gentry
Sally Struthers
Rhonda Fleming
Julia Child
Maureen O'Hara
Jill St. John
Coco Chanel
Carrie Fisher
Peggy Fleming
Gracie Allen
Loni Anderson
Lana Cantrell
Lina Wertmuller
Bella Abzug
Phyllis Schlafly
Lillian Carter
Dorothy Parker
Joan Mondale
Dolores Del Rio
Dorothy Hamill
Myrna Loy
Queen Mother Elizabeth
Mata Hari
Me

MEN

Aldous Huxley
Carl Jung
Carroll O'Connor
Napoleon
Norman Lear
George Bernard Shaw
Tony Bennett
George Hamilton
Yves Saint Laurent
Dustin Hoffman
Andy Warhol
Mike Douglas

"Diamond Jim" Brady
John Derek
Peter Duchin
William Powell
Menachem Begin
Fidel Castro
Robert De Niro
Robert Redford
Malcolm Forbes
Gene Kelly
Rafer Johnson
Neil Armstrong
Robert Mitchum
Dino de Laurentiis
Herbert Hoover
Peter Bogdanovich
Benito Mussolini
Stanley Kubrick
Cecil B. De Mille
Alfred Hitchcock
Milton Goldman
Spencer Christian
Sam Goldwyn
Henry Ford, Sr.
Eddie Fisher
Alexander Dumas

CELEBRITY COUPLES AND ROMANTIC PAIRINGS

Jacqueline (Leo) and John F. Kennedy (Gemini)
Mick Jagger (Leo) and Bianca (Taurus)
Rhonda Fleming (Leo) and Tom Mann (Aries)
Eugenia Sheppard (Leo) and Earl Blackwell (Taurus)
Robert Taylor (Leo) and Greta Garbo (Virgo) in *Camille*
Ian (Leo) and Ellen Graham (Virgo)
William Powell (Leo) and Jean Harlow (Pisces) in *Wife vs. Secretary*
Robert Taylor (Leo) and Barbara Stanwyck (Cancer)
Napoleon (Leo) and Josephine (Cancer)
Prince Egon von Fürstenburg (Leo) and Lynn Marshall (Cancer)
Rosalynn (Leo) and Jimmy Carter (Libra)
John Derek (Leo) and Linda Evans (Scorpio) and Bo Derek (Scorpio)
"Diamond Jim" Brady (Leo) and Lillian Russell (Sagittarius)
Elizabeth Hanford Dole (Leo) and Robert Dole (Leo/Cancer cusp)
Gracie Allen (Leo) and George Burns (Capricorn/Aquarius cusp)
Joan Mondale (Leo) and Walter Mondale (Capricorn)
Princess Margaret (Leo) and Anthony Armstrong-Jones (Pisces)
Eddie Fisher (Leo) and Elizabeth Taylor (Pisces)
Eddie Fisher (Leo) and Debbie Reynolds (Aries)
George Bernard Shaw (Leo) and Ellen Terry (Pisces)
Geoffrey Holder (Leo) and Carmen de Lavallade (Pisces)
Jill St. John (Leo) and Robert Wagner (Aquarius)
Jacqueline Kennedy (Leo) and Aristotle Onassis (Capricorn)
George Hamilton (Leo) and Alana (Taurus)
Gene Kelly (Leo) and Rita Hayworth (Libra) in *Cover Girl*
William Powell (Leo) and Myrna Loy (Leo) in *The Thin Man* series

LUCKY LEO PLACES TO BE

Colorado
New York State
Texas
Los Angeles
Hawaii
Missouri
Italy
Rome
France

3 SAGITTARIUS— THE GLOBE-TROTTING GAMBLER

(November 22-December 21)

The song, "Taking a Chance on Love," must have been written for a Sagittarius. (It was recorded beautifully by Frank Sinatra, one of my favorite Sags.) You are the romantic gamblers of the zodiac and love is your favorite game. Always on the move, Archers rarely take love too seriously or, heaven forbid, take time out to commit themselves!

Sagittarians are ruled by Jupiter, the planet of good fortune. You are usually lucky in all you undertake. (Just be sure you don't take on too much and dissipate your energies.) Your symbol is the archer with his arrow aimed skyward, which is where your aspirations are headed. You're a straight shooter — seemingly compelled to speak your mind — as well as a born leader and pacesetter. You aim for the stars, but your feet are usually on the ground.

Your slogan is "I see"; your key word is "prophesy." (You can pontificate for hours on that subject!) Though Sagittarians *are* the philosophers of the zodiac, they brim over with vitality, generously spreading warmth, friendliness, and love so natural to their expansive personality. You're the original "roving eye" with a lover in every port. Jupiter gives you upbeat good cheer. Sex for you is fun and lighthearted — those dreary intense relationships are not for you. (Thoughts of being tied down make you run for the next plane!)

How does a lighthearted lover like you build a solid, lasting relationship? It *is* possible, if you choose your mate on the basis of shared interests (sports, travel, community activities) and friendship. You are innately idealistic and explore everything with insatiable curiosity. When you find a true companion to share these interests, your chances for a lasting love affair are excellent.

Jane Fonda is the perfect example of a wandering Sag who found a friend, lover and fellow idealist in her husband, the liberal politician Tom Hayden (another Sag). She supports him wholeheartedly in his career, and he lets her do her "own thing" as a highly successful actress and

founder of a nationwide chain of exercise studios (Sags are fitness fanatics!).

The more intellectual interests you Sags share with your mate, the better your chances for a long-lasting relationship (passions burn fast and furiously with Sag . . . and frequently burn out!).

Which brings us to the famous Sagittarian gift of gab. You make great salesmen — you can talk anybody into anything and usually back up your convictions with action. You are not, however, known for your tact or diplomacy.

You hate to take orders and, if you can't be boss, you'd rather not have any part of a relationship. You should work to develop a spirit of cooperation and, at least, a *small* sense of humility. You're a vibrant and a clever person, but other people have good qualities, too.

When choosing a mate, your mind rather than your heart is your guide. Once you've decided that a person is your intellectual equal, shares your interests, and has the proper background, then you *may* consider marriage. What's more, you're likely to tell these sentiments to your lover. Don't! Nothing could put the damper on the spirits of ardent romanticists (especially if they're Water or Earth signs), more than bluntness at one of life's most poetic moments.

Your life may be strewn with broken engagements and disappointments in love, which could make you wary of becoming involved again — until the next time! You'll hide your disappointments with a laugh and even relate humorous anecdotes about your lost love. Just be careful you don't end up alone — a perennial extra man or woman, unable to trust anyone enough to marry them.

THE SAGITTARIUS/SCORPIO CUSP (November 19-24)

As a Sag, you have high ideals and optimism while Scorpio gives you realism and perseverance. You'll track down your ideal love . . . and make him or her yours no matter what the odds! Your curiosity and need to get to the bottom of things could make you search deeply into your lover's past. (Better leave those skeletons in the closet and concentrate on the future.) This cusp equips the Sag sense of humor with a Scorpio sting. (Use your rapier wit to entertain, not to maim!) Spontaneous and enthusiastic, you've got enough drive and passion to fulfill many a lover's dreams!

THE SAGITTARIUS/CAPRICORN CUSP (December 19-24)

You're an optimist who's determined to make things work . . . an attitude that bodes well for developing a long-term relationship. Freedom-loving Sagittarian traits are balanced here by Capricorn ambition and sense of responsibility . . . you're serious about your goals! In love, you'll speak with action as well as words. And, your chances for success in business are great, promising your partner a comfortable, secure lifestyle (something most Sags have trouble delivering). Your conviction that you know the truth (and must tell it like it is!) coupled with your Capricorn need to be an authority figure can make you a bit of a tyrant. Let your lover have a fair say in all matters . . . you'll both be happier for it!

THE SAGITTARIUS MAN

He's a romantic wanderer (they say Don Juan was a Sag), but he's such fun, every woman should have one at some point in her life.

He adores beautiful women, especially those with gorgeous gams (bring on those revealing side-slits and miniskirts). He loves to travel, so keep your suitcase packed. When he does succumb to marriage, it won't be the conventional kind. He doesn't mind a working wife so long as she doesn't neglect him. But a Sagittarian man is usually very successful and puts *his* work before personal interests.

He's not the domestic type. He's adventurous, adores sports, horses, gambling and games. A Fire sign, he has a fiery temperament but forgives easily (look helpless during his tirades). He has an extremely good sense of humor, something he also appreciates in his women. His nature is honest but blunt. Help him to cultivate diplomacy and tact (and don't dissolve in tears when he comments on your excess poundage — get to the gym, fast!).

He's highly idealistic about love and has no intention of "throwing his heart away." If you *do* land him, don't disappoint him. He expects a lot from you. As a lover, he's a marvelous companion (you'll never be bored!). As a husband, you'll need roller skates to keep up with him.

HOW TO TURN ON THE SAGITTARIAN MAN

- He's the perennial bachelor of the zodiac, but once committed, he'll be yours if you're not possessive.
- He gets his kicks from beautiful legs, so stock up on super sheer pantyhose and sexy shoes.
- He loves to travel, so keep your passport updated.
- Take an interest in his work, but don't try to run his life.
- Wear the latest styles. He loves deep red, blue and purple — also filmy lingerie and sleepwear.
- Laugh at his jokes. He has a great sense of humor and, though a philosophical type, doesn't take life — or love — too seriously.
- Be a good listener (even when he philosophizes *at length*!).
- Take an interest in sports. He's very athletic.
- Don't make jealous scenes. He has an incurable roving eye . . . but he won't follow through unless you *cling*.
- Be diplomatic. He needs someone to smooth things over when he's been too blunt.
- Never lie — he can never forgive a falsehood.
- Plan a rendezvous on a deserted tennis court . . . or in an abandoned stable.
- He's a great dancer! Make sure you know the latest steps!

HIS LESSONS TO LEARN

- Temper your truth-telling with tact! There is another way to tell her you hate her hairdo besides making her feel like the wrong end of a floor mop!
- Find a woman you can stick to for at least a year!
- Establish a secure home base. This is important for most women. Not everyone dreams of living in a camper van.
- Base your love on solid friendship and common interests.
- Don't promise more than you can deliver. You're one of the great salesmen of the zodiac and not above making extravagant gestures (or promises) — without the paycheck to back them up!
- Don't complicate your love life. It takes two to tango, not three or four. (Sag likes juggling half a dozen ladies at the same time, usually with disastrous results!)

THE SAGITTARIUS WOMAN

The Sagittarius woman looks like the outdoor type and most Sags *are* (skiier Suzy Chaffee and tennis stars Chris Evert and Tracy Austin, for instance). She also loves sports that involve animals (Sags are the great horse-lovers of the zodiac).

Sometimes she takes her sports more seriously than she takes her man (tough on the male ego!). And she's sure to be attracted to someone who's even better than she at her favorite outdoor activity (that's the quickest way to get her indoors!).

The Sag woman is the perfect companion. She can take part in even the most masculine activities such as fishing and hunting. She's the gal who can handicap the races and pick the top-running stock. She's not a domestic creature and will do her best to hurry through her daily chores (or better yet, hire someone else to do them) so she can be off to more exciting adventures. You'll often find a Sag woman running her own business or in a top sales job . . . she has a gift of gab and is forever on the telephone. (Better be sure she has her own private line!)

Her family is important to her, but she won't devote her entire life to husband and children as Moon Children do. She would rather be out where the action is. She looks at sex as one of her favorite sports and practices it often, but promiscuity is not her style. For happiness, she needs a solid home base with a partner who is a good friend as well as lover. (It helps if he plays tennis, too!)

TO EXCITE THE SAGITTARIUS WOMAN

- Take her on a horseback-riding trip . . . to the Peruvian Andes.
- Give her a push-button phone with her own private line . . . or two or three!
- Back her in her own business, help produce her play or promote her exercise studio.
- She'll be faithful if you're not jealous or possessive.

- Give her a set of designer luggage and a plane ticket for two!
- She loves to play games, so lead her on a merry chase.
- Rendezvous in a camper van or on a jogging track!
- Here's the girl you can take to sporting events. She might flirt with the star athlete, but she'll always come back to you.
- Give her rubies or turquoise jewelry and send her long-stem red roses.
- Make love on purple satin sheets.
- She has a great sense of humor, and loves to be seen in the "right" places . . . so take her to a good comedy . . . or to the latest disco.
- Country and western music appeals to her cowgirl instincts.
- She's looking more for a playmate than a provider. Show her playmates can be partners, too!

HER LESSONS TO LEARN

- Keep the home fires burning! You'd rather fight for a cause or travel to where the action is than stay at home. Make *home* where the action is or you'll have no one to come home to!
- Learn to build your lover's ego. This is especially important if you're involved with another Fire sign. You tend to tell the unvarnished truth (as you see it) with little regard for diplomacy.
- Plan things you can do together. Try some indoor sports for a change. Or exercise together. You'd be surprised how well it works out.
- Look before you leap into a relationship. You dislike restrictions or commitments of any kind, so choose someone who will give you the freedom you need.

YOUR SAGITTARIUS SUN-CAST

With celebrity couples and romantic pairings . . . for better or for worse . . . from the stage, screen, television, and real life.

WITH AIR SIGNS: You travel fastest with Air signs. But one of you has to know for sure in which direction you're going!

GEMINI-SAGITTARIUS

Marilyn Monroe and Joe DiMaggio
Beatrice Lillie and Noel Coward

SMILING SUN: A scintillating couple, you're a party all by yourselves. You love being on the go together. And sexually, your Gemini is a walking harem (your eye will never have time to rove). You'll philosophize all through the night 'til you put those words into action.

CLOUDS: A bit hard on the nerves . . . and glib Gemini has a clever way of twisting the truth to his or her advantage. Gemini withdraws from your fiery temper tantrums and avoids confrontations. You demand all cards on the table. Gemini always has an ace up the sleeve!

LIBRA-SAGITTARIUS

Melina Mercouri and Jules Dassin

SMILING SUN: You're both mentally and physically agile, debating and deliberating through the night. Libra ideas make your flames dance. Librans will help you aim your Bow of Truth with a diplomatic hand . . . and will smooth over any rough situations your bluntness may cause. And they're so good looking!

CLOUDS: Libran indecision and constant weighing and measuring may drive straight-shooting you to other targets. Your bluntness ruffles Libran's feathers. Librans are marriage-minded (they operate best in tandem) while you're a freedom-loving rolling stone. Oh, my!

AQUARIUS-SAGITTARIUS

Abraham Lincoln and Mary Todd
Mia Farrow and Woody Allen

SMILING SUN: You're both freethinkers and very independent. This makes for some highly eccentric goings-on in the bedroom, if you're ever in the same place at the same time. Unpredictable, brilliant, fun-loving Aquarius could be the traveling companion of your dreams . . . and your blunt verbal thrusts will be expertly parried by Aquarian wit.

CLOUDS: Aquarius is a bit too *detached* for you. You're both fast talkers and expect others to pay attention. Get two (or more) telephones: you'll need a few listening ears. Could be more "static" than ecstatic!

WITH OTHER FIRE SIGNS: Your fellow Fire signs turn up the heat of romance. You really ignite each other . . . but watch out! Their jealous nature could curb your roving eye.

ARIES-SAGITTARIUS

My mother and father

SMILING SUN: You may start as friends, then find you can't live without this energetic soulmate. They're spontaneous and adventurous (like you) and will take off on the spur of the moment, without a backward glance. Busy with their own plans, they'll give you plenty of space for yours!

CLOUDS: While you're both off on tangents, someone has to watch the budget. (Get a good Virgo accountant.) Both of you may get weary from juggling so many projects — try to team up professionally and share the load. If you deflate the Aries ego with one of your sharp Sag barbs, get ready for an explosion. Nevertheless, a winning combination.

LEO-SAGITTARIUS

"Diamond Jim" Brady and Lillian Russell
Robert Redford and Jane Fonda in *The Electric Horseman*

SMILING SUN: The Lion glamour draws you like a magnet. And your sunny nature promises some roaring good times. Leo could be your best playmate. A hot combo in bed and a dazzler on the social scene. One who will love to jet with you to all the best places.

CLOUDS: Leo wants your attention exclusively. You'll have to curb your tendency to flirt and carry on or you're going to have some rip-roaring bonfires. Although you are openhearted you can be penurious with money . . . a definite Leo turn-off. Also, you're rather unconventional in your dress and behavior (there *are* times when a jogging suit just won't do!). Still, this one's a good bet!

SAGITTARIUS-SAGITTARIUS

Jane Fonda and Tom Hayden

SMILING SUN: Here's a friend/lover who'll never disappoint you. You'll search for adventure together, share each other's ideals and give each other lots of room to grow! You'll have a spirited and spiritual relationship that grows deeper with the years . . . two wanderers who feel completely "at home" together!

CLOUDS: Both of you risk takers need someone to mind the store and follow up on the details as you race ahead. Fine . . . as long as you don't expect your Sag mate to mind the budget! (Hire some help!) Arrange to do your traveling together: your mate will hate to be "left behind" . . . and that Sag eye might start to wander . . .

WITH EARTH SIGNS: Opposites attract and you sense that these earthy signs have their feet on the ground. A close association can make exciting things happen for you both.

TAURUS-SAGITTARIUS

Bing Crosby and his Kathryn

SMILING SUN: Taureans love your sense of humor and flair for salesmanship. You love their sound, good sense and sensuality. When Jupiter luck teams with Venus love of beauty and possessions, you could reap a landfall!

CLOUDS: Taurean caution could put a damper on your fiery enthusiasm, since conservative Bulls pale at Sag's risk-taking. Bulls like the sure things; you like surprises! Taurus possessiveness could ground your fancy flights. It's a gamble for you both.

VIRGO-SAGITTARIUS

Cliff Robertson and Dina Merrill
Sophia Loren and Carlo Ponti

SMILING SUN: Precise Virgos make you back up those sweeping Sag promises with facts. And they'll want all the details! You communicate easily (both talkers) and both move around a lot (could be lively after dark). Purist Virgos could be moved by Sags' love of truth.

CLOUDS: Virgo may try to cure you of your restless ways and organize every minute of your life (that's good!). You'll have some tense moments, though, when Virgo's criticism jars Sag's bluntness. Virgo will bring you down to earth when you want to take off. This combo's a challenge.

CAPRICORN-SAGITTARIUS

Ava Gardner and Frank Sinatra
Diane Keaton and Woody Allen
Aristotle Onassis and Maria Callas

SMILING SUN: Capricorns put the ever-wandering Sag on a straight and narrow path to achievement. Their realism tempers your brutal frankness and their advice is definitely to your benefit. A good target for your bow and arrow (you'll take earth-bound Capricorns on flights of fancy beyond their wildest dreams.)

CLOUDS: Capricorn's a pessimist; you're an optimist. Those dark Saturn clouds could smother your enthusiasm. Plan-ahead Capricorn is the antithesis of spontaneity — likes to make love on schedule. You're the spur-of-the-moment type. Capricorn can be tight-fisted with money; you're a high roller. A test-y couple!

WITH WATER SIGNS: Creative Water signs can inspire or infuriate you. They rarely say what they really think (which could keep your curiosity alive) and they're extremely possessive. Skim the sexy surface and watch out for murky depths.

CANCER-SAGITTARIUS

Ingmar Bergman and Liv Ullmann
Donald Sutherland and Jane Fonda in *Klute*

SMILING SUN: Cancer sensitivity and sympathy touch your emotions and smooth over your rough edges. You inspire Cancers to create on a large scale. Domestic Cancers could create the home you'll want to come back to.

CLOUDS: Cancers collect *things* while you collect *experiences*. They're the home-lovers of the zodiac; you're the wanderers. They're supersensitive; you send out sharp, wounding barbs unknowingly. Watch out for flash floods.

SCORPIO-SAGITTARIUS

Ike and Tina Turner
Ruth Gordon and Garson Kanin
Marlo Thomas and Phil Donahue

SMILING SUN: A real sizzler in bed . . . at first! Scorpio can match or even top any sexual adventures you've had before. You skim the surface of life; Scorpios give you depth. Their energy is boundless, too. You'll both enjoy outdoor (as well as indoor) sports.

CLOUDS: Scorpio is possessive and intense; you take life and love lightly. Watch out for Scorpios' sting. These are not lovers to trifle with! You'll resent their constant suspicion, which is usually on target (they can even read your thoughts) and their desire to control and manipulate. A steamy combination — both hot and cold.

PISCES-SAGITTARIUS

Harry James
and Betty Grable

SMILING SUN: Two restless, mutable signs make for a lot of action and quick changes. Pisces has the same mental, spiritual, and sexual wanderlust, with a decided taste for the exotic. Pisces's self-sacrificing nature will help you become more considerate of others. Your super-salesmanship provides the arrows to guide Pisces's creative ideas to their target.

CLOUDS: Pisces negativism can dampen your fire. Neither of you keeps an eye on the budget when it comes to the pursuit of life's pleasures. You could even go bankrupt together! Pisces has a strong sense of privacy. You want everything out in the open. When it's good, it's great — otherwise . . .

OTHER FAMOUS SAGITTARIUS PERSONALITIES

WOMEN

Maria Callas
Jane Fonda
Suzy Chaffee
Sunny Griffin
Dina Merrill
Tracy Austin
Patty Duke Astin
Lee Remick
Dionne Warwicke
Kathryn Crosby
Tina Turner

Caroline Kennedy
Bette Midler
Charlene Tilton
Lillian Russell
Natalia Makarova
Dorothy Lamour
Christina Onassis
Liv Ullmann
Betty Grable
Rita Moreno
Connie Francis

Lynn Fontanne
Ellen Burstyn
Chris Evert Lloyd
Margaret Mead
Eleanor Roosevelt
Mary Martin
Julie Harris
Louisa May Alcott
Melanie Kahane

MEN

Andy Williams
Mark Twain
Garson Kanin
Joe DiMaggio
Ricardo Montalban
John F. Kennedy, Jr.
David Merrick
Bruce Lee
Tom Hayden
Sir Charles Mendl
Winston Churchill
Woody Allen
Lee Trevino
Adolph Green
Jean-Luc Godard

Otto Preminger
Jules Dassin
Douglas Fairbanks, Jr.
Chet Huntley
Carlo Ponti
Frank Sinatra
Noel Coward
Sir Ralph Richardson
Kirk Douglas
Beau Bridges
Edward G. Robinson
Alexander Haig
Phil Donahue
William F. Buckley, Jr.
Henri de Toulouse-Lautrec

James Thurber
David Susskind
Adam Clayton Powell
Alexis Lichine
Harpo Marx
John Milton
John Lindsay
Walt Disney
Sammy Davis, Jr.
Benjamin Disraeli
Dale Carnegie
Andrew Carnegie
Leonid Brezhnev
Billy the Kid
George Segal

CELEBRITY COUPLES AND ROMANTIC PAIRINGS

Mary Todd (Sagittarius) and Abraham Lincoln (Aquarius)
Woody Allen (Sagittarius) and Mia Farrow (Aquarius) in *Stardust Memories* (and in real life)

Joe DiMaggio (Sagittarius) and Marilyn Monroe (Gemini)
Melanie Kahane (Sagittarius) and Ben Grauer (Gemini)
Jules Dassin (Sagittarius) and Melina Mercouri (Libra)
Lillian Russell (Sagittarius) and "Diamond Jim" Brady (Leo)
Jane Fonda (Sagittarius) and Tom Hayden (Sagittarius)
Kathryn (Sagittarius) and Bing Crosby (Taurus)
Dina Merrill (Sagittarius) and Cliff Robertson (Virgo)
Carlo Ponti (Sagittarius) and Sophia Loren (Virgo)
Frank Sinatra (Sagittarius) and Ava Gardner (Capricorn)
Maria Callas (Sagittarius) and Aristotle Onassis (Capricorn)
Woody Allen (Sagittarius) and Diane Keaton (Capricorn) in *Annie Hall* (and in real life)
Liv Ullmann (Sagittarius) and Ingmar Bergman (Cancer)
Tina Turner (Sagittarius) and Ike Turner (Scorpio)
Garson Kanin (Sagittarius) and Ruth Gordon (Scorpio)
Phil Donahue (Sagittarius) and Marlo Thomas (Scorpio)
Betty Grable (Sagittarius) and Harry James (Pisces)
Frank Sinatra (Sagittarius) and Barbara Marx (Pisces)
Frank Sinatra (Sagittarius) and Mia Farrow (Aquarius)
Julian Earl (Sagittarius) and Phyllis Earl (Sagittarius)

LUCKY SAGITTARIUS PLACES TO BE

Australia
Delaware
Indiana
Mississippi
Thailand
Alabama
Finland
Illinois
New Jersey
Spain
Chile
Hungary
Monaco
North Carolina
Pennsylvania

The element of Earth, astrologically speaking, stands for all that is solid and practical. People influenced by this element only believe in what they can see, smell, hear, touch and taste, therefore, all five senses are highly developed. They are the zodiac realists and live in the present tense. Rather than analyze how reality *might* be or is *felt,* Earth signs care about how it *works*.

The three Earth signs — Taurus, Virgo, and Capricorn — are the builders and organizers of the zodiac: productive, practical, and responsible. Although they are earthy, sensual people who are stimulated by the tangible, elegant, and luxurious, they are capable of Spartan self-discipline. They are observers of the comings and goings of life, always protecting themselves from too much dangerous involvement with dark, emotional and eroding forces (even though they are attracted to mystical emotional *partners*).

Taurus, the first Earth sign (April 20-May 20), is ruled by Venus, the planet of love and beauty, and is symbolized by the bull . . . a very patient and easy-going animal, until he's aroused! Because their senses can be stimulated easily, Taureans have strong appetites and must be careful not to overindulge themselves at the table or in the bedroom.

The Taurus woman is affectionate, feminine and a collector of beautiful things. The Taurus man is virile, possessive, a gourmet (or gourmand) and a good provider. Both sexes love to sing, appreciate beauty, want financial security, and are lucky with property investments. They also have a wealth of the spirit. The way to their heart may be through your pocketbook. They love all green things: emeralds, the green countryside, and money — especially.

Two perfect examples of Taurean style and harmony: Glen Campbell and Cher.

Virgo, the second Earth sign (August 23-September 22), is ruled by Mercury, planet of communications. Virgos are the perfectionists of the zodiac. They love to talk and to analyze everything. They must learn not to talk themselves out of love, to praise as well as criticize. The Virgo lady is elegant, disciplined, organized and has a secret fantasy life. She can even be a sex symbol (Raquel Welch and Sophia Loren). The Virgo man can spend so much time looking for the perfect woman that he may never marry at all. He is success-oriented, idealistic and analytical. He prefers the quiet, intelligent beauty who doesn't make waves. Two vibrant Virgos are Sean Connery and Jacqueline Bisset.

Capricorn, the third Earth sign (December 22-January 19), is ruled by Saturn, the planet of duty and hard work. (That's probably why they make great executives.) Capricorns are symbolized by the mountain goat. Instead of always keeping their eyes on the summit of the mountain, Capricorns must learn to enjoy the scenery along the way and kick up their heels more! They're health-conscious, live the longest of any of the signs of the zodiac and seem to have discovered the fountain of youth (Cary Grant and Marlene Dietrich).

The Capricorn woman loves status. She's an elegant hostess and a super businesswoman. The Capricorn man is dignified, ambitious, dependable, and traditional. He's also a loner — just be sure he's not alone with your best friend! All Capricorns look for a mate who'll help them on their way up.

Everyone's horoscope contains a mixture of the elements, so most of us have some planets in Earth signs. If our lovers have the Sun or one of the major Love planets (Moon, Mars or Venus) in Earth signs, they will relate harmoniously to our Earth placements. If their Sun or Love planets fall in *other* elements, they will challenge or stimulate our Earth placements.

For instance, Earth signs, which tend to be cautious, plodding and systematic, are often fascinated by the impulsive, dynamic and exciting Fire signs — Aries, Leo and Sagittarius. On the surface, it would seem this combination would be doomed to failure. Far from it! Earth signs can make the idealistic visions of Fire materialize. They can provide a strong, sure base for Fire's pioneering projects . . . the follow-through and attention to detail that Fire signs usually lack.

On the other hand, this relationship requires much understanding. Earth must be careful not to suffocate Fire's flame . . . not to contain it so tightly that "security" becomes a cage. And Fire must understand that Earth needs "roots": a place in society, a strong home-base and a way to pay the bills. Strongly individualistic Fire signs don't care a fig for tradition (except Leo) or what people think. Each element both desires and rejects the other's values. ("What does all that running around accomplish?" asks Earth of Fire, all too frequently.) Of course, for a truly successful pairing, much depends on other planetary placements and how willing *both* are to give and take.

Earth signs challenge their Air sign partners (Gemini, Libra and Aquarius) to give their ideas value and definition. (They literally pull the Air signs "down to Earth.") Since Earth is concerned about *physical* needs and Air about *mental* stimulation, these signs have much to teach each other. Earth adds reality to Air signs' theories, turning them into "doers" as well as "thinkers." The more controversial and abstract Air signs may find Earth's constant materialism suffocating; while Earth signs' warm sensuality may not jibe with Air signs' cool detached approach to sex (or their sometimes unconventional experiments).

Earth signs are possessive and possession-minded; Air signs can float away into a purely mental world, leaving Earth signs feeling stranded in the nest. Practical Earth tries to give substance to volatile, breezy, shifting Air. A challenge or a waste of time? These elements have much to give each other: perspective, achievement, brilliance, creativity. It's up to both to work it out.

The creative, emotional Water signs are said to be natural foils for Earth. Water makes Earth productive, while Earth gives shape to Water. Water people tend to look for someone to take care of them, which Earth does happily. Intuitive Water also appeals to Earth's sensual nature, knowing almost instinctively how to please Earth people. It's hard to see where they could go wrong. *But* sometimes too much Earthy realism smothers the romantic Water creativity. (The resulting deluge of emotion can cause floods . . . of tears!) Water can also stray sexually, which can quickly erode an otherwise solid relationship.

To succeed, each partnership must have a mixture of diversity and communion in unequal proportions. Much depends on having a similar *definition* of love. If you can't accept or provide what your mate really wants, and vice versa, forget it! But bear in mind that even the most *diverse* elements can succeed if a *stimulating* and dynamic life is what they both want. Sometimes the most "compatible" elements *miss* because too much tranquility and ease of relating become *boring*.

4

TAURUS—THE ZODIAC'S SENSUALIST

April 20–May 20

Taurus is wealth. Not just the richness of material possessions, but also the wealth of the spirit. The slogan for Taurus, the first Earth sign of the zodiac, is "I possess," and the key word is "establish" . . . which gives you some important clues to this powerful Taurus personality. The symbol for Taurus is the bull, and you Taureans can certainly be bullheaded when it comes to getting your own way. ("Stand back, Evita!")

Ruled by Venus, the planet of love and beauty, you're extremely sensual . . . all five senses are highly developed. Taurus rules the throat. (Every astrological sign rules a certain part of the body.) That's why there are so many wonderful singers born under this sign, like Barbra Streisand and Ella Fitzgerald. James Mason and Orson Welles are famous for their beautiful, distinctive speaking voices (they usually know what to say to make you feel good, too!).

Taureans know what they want . . . and when they want *you*, nothing can deter them. The male of this sign is virile, family-oriented and a good provider (he often accumulates wealth and property in later years). He must have a beautiful wife and a comfortable home. The Taurus woman loves beauty in all things and has expensive tastes. She makes a marvelous decorator with her unique sense of color. (Some of the most sensual bedrooms in the world belong to Taurean love-goddesses.)

You Venus-ruled Taureans are constant in your affections and guided more by emotions than by thought or reason. While you're highly susceptible to beauty and to your surroundings (dingy rooms can actually make you ill!), you maintain a practical perspective. Determined and possessive, once you've acquired what you want, be it a husband or a precious jewel, no one can pry you loose from what you feel is rightfully yours!

Taurus is a persevering sign — no matter what opportunities and obstacles you may encounter. Barbra Streisand is the best example I know of the determined, triumphant Taurean. Barbra, the ugly duckling who turned into a swan, was "Cinderella at the Ball" without the help of a fairy godmother. She alone is responsible for her superstar fame. Her incredible talent, combined with originality and determination, caused her to triumph over great odds. She believed in herself. She dared to be different.

You Taureans attract many people with your imaginative ideas and your Earthy sensual charm. (Your mates must be able to deal with this powerful persona.) You hate to be rushed and insist on being in control at all times.

Although you rarely show violent emotions — you prefer to maintain a calm, placid exterior — when you're pushed to an extreme or feel you've been dealt with unfairly, watch out! The Taurean temper is famous for being one of the most devastating in the zodiac.

One of your greatest assets is your staying power. You have all the patience in the world, and will pursue a goal through thick and thin until you finally achieve it. (Your sexual stamina is also legendary . . . you're the lover who never tires!)

THE TAURUS/ARIES CUSP (April 18-23)

The gentleness of Taurus combines with the self-confidence of Aries, creating a very unique personality. When the energy of Mars joins the sweetness and sensuality of Venus, you're capable of great love, sustained throughout a lifetime. Your temperament, however, is volcanic (so is your passion!). You're both hard to resist and hard to live with! But there is no denying your talent and dynamism.

THE TAURUS/GEMINI CUSP (May 18-23)

This is a very creative cusp: Gemini's mental agility combines with Taurus's artistic talent. You have a mind that soars on imaginative wings and a body that delights in earthly pleasures. You're both sensuous and experimental in bed (you've got something for everybody). You can be very successful financially using your creative way with words, your practical Taurus savvy, and your love of music and song (a songwriter?).

THE TORRID TAURUS MALE

The Taurus man has a thoughtful, emotional nature and values his home over almost everything else in life. He'll take very good care of his love — financially and physically. His life centers around his family, which makes him a very good husband.

In return, he expects a home in good taste that is well cared for and has, above all, good food. Here's one of the zodiac gourmets! An excellent amateur chef, he would love you to let him help prepare a romantic, candlelit dinner for two. He's the epitome of a man whose heart can be won through his stomach, so if you can't cook, learn. And, since all five of his senses are so highly developed, be sure the meals *look* as attractive as they *taste*.

Venus rules this Earth sign . . . that's why he loves everything that's beautiful (especially women). Always look your most alluring. He's possessive, but doesn't like possessiveness in women. Let him know you care, but don't smother him. He loves the outdoors, so be a good sport and a good partner.

Though he tends to save money, Taurus can be very generous with those he loves (and he loves to see his mate looking her best in beautiful clothes). But he will insist on top quality as well as *value* in his purchases.

Though he's extremely protective of his loved ones, that same protectiveness provides camouflage for his very jealous nature. He's not above checking up on his mate from time to time, so watch it! But when he knows he is loved, and has a secure and comfortable home, the Taurus male is the most contented, devoted, and loving partner a woman could want.

HOW TO ROUND UP THE TAURUS KING OF HEARTS

- Let him sing you to sleep!
- Bombard all five of his senses! (He's highly developed on every level.) Give him something soft to touch that smells good and tastes good . . . and you'll have a very loving Bull.
- Develop the artist in you. Make your home a work of art and he'll stay to admire it.
- He's a good provider . . . and loves to watch his fortune pile up! (He'll share it with you if you show your appreciation.)
- Take lessons in cordon bleu cuisine . . . and get cooking together. (Then cook up something sensual later on!)
- Cover him with affection, but don't smother him.
- Put a love note in his briefcase . . . along with a gourmet lunch for the office.
- He'll follow a fabulous fragrance. (Be sure it's yours!) His favorite is rose scented.
- Wear shades of blue and green . . . and he won't look for greener pastures elsewhere.

HIS LESSONS TO LEARN

- Talk out your problems . . . don't just sit and brood over them at length — letting them build up to a devastating earthquake!
- Don't resent your mate having outside activities. You were attracted to that sparkling creature, right? Well, don't put out the light in her eyes!
- Control your jealousy. The green-eyed-monster act implies that your partner has no integrity. (But she chose YOU, didn't she?) Don't check out her every move.
- Get out and party once in a while . . . even if you'd rather watch the football game in a big comfy chair than visit friends or dance in a noisy disco . . . THE CHANGE OF PACE WILL DO YOU GOOD.

THE TAURUS BEAUTY

Love of the esthetic, attraction to beauty in all its forms, is the strongest influence in the life of a Taurus woman. She is warm, sensitive, loving, and extremely feminine and although she indulges her love of luxury, she is also down to earth.

You lovely Taureans are uncomplicated, straightforward, natural, and rather conservative. You're willing to work hard for success. Yet you sincerely care about *others* and can give (and take) a great deal of affection. You're one of the maternal signs of the zodiac (like Leo and Cancer), and truly adore taking care of people (you make them delicious meals), pets, and children. You especially love taking care of the man in your life!

You have a wonderful, unique, fashion sense (Candice Bergen, Bianca

Jagger, Cher, and Audrey Hepburn) that is distinctively right for your face and figure. It frequently extends to collections of fabulous jewelry: emeralds, green malachite, and jade . . . also green things that *grow:* plants and money!

Your home will be filled with sensuous textures, beautiful colors, and bowls of potpourri to scent the air. And there will always be beautiful music on the stereo and something delicious to eat. (Tough competition for your less domestic rivals!)

Your problems with men usually stem from your possessiveness and desire to control them. The Taurean lady likes to get her own way and can't stand even a hint of indecision or insecurity. You're a planner who knows exactly what you want and where you want to put it.

Land and pastoral landscapes attract you, and you should always keep green growing things around: a beautiful garden or at least a room full of colorful flowers and exotic plants . . . to treat with your magical green thumb.

HOW TO EXPLORE YOUR SENSES WITH A GORGEOUS TAURUS WOMAN

- Help her make things grow . . . plants, flowers and her bank account!
- Inspire her to cook for you . . . by trying out the newest gourmet restaurants, first!
- She's an old-fashioned girl, so send her a nosegay of forget-me-nots and miniature pink roses.
- She likes the solid comforts of life . . . country property, a portfolio of stocks and bonds, a herd of prize cattle!
- She's an earthy woman who likes to collect jade, lapis lazuli and emeralds. Take the cue and give her a glittering bauble for her collection.
- Bring your romance back to flower with a romantic walk in the country.
- She likes a man of means . . . show her you *mean* what you say. Light flirtations are for other signs!
- She has a tendency to put on pounds . . . so give her her weight in carats, not calories. (Help her work off those extra pounds with lots of indoor exercise!)
- Make love to music! Be Tristan to her Isolde. She's inspired by opera, rock concerts and jazz. Vocalize together!

HER LESSONS TO LEARN

- Taurus women can be positively tyrannical (shades of Evita Perón!).
- Develop more subtle techniques to get your way. Don't resort to bossiness or obvious manipulation. (You could lose some warm friends.)
- Don't become possession-oriented. Security means a lot to you, but you sometimes give the impression that you're more attracted to *things* than to *people*.
- Be flexible! Do something to shake yourself up (try a Gemini lover!). A little flexibility never hurt and could put you in an interesting new position.

• Watch your weight . . . you could be too much of a good thing!
• Admit you're wrong. Stubborn Taurus hates to give in almost as much as Aries and Leo.
• Don't be too possessive . . . you could drive your lover into the arms of another!

YOUR TAURUS SUN-CAST

With celebrity couples and romantic pairings . . . for better or for worse . . . from the screen, stage, television, and real life!

WITH OTHER EARTH SIGNS: Common sense tells you this could be a mutual admiration society . . . but also that variety is the spice of life . . . and you do love spice!

TAURUS-TAURUS

Patrice Munsel and Robert Schuler
Audrey Hepburn and Albert Finney in *Two for the Road*

SMILING SUN: Two immovable objects are hit by an irresistible force! Here is someone to share your dreams. You're both sentimental, love your home and possessions and are sizzlingly sensual in bed.

CLOUDS: You're both stubborn and unrelenting in arguments. (Fortunately, you'll agree on most things.) This pairing could get a bit boring and you'll be tempted to stray to more exciting pastures. Your partner, however, will NOT forgive and forget!

VIRGO-TAURUS

Kathy and Darren McGavin

SMILING SUN: You sense that underneath Virgo's cool, chatty exterior are some white-hot fantasies well worth exploring . . . and you're right! Virgo responds to your romantic, sentimental side. You provide the comfort, calm, and peace to soothe Virgo's nerves. You could build a beautiful life together.

CLOUDS: You love Virgo's lively mind, but may find this sign a bit cool and uptight. Temperamentally you could irritate each other, too. Virgo gets upset over little things while Taurus opts for calm at all costs. Virgo's complaints, hypochondria attacks, and nagging may turn you into a Raging Bull. Still, it's worth the effort.

CAPRICORN-TAURUS

Martin Luther King and Coretta King
Rod and Alana Stewart

SMILING SUN: You two share a love of home and order. You also have similar goals in life. You understand each other without trying. Both know exactly where you're going (to the top!) and can help each other get there.

CLOUDS: Even-tempered Taurus might find Capricorn's fluctuating highs and lows a bit of a downer. You also suspect that Capricorn's business and social-climbing are more important than you are. Capricorn might not appreciate your bullheaded stubbornness and attempts to take what you want. Hmmmmmmmmmmmmmm.

WITH AIR SIGNS: They like the invisible (ideas, excitement) and you like the visible (things, sensual pleasures). You have much to give each other . . . but just watch out for strong winds and immovable mountains.

GEMINI-TAURUS

Prince Philip and Queen Elizabeth II
Marion Davies and William Randolph Hearst

SMILING SUN: Good-looking, socially graceful Gemini is compelling to Taurus . . . and fun, with a super sense of humor. They're just the lovers to lure you away from the roost. And their brilliant ideas (especially in bed) can turn you on!

CLOUDS: Gemini is not known for fidelity, can't stay attached to anything or anyone for long, while Taurus never lets go! Taurus has to make some difficult adjustments to stick with Gadfly Gemini and must stifle any jealous, possessive tendencies. Improbable, but not impossible.

LIBRA-TAURUS

Juan and Evita Perón
Rita Hayworth and Glenn Ford in *Gilda*
Rita Hayworth and Orson Welles

SMILING SUN: Both Venus-ruled, you communicate beautifully. Libra's good looks and style never fail to dazzle you. The chemistry is magic — at first, anyway. Libra's ethereal sexuality blends beautifully with Taurus's earthy sensuality. And Taurus helps provide the solid cash they need for a decidedly luxurious lifestyle (with lots of beautiful clothes!).

CLOUDS: Libra loves to flirt (though it's often harmless) while Taurus must feel like the One and Only *all the time.* Watch out for the green-eyed monster here. Libra's constant indecision can drive Taurus wild. A good bet, however.

AQUARIUS-TAURUS

Sonny and Cher Bono
Lana Turner and Tyrone Power

SMILING SUN: Aquarius likes to explore uncharted erotic territory, which intriques sensual Taureans. Aquarian brains plus sexy Taurean know-how could take them far. Expect the unexpected here . . . this could be just the love to jolt the Bull out of a rut!

CLOUDS: Money means little to Aquarius — a lot to Taurus. Aquarians have many friends and aquaintances (they need a telephone handy to keep in constant touch), while Taurus opts for a few close relationships. Aquarians would rather be out in the world crusading for causes than cozily nesting in the Taurus-ruled domain. Major adjustments are necessary to make this one work.

WITH FIRE SIGNS: This could be a consuming passion. Action-oriented Fire gets you moving. There could be quite a few explosions, however . . . both pleasant and otherwise.

ARIES-TAURUS

Omar Sharif and Barbra Streisand in *Funny Girl*
Gregory Peck and Audrey Hepburn in *Roman Holiday*

SMILING SUN: Taurus provides stability and security, and Aries adds a zap of energy. Taurus keeps gadabout Aries on the right track. Together, you can make things happen. You're a powerful combination of willpower and determination.

CLOUDS: Aries is impulsive; Taurus is deliberate. Aries's rash enthusiasm could turn Taurus off. And when Aries pushes, Taurus digs in his (or her) heels. Aries could try Taurus's patience with a flurry of unproductive activity. Watch out when the Ram and Bull lock horns!

LEO-TAURUS

George Hamilton and Alana
Mick and Bianca Jagger

SMILING SUN: You provide the setting for Leo to shine. You both love a social life with the "elite" of your worlds. And Taurus lavishes praise and gifts on Leo, while Leo promotes Taurus's schemes on a grand scale.

CLOUDS: Leo commands, Taurus resists! Taurus is not about to give Leo unquestioning obedience! Leo's extravagance can cause Taurus to tighten the purse strings. Then Leo will roar and Taurus will charge! STAND BACK!

SAGITTARIUS-TAURUS

Nancy Kovak and Zubin Mehta
Kathryn and Bing Crosby

SMILING SUN: Could be worth the gamble. Lucky Jupiter-ruled Sag and Venus-ruled Taurus play for high stakes. Both like to get directly to the point. Archers and Bulls love the great outdoors, and could have "happy hunting" in bed, too, with lots of sexual adventures.

CLOUDS: Home-loving Taurus might attempt to tie down the wandering Sag. (The more rope you give Sags, the more likely they are to return.) Sag has a roving eye, too . . . which is like waving a red flag at the Bull. Lots of compromises could make this combo work.

WITH WATER SIGNS: It's a fertile climate for love: lots of hearts to give and flowers to grow. But Water's emotional nature needs tending to keep this one blossoming.

CANCER-TAURUS

Phil Harris and Alice Faye
Ginger Rogers and Fred Astaire in *Flying Down to Rio, Top Hat*

SMILING SUN: You'll both face the music and dance! An enduring partnership, especially in creative endeavors. Cancer's warm emotions flower under Taurus's tender loving care. You'll stabilize Cancer's moody tendencies and love their sharp intuition about finances (Cancers are some of the great money-earners of the zodiac!).

CLOUDS: You both tend to hold in your anger and brood (very few cataclysmic rages here!) but expect some pouting and sniffling from time to time. Taurus may also find it difficult to understand Cancerian ups and downs, preferring the solid middle ground. But you can work it out!

SCORPIO-TAURUS

Louis Malle and Candice Bergen
Linda Christian and Tyrone Power

SMILING SUN: This is one of the zodiac's great love matches. Scorpio's emotional depth and intensity blends with Taurus's stamina and sensuality for a match that smoulders indefinitely. You could keep each other from *ever* straying. (You'll have to get out of bed sometime, however!) You admire Scorpio's penetrating insight (they can guess all your secrets) and they admire your inner calm.

CLOUDS: You're both ultra-possessive (but hate to be possessed). You're not above checking up on each other. Scorpio's devious tactics go against your grain. You have your own style of manipulating. Settle the question of *control* in this relationship fast! Then enjoy it!

PISCES-TAURUS

Elizabeth Barrett Browning
and Robert Browning
Rudolf Nureyev and Margot Fonteyn
Rex Harrison and Audrey Hepburn in *My Fair Lady*

SMILING SUN: Good prospects for an ardent and lasting relationship. Creative Pisces is a marvel in bed and loves the good things in life (just like you!). Steady Taurus gives elusive Pisces substance — and keeps an eye on the cash flow! And you're so protective of Pisces's sensitive feelings.

CLOUDS: You may find this sign a bit difficult to handle out of the bedroom. If you try to control them, they slip away mysteriously and do their own thing anyway. Pisces are natural drifters (they can't stand being pinned down), which could make the Bull see red. Poetic or pathetic?????

OTHER FAMOUS TAURUS PERSONALITIES

WOMEN

Queen Elizabeth II
Eva Perón (Evita)
Golda Meir
Dolly Madison
Bess Truman
Audrey Hepburn
Candice Bergen
Jill Clayburgh
Danielle Darrieux
Anne Baxter
Glenda Jackson

Birgit Nilsson
Patrice Munsel
Barbra Streisand
Catherine the Great
Bianca Jagger
Alana Stewart
Toni Tennille
Tammy Wynette
Rita Coolidge
Judy Collins
Ann-Margret

Shirley MacLaine
Ella Fitzgerald
Margot Fonteyn
Zizi Jeanmaire
Carol Burnett
Cher
Betty Comden
Shirley Temple Black
Martha Graham
Leslie Uggams
Martha Reed

MEN

Bing Crosby
Perry Como
Irving Berlin
Burt Bacharach
Glen Campbell

Jules Stein
Liberace
Billy Joel
Christopher Barker
Zubin Mehta

Sergei Rachmaninoff
Johannes Brahms
Sergei Prokofiev
Pëtr Ilich Tschaikowsky
Tyrone Power

Gary Cooper
Glenn Ford
Al Pacino
Orson Welles
James Stewart
Halston
Valentino
Balmain
Giorgio di Sant-Angelo
Karl Marx
Nikolai Lenin
Ho Chi Minh
Ayatollah Khomeini
Adolf Hitler
Sigmund Freud
Mike Wallace
Tom Snyder
Earl Blackwell
Anthony Quinn
Albert Finney
Niccolò Machiavelli
Eddie Albert
Ezio Pinza
Darren McGavin
Rudolph Valentino
Roberto Rossellini
Leonardo da Vinci
Salvador Dali
Rod McKuen
Willie Mays
James Mason
Sugar Ray Robinson
William Shakespeare
Socrates

CELEBRITY COUPLES AND ROMANTIC PAIRINGS

Barbra Streisand (Taurus) and Omar Sharif (Aries) in *Funny Girl*
Audrey Hepburn (Taurus) and Gregory Peck (Aries) in *Roman Holiday*
Queen Elizabeth II (Taurus) and Prince Philip (Gemini)
Jimmy Stewart (Taurus) and his wife Gloria (Gemini)
Fred Astaire (Taurus) and Ginger Rogers (Cancer) in *Top Hat, The Gay Divorcee*, etc.
Earl Blackwell (Taurus) and Eugenia Sheppard (Leo)
Bianca (Taurus) and Mick Jagger (Leo)
Barbra Streisand (Taurus) and Elliot Gould (Virgo)
Evita (Taurus) and Juan Perón (Libra)
Orson Welles (Taurus) and Rita Hayworth (Libra)
Tyrone Power (Taurus) and Linda Christian (Scorpio)
Candice Bergen (Taurus) and Louis Malle (Scorpio)
Henry Fonda (Taurus) and Katharine Hepburn (Scorpio) in *On Golden Pond*
Cher (Taurus) and Gregg Allman (Sagittarius)
Bing (Taurus) and Kathryn Crosby (Sagittarius)
Coretta (Taurus) and Martin Luther King (Capricorn)
Alana (Taurus) and Rod Stewart (Capricorn)
Tyrone Power (Taurus) and Lana Turner (Aquarius)
Cher (Taurus) and Sonny Bono (Aquarius)
Margot Fonteyn (Taurus) and Rudolf Nureyev (Pisces)
Robert Browning (Taurus) and Elizabeth Barrett Browning (Pisces)
Audrey Hepburn (Taurus) and Rex Harrison (Pisces) in *My Fair Lady*

LUCKY TAURUS PLACES TO BE

Greece
Greenland
Louisiana
Iraq
Minnesota
Iran
Maryland

5 VIRGO—THE PASSIONATE PERFECTIONIST

August 23-September 22

Some of the world's sexiest people were born under the sign of Virgo, symbolized by the Virgin and ruled by the planet Mercury (Sean Connery, Raquel Welch, Sophia Loren and Jacqueline Bisset). Many stay single . . . but that's because they're VERY choosy. (They manage to have a bit of fun in the meantime however!)

The slogan for Virgo is "I analyze," and the key word is "discriminate." Virgo is the most critical and discriminating sign of the zodiac. Virgo standards are so high they have trouble reaching them themselves . . . which makes them angry and often very difficult to live with (particularly since they take their anger out on those closest to them!). Virgos can be very mysterious about their private life (Greta Garbo). But they make very devoted, loyal, and helpful mates for the "right" person.

Sincerity, discipline, and devotion mark this sign. Virgos are the embodiment of perfected skill and refined talent.

If you're looking for a Virgo, try working late at the office. They're as demanding of themselves as of others and put in long hours on the job. Or try a health food store. Virgos are the most health-conscious sign of the zodiac, always stocking up on vitamins and minerals. (Many doctors and nurses are found in this Sun sign.) You'll also find Virgos in libraries, meticulously researching fascinating subjects to polish their naturally brilliant minds.

Their careers are of utmost importance to them and they're usually very successful. (Interestingly, two Virgos starred in succession in Broadway's *Woman of the Year* — Lauren Bacall and Raquel Welch — the story of a highly successful television journalist, a Mercury-ruled profession!)

Virgo never bestows affection lightly and is not one for impulsive romances. However, Virgo does dream of the ideal love and often fantasizes about that perfect mate. This is not often the type Virgos choose in real life, however; their fantasy love is a good deal racier! Some Virgos live out their fantasies in secret, but more relive them through the pages of steamy novels or television soap operas.

Virgos are super-organized and hate *anything* to disrupt their prescribed routine. If Thursday is their night for the health club, then they're not likely

©83 L+D DILLON

to accept a spur-of-the-moment dinner invitation or, heaven forbid, a blind date. (Virgo will want to know all about this date ahead of time!)

When they finally find the perfect mate (or as close as possible), Virgos settle down. (It's so much more organized and dependable that the single life.) The home will be neat and well run (or else!). And if their lover is attached to someone else, they'll find a way to be with them. (Virgo Ingrid Bergman risked everything for her Italian love, director Roberto Rossellini, remember?) They are indifferent to public opinion and are capable of a love that moves mountains. (Sophia Loren lived for years with her great love, Carlo Ponti, before the law allowed them to marry.)

THE VIRGO/LEO CUSP (August 21-26)

You're a fascinating mix of reserve and showmanship, outgoing one minute and retiring the next! You're energetic and hard-working, carefully navigating your ship of fortune toward power. With your mercurial gift-of-gab and your Leo salesmanship, you can inspire others to help you achieve anything. Your sunny disposition and a genuine desire to be of service make you very popular. You could run an organization that would be of great benefit to society. You also have a talent for public relations and advertising. Conductor-composer Leonard Bernstein, born on this cusp, combines the Virgo analytical quality with Leo showmanship to a superlative degree.

THE VIRGO/LIBRA CUSP (September 21-26)

You do everything in the best of taste, with Venus-ruled Libra, the zodiac's lover of beauty, combined with discriminating Mercury-ruled Virgo. You instinctively create beauty around you as an artist, designer, decorator or art critic. Your mind is first-rate; and you're articulate, charming and tactful. You have a double dose of idealism, but Virgo's practicality can put Libra's dreams into action. Your problem is in choosing *which* project or lover to take on!

THE VIRGO MAN

The Virgo male is a perfectionist, forever seeking the perfect woman. A large percentage of Virgos are bachelors. They have impeccable taste and expect their woman to have it, too. (That's why Virgos often mate with other Virgos.) A Virgo is not wildly passionate and prefers a woman with whom he can discuss a wide variety of subjects, a quiet intelligent beauty who "doesn't make waves."

Virgo's concept of marriage is rather like a business arrangement, but he'll take good care of his home and family and he'll expect you to keep his house immaculate (and keep the skeletons in the closet, as well). He can't stand disorder or women who are late for appointments. Play it cool, be competent and conventional if you want to please him.

He usually shuns displays of emotion. Wild displays of passion horrify him in reality (but he *does* fantasize!). He'd love to be James Bond (Virgo

Sean Connery actually *is*!). The zodiac hypochondriac, he often goes into the field of medicine. Our Mercury-ruled lover has a dry sense of humor, loves a good discussion, is usually up on the latest world happenings and has opinions about everything. (He likes to have the last word.)

The Virgo man is a master of subtle seduction and mental games. Underneath that cool exterior, he hints at a lusty libido . . . and a love that never wavers. If you're his ideal woman, he'll move mountains to get and keep you!

HOW TO TURN ON THE VIRGO MALE

- Wear an immaculate white tailored linen suit . . . and he'll take you to Casablanca.
- Give him a beautiful leather-bound romantic biography . . . then be his heroine (invent a few X-rated chapters!).
- Take him to an art exhibit and color yourself in navy, gray or yellow.
- Be on time. If you're late, he won't wait . . . if he does, he'll fume. (Take note, Leo and Gemini!)
- Wear a fragrance with violet notes . . . this will appeal to his scent-iments.
- Give elegant little sit-down dinner parties (he hates buffets). Invite brilliant, witty people and encourage conversation.
- Serve fresh fruits and vegetables. They'll bring on his healthy urges.
- Seduce him in a dusty library stack or a hot tub.
- He loves classical music. Go for baroque together.
- Help him do the Sunday crossword puzzle in bed. He'll finish it in record time.
- Encourage his flair for detail. Get him the newest gadget (then show him how to press your buttons!).
- Take him to a concert, opera or Japanese film; then stage a little encore in your bedroom for more applause.

HIS LESSONS TO LEARN

- Learn to love a woman in spite of her faults (and don't remind her of them constantly). Perfection can never be attained, except in your erotic fantasies.
- Relate to people and make allowance for human nature . . . nobody likes to be constantly scrutinized or discriminated against.
- Don't be a workaholic, creating a mind-boggling schedule of activity to keep you from dealing with your emotions.
- Learn to relax and have a good time. You know what they say about all work and no play!
- Give a few compliments once in a while. Your standards are very high — and very few can reach them, including yourself.
- Arrive ten minutes late for a date or social engagement once in a while. Your lover or hostess will be most grateful.
- Do something on the spur of the moment. You'll be surprised what a good time you'll have.

THE VIRGO WOMAN

One of the zodiac's most tantalizing creatures, the Virgo woman is a sexy paradox. She's the voluptuous sexpot who is ever faithful to her man. She's the cool, elegant "loner" who'll risk everything for True Love. One thing is for sure, Virgo knows exactly what she is doing, when she finally finds the man who measures up to her very exacting qualifications.

Virgo sets her own standards and often those of society, as one of its chief critics. But she never lets public opinion interfere with her choices when she comes across her ideal. He can be married (so can she), of a different race, religion, or society. Virgo will cut through all ties coolly to live with her lover. It takes time and effort to win her, but once she's yours, she'll stay with you through thick and thin, organize your life, take care of you when you're ill . . . and help you up the ladder of success by attending to all the intricate details.

Her negative traits can be trying, however. She'll spot a flaw a mile away and let you know about it immediately. If you don't take action, she'll nag. Her hyper-organization and extreme cleanliness can be a turn-off (especially when she insists on rinsing out her lingerie when you want to make love!). If you can straighten out her priorities in that area, you'll have a sensual treasure to be envied by many men!

HOW TO HAVE A PERFECT RELATIONSHIP WITH YOUR VIRGO WOMAN

- Brush up on your manners and your language (save naughty words for naughty places).
- Let her balance the budget. She's got a good head for figures.
- She may look like a *Playboy* centerfold, but tell her you appreciate her *mind*!
- If she's angry, pacify her with a bouquet of violets or forget-me-nots.
- Move *slowly*. She'll want to check you out thoroughly.
- She likes *everything* to function well. So stock up on vitamin E. Let her plan your diet and exercise regime.
- Although she's basically tame . . . her fantasies are wild!
- Fly her to Paris for some nouvelle cuisine. That should get her cooking. Or try a beach in Turkey, the Parthenon in Greece (or some beans in Boston).
- All Virgos have a fetish for cleanliness. Make love in a bubble bath with lots of white towels nearby. Then move on to fresh white sheets.
- And remember to shave often. Virgos hate to be rubbed the wrong way!

HER LESSONS TO LEARN

- Learn to express your feelings as well as your mind. (Though the "true you" may be sexy, you sometimes come on a bit too cool.)
- Don't make mountains out of molehills. Every job is not a major task. And not every problem is worth hours of worry and deliberation.
- Be tolerant of your lover's occasional disorganization. There is a difference between being neat and being a fanatic.
- Be as understanding of your lover as you are of your friends. Tone down the criticism . . . he has his OWN standards to live up to.

- Don't pick your love apart; you may send him fleeing.
- Learn to relax and enjoy life; you don't have to work every day to prove yourself.
- Do something outrageous once in a while. That way, your friends and lovers won't always take you for granted.
- Live out a few of your wilder fantasies with him . . . don't just leave them between the pages of your well-read novels.

YOUR VIRGO SUN-CAST

With celebrity couples and romantic pairings . . . for better or for worse . . . from the screen, stage, television, and real life.

WITH OTHER EARTH SIGNS: You could bury this romance with boredom or build a relationship that lasts.

TAURUS-VIRGO

Toni Tennille and "Captain" Darryl Dragon
Roberto Rossellini and Ingrid Bergman
Darren and Kathy McGavin
Audrey Hepburn and Mel Ferrer

SMILING SUN: Beauty-loving, successful, ambitious Taurus gives you soothing stability. Here's a really workable relationship. Taurus brings out your sensuality and loves to play house with you. You'll spend lots of time organizing and working on projects together.

CLOUDS: You need lots of mental stimulation, so Taurus could be a bit too physical for you. You're a restless type, not one for contented ruminating. Taureans have their own standards to follow and won't be pushed or nagged. But definitely worth a try.

VIRGO-VIRGO

John and Martha Mitchell

SMILING SUN: Can two perfectionists live together happily? You bet! These two understand each other perfectly . . . are much less likely to have those annoying little habits that bother the other so much. A love relationship to a Virgo means far more than mere passion . . . lifelong devotion and mental harmony count, too!

CLOUDS: You both could get caught up in trivia. And, though you love to dish out criticism, you're not too happy about receiving it. Iron this one out and put a bit of variety into each other's life.

CAPRICORN-VIRGO

Cary Grant and Sophia Loren in *Houseboat*
Lady Bird and Lyndon Johnson

SMILING SUN: This combo could give you a happy, well-ordered life; you'll both be working hard and achieving much. You can be of good, solid assistance to each other and the sexual magnetism is terrific.

CLOUDS: Could be a bit too solid, sending you both off looking for excitement elsewhere. You'd like someone who also has time for intellectual and cultural interests, while Capricorn's whole life is getting down to business (one way or another). Still, it's a good bet!

WITH FIRE SIGNS: If you learn to build their ego, the relationship can stay very warm. If you smother them with criticism, you'll be out in the cold.

ARIES-VIRGO

Dudley Moore and Tuesday Weld
Gloria Swanson and Joseph Kennedy, Sr.

SMILING SUN: An affair full of energy. Lots of stimulating talk and action. Virgo loves to talk up Aries's ideas. Aries brings out Virgo's hidden spirit of adventure, takes you to thrilling new places. It's a good thing you like to handle details . . . Aries always leaves lots of loose ends.

CLOUDS: Aries likes to be boss, while Virgo can't be put down. And Virgo can't resist picking holes in some of Aries's more outrageous schemes (here's someone who should be brought down to earth, you think). You like to be of service, but Aries's selfishness grates. You both like to run things in different ways.

LEO-VIRGO

Robert Taylor and Greta Garbo in *Camille*
Princess Margaret and Peter Sellers

SMILING SUN: Virgos can bring out roars of Leonine laughter with their subtle wit. (They can say the nastiest things in the funniest ways!) The Lion appreciates Virgo's attention to details. Virgo also loves the Leonine charisma, how Leo catches and holds the spotlight with natural poise . . . such a social asset!

CLOUDS: The Lion doesn't take criticism lightly, so brace yourself for a few roars when you point out some flaws. Leos tend to be rather extravagant and self-centered, too, which goes against your grain. Flamboyance is not really your style. You'd rather be home with a good book than out on the town every night. Watch this one.

SAGITTARIUS-VIRGO

Carlo Ponti and Sophia Loren
Dina Merrill and Cliff Robertson

SMILING SUN: Here's someone to go out on the town with . . . be it Paris, London, or Palm Beach. Virgo's impeccable manners smooth over Sag's blunt bloopers, while Sag's jovial good humor warms up Virgo's often frosty nature. You help Sag get organized, so those great ideas bring in cash.

CLOUDS: Sag can be a gambling wanderer and prudent Virgo has NO tolerance for infidelity or taking risks with hard-earned cash. Sag's approach to love is decidedly happy-go-lucky! Virgo takes love very seriously. If you keep the communication lines open, you MIGHT work out a compromise.

WITH AIR SIGNS: Don't try to tie them down. You could end up with a lot of rope. But they do need someone with feet on the ground.

GEMINI-VIRGO

Jerry Stiller and Anne Meara
Queen Victoria and Prince Albert
Frederick Loewe and Alan Jay Lerner of *My Fair Lady*

SMILING SUN: Both Mercury-ruled, you find all the mental stimulation you need in each other. You could (and do) talk for hours! You'll need at least two telephones for all the goings-on. Gemini needs Virgo to keep track of the details while Gemini creates. You could both write a book about this romance. (Shades of *My Fair Lady*!)

CLOUDS: You'll both be very hard to get . . . and hold on to! This could be wearing on the nerves . . . Virgo needs a steadying influence, and doesn't find it with Gemini. And dedicated Virgo will find Gemini a flirt with much straying power. Tranquilizers are in order for this combo.

LIBRA-VIRGO

Pierre and Margaret Trudeau
George Peppard and Elizabeth Ashley

SMILING SUN: Handsome, charming and oh-so-intelligent Libra has a diplomatic way with words. You also love Libra's cool logic and loving, affectionate manner. You're great together on the social scene and can make beautiful music together at home.

CLOUDS: The Libran scales are caught off balance with Virgo criticism. Pointed words undermine their self-confidence . . . and an unbalanced Libra is no fun to have around. Libra is also inclined to flirt to reinforce feelings of attractiveness . . . which makes Virgo very nervous and a bit of a nag.

AQUARIUS-VIRGO

Jeanne Moreau and William Friedkin
Lorenzo Lamas and Michele Smith
Clark Gable and Claudette Colbert in *It Happened One Night*

SMILING SUN: The route to both your hearts is through your heads! Virgo will love Aquarius's original ideas and visionary approach (some of those ideas might be the same ones you've dreamed about). Virgo also loves helping Aquarius in business, making those ideas happen. Could be a winning team.

CLOUDS: Erratic Aquarius can try Virgo's patience. (When WILL they get organized?) Aquarius can also be emotionally aloof . . . just when Virgo needs to be cuddled. Virgo must supply all the practical thinking here. But it's definitely a star attraction!

WITH WATER SIGNS: They'll give you depth and send you flowers. You'll keep growing fonder of each other. These emotional signs need your practical sense.

CANCER-VIRGO

John Gilbert and Greta
Garbo in *Flesh and the Devil*

SMILING SUN: Cancer gives you the affection and appreciation you need . . . and your home will always be a haven, exactly the way you want it! Cancers sense how to please you . . . their subtle sensitivity in bed brings out your passionate nature. You both come out of your shells and into the moonlight. A sexy combo!

CLOUDS: Your critical tongue wounds Cancer's tender feelings (Cancer cannot take much criticism). If you don't learn to give them emotional support, instead of verbally tearing them down, there will be lots of damp weather.

SCORPIO-VIRGO Hedy Lamarr and Charles Boyer in *Algiers*

SMILING SUN: You can live out your fantasies with this sign, which can be placid on the outside, smoldering inside (just like you!). You both also demand fidelity of your partner (though Scorpio might not always give it!). Scorpio is intense, dedicated and has great stamina . . . all of which you appreciate to the fullest.

CLOUDS: Your cool logical reasoning can't fathom the emotional games Scorpio plays at times. You're finely tuned and don't like emotional upsets . . . while Scorpio actually enjoys intrigue. Your critical barbs are not appreciated by the Mars-ruled lover, who retaliates with a sharp sting! Ouch!

PISCES-VIRGO Merle Oberon and Sir Alexander Korda
Rex Harrison and Rachel Roberts
Tommy Tune and Twiggy in *The Boy Friend*
Ursula Andress and Sean Connery in *Dr. No*

SMILING SUN: Pisces make intelligent and intuitive lovers, sensing just *when* you need affection and *how*. They will treat you with finesse and give you the tender caring concern you need. In return, you'll keep track of the practicalities and push Pisces to develop their fantastic creativity.

CLOUDS: Negative criticism sends Pisces into a deep murky mood. Be sure to make your point gently or the Fish will swim away to safer waters.

OTHER FAMOUS VIRGO PERSONALITIES

WOMEN

Greta Garbo
Sophia Loren
Raquel Welch
Jacqueline Bisset
Lauren Bacall
Elizabeth Ashley
Twiggy
Ingrid Bergman
Tuesday Weld
Anne Bancroft
Margaret Trudeau
Joan Kennedy
Marge Champion
Carol Lawrence
Taylor Caldwell
Claudette Colbert
Pia Lindstrom
Lily Tomlin
Valerie Perrine
Mitzi Gaynor
Barbara Bain
Debbie Boone
Louise Nevelson
Shirley Booth
Ellen Graham
Martha Raye
Grandma Moses
Martha Mitchell
Shirley Lord
Anne Meara
Barbara Eden
(Leo/Virgo cusp)

MEN

Leonard Bernstein
(Leo/Virgo Cusp)
Mel Ferrer
Van Johnson
Sean Connery
Lyndon B. Johnson
Charles Boyer
Ben Gazzara
William Friedkin
Regis Philbin
Jean Claude Killy
Geoffrey Beene
James Galanos
Ted Williams
Alan Jay Lerner
Arthur Godfrey
Barry Gibb
Henry Ford II
Jimmy Connors
Ray Charles
Rod Laver
Arnold Palmer
Maurice Chevalier
Larry Hagman

John Ritter
Rossano Brazzi
Peter Falk
Bobby Short
Mel Torme
Dr. Michael DeBakey
Elia Kazan
Joseph P. Kennedy, Sr.
Sid Caesar
Jesse James
Alan Ladd
D. H. Lawrence
John Mitchell
H. G. Wells
Hank Williams
O. Henry
J. C. Penney
Cardinal Richelieu
William Saroyan
Leo Tolstoy
Cornelius Vanderbilt
Alvin "Bud" Lindsay

CELEBRITY COUPLES AND ROMANTIC PAIRINGS

Joseph Kennedy, Sr. (Virgo) and Gloria Swanson (Aries)
Tuesday Weld (Virgo) and Dudley Moore (Aries)
Mel Ferrer (Virgo) and Audrey Hepburn (Taurus)
Anne Bancroft (Virgo) and Mel Brooks (Cancer)
Marge (Virgo) and Gower Champion (Cancer)
Margaret (Virgo) and Pierre Trudeau (Libra)
Elizabeth Ashley (Virgo) and George Peppard (Libra)
Charles Boyer (Virgo) and Hedy Lamarr (Scorpio) in *Algiers*
Ruby Keeler (Virgo) and Dick Powell (Scorpio) in *42nd Street*
Carol Lawrence (Virgo) and Robert Goulet (Sagittarius)
Sophia Loren (Virgo) and Carlo Ponti (Sagittarius)
Cliff Robertson (Virgo) and Dina Merrill (Sagittarius)
Sophia Loren (Virgo) and Cary Grant (Capricorn) in *Houseboat*
Michele (Virgo) and Lorenzo Lamas (Aquarius)
Claudette Colbert (Virgo) and Clark Gable (Aquarius) in *It Happened One Night*
Sean Connery (Virgo) and Ursula Andress (Pisces) in *Dr. No*
Rachel Roberts (Virgo) and Rex Harrison (Pisces)
Twiggy (Virgo) and Tommy Tune (Pisces) in *The Boy Friend* and *My One and Only*
George Montgomery (Virgo) and Dinah Shore (Pisces)
Anne Meara (Virgo) and Jerry Stiller (Gemini)
Ruth (Virgo) and Dr. Norman Vincent Peale (Gemini)

LUCKY VIRGO PLACES TO BE

Athens
Boston
California
Turkey
Paris!
Washington, D.C.

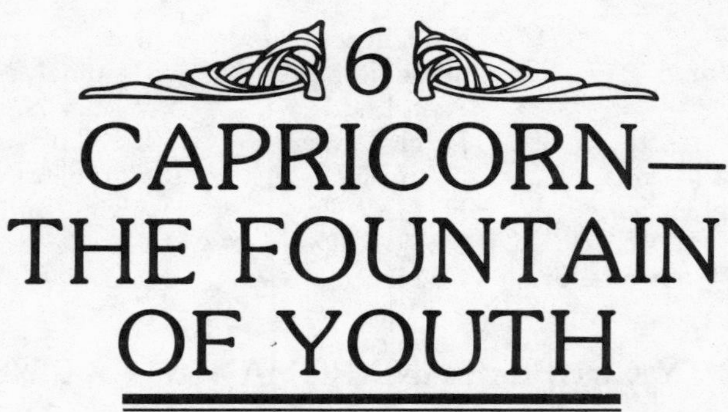

6 CAPRICORN—THE FOUNTAIN OF YOUTH

December 22-January 19

Saturn-ruled Capricorn is one of the luckiest signs of the zodiac . . . Capricorns seem to have discovered the fountain of youth! Maybe that's because they take good care of themselves and are moderate and conservative in everything they do. (Well, almost!)

The mountain goat is the symbol for this sign and with good reason. Capricorns love high places and are always striving to better their careers and lifestyles. Like the mountain goat, they can overcome all obstacles; when Capricorns set out to win something or someone, they never give up, no matter how long it takes. Saturn is the planet of self-preservation, discipline, duty, and hard work, so you'll find Capricorns anywhere they can advance or improve themselves: in gyms, health clubs, universities and business schools.

The slogan for this sign is, "I use"; the key word, "organize." It is the symbol of success through perseverance. It incorporates reason into living and depth into loving. If you're a Capricorn, you'll make a wonderful lover or partner for someone who understands your ambition and who not only encourages you to *work* but shows you how to have *fun* afterwards. (Who wouldn't love to romp around with Cary Grant, Victoria Principal, Crystal Gayle, Dolly Parton, or John Denver?)

Capricorns are always interested in those who can give them a boost up the mountain . . . particularly if they happen to be marriage material. They size up their mates carefully, taking into account family, position, prestige, and, of course, their bankbooks, before committing themselves. You rarely find a Capricorn married to a flamboyant personality who is NOT a social asset. Remember how Capricorn Elvis Presley dodged starlets to marry the proper young daughter of an army officer? Capricorn Muhammad Ali is also traditional and proper when it comes to his marriage and home life. He keeps his very beautiful wife very much in the background most of the time.

Many Capricorns are renowned for their star quality, but few are really the partygoing type. They enjoy the social scene, but prefer to entertain at home, giving intimate little dinners, or in an exclusive club. (You'll find many Capricorn women happily engaged in running socially prominent charity or club events.)

Capricorns are very well organized and like to schedule everything, including lovemaking. Spontaneity is a problem for them and, for this reason, they are often attracted to the more fancy-free signs of the zodiac. Their ideal lover, however, must fit into their life style (or the style in which they intend to live), so be sure your goals are the same. A good partner must be proper and traditional, must like fine wood and antique furniture, dress appropriately (usually conservatively), and favor the status designers and symbols. Their great love must take commitments seriously, as Capricorns will observe every contract to the letter. Though emotions and sex are very important to them, they're usually not top priority.

It's a bit difficult to please the discriminating Goat, but, once committed, this Saturn-ruled sign makes a loyal, supportive, successful and devoted mate.

THE CAPRICORN/SAGITTARIUS CUSP (December 20-25)

When the warm fire of Sag meets the dynamic earth of Capricorn, great achievement and leadership are possible. You are both generous and restrained, traditional and freedom-loving, independent and cautious . . . producing a slight conflict between your inner and outer personality. Your natural congeniality is blended with good judgment and foresight, so you can usually make your dreams come true. You make a formidable partner who has the star power to soar romantically, yet give solid support.

THE CAPRICORN/AQUARIUS CUSP (January 18-23)

You're an inventive genius with a streak of common sense! You've got your eye on the future, but you learn from the past. With your strong humanitarian ideals and your leadership and organizational ability, you'd make a sensational politician. Your Capricorn side could hold back your Aquarius tendency to race ahead willy-nilly, and you'll have the patience to see the tough times through. You love working with others for their own benefit (much appreciated by your love partner) and are witty and articulate, with a talent to amuse (also appreciated by the opposite sex).

THE CAPRICORN MAN

The Capricorn man makes a good husband and provider. He loves his home. He's companionable, but likes things "just so" and can be critical and demanding. He's conservative, hard-working, and thoughtful. He loves good food and, since he's an Earth sign, the great outdoors. He makes an excellent host and will expect you to be a good hostess.

How to appeal to him? Feed him. He's a gourmet, so start collecting cookbooks and learn how to make some unusual dishes. (He doesn't usually have to worry about weight.) When you invite him for dinner, serve exotic fruits that are out of season or splurge on a pheasant from Scotland. (Just know how to prepare it.)

He likes a tasteful, comfortable home, done in earth tones (browns and sands, beiges, and greens, with accents of yellow or orange). He also vibrates to black and white with a dash of wine red. Provide a cozy, traditional setting for him.

He'll be as hard a taskmaster of himself as he is of everyone else, but he's great in a crisis, sympathetic to your problems, and able to offer some solid assistance. He knows how to make the best of a difficult situation and can teach you to do it, too.

He is very serious about life and can become a real workaholic in his younger years. As he grows older, however, he'll learn to kick up his heels (with your help) and seem, paradoxically, to grow younger! He comes across as the strong, silent type, but, in truth, he has a terrific, dry sense of humor and, on occasion, can even laugh at himself. He's not one to rush into romance. He's the slow-but-sure type who'll want to check you out first. Then, at the right moment, he'll sweep you off your feet, if you have the right QUALITY.

HOW TO TURN ON THE CAPRICORN MAN

- Take him to Switzerland and make love on an Alp!
- Feed him the best of everything. And serve it on fine china and Irish linen.
- Make love in a canopy bed . . . with the curtains drawn. (He loves privacy.)
- Take up flamenco dancing and take him along. (He has a passion for Spain and Spanish costumes.)
- Plant some new ideas in his head . . . wear a down-to-earth woodsy-mossy fragrance and his imagination will blossom.
- Frame his first dollar bill . . . and teach him how to spend the rest!
- Always dress as if you were going to meet his mother, in conservative good taste, nothing flashy. (But wear black lace lingerie underneath!)
- He's secretly a romantic, but hates public displays of affection. (Hold hands when no one is looking.)
- Prepare him gently for changes . . . he hates to be taken by surprise.
- He's looking for perfection and pedigree. So trot out the family tree and dress with a touch of class. He'll repay you with lots of staying power.
- Give him a unicorn carved out of solid onyx to add to his rock collection.

HIS LESSONS TO LEARN

- Don't be afraid to express yourself romantically, with a few well-chosen words of love. You'll be surprised at the magic effect they'll have.

- Don't make too many demands on your partner. She can't always be the perfect wife, mother, mistress and business associate.
- You often expect your mate to dedicate herself to YOUR upward climb. If you allow her to have some interests of her own, she'll have more to contribute to the relationship . . . and you won't get bored!
- Don't try to control her totally. You'll only succeed in making her rebel. (You fell in love with her WILD side, remember?)
- Unbend from time to time. Relax and do something unexpected. You love to plan everything, but some spontaneity is good for you both.
- Spend a little cash on frivolous things once in a while . . . it could just snap you out of one of those murky Saturn moods.

THE CAPRICORN WOMAN

Gifted with the kind of beauty and sex appeal that endures (Marlene Dietrich, Loretta Young, Ava Gardner), the Capricorn woman is often a late bloomer. She has a natural reserve, but once you've broken down her barriers, watch out! She loves with intensity of purpose.

Frequently a loner, she's dedicated to her career, but as she grows older and more mature, she grows younger in attitude. Expect her to take up a new, daring hobby, like sky diving or sports car racing in her forties.

She is very selective about her lovers, often choosing men of importance and substance who can help her attain her goals. She's traditional about her home and family and makes an excellent partner and outstanding hostess (Elsie de Wolfe) for an ambitious man. She'll happily help him climb the ladder of success.

Her ruling planet, Saturn, makes her persevere throughout difficult times, always making the best of things and working to better the situation. She'll use her beauty and sexuality as a lure to ensnare the one she loves (her keynote is "I use") and she'll use her other talents equally well. She has the kind of classic magnetism that attracts and holds.

HOW TO TURN ON THE CAPRICORN WOMAN

- Give her something to race her motor . . . like her own Lear jet!
- Make her a part of your rise to success . . . she'll be your biggest asset.
- She has a talent in the kitchen . . . help her move it to the bedroom.
- Status turns her on . . . take her for a long stroll through Gucci and Cartier.
- Surprise her with deep wine-red roses (and include a bottle of her favorite fragrance). She adores thoughtful men.
- She may appear depressed when she's really bored. Clear the air with a walk in the woods.
- Take her to a VIP function. She'll make you feel like running for president!
- Give her some certificates of merit . . . like stocks and bonds.
- Highlight her beautiful neckline with an emerald necklace.
- Bring your boss home for dinner. She's a fabulous hostess and is bound to get a raise out of him!

- Give her something to remember you by . . . like the deed to your family estate.
- Don't move too fast — she's not one for instant sex. Become her friend first.

HER LESSONS TO LEARN

- Show him you care . . . wear your heart on your designer sleeve.
- Don't let ambition keep you from enjoying the lighter side of life.
- Dally with a lover who appeals to your emotions — not just to your pocketbook!
- It's your talent to "use," but don't mis-use your friends.
- Let *him* make the decisions for a change (keep your take-charge tendencies under control).
- Express your love in little ways — slip a love note between the pages of his breakfast paper or tuck one into his stocking drawer.
- Part with some of your savings . . . treat him to a night on the town.
- Don't neglect artistic or spiritual values in your climb to the top.

YOUR CAPRICORN SUN-CAST

With celebrity couples and romantic pairings . . . for better or for worse . . . from the screen, stage, television, and real life!

WITH OTHER EARTH SIGNS: A cosmic communication or a crashing bore . . . two Earth signs can move mountains together. But they need something or someone to shake them up!

TAURUS-CAPRICORN

Albert Finney and Diane Keaton in *Shoot the Moon*
Gary Cooper and Marlene Dietrich in *Morocco*

SMILING SUN: Tender Taurus puts you in your element. You both love beautiful possessions and together can earn enough to afford them. Taurus is rock-steady and reliable and a sensual nonstop lover. Here's a love that could endure.

CLOUDS: You could get into a rut together and start taking each other for granted. (Where's that Capricorn ambition?) You have to spur each other on, not lock horns. This combo might pall in the long run and have you both looking for more lively pastures.

VIRGO-CAPRICORN

Lauren Bacall and Humphrey Bogart
Sylvia Fine and Danny Kaye
Lyndon B. Johnson and Lady Bird

SMILING SUN: A mutual understanding that could last. You love Virgo's analytical mind and sense there's much to uncover here. Virgo appreciates your drive for success and will help you to the top.

CLOUDS: Virgo's perfectionist tendencies could get your goat! Not given to fantasy, you prefer to keep your smoldering passion straight, while Virgo's fantasy life could get a bit naughty. Virgo's obsession with details could leave you yawning.

CAPRICORN-CAPRICORN Dyan Cannon and Cary Grant

SMILING SUN: You both get down to earth together. You're practical and thirfty enough to build a mountain. And persevering enough to move one! Mutual respect builds a sturdy foundation.

CLOUDS: You both want to take the lead (maybe in different directions?). And in bed, there's not enough innovation to keep you interested. You might spend more time on business than on pleasure. Ho hum.

WITH AIR SIGNS: Your practicality could make their airy dreams come true. They are a bit flighty, however . . . so watch out for dust storms!

GEMINI-CAPRICORN Gena Rowlands and John Cassavetes

SMILING SUN: If you're looking for a light, playful love, Gemini will provide plenty of excitement and could liven up your murky Saturn melancholy in a flash. Gadabout Gemini loves people and a lively social life. A Gemini mate is a super asset at parties, charming *everyone* while you seek out the powerful business connections. You could both entertain beautifully with parties that make the social page.

CLOUDS: Not the love to give you stability and security. Gemini flirts while you fume. If you can do your own thing, mercurial Gemini will keep coming back. Control your domineering tendencies . . . Gemini hates to be bossed.

LIBRA-CAPRICORN Marcello Mastroianni and Faye Dunaway

SMILING SUN: The zodiac charmer, Libra has style and good looks that enchant you, while you, decisive Capricorn, give Libra direction. (How you love to make decisions!) If Libra is well placed socially or careerwise, there could be great benefits for you both.

CLOUDS: Libra can be a bit lightweight for the serious Saturn-minded. You're bent on success and Libra likes the good life, but may be too lazy to work for it. Lack of ambition on Libra's part or too much on your part could upset the balance here.

AQUARIUS-CAPRICORN Mikhail Baryshnikov and Gelsey Kirkland in the American Ballet Theater
Burt Reynolds and Dolly Parton in *The Best Little Whorehouse in Texas*
Clark Gable and Loretta Young in *Call of the Wild*
Drs. William Masters and Virginia Johnson

SMILING SUN: "Lone Wolf" Capricorn and "Maverick" Aquarius could find each other in some exotic places and predicaments. When you work together for a cause, you'll provide the strong organizational backup Aquarius needs. They'll provide the Uranus-ruled flair for mass communication. Together you could scale the political or entertainment world heights.

CLOUDS: Definitely not homebodies, Aquarians are constantly out feathering their own nests, while you're home brooding. Aquarians are everybody's pals, while you're selective about yours. When you need comfort and coziness, you'll find them quite detached and maddeningly aloof. Better stick to business partnerships.

WITH FIRE SIGNS: The conflicts are part of your intense attraction! Just don't let them take over. You could be their rock of Gibraltar . . . or just rock THEIR boat!

ARIES-CAPRICORN

Goddard Lieberson and Vera Zorina
Warren Beatty and Diane Keaton in *Reds*

SMILING SUN: A spirited combination: you bring Aries's dreams down to earth. They're as ambitious and energetic as you are. You can give them the "follow through" to complete their projects. Could be a winning team.

CLOUDS: You're far more capable with finances than Aries . . . and they hate to let you "run things." A delicate ego problem here. You need substance . . . and you're not much interested in great ideas that just won't happen. Aries likes to burn the candle at both ends . . . and in the middle! You're the conservative type. Still, an interesting combination.

LEO-CAPRICORN

Jacqueline Kennedy Onassis
and Aristotle Onassis

SMILING SUN: You both want the best out of life . . . and Leo has that star quality to rise to the top. You'll provide the setting for Leo to shine. And they will be appreciative. Leo's charm and magnetism plus Capricorn's distinguished air of authority and background make a formidable social or business combination.

CLOUDS: Conservative Capricorns can be a bit too tight with cash for Big Spender Leo. When this happens, watch the fur fly! Capricorn turns a cold shoulder to Leo's temper tantrums. You're a loner who needs your own space, while Leos like to entertain and be surrounded by their own entourage. Difficult, but could be worth it!

SAGITTARIUS-CAPRICORN

Sir Charles Mendl and
Elsie de Wolfe
Maria Callas and Aristotle Onassis

SMILING SUN: The Sagittarian is a merry mover who can show you the lighter side of life. (You can give them the "wheels" — financial and organizational — to get them where they're going.) The Centaur and the Goat could climb in tandem if they have the same ideals and causes.

CLOUDS: Sagittarian bluntness could raise Capricorn's eyebrows (and temper), especially when they gamble with your hard-earned cash. Most of your fights could be over money . . . or Sag's fickle ways. Fidelity is a MUST for Capricorn. Watch out!

WITH WATER SIGNS: This relationship can bear the sweetest fruit. But watch out for muddy waters . . . water signs are ruled by emotions, while you're a pragmatist.

CANCER-CAPRICORN

Bob Fosse and Gwen Verdon
Prince Egon von Fürstenberg and Diane
Marlene Dietrich and Ernest Hemingway

SMILING SUN: The romantic and gallant Moon Child also has a fine flair for finance, which delights thrifty Capricorn. And Cancers are so protective and home-loving. Also fine foils for entertaining business friends. A very promising union.

CLOUDS: The Moon Child's moods may ruffle your sense of order. You don't always have time to coddle the zodiac's crybaby. (You're more interested in your career than in mothering anyone.) And when Cancer's constant complaining gets to your Saturn melancholy, those murky depths could be just toooo much!

SCORPIO-CAPRICORN

Grace Kelly and Cary Grant
in *To Catch a Thief*

SMILING SUN: You will be magnetically drawn to the intense Scorpio passions. At last you've found someone to take your mind off business — for a while, anyway. You both love power, are ambitious and lusty. Could be an unforgettable love affair.

CLOUDS: In the long run, this combo could get *too* intense! You both want to control every situation and the Saturn-ruled Goat may resent Scorpio's possessiveness and jealousy (even when given no cause!). You're not one to play emotional games (or any other kind). Warning: handle with care!

PISCES-CAPRICORN

Cyd Charisse and Tony Martin
Patricia Nixon and Former President Richard M. Nixon

SMILING SUN: Dreamy Pisces fascinates you. They can relax and turn you on to new experiences (they're so original in bed). *You* give Pisces solid security and protection from the cold cruel world that never quite understands them. You exchange your best qualities. They'll soften your craggy edges; you'll give them stability.

CLOUDS: Realistic you and dreamy Pisces have many differences in basic philosophy. Pisces could demand more emotional surrender than you (or anyone!) can deliver. You may prefer to stay on firm ground rather than to drift along with this one. (But think of all the fun you'll miss!)

OTHER FAMOUS CAPRICORN PERSONALITIES

WOMEN

Ava Gardner
Loretta Young
Marlene Dietrich
Faye Dunaway
Pola Negri
Dyan Cannon
Anna Pavlova
Vera Zorina
Gelsey Kirkland
Dolly Parton
Crystal Gayle
Joan Baez
Janis Joplin
Eartha Kitt
Sophie Tucker
Lady Bird Johnson
Sissy Spacek
Barbara Mandrell
Victoria Principal
Diane Keaton
Diane von Fürstenberg
Madame Pompadour
Mary Tyler Moore
Jane Wyman
Ethel Merman
Nancy Lopez
Shirley Bassey
Grace Bumbry
Marilyn Horne
Adrienne Cleere
Joan of Arc
Helena Rubinstein

MEN

Elvis Presley
David Bowie
Johnny Ray
Rod Stewart
Little Anthony
Walter Mondale
Alvin Ailey
Robert Duvall
Martin Luther King
Henry Miller
George Balanchine
Barry Goldwater
Former President Richard M. Nixon
J. Edgar Hoover
Howard Hughes
Anwar el-Sadat
Tony Martin
Dr. William Masters
Jon Voight
Rex Allen
John Denver
Humphrey Bogart
Aristotle Onassis
Cary Grant
Benjamin Franklin
Edgar Allan Poe
Danny Kaye
Muhammad Ali
Maurice and Robin Gibb
Fernando Lamas
Steve Allen
Konrad Adenauer
Nat King Cole
James Earl Jones
Alan King
Rudyard Kipling
Nostradamus
Sir Isaac Newton
Louis Pasteur
Joseph Stalin
Danny Thomas
Woodrow Wilson
Daniel Webster
Carl Sandburg
Leo Arthur Kelmenson

CELEBRITY COUPLES AND ROMANTIC PAIRINGS

Diane Keaton (Capricorn) and Warren Beatty (Aries) in *Reds*
Pola Negri (Capricorn) and Rudolph Valentino (Taurus)
Marlene Dietrich (Capricorn) and Gary Cooper (Taurus) in *Morocco*
Howard Hughes (Capricorn) and Jane Russell (Gemini)
Diane (Capricorn) and Prince Egon von Fürstenberg (Cancer)
Aristotle Onassis (Capricorn) and Jacqueline Kennedy Onassis (Leo)
Humphrey Bogart (Capricorn) and Lauren Bacall (Virgo)
Cecil Beaton (Capricorn) and Greta Garbo (Virgo)
Danny Kaye (Capricorn) and Sylvia Fine (Virgo)
Faye Dunaway (Capricorn) and Marcello Mastroianni (Libra)

Cary Grant (Capricorn) and Grace Kelly (Scorpio) in *To Catch a Thief*
Aristotle Onassis (Capricorn) and Maria Callas (Sagittarius)
Dolly Parton (Capricorn) and Burt Reynolds (Aquarius) in *The Best Little Whorehouse in Texas*
Loretta Young (Capricorn) and Clark Gable (Aquarius) in *Call of the Wild*
Cary Grant (Capricorn) and Dyan Cannon (Capricorn)
Former President Richard M. Nixon (Capricorn) and Pat (Pisces)
Gelsey Kirkland (Capricorn) and Mikhail Baryshnikov (Aquarius)
Drs. William Masters (Capricorn) and Virginia Johnson (Aquarius)
Steve Allen (Capricorn) and Jayne Meadows (Libra)

LUCKY CAPRICORN PLACES TO BE

Alaska
Afghanistan
Iowa
Utah
India
Georgia

The element of air stands for all that is light, mental, sociable and versatile. Those influenced by this element desire contact and communication in a relationship. They are the zodiac communicators: original thinkers who speak to us through their use of words, color, style and beauty. They thrive on human contact and are definitely not ones to take to a deserted island!

The three Air signs — Gemini, Libra, and Aquarius — add change and versatility to life and provide a beautiful atmosphere for other elements to enjoy. It is through these signs that we can explore human intelligence and experience.

Gemini, the first Air sign (May 21-June 21), is ruled by Mercury, the planet of communication and symbolized by the Twins. Glamorous Geminis (like Brooke Shields and Clint Eastwood) have two different sides (at least!) and both can be fascinating. They truly believe that "variety is the spice of life." They must learn to think before they speak, or that line of theirs could get them into trouble! (Geminis can also speak on many levels with their hands — this sign rules the hands.)

The Gemini woman is charming and witty, creative, adaptable, and many faceted . . . like a diamond! The Gemini man usually has two of everything (including playmates). He's quick-witted, fun, a gadabout, and a jack of all trades. Neither is a stay-at-home type . . . unless you have more than one home!

Libra, our second Air sign (September 23-October 23), is ruled by Venus, the planet of love and beauty, and symbolized by the scales of justice. (They seek balance in everything.) Librans are the diplomats of the zodiac and love to be surrounded by beautiful things. Their lesson to learn: not to procrastinate. They weigh the pros and cons of any issue endlessly, to be sure to make "the right decision."

The Libra woman is a Love Goddess. She's usually beautiful, charming, and sociable. Though she may be fun loving, she's never vulgar. The Libra man, like his female counterpart, seeks a harmonious atmosphere. He can't stand conflict or scenes of any kind, and *loves* to be married. Two beautifully balanced and happily married (but not to each other) Librans are Charlton Heston and Greer Garson.

The third Air sign, *Aquarius* (January 20-February 19), is ruled by Uranus, the electrical planet of sudden change. Symbolized by the water bearer, Aquarians are the humanitarians of the zodiac, always eager to help people in need. Their lesson to learn: to make their lover their special cause. (They sometimes love groups more than individuals — and some of the other elements love *things* more!)

The Aquarius woman is dynamic, a trend setter, and a crusader. She's clever and witty, and not afraid to be controversial (she just loves to gossip). The Aquarian man is an idealist . . . articulate, gregarious, and a great politician. He's got original ideas about everything. The only drawback: he may be more interested in mankind as a whole than in you as an individual. Both sexes want their lovers to be good friends, as well as good bedmates. Two of our celebrity Aquarians are Burt Reynolds and Vanessa Redgrave.

Though our Sun sign (which governs our character) is usually the most powerful in our horoscope, there are other factors that influence whether or not we have a harmonious relationship with our lovers . . . such as the placement of our "Love planets" — the Moon, Venus, and Mars. It's also true that sometimes you can love someone BECAUSE the elements in that person's horoscope CONFLICT with yours, creating a dynamic tension. I hope, through this book, you'll learn to understand your lovers a little better, so their imperfections will make them more endearing or, at least, you'll be able to cope with them!

In theory, the Air and Fire signs are ideal for each other . . . Air gives Fire oxygen to burn more brightly; Fire gives Air power to create a mistral or a heavenly breeze. On the other hand, too much Air blows out Fire's flame and too much Fire creates a lot of "hot air." Air sign communicators can spread Fire's enthusiastic schemes . . . or blow them away with cool logic.

Two Air signs get along beautifully . . . creating a lot of breezy companionship. But they may have difficulty moving from talk to action, without the initiative of Fire, the practicality of Earth, or the inspiration of Water. (They'll spend too much time debating the problems before solving them!)

Earth signs have strong physical needs, while Air signs are primarily mental. Air likes to experiment with ideas while Earth wants to get down to business. It's when they help your ideas materialize and your dreams come true that you begin to build a solid relationship.

Water signs are intensely emotional, something you'd rather not deal with, but wait! Instead of skimming the surface of love, Water signs help you delve deep, and can give you a mystical and total union you thought was only possible in your mind's eye. Water's natural creativity (which comes from emotion and intuition, not logic) has intense power. Together you could reach new levels of understanding and communication.

When you examine the SUN-CAST which follows the description of each sign, you'll see many successful celebrity pairings that were NOT in their so-called "compatible" element (and some that were supposed to be "ideal" . . . and alas, did not last!). So, you Aquarius/Cancer, Libra/Capricorn, Gemini/Pisces couples . . . take heart! Even the most diverse elements can succeed if a stimulating and dynamic life is what they *both* want. Those "perfect" star-kissed lovers may have become star-*crossed* because too much tranquility and ease of communication can create boredom . . . wandering minds and straying bodies!

7 GEMINI—THE MERCURIAL MADCAP

May 21-June 21

If you want excitement, charm, intelligence, and never a dull moment, look for a Gemini lover! Gemini, ruled by Mercury, the planet of communication, and symbolized by the Twins, is really two people . . . or maybe more. Some men say the Gemini woman is a walking harem. She's never the same way twice. You can predict that Gemini will be unpredictable, charming, intelligent, changeable, and always fascinating. If you can learn to enjoy them and let them float free and keep them guessing about YOU . . . you'll love having a Gemini (or two) in your life.

The Gemini slogan is "I think"; their key word is "communicate." Geminis are brilliant communicators: they've got a line for every occasion. The mind is quick and advanced, and has a lightning-like ability to assimilate data. It is the sign for writing or speaking.

They're wildly inventive . . . you'll never be bored in bed! But don't you be boring either. Gemini rules the hands and this is a sign that knows just how, when, and where to use them. They're wonderful masseurs, so keep some oils and lotions handy to take advantage of their special talents. They like to be touched too, as long as you're not heavy-handed.

Jealousy, possessiveness, and too much staying at home won't work with Gemini. Their quicksilver minds need constant stimulation. They adore parties, telephones, and anything that enables them to communicate with the outside world! They have an insatiable hunger for human interchange and are geared to enjoying life to the fullest by finding a means of expressing the inner self to the outside world.

To Gemini, as with the other Air signs, mental compatibility is actually more important than physical and emotional stimuli (though you'd never guess it by the quantity of admirers).

Their love life is lighthearted and full of pranks; they have a light, quick wit, with a satiric comic twist. My favorite Gemini prankster was the devastating Errol Flynn, who could not resist flirting with every pretty actress

who crossed his path. Our paths crossed many times and he delighted in shocking me, especially if there were photographers around to record my horrified (but deceptively smiling) face as he grabbed me in an embarrassing place!

Geminis have many faces, and make wonderful actors and mimics. Laurence Olivier has the Gemini subtlety and genius for grasping the nuances of every role he plays. The late Judy Garland and Marilyn Monroe had the Gemini duality of strong presence combined with fragile vulnerability . . . fascinating paradoxes that often underline these complicated personalities.

It's not easy to persuade Gemini to enter any binding relationship. Generally, the more freedom you give them, the more likely they are to stay with you. They're always tempted by new experiences, but will stay with someone who intrigues them. (They have to feel they'd be missing some fascinating experiences by not sticking with YOU.) Anyone who tries to mold them to their pattern, tie them to tradition, or fence them in with domesticity had better think more than twice about getting involved.

THE GEMINI/TAURUS CUSP
(May 19-25)

Gemini's quick mind combines with Taurus's strength of purpose to achieve much! You're both sensual and inventive (a fascinating partner in bed!). Your physical strength and quick reflexes make you a super athlete . . . but sometimes your mind will move faster than your body! (Watch a tendency to be accident-prone.) Your sociable nature (you have a way with words) and wicked sense of humor, plus your earthiness, make you a joy to be with. You could be a great statesman (Henry Kissinger), diplomat, author, or composer. With your Gemini need to communicate and socialize, you'd also enjoy managing a resort or health spa.

THE GEMINI/CANCER CUSP
(June 20-26)

Emotional, intuitive Cancer combines with creative and literate Gemini to form great material for a romantic novel. Your life should never be dull. You're a "people" person who loves to nurture your friends. You're always surrounded by admirers, family, and business associates, who can't wait to get invitations to your next stimulating party. You could have a career as an interior decorator (you're color-oriented) or cookbook author (you're a great chef). You have tremendous communication skills and could also be a fine journalist or novelist.

THE GEMINI MAN

He's a gadabout who simply can't bear monotony. Variety is truly his "spice of life." The worst thing you can do is bore him. In fact, you'd hardly get a chance because at the first sign of ennui, he's off! He looks for a woman who can share his interests. (Learn what they are.) He wants someone who's bright, quick-witted, and willing to move about. He loves to travel.

The planet Mercury rules Gemini, which makes this man a dilettante — a jack of all trades. He's flirtatious because he can't resist a new face (and figure). When he strays, leave him alone and he'll come home wagging his tale of woe behind him.

He has a chameleon character that can blow hot one minute, cold the next. Don't go for this one if you're looking for stability and security. Money is not necessarily important to him . . . ideas, intellectual stimulation and a good role are!

Sexually, Gemini is full of tricks, and some of them can be a bit quirky. He needs constant variety — and gives it, too. He is anxious to explore all of his different facets. Don't expect him to take sex too seriously, though he's always ready for any fun and games you can think of. If this doesn't make you nervous, he might be the man for you!

HOW TO HANDLE THE MERCURIAL GEMINI MAN

- Be experimental. This man will make love anywhere. Try a mountaintop, an airplane, or deserted cabin.
- Geminis love to be touched but not strangled. Curb your jealous tendencies when he flirts. (And he will!)
- Stay in tune with the newest trends, the latest IN restaurant, wear the newest fashions. This man is WITH IT. He loves to try new things!
- Join him in mental adventures. Take a class in mind control or meditation.
- Make sure your hands are beautifully tended and use them well . . . he loves to be caressed.
- Don't demand permanence, only permanent excitement. Have your suitcase packed and passport ready to travel at a moment's notice. He can literally spin on a dime and expects you to keep up.
- He usually has too much nervous energy. Think up some wonderful ways to relax him — start with a good massage.
- Geminis always look for greener pastures "over the rainbow." Be ready to go with him and you could have a wonderful trip. Try to tie him down and you'll end up with a lot of rope.
- Remember, variety is the spice of this lover's life!

HIS LESSONS TO LEARN

- Learn the difference between motion and action. (Most women prefer a man who takes his time!)
- Enjoy the bird in your hands . . . that pretty girl across the room is not necessarily sexier or brighter than the one you already have.

- Learn to value your home. Always on the go, you *do* need to rest and refuel once in a while. Explore the erotic potential of every room in the house!
- You must have two of everything, including loves! Make sure they don't find out about each other, or you could end up with ZERO.
- That green stuff just slides through your mercurial fingers, so get a good financial manager. (Or marry a Taurus, Capricorn or Virgo!) You'd prefer to deal with high finance in the abstract.
- Learn to take your commitments more seriously . . . or you could end up out of pocket and out of favor.

THE GEMINI WOMAN

The words "fascinating" and "flirtatious" describe the scintillating Gemini woman. Always alluring, Geminis have expressive faces and good figures. They need romance in their lives and will probably have dozens of love affairs (a few of them serious). Geminis have no trouble attracting people with their wit and charm . . . and make excellent conversationalists (though sometimes they talk too much and become gossipy).

They enjoy arguments! Born under this "double" sign, they can even argue both sides at once! It certainly isn't difficult for them to change their mind halfway through the conversation; changeability is the keynote of Gemini. Because they are articulate, clever, and have the ability to see both sides of a question — they make good lawyers.

The marvelous Gemini sense of color and proportion, and their ability to mix diverse styles and shades, make them excellent interior designers. If the mercurial nature of their affinities seems confusing, it may help to know that Gemini often have two occupations during their lifetime. (Actually, Gemini likes to have two of everything — sometimes simultaneously!)

The Gemini woman's life is frequently full of changes, of nonstop ups and downs. This applies to her finances, too. She should make provisions for lean times (or get a good financial manager) and subscribe to a regular system of savings and other programs that will ensure security when business isn't going great guns.

In love, it is difficult for a Gemini to remain faithful over a long period of time. Often she will marry a man on impulse, then tire of him quickly and search for excitement outside of marriage. When she finds a man who can be a real partner (and if she applies her formidable mental capacities to make the union special), she can finally have a lasting romance of which legends are made — like Wallis Warfield Simpson, Duchess of Windsor!

TO WIN YOUR GEMINI SWEETHEART

- She loves doing two things at once . . . and she's one who can do them both well! Give her plenty of things to keep her lovely hands busy.
- She's at least two women, so if you don't like the first, wait an hour or two . . .

- Don't expect her to stay home while you have all the excitement in business . . . she'll want to share your adventures all the way!
- She may scatter money to the wind, so salt away some cash discreetly.
- She's a romantic who loves short weekend jaunts to unexpected places. Surprise her by chartering a small jet and taking off to a mysterious destination!
- She's always seeking the ideal man, who's not threatened by her brilliant mind or her roving eye!
- Give her her own telephone . . . with two lines and lots of "hold" buttons. (She may have all the lines working at once!)
- She needs occasional flights of freedom . . . but she's sure to fly back if her wings are not clipped.
- She loves to sleep late . . . surprise her with breakfast in bed!
- She generally likes more than one position . . . you'll love them all!

HER LESSONS TO LEARN

- You're a walking harem — find yourself a Sultan who appreciates your many facets!
- Learn to fall in love with a MAN, instead of an ideal. (And try being a little truer yourself!)
- Slow down and enjoy the scenery instead of always planning your next adventure.
- Your love of words can make you a nonstop (if fascinating) chatterbox. Learn to listen *some* of the time.
- You're famous for being fickle and prefer juggling a multitude of lovers to settling down with one. Find an undemanding mate . . . not a domineering one; you'll be happier.
- When you find out that life is more than fun and games, don't get suicidal, get help!

YOUR GEMINI SUN-CAST

With celebrity couples and romantic pairings . . . for better or for worse . . . from the stage, screen, television, and real life!

WITH OTHER AIR SIGNS: Two Air signs can create a lot of wind! You could soar to heavenly heights . . . or blow each other away!

GEMINI-GEMINI

Bob Hope and his Dolores
Marilyn Monroe and Tony Curtis
in *Some Like It Hot*

SMILING SUN: At last, a true soulmate to share your nearly limitless range of interests. And with two double signs, there should be enough variety to please your many facets! Luckily, neither is the jealous type; and there'll be so much going on that you'll never get bored!

CLOUDS: Both of you may have trouble making up your minds. There are so many fascinating things to do and people to know (and love), you may never actually get together! You both are children at heart playing many roles, and need a stabilizing influence. (Someone has to deal with the nitty-gritty of life!) Both of you will have to take turns playing the parent role to make this pairing work.

LIBRA-GEMINI

Linda and Paul McCartney
Arthur Miller and Marilyn Monroe
George C. Scott and Colleen Dewhurst

SMILING SUN: A delightful combination of romance, charm, and wit. Your temperaments complement each other and there is much mutual understanding. You're both social beings, who love excitement and people . . . you'll gad about together happily and turn each other on mentally and sexually.

CLOUDS: Too much "gadding about" from Gemini could upset the Libran balance — Librans need continual attention and affection. Libra's constant weighing of every situation and Gemini's indecisiveness could keep *anything* from really happening. Financially, you'll both need someone with both feet on the ground to keep from running into trouble.

AQUARIUS-GEMINI

John Forsythe and Joan Collins
in TV's "Dynasty"
Clark Gable and Marilyn Monroe
in *The Misfits*

SMILING SUN: You understand each other's need for freedom and give it happily. No possessiveness here to fence you in! And mentally, you fascinate each other with an incredible range of interests. Good news sexually, too . . . Aquarius will respond favorably to Gemini experiments, and vice versa!

CLOUDS: You two could easily drift away from each other since neither gets that emotionally involved (someone has to CARE!). Or you might prefer to be loving friends. There's not too much chemistry here for the Grand Passion (not that you'd really want that sort of thing). But somehow you get each other's message in this airy combination.

WITH EARTH SIGNS: Earth signs make you put all that talk into action! Together you're a cyclone of activity. Just don't let them fence you in!

TAURUS-GEMINI

Queen Elizabeth II and Prince Philip
William Randolph Hearst and Marion Davies
Judy Collins and Stacy Keach

SMILING SUN: Home-loving Taurus could give Gemini the beautiful surroundings and base of operations they need to pursue their many projects. And Gemini's salesmanship could push Taurean talent. Also, Taurus can give Gemini a strong shoulder to cry on when some of their many projects don't pan out, plus some pretty green pastures (of cash) to fall back on.

CLOUDS: Gemini treasures freedom and privacy. Taurus loves to fence them in and show them off! Gemini loves to flirt (and stray), which makes the Bull see red! Taurus moves slowly and deliberately straight ahead . . . Gemini moves quickly and subtly in circles. A frustrating combination!

VIRGO-GEMINI

Anne Meara and Jerry Stiller
Prince Albert and Queen Victoria

SMILING SUN: Both of you are bright, stimulating and quick witted! You'll always have lots to talk about. Sensible Virgo could give efficiency to Gemini's helter-skelter existence, while Gemini squires Virgo out and about. Gemini listens to Virgo's criticisms and may even heed them.

CLOUDS: Fast-paced Gemini has to contend with Virgo precision and perfectionism. While Gemini speeds by seeing only the forest, Virgo counts the trees. Too much organization irritates Gemini; they prefer to do things on the spur of the moment, while Virgo likes to plan months (even years) in advance. Spontaneous lovemaking is not on Virgo's schedule either. A mercurial combination: lots of highs and lows.

CAPRICORN-GEMINI

Simone de Beauvoir and Jean-Paul Sartre
Jose Ferrer and Rosemary Clooney
Gena Rowlands and John Cassavetes

SMILING SUN: With Capricorn, the zodiac achiever, your brilliant ideas are bound for success. Geminis lighten the load of Capricorns who always appear to be carrying the weight of the world on their shoulders. Your sense of humor adds spice to their life, and your interesting approach to sex brings out their animal instincts.

CLOUDS: The Goats may be a bit heavy going for the Twins. They're also a bit too close with the dollar. They would rather stay home and save money than be out on the town (unless it's on business). Gemini can seem too flighty and superficial for Cap, while the Goat can be a bit of a bore to Gemini . . . Ho hum!

WITH FIRE SIGNS: You can fan Fire's flame or blow it out! Decisive Fire signs could make your brilliant ideas soar! (A super takeoff, but guard against crash landings!)

ARIES-GEMINI

Warren Beatty and Joan Collins
Gloria Swanson and Bill Dufty

SMILING SUN: Fast-moving Aries and fast-thinking Gemini can make a fascinating team! Gemini loves the way Aries takes control and makes decisions. Aries never get bored with Geminis, who lead them on a merry chase. The razzle-dazzle Ram has all the verve and energy you need in a partner. Bonus: in bed you can build a big bonfire.

CLOUDS: This combo can be hard on the nerves. Gemini flirts outrageously, while Aries insists on being Number One at all times. And trying to control mercurial Gemini could be an exercise in frustration. It may be a matter of who takes off first!

LEO-GEMINI

Jacqueline and John F. Kennedy
Norma Shearer and Irving Thalberg

SMILING SUN: Gemini charms and flatters Leo; Leo shines brightly for Gemini. Both love to live in style, with a glorious social life. Leo will promote Gemini's schemes and attract much-needed financial resources. But Leo won't settle for less than the best . . . a real challenge for Gemini to PRODUCE.

CLOUDS: The more Gemini ignores Leo's royal airs, the more Leo roars! Then Gemini looks elsewhere for a playmate (or two or three) bringing on more Leonine pouts. The Leo pride could take a battering here . . . and so could Gemini's nerves. This could be a hit or a miss!

SAGITTARIUS-GEMINI

Joe DiMaggio and Marilyn Monroe
Noel Coward and Beatrice Lillie

SMILING SUN: Both are fun loving, neither takes life (or love) too seriously. You're friends as well as lovers and great traveling companions — explorers of exotic places and erotic fantasies. You're two blithe spirits who can reach great heights together.

CLOUDS: You could give each other too much rope and swing away! You both change your mind so often that the resulting nervous tension could drive you (and others) up the wall. It could be a case of keeping up with each other or running off in different directions. You need a cause, a job, or a project to tie you both together.

WITH WATER SIGNS: All those water-y emotions baffle you . . . you'd prefer to live life on the lighter side. But water signs give bubbly you some *depth* and make you sparkle like vintage champagne!

CANCER-GEMINI

The Duke and Duchess of Windsor
Harding Lawrence and Mary Wells
Hume Cronyn and Jessica Tandy
Nelson and Happy Rockefeller
Nelson Eddy and Jeanette MacDonald in *Naughty Marietta*

SMILING SUN: An oddly successful combination. Somehow Gemini wit and Cancer humor rescue this match. You function beautifully *in business*, where Gemini communicates and Cancer creates (money); *in the arts*, where Cancer moves the emotions and Gemini scintillates; and *in social life*, where Gemini entertains and Cancer plays host (or hostess).

CLOUDS: Gemini is light and airy while Cancer is emotional and possessive. Gemini is the zodiac's partygoer, while Cancer prefers to stay home and putter in the garden or the kitchen. Gemini is the perennial child — Cancer the perennial parent.

SCORPIO-GEMINI

Billy Graham and Ruth
Vivien Leigh and Laurence Olivier

SMILING SUN: Intriguing chemistry! Gemini fascinates Scorpio; you're one sign Scorpios can't possess . . . but how they love to try! You'll stimulate each other in every way! Your versatile sexuality and Scorpio's sizzling intensity create some sensational bedroom scenes. This could be just the sign to keep fickle Gemini faithful!

CLOUDS: And you'd better be faithful or watch out! Scorpio jealousy is not to be taken lightly! They'll retaliate in ways you can't imagine (you've heard of the Scorpion sting, I'm sure). And Scorpio possessiveness could clip your wings forever. Lots of ups and downs here, so evaluate carefully.

PISCES-GEMINI

Paula Prentiss and Richard Benjamin
Vincente Minnelli and Judy Garland
Rex Harrison and Lili Palmer
Fred Brisson and Rosalind Russell

SMILING SUN: Another fascinating combination. Romantic, imaginative Pisceans can excite you mentally and stimulate you sexually (they're as versatile and creative as you are!). They love your crazy ideas and can change to suit the occasion . . . so can you! You're great companions — as well as lovers who never seem to bore each other.

CLOUDS: Pisces is emotionally oriented and you're mentally oriented. So you really live in two different worlds. From time to time you may find it impossible to meet each other's needs. Pisces needs financial and emotional security to thrive; you need financial and emotional freedom. You hide your emotional nature behind a detached exterior which can drive a sensitive Pisces to drink! Still, it's worth a try!

OTHER FAMOUS GEMINI PERSONALITIES

WOMEN

Jeanette MacDonald
Sylvia Porter
Judith Crist
Katharine Graham
Rosalind Russell
Rachel Carson
Lillian Hellman
Beatrice Lillie
Queen Victoria
Brooke Shields
Joan Collins
Marilyn Monroe
Judy Garland

Rosemary Clooney
Jane Russell (Gemini/Cancer cusp)
Happy Rockefeller
Mary Wells Lawrence
Christine Jorgensen
The Duchess of Windsor
Jessica Tandy
Paulette Goddard
Gena Rowlands
Josephine Baker
Nancy Sinatra
Dorothy McGuire
Peggy Lee

MEN

Brigham Young
Frank Lloyd Wright
Hubert Humphrey
Henry Kissinger
Paul McCartney
Prince Philip
Dean Martin
Joe Namath
Robert Preston
Vincent Price
Basil Rathbone
Dr. Norman Vincent Peale
Cole Porter
Mike Todd
John Wayne
Tony Curtis
Errol Flynn
Bob Hope
F. Lee Bailey
Frank Blair
Louis Jordan
Pat Boone
Bob Dylan
Sir Anthony Eden
Marvin Hamlisch
Ian Fleming
Jacques Cousteau
John Dillinger
Bennett Cerf
Jerry Stiller
Marvin Hamlisch

CELEBRITY COUPLES AND ROMANTIC PAIRINGS

Bob Hope (Gemini) and his Dolores (Gemini)
Marilyn Monroe (Gemini) and Tony Curtis (Gemini) in *Some Like It Hot*
Paul McCartney (Gemini) and Linda (Libra)
Colleen Dewhurst (Gemini) and George C. Scott (Libra)
Jean-Paul Sartre (Gemini) and Simone de Beauvoir (Capricorn)
Jane Russell (Gemini) and Howard Hughes (Capricorn)
Rosemary Clooney (Gemini) and Jose Ferrer (Capricorn)
Gena Rowlands (Gemini) and John Cassavetes (Capricorn)
Prince Philip (Gemini) and Queen Elizabeth II (Taurus)
Marion Davies (Gemini) and William Randolph Hearst (Taurus)
Stacy Keach (Gemini) and Judy Collins (Taurus)
Queen Victoria (Gemini) and Prince Albert (Virgo)
Bill Dufty (Gemini) and Gloria Swanson (Aries)
Joan Collins (Gemini) and Warren Beatty (Aries)
John F. Kennedy (Gemini) and Jacqueline Bouvier (Leo)
Irving Thalberg (Gemini) and Norma Shearer (Leo)
Marilyn Monroe (Gemini) and Joe DiMaggio (Sagittarius)
Beatrice Lillie (Gemini) and Noel Coward (Sagittarius)
The Duchess of Windsor (Gemini) and the Duke (Cancer)
Mary Wells Lawrence (Gemini) and Harding Lawrence (Cancer)
Jessica Tandy (Gemini) and Hume Cronyn (Cancer)
Happy Rockefeller (Gemini) and Nelson Rockefeller (Cancer)
Paulette Goddard (Gemini) and Erich Maria Remarque (Cancer)
Laurence Olivier (Gemini) and Vivien Leigh (Scorpio)
Richard Benjamin (Gemini) and Paula Prentiss (Pisces)
Judy Garland (Gemini) and Vincente Minnelli (Pisces)

Lilli Palmer (Gemini) and Rex Harrison (Pisces)
Rosalind Russell (Gemini) and Fred Brisson (Pisces)
Marvin Hamlisch (Gemini) and Cyndy Garvey (Cancer)

LUCKY GEMINI PLACES TO BE

Arkansas
South Carolina
Egypt
Tennessee
Wales
Rhode Island
Wisconsin

8 LIBRA—THE PLEASURE LOVER

September 23-October 23

Libra is the sign of human relationships, marriage, equality, and justice. It symbolizes the need of one human being for another; one with whom to share all that life has to offer. It is the essence of union on all levels — mental, sexual, emotional, or business. Libra is a pleasure seeker who is always searching for the perfect balance of heavenly bodies! (It could be pronounced Lie-bra — because Librans never stand when they can sit, never sit when they can lie down!)

Those of you born between September 23rd and October 23rd are ruled by Venus, the planet of love and beauty, symbolized by the golden scales of justice. This means that having an argument with you is tough . . . you're liable to argue for both sides at once or just vanish into thin air. You also have difficulty in making up your mind. But not when it comes to beauty. You'll go for the best and most extravagant every time!

To keep your interest, the target of your affection must be intelligent as well as attractive. Libra is known as the marriage sign of the zodiac. Even if you are a confirmed single, you prefer living with someone and doing things in tandem. (The bicycle built for two was probably designed by a Libran!)

Like the scales, Libra is always swinging and dipping, trying to keep the balance. Your slogan is "I weigh" and your key word, "cooperate." Librans are one of the best looking signs of the zodiac, with devastating dimples here and there.

They will always work for peace and harmony. Though every Libran likes to be in charge, instead of ordering you around, they'll diplomatically convince you to do things their way. Librans have the capacity to recognize the needs of others and to develop to the fullest our powers of diplomacy, good taste, and refinement.

The ladies of this sign are deceptively fragile (the iron fist in the velvet glove). They're naturally co-operative except when their sense of fairness is challenged, they can then be extremely stubborn. They love a good discussion on an intellectual plane, but if it becomes personal and argumentative, they'll fly away fast! (This sign will go to any length to avoid a nasty scene.)

Librans make perfect hosts and guests. Their graciousness and diplomacy sparkles in embassies and scintillates in salons. In addition to the influence of Venus, Librans are also affected by the rather serious planet, Saturn. They can become moody and worrisome at times. (When this happens, they should take a long walk in the fresh air until the mood passes.) But Saturn's good side gives them both persistence and manual dexterity. They excel at creative arts and crafts and have tremendous powers of concentration. They can work for long periods of time, seemingly without tiring. (If Librans have fascinating jobs or interests, their work can engross them completely.)

If they have a handicap in a career or in their love relationships, it's a tendency to be too meticulous, too fastidious. They want everything to be absolutely perfect, and while perfection is an admirable goal, they have to be willing to compromise to gain peace and relaxation in their home or office. They love to work at home (in bed) with all their papers spread about and a telephone handy.

In addition to their keen sense of beauty and desire for perfection, they have rather expensive tastes and must curb a tendency to spend too much. Like others born under Air signs, they are impulsive buyers who just can't resist an object of beauty. They should use their innate sense of balance and reason to keep from overspending (or else have a partner who watches the budget!).

Librans are easily influenced, perhaps because they're basically so agreeable that they find it most difficult to say "no," and sometimes make an unfortunate first marriage simply because they hate to hurt people's feelings. They can be faithful during a love affair or marriage, but, once it's over, they lose little time before starting another. Hopefully, mature judgment will prevail, helping them to think things through carefully the second time around and choose a partner who balances them beautifully.

THE LIBRA/VIRGO CUSP (September 21-26)

You're all charm on the surface, but underneath there's a sharply critical mind. You combine taste with discrimination. Your love for beauty and first-rate brain could make for super-success as a decorative artist or interior designer. Virgo's desire to give service to others will balance Libra's tendency to self-indulgence. Both Virgos and Librans are perfectionists, though in different ways, so you could be very demanding of others as well as yourself. If you can resolve the conflict between Virgo's practicality and Libran's airy extravagance, you could have a big success in both love and money.

THE LIBRA/SCORPIO CUSP (October 22-27)

You are a potent mixture of romantic charm and sex appeal, diplomacy and daring . . . quite a dazzling combo!

With Libra's love of beauty and Scorpio's intensity of purpose, you are bound to succeed in all you undertake. You have deep feelings, strong intuition and an uncompromising sense of justice. Fascinated by mystery and power, you sometimes choose unusual (offbeat) friends. Control your emotions, temper your tantrums, and the world (and your mate) will reward you with all the good things in life.

THE LIBRA MAN

The Libra man is a marvelous lover. He looks for a responsive woman and, when he finds her, makes a wonderful husband. He loves luxury and elegance, which he wants reflected in his home and his mate.

He isn't easy to please, however, though he can be reasonable. He'll do his best to keep life going along smoothly and despite his low tolerance for monotony, he'll put up with a certain amount of it for the sake of peace and harmony. He hates scenes of any kind.

Ruled by Venus, Libra men, like Taureans, have highly developed senses. They have an innate sense of color and style and enjoy shopping for clothes and furniture (for themselves and you!). Like Leos, they need to be appreciated and are more than a little susceptible to flattery.

Libra men have keen analytical minds and love to solve problems (though they may spend a great deal of time weighing both sides of the matter first). Don't expect automatic sympathy when you come to them with a tale of woe, either. They'll want to know the other side of the story, too! Chances are, their solutions will be both fair and logical (though not always as favorable to YOU as you'd like!).

The Libra man enjoys a good social life, is an excellent dancer, and appeals to men as well as women (Charlton Heston). He loves to entertain at home and will expect his mate to be a beautiful and gracious hostess. He'll flirt with the ladies, but won't necessarily follow through. (You may have trouble getting him ALONE!) One thing you *must* know — he'll never retire from romance, which gives you a lot to look forward to!

HOW TO KEEP YOUR BALANCE WITH A LIBRA MAN

- ALWAYS look your best. Beauty and good grooming are essential to him (he'll notice if there's a spot on your dress or dandruff on your collar!).
- Let him dress and un-dress you! He appreciates femininity in all its splendor.
- Think pink and wear it often to put him in a good mood.
- Make elegance your keynote. Always be feminine and subtle . . . aggressive ladies throw him off balance.
- He has a nose for fragrance . . . turn him on with a light (subtle) floral perfume that has a rose base.
- Let him help you with your problems (as long as he's not one of them!). He'll be fair.
- Keep his home beautifully decorated and running smoothly. Pay attention when he complains that the curtains don't match the rug. Dis-

harmony in his environment can actually upset him physically. Entertain graciously with your finest china and crystal.

- When he frets over trifles, distract him with sensual pleasures.
- When he flirts with other women . . . don't worry. He's just practicing his charm.
- He's sentimental. Remember his birthday. Arrange a trip to China, Latvia or Tibet — all Libra-ruled countries — or listen to violins in Vienna. Music soothes his psyche.
- Keep in step with him; sign up for dancing lessons and learn new ones to do together.

HIS LESSONS TO LEARN

- Your scales of balance can be upset by any sign of discord or disharmony. Air your problems with a long walk or a discussion with a neutral friend.
- You love being loved (sometimes more than you love loving!). Don't pout when you don't receive constant adoration (or when instead you get criticism) from your mate!
- Get your dislikes and grievances out in the open and over with. A quick confrontation is better than a long brooding silence.
- Sometimes you pay more attention to a woman's surface appearance than her inner makeup. (Remember, you need empathy and tender loving care as well as a pretty face!)
- Watch your extravagant tendencies or you'll court financial disaster, which could upset *your* scales (and others) a lot!
- Develop a calm, inner philosophical core to help you weather all storms.

THE LIBRA WOMAN

The Libran lady is harmony, grace, esthetic sensibility, and the personification of the spirit of companionship.

There are two distinct types. One is the "love goddess" symbolized by Rita Hayworth, Angie Dickinson, and Brigitte Bardot. The other is more "subtle" and esthetic like Catherine Deneuve, Julie Andrews and Deborah Kerr. Whether seductive or subtle, they're always charming and feminine.

If she's a housewife and mother, the Libra lady is likely to devote herself to it full time, sometimes to the exclusion of other interests. Many of this sign find their fulfillment in a career later in life, like Libran Eleanor Roosevelt. Although she contributed a great deal to her husband's public life, she worked chiefly behind the scenes to help him help himself and busied herself bringing up her large family. Only after the children were grown and her husband had achieved extraordinary eminence did she launch her own public career, which continued successfully until the day she died.

A Libran is sometimes difficult to define, since she is constantly weighing and balancing the many different sides to her personality. With her intelligence, ready laughter, appealing face (and dimples), she usually has an endless supply of male admirers throughout her life. She'll either lavish attention on her man, becoming the perfect playmate, hostess, fashion plate and intellectual companion, or she'll avoid emotional entanglements altogether, maintaining only superficial flirtations to avoid any sort of emotional discord.

The Libra lady is a master at anticipating another's needs and reactions. When her scales are balanced, she's the ideal mate: sentimental, affectionate, sexy, and ladylike — charming and talented, sociable and homeloving. What more could a man ask???

TO PAY YOUR LIBRAN LOVE GODDESS HOMAGE

- Always dress like a leading man!
- Indulge her expensive tastes with satin sheets, pink roses, pink diamonds, and opals to reflect her beauty and personality.
- She loves to be the Belle of the Ball. So show her off! And don't forget to mention how lovely she looks!
- Tell her you love her . . . at least twice a day! (She needs assurance.)
- She's a bit lazy . . . and loves to do everything in bed. Why not give her a vibrating mattress — then help it along.
- Be prepared to make up her mind for her . . . after she's debated the pros and cons of the situation.
- She's an old-fashioned girl and loves to be embraced while dancing. (She'd rather waltz than disco!)
- Remember her birthday and your anniversary — send flowers! She's very sentimental.
- "Treat" her often and she'll always be your Fair Lady!

HER LESSONS TO LEARN

- Lazy Libran that you are . . . find a playmate to lie with . . . but be sure he doesn't belong to someone else!
- The single life is not for you, but choose your partner (or partners) carefully for MENTAL compatibility as well as beauty. (Libra often flips her scales over a handsome face and physique!)
- You're an unabashed flirt! Enjoy yourself, but watch out for a jealous husband or wife who may take you seriously. Mischievous Venus Girl, are you *sure* you're as innocent as you seem?
- Don't be shallow or superficial. Develop the spiritual side of your nature.
- You love to be taken care of. But, careful! That protective huggy-bear could turn out to be a possessive strangler.
- Venus-ruled, you must have beautiful surroundings at all costs! But be sure you (or your partner) can pay the bill.
- You need a steady influence to stay on an even keel . . . find someone who won't rush you (especially when you're trying to make up your mind!).
- Don't court men at the expense of your women friends! (You don't need a stable full.)

THE LIBRA SUN-CAST

With celebrity couples and romantic pairings . . . for better or for worse . . . from the stage, screen, television, and real life!

WITH OTHER AIR SIGNS: You could soar together — and crash — or spend your time talking. Nevertheless, you'll have *lots* to say to each other . . . but you need outside help to make things happen!

GEMINI-LIBRA

Ali Khan and Rita Hayworth
Marilyn Monroe and Arthur Miller

SMILING SUN: Gemini is such fun to be with that you're never bored. You both love to flirt . . . but that only keeps the situation lively. And there's no end to the fun in bed. This romance is almost too good to be *true* (which neither of you are).

CLOUDS: Libra likes being taken care of and has expensive tastes. Gemini is creative financially (but not always quick to supply cash or affection on demand). The Gemini gadabout could make Libra a bit nervous and destroy your fragile ego (somehow you never quite trust each other). With time (and effort), however, this could work out.

LIBRA-LIBRA

Catherine Deneuve and
Marcello Mastroianni

SMILING SUN: You're everybody's ideal couple: goodlooking, stylish, amusing, and charming. A double dose of Venus. You understand each other's need for togetherness and give each other mutual support.

CLOUDS: Someone's got to make a decision now and then . . . deciding *which* one could be a crisis. Libra needs substance to keep its scales in balance: alas, you won't get it from each other. Too much glamour and no guts! A lightweight combination that could easily drift apart.

AQUARIUS-LIBRA

Yoko Ono and John Lennon
Franklin D. Roosevelt and Eleanor
Clark Gable and Carole Lombard
Jack Lemmon and Felicia Farr

SMILING SUN: Lots of happy talk here that could grow into a meaningful relationship. You create as well as make love together. Aquarius keeps Libra guessing (which keeps them from being bored). Libra appreciates Aquarians' innovations and talks them out of their unrealistic ventures. Independent Aquarius will never fence Libra in!

CLOUDS: Librans love to be married and have a working partnership. Aquarius must be independent and free! Your relationship may be more mental than physical. Libra's spending on luxury may seem too superficial to humanitarian Aquarius. Libra needs lots of compliments and attention; Aquarius can't be bothered. With a little work, however, this relationship could blossom.

WITH EARTH SIGNS: They'll keep your feet on the ground; you'll keep their head in the clouds. You'll also give them some exciting new ideas to ponder. Watch out for tornados when things go awry.

TAURUS-LIBRA

Burt Bacharach and Angie Dickinson
Glen Campbell and Tanya Tucker
Evita and Juan Perón

SMILING SUN: You're attracted to Taurean strength and sensuality (you're both Venus-ruled) and Taurus can provide the cash for your luxury-loving lifestyle. (Beautiful surroundings are crucial to you both.) Taurus melts over your innate style and good looks and gives your swinging Libra scales much-needed solidity.

CLOUDS: Libran mood swings could irritate the steady Bull. Taurean rages could send Libra scurrying for shelter. Taureans know what they want and won't consider alternatives, while you're forever deliberating. This combo could swing either way.

VIRGO-LIBRA

Peter Sellers and Britt Eklund
Margaret and Pierre Trudeau
Elizabeth Ashley and George Peppard

SMILING SUN: You're both idealistic perfectionists and super-critical . . . you'll have lots of lively chitchat as you debate the merits of every situation (and gossip about everyone!). Libra can live up to Virgo's standards and vice versa.

CLOUDS: Virgo nags when displeased and loves a good argument, which can drive Libra crazy. The Libran love of luxury could cause Virgo to sit solidly on all assets . . . spendthrifts they're not! Problems could arise when Virgo's sex fantasies throw Libra completely off balance.

CAPRICORN-LIBRA

Faye Dunaway and
Marcello Mastroianni
Howard Hughes and Jean Peters
Steve Allen and Jayne Meadows

SMILING SUN: Capricorn is charmed by Libra: your diplomacy and refinement can help the Goat reach the top of the professional and social ladder. And Libra's ambitious, too! Both of you love the good life in a somewhat traditional vein. In bed, Libra gives Capricorn a mad whirl, lighting up their dark corners and bringing them welcome relief from the usual intensity of feeling.

CLOUDS: Capricorn is known to be one of the zodiac stingies, while Libra's a Big Spender. Oh-oh! Libra needs lots of pretties and parties; Capricorn needs lots of work and time alone. To Capricorn, Libra is superficial; to Libra, Cap's a killjoy. Better think twice about this one.

WITH FIRE SIGNS: This could be your hottest romance! But too much wind can blow out the fire! So, use your charm to fan the flames.

ARIES-LIBRA

Harry Reasoner and Barbara Walters
Simone Signoret and Yves Montand

SMILING SUN: Opposites attract and intrigue each other. Aries forges ahead with pioneer spirit and dynamic energy, while Librans use charm and diplomacy to reach their goals. The Venus-ruled smooth over the Ram's rough edges (making beautiful music and beautiful surroundings). Aries can put a lot of action into your love life!

CLOUDS: Reckless Aries is just the one to set Libra's scales swaying dangerously. You resist domination and always want to have the last word. Aries jumps into things without looking, while you insist on seeing all sides of the question before making a move. Libra won't *move* and Aries won't *wait*! There could be some very heated arguments here!

LEO-LIBRA

Blake Edwards and Julie Andrews
Gene Kelly and Rita Hayworth in *Cover Girl*

SMILING SUN: Leo's solar flair blends beautifully with Libra's high style . . . and you both can live it up together. Your social life will shine and your sex life will smolder as Leo's sunny, optimistic nature keeps Libra in beautiful balance. You'll both give each other the praise and support you need.

CLOUDS: Leos and Libras are big spenders (Leo never does anything small) so watch out for financial crises! Libra will get stuck with balancing the budget (not your favorite pastime). Though you love to bask in Leo's sunny rays, make sure you don't have to fight for the spotlight. Could be a winning combination, though.

SAGITTARIUS-LIBRA

Jules Dassin and
Melina Mercouri

SMILING SUN: The lovable, attractive, gregarious Sagittarius really appeals to you. Sag is forward-thinking, idealistic and, like you, a lover of truth. In bed, Libra fans Sag's flame, creating a warm circle of fire. Sag's good humor laughs at your insecurities and somehow you know everything will turn out well. There could be a happy ending.

CLOUDS: Sag is forever taking chances on love and money. (Here, too, Libra may have to take on the distasteful chore of balancing the budget.) While Librans merely flirt with admirers, Sags take *action* . . . sometimes acting before they *think*. To Libra, "He who hesitates . . . sometimes makes the best choice." You might choose to leave this one alone.

WITH WATER SIGNS: Bubbles or troubles! Their creativity and your ideas could take off! On the other hand, you'll never quite understand their emotional natures. Watch out for hurricanes!

CANCER-LIBRA

Babe and Bill Paley

SMILING SUN: You both have a great sense of style and flair and can blend beautifully together. Cancer is intuitive; you are logical. You love to pamper each other, creating a beautiful home together and entertaining exquisitely.

CLOUDS: Libra can wound Cancer's tender feelings unknowingly. And Cancer's possessiveness is just TOO much for Libra. When they suspect they've been wronged, Cancer will pull a guilt trip that will send Libra flying out the door. The more Cancer clings, the more Libra flaps its wings!

SCORPIO-LIBRA

Mamie and Dwight Eisenhower
Dick Powell and June Allyson
King Edward VII and Lily Langtry

SMILING SUN: Scorpios fascinate and tantalize you with their intensity. They also gobble up your sweet charm and shower you with attention. And, Happy Day, Scorpio will take charge and make all those painful decisions for you . . . while Libra's charm and diplomacy will lighten Scorpio's heavy moods.

CLOUDS: When you flirt (even innocently!), Scorpio stings! So fly away while you can if you're not prepared to be faithful. Scorpios want freedom, too, but only for themselves! It does seem a bit unfair, but may be worth it. Boring it's not.

PISCES-LIBRA

Trish Van Devere and George C. Scott
Lynn and Charles Revson
Kurt Weill and Lotte Lenya

SMILING SUN: These two creative signs can do beautiful things together. This partnership seems to work best if they mix love and business (you'll know how to please each other on both levels). Pisces boosts Libra's ego with tender words, while Libra's adoration makes Pisces feel secure.

CLOUDS: If Libra flirts too much, this boat could rock! (Neither sign is known for fidelity.) Pisces gives their all . . . Librans hold back — running hot and cold. Takes some work. On the bread-and-butter level, both their tastes for luxury could sink the financial ship.

OTHER FAMOUS LIBRA PERSONALITIES

WOMEN

Julie Andrews
Rona Barrett
Brigitte Bardot
Arlene Francis
Helen Hayes
Rita Hayworth
Deborah Kerr
Catherine Deneuve
Carole Lombard
Jayne Meadows
Emily Post
Eleanor Roosevelt
Barbara Walters
Angie Dickinson
Susan Sarandon
Felicia Farr
Britt Eklund
Shana Alexander
June Allyson
Tanya Tucker
Greer Garson
Anita Ekberg
Lily Langtry
Jean Peters

Angela Lansbury
Linda Darnell
Suzanne Somers
Margot Kidder
Jean Arthur
Dr. Joyce Brothers
Joan Fontaine
Constance Bennett
Olivia Newton-John
Madeline Kahn
Margaret Thatcher
Melina Mercouri
Lotte Lenya
Victoria Lamas

MEN

Art Buchwald
Truman Capote
Montgomery Clift
Former President Jimmy Carter
Dwight D. Eisenhower
F. Scott Fitzgerald
George Gershwin
Mohandus K. Gandhi
David Ben-Gurion
Charlton Heston
Buster Keaton
John Lennon
Franz Liszt
Yves Montand
Marcello Mastroianni
Arthur Miller
Eugene O'Neill
Mickey Rooney
Ed Sullivan
Pierre Trudeau
Gore Vidal
Anthony Newley
Christopher Reeve
William Paley
Gene Autry
Michelangelo Antonioni
Peter Finch
Jerry Lee Lewis
President Rutherford Hayes
President Chester Alan Arthur
Arthur Schlesinger, Jr.
Dick Gregory
Luciano Pavarotti
Charles Revson
Cesare Borgia
Timothy Leary
George Peppard
Walter Matthau
Marc A. Rosen

CELEBRITY COUPLES AND ROMANTIC PAIRINGS

Barbara Walters (Libra) and Harry Reasoner (Aries)
Yves Montand (Libra) and Simone Signoret (Aries)
Rita Hayworth (Libra) and Ali Khan (Gemini)
Arthur Miller (Libra) and Marilyn Monroe (Gemini)
John Lennon (Libra) and Yoko Ono (Aquarius)
Eleanor Roosevelt (Libra) and Franklin Delano Roosevelt (Aquarius)
Carole Lombard (Libra) and Clark Gable (Aquarius)
Felicia Farr (Libra) and Jack Lemmon (Aquarius)
Walter Matthau (Libra) and Jack Lemmon (Aquarius) in *The Odd Couple*
Catherine Deneuve (Libra) and Marcello Mastroianni (Libra)

Angie Dickinson (Libra) and Burt Bacharach (Taurus)
Tanya Tucker (Libra) and Glenn Campbell (Taurus)
Juan Perón (Libra) and Evita (Taurus)
Britt Eklund (Libra) and Peter Sellers (Virgo)
Pierre Trudeau (Libra) and Margaret Trudeau (Virgo)
George Peppard (Libra) and Elizabeth Ashley (Virgo)
Marcello Mastroianni (Libra) and Faye Dunaway (Capricorn)
Jean Peters (Libra) and Howard Hughes (Capricorn)
Jayne Meadows (Libra) and Steve Allen (Capricorn)
Julie Andrews (Libra) and Blake Edwards (Leo)
Rita Hayworth (Libra) and Gene Kelly (Leo) in *Cover Girl*
Melina Mercouri (Libra) and Jules Dassin (Sagittarius)
William Paley (Libra) and his wife Babe (Cancer)
Dwight D. Eisenhower (Libra) and his wife Mamie (Scorpio)
June Allyson (Libra) and Dick Powell (Scorpio)
Lily Langtry (Libra) and King Edward VII (Scorpio)
George C. Scott (Libra) and Trish Van Devere (Pisces)
Charles Revson (Libra) and his wife Lynn (Pisces)
Lotte Lenya (Libra) and Kurt Weill (Pisces)
Olivia Newton-John (Libra) and John Travolta (Aquarius) in *Grease*

LUCKY LIBRA PLACES TO BE

China
Latvia
Vienna, Austria
Tibet

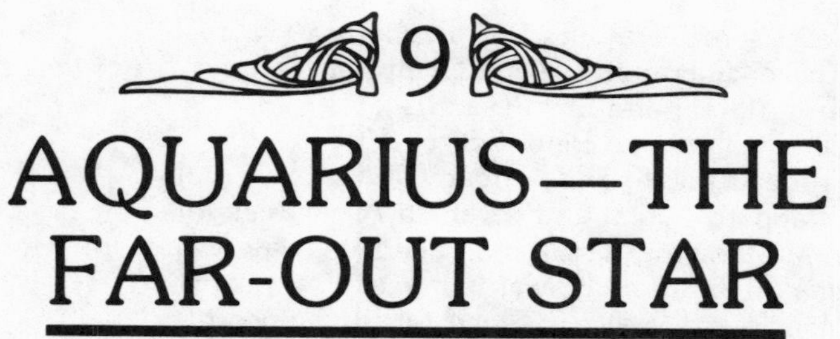

9 AQUARIUS—THE FAR-OUT STAR

January 20-February 19

Aquarius, the Water Bearer, is one of the most exciting, original, and altruistic signs in the zodiac. To this Air sign, making love is as natural as breathing! And speaking of air, you do like to talk a bit. But then, a lot of people like to *listen* to your creative and revolutionary ideas!

You thrive on hustle and bustle, and if there's a worthy cause around (or crossword puzzle) you work on it. Your slogan is "I solve" . . . your key word, "coordinate." You are the child of the future working toward the betterment of the human race. You seek better living conditions and better communications among all the world's people.

You have a progressive and perceptive mind (you can see through people at a glance). Ruled by the electrical planet, Uranus, you love new ideas and can be expected to do the unexpected. You're the visionary of the zodiac, a marvelous communicator! You gobble up words and go through books in record time.

Aquarians make the most fascinating lovers. Since they're an Air sign, a meeting of minds is just as important to them as sexual compatibility. The typical Aquarian is an outgoing, extroverted nonconformist who can tickle your fantasy. (These people have a great sense of humor and a winning smile!) Some of our best politicians — Abraham Lincoln, Franklin D. Roosevelt, and Ronald Reagan — were born under this sign. Their charismatic good looks won them a lot of votes.

The Aquarian male sometimes finds it hard to discover that perfect combination of brains and beauty, but when he finally does, he settles down and makes a loyal, devoted partner. The ideal Aquarian mate must be a friend as well as a lover, someone who can share a partner's concern for humanity. An Aquarian will give away the shirt off his back to someone with a good sob story (just be sure he doesn't give away yours, too!) and their mates must not be too possessive. This sign needs lots of time to pursue important causes and political interests, campaign for their candidate (or for themselves), and lend detached but sympathetic ears to their friends' troubles.

Aquarians have scads of friends (though few get REALLY close) and move in and out of different and divergent groups with ease. Paradoxically, they're loners who hate to be alone!

The Uranus-ruled are visionaries who love to experiment and open themselves up to new experiences. They'll try anything ONCE (they hate to miss anything in life!), but it takes a lot to get an Aquarian truly involved in a one-to-one relationship. (Sometimes, when truly caring, they'll pretend aloofness to keep their emotional perspective.) They'd prefer to deal with abstract concepts that don't involve tricky emotions.

However, once committed emotionally, Aquarians will remain your friends for life. Often, they'll keep ex-lovers and spouses as friends long after the romance or marriage is over. (Mates of Aquarians may have a problem with ex-lovers who are now favored chums!)

Aquarians have a nose for the spotlight, both for themselves and for their favorite causes . . . and have no hesitation about speaking out on controversial issues. Often they'll use their talent in one area to push a favorite cause in another. (Vanessa Redgrave has become as famous for her controversial issues as she is for her acting talent.)

Restless Aquarius is moving into the mainstream of the '80's. On the screen, a devastating array of Aquarian male stars are competing to succeed Clark Gable as "The King": Paul Newman, Alan Alda, John Travolta, Placido Domingo, Tom Selleck, Burt Reynolds! On the distaff side, the Aquarian woman's seductive combo of beauty and brains has made new stars of Morgan Fairchild and Farrah Fawcett, as well as the one who "has it all," *Cosmopolitan* editor and sexual guru Helen Gurley Brown.

THE AQUARIUS/CAPRICORN CUSP (January 18-24)

With Aquarius's abstract mind and Capricorn's practicality you're one of the great problem solvers of the zodiac! You'll sniff out trouble and invent a totally new way to deal with it. You're concerned about freedom and will campaign for social structures that guarantee it for everyone (Vanessa Redgrave). In love, however, you're often a bit detached . . . with little sympathy for emotional difficulties: you want to get on with it! Sometimes you can get so involved with humanity that you neglect those closest to you. You're a hard worker who can concentrate on a goal and persist until you reach it (Placido Domingo).

THE AQUARIUS/PISCES CUSP (February 18-24)

One of the most talented of all cusps, you combine the creative Piscean ability to fantasize with brilliant Aquarian logic. Great poets (Edna St. Vincent Millay), composers (Chopin), actors (Cedric Hardwicke), philosophers (Schopenhauer), and world leaders (George Washington and Alexei Kosygin) were born on this cusp. Your mind can literally fathom the depths of the universe (Copernicus), go beyond logic into the higher realms. If you can integrate the creative and logical aspects of your nature, you can be one of the zodiac's greats. On the other hand, it's easy for you to be "spaced out" . . . so involved in the intricacies of the mind and beyond that you may have trouble surviving in the real world.

THE AQUARIUS MAN

Magnetic, virile and crackling with charisma, many of the world's leading men were born under this star-powered sign. The Aquarian male kilowatts reached top voltage with the late Clark Gable. Since then, a centerfold physique (Burt Reynolds), a devastating grin with dimples (Tom Selleck), electric blue eyes (Paul Newman), a cutup sense of humor (Alan Alda), and two high jumpers (Mikhail Baryshnikov and John Travolta) have turned women on the world over.

Electric, exciting and unpredictable, the Aquarian male is also a visionary, an innovator, and a nonconformist. The bold and the offbeat appeal to his senses. He seeks a mental challenge and pursues it regardless of what others might think.

The adventurous Aquarian man makes powerful waves, which can charge your batteries fast. Tall, with a strong, healthy outdoor look, he has a dazzling smile, sometimes framed by a mustache and always accompanied by flashes from those laser-beam eyes.

To "land" the elusive male of this sign, you must realize that his passion is mental as well as physical. Get involved with his projects (take a tip from first lady Nancy Reagan). And be his good friend *first* (Carole Lombard was Gable's hunting companion as well as his lover). Then let nature take its course.

HOW TO GIVE YOUR AQUARIAN MAN THAT "SATURDAY NIGHT FEVER" ALL WEEK

- Turn him on by wearing his favorite colors: electric blue, stark white, plaids, and bright psychedelic shades! This is one man who really appreciates the latest fashions.
- Appeal to his love of adventure. Give him something new and exciting to do . . . with you!
- Give him lots of freedom and a night out with the boys. (Fences only make Aquarians want to jump over them!)
- Be as much of a humanitarian as he is. Get out and campaign for him!
- Choose a modern, Greek or Roman-type house, and furnish it with abstract fabrics and modern furniture. Aim for utter simplicity, no clutter!
- He goes for the newest electronic gadgets and stereo equipment. Experiment together!
- Be flexible and prepared to make sudden changes in plans. He may take up sky diving one minute, scuba diving the next — and want you to come along.

- Make sure he eats properly. (Usually he's too busy to think about food.) He's basically a steak and potatoes man, but he'll experiment with the newest Oriental or Mexican dishes.
- Wear a light, heady fragrance like white lilacs and you might give him ideas worth exploring together.
- Warm up both of you with a deep massage. It's good for his circulation (which is usually poor) . . . and yours!
- Keep your suitcase packed and passport updated; he's spontaneous and loves to travel at the drop of a hat.

HIS LESSONS TO LEARN

- Learn to give compliments. (Yes, it's her *inner* self that matters, but she needs to know she *looks* gorgeous, too!)
- In spite of your breezy, friendly manner, you are difficult to get to know on a one-to-one basis. Don't be afraid to reveal your true feelings instead of hiding them or expressing the opposite of what you feel. Then you'll be able to build a rewarding and honest relationship.
- Stop analyzing *everything* . . . it kills romance!
- You're not the jealous type . . . but don't shrug off your lady's flirtations. It usually means she needs more attention from YOU.
- Give some thought and time to your home life (or you won't have one!).
- Make HER your favorite cause . . . and you'll be the winner!
- Don't talk about your past loves (or extracurricular sexual activities). Write it down while you live it up and you'll have a successful novel!
- Make sure your partner is interested in the wilder shores of love before you suggest eccentric sexual experiments. (Sometimes shock tactics can short-circuit romantic impulses.)

THE AQUARIUS WOMAN

Here's a woman who knows how to be both naughty and nice. Diamonds may be her best friend (both Zsa Zsa and Eva Gabor concur) but she'll auction them off as her contribution to a truly worthy cause. Romance comes naturally to her, but not *commitment*! Aquarian ladies find it easy to marry, but difficult to stay that way. Sometimes they'll choose unlikely loves, since they're ruled by an idealistic spirit, not conventional morality.

Maddeningly elusive, this Uranus siren prefers dealing with emotions in the abstract. She'd rather be your best friend, and she'll often remain so even after your romance is over! She's not necessarily the jealous type . . . and she'll be in tune with some of your most unusual and original ideas. She does, nevertheless, have high moral principles (though they may not be conventional) and will expect you to adhere to them.

You'll rarely find an Aquarian woman at home, coping with menial chores. She prefers the ambience of a stimulating intellectual gathering, a political rally, or a charity event. She has a way with words (often humorous). You'll most likely hear or see her broadcasting them via the electronic media.

She's interested in people who are doing things, who contribute to life. She's an adventuress, always dashing off to new places — to explore darkest Africa or to meditate with a guru in deepest India. If you share her interests, you'll find her steadfast, loyal, and supportive . . . a partner who never gets dull with time; a great companion who is tuned in to the newest wave of exciting, forward-thinking ideas and concepts.

HOW TO MAKE SPARKS WITH THIS ELECTRIC FEMALE

- Turn her on with an electrical gadget . . . and find some exciting new ways to use it.
- Take her to a lecture on relativity or a rally for her favorite cause.
- She'll welcome a generous gift or two . . . like a sable, mink, or diamond (Aquarian Carol Channing believes "diamonds are a girl's best friend," remember?)
- She hates to be tied down to a schedule. So don't insist that she have dinner on the table the same time every night.
- She's an adventuress. Surprise her with electric-blue leather luggage and tickets to Bali for two!
- Install plenty of telephones in the house (give her a private one hidden in a suitcase) . . . telephones are her lifeline to the outside world.
- Be her worthy cause . . . then put out the lights and turn on Ravel's *Bolero*.
- Send her white lilacs (her flower) or a modern abstract fragrance with a white-lilac base. You'll be rewarded beautifully.
- She often has cold feet (poor circulation). Give her a warm massage starting with her toes.

HER LESSONS TO LEARN

- You're extremely temperamental, blowing hot and cold at intervals. Control your temper . . . or it will control you!
- You don't have to take or make telephone calls at all hours and times. It could interrupt a good thing.
- Force yourself to be sentimental and thoughtful. (Water and Earth signs expect you to remember their birthdays, anniversaries, day you first met, etc.)
- Don't talk about your past loves (especially with Leo, Taurus, or Scorpio!) — even though they're now your Best Friends.
- Make sure your mate understands your need for privacy and freedom to pursue your causes and career BEFORE you marry him!
- Give compliments — especially to Libras, Pisceans, Leos and Arians. Everyone needs frequent words of appreciation and love.
- Concentrate on a balanced diet and regular meals, with periods of relaxation and regular exercise . . . or your body won't keep up with your mind!
- You are known to be fickle; concentrate on one man at a time.
- And don't gossip — you'll make more enemies than friends.

YOUR AQUARIUS SUN-CAST

With celebrity couples and romantic pairings . . . for better or for worse . . . from the stage, screen, television, and real life.

WITH OTHER AIR SIGNS: You could communicate beautifully or blow each other away. If you can put your way with words to good use, you'll both have a high old time!

GEMINI-AQUARIUS

Joan Collins and John Forsythe in "Dynasty"
Marilyn Monroe and Clark Gable in *The Misfits*

SMILING SUN: Gemini's as freedom-loving as you (for once you get all the space you need). Mentally, you're both in tune and can talk for hours — a blend of invention and creativity. Aquarius can teach Gemini some new tricks, and their unpredictability is just the stimulation restless Gemini needs. Neither will try to change or chain the other. Wheeee!

CLOUDS: Aquarius explores ideas in depth while Gemini skims the surface (and may seem a bit shallow). Aquarians are passionate about their causes; Geminis rarely get too involved in anything (so don't expect them to march in your demonstration!). Geminis' criticism can be stinging . . . especially when they make fun of some of your more eccentric (but treasured) friends. The trouble may lie in getting together in the *first* place!

LIBRA-AQUARIUS

Carole Lombard and Clark Gable
Cheryl Tiegs and Peter Beard
Brigitte Bardot and Roger Vadim

SMILING SUN: The two of you have so much in common! You both adore people in groups, love travel, and doing exciting and stimulating things (together and to each other!). Harmony-loving Librans won't criticize or nag Aquarius; both love beauty in its purest form and are seekers of truth.

CLOUDS: You're both so busy with outside interests you may have to plan time to be together (a good idea). Libra, though a truth seeker, needs flattery and personal attention . . . and isn't likely to get much of either from Aquarius. Aquarius doesn't care what others think and says so. Libra is the diplomat of the zodiac, always smoothing things over. Nevertheless, it's worth a try.

AQUARIUS-AQUARIUS Clark Gable and Lana Turner in *Honky Tonk*

SMILING SUN: One thing's for sure, you'll give each other lots of space. Sexually, you'll never tire of each other's amorous exploits . . . nothing shocks either of you. You're both mental and physical wanderers but you'll know when to be there for each other . . . equal partners in every respect.

CLOUDS: Since neither one of you is terribly emotional, you could let this romance slip by without even noticing it. Neither of you really challenges the other to grow (expanding your mind is your favorite hobby) so you simply drift off in different directions. A shared interest or humanitarian cause could bring you back together.

WITH EARTH SIGNS: They'll bring *you* down to earth; you'll get *them* off the ground! They can help you accomplish much.

TAURUS-AQUARIUS Harry S Truman and Bess; Lee Majors and Farrah Fawcett

SMILING SUN: Aquarius is challanged by Taurus and vice versa. You force Taureans to look beyond the material, while they tantalize you with sensual promise and practical know-how. You'll show Taureans some green pastures they never dreamed of! It could profit you both!

CLOUDS: Money troubles could spill over into romance (Taurus wants to put down roots; YOU want to run from them). Both of you have great schemes and different goals. Better make your position clear from the start. Taurus could find your plans a bit spaced out, while you find *them* too stodgy. It's hard to get a meeting of minds here.

VIRGO-AQUARIUS Michele and Lorenzo Lamas; Lily Tomlin and John Travolta in *Moment to Moment*

SMILING SUN: You both have finely tuned minds and Aquarians can actually enjoy Virgo's critical ability (if they don't take it too personally). Aquarians bring out Virgo's fantasy life with their inventive ways. Then too, health-conscious Aquarians and hypochondriac Virgos are almost kindred spirits. Hmmmm!

CLOUDS: Neatnik Virgo is forever picking up after Aquarius, who could care less about a squeaky-clean house or closet. *People* are more important than *things* to Aquarius, a problem when Virgo starts tallying the telephone bills. Virgo works to earn money . . . Aquarius works to spend it for a worthy cause. Guess who pays the bills?

CAPRICORN-AQUARIUS Ava Gardner and Clark Gable in *Mogambo and The Hucksters*; Gelsey Kirkland and Mikhail Baryshnikov in the American Ballet Theater

SMILING SUN: The disciplined, ambitious Capricorn could give you the direction you need. Aquarius admires Cap's capacity for achieving great heights. While Capricorn admires Aquarian brilliance and originality. You could go places together.

CLOUDS: Aquarians' disregard for convention could shock the traditional Capricorn, while Capricorn's status-seeking tendencies turn Aquarians off. (Who cares about all those clubs and wearing someone else's initials?). Aquarians could spend Capricorn's carefully accumulated cash without a thought. This could be a case where opposities *repel* and rebel.

WITH FIRE SIGNS: This could be a bonfire or a holocaust! You've got the power to create flaming energy together or a Big Blowout!

ARIES-AQUARIUS

Ryan O'Neal and Farrah Fawcett
Philippe Junot and Princess Caroline
Rod Steiger and Claire Bloom
Hugh Hefner and Barbi Benton

SMILING SUN: Arians are fascinated by unpredictable Aquarians. (They can't figure them out). You lead Arians on a merry chase, which they love. Aquarians love Arians' energy (especially in bed, where they respond to your most inventive urges).

CLOUDS: Arians are traditionalists who want their mate to toe the line. Not the thing for liberated you who insists on going your merry way. Then, too, Aquarius can be emotionally too cool for hot-blooded Rams, who want your exclusive devotion (forget that *other* worthy cause!). Can be a flaming love affair, but marriage is risky!

LEO-AQUARIUS

Tom Meyer and Fleur Cowles Meyer
David Brown and Helen Gurley Brown
Loni Anderson and Burt Reynolds

SMILING SUN: Aquarius is witty, intelligent, and great-looking, which appeals to Leo. Leo is generous, sexy, an attention-getter — which Aquarius loves. You both know how to impress each other. Aquarius knows how to think *big*, which intrigues Leo. Sounds like a star-kissed match.

CLOUDS: Aquarius wants to spend money to improve humanity . . . Leo wants to spend it on living royally. Leo requires lots of attention and admiration . . . Aquarius is a loner who loves people in groups. When the party's over, these two have their work all cut out for them!

SAGITTARIUS-AQUARIUS

Woody Allen and Mia Farrow
Geraldine Page and Rip Torn
Mary Todd and Abraham Lincoln

SMILING SUN: Two of the zodiac philosophers get together for a rewarding combination. Neither is too possessive, since both have plenty of outside interests. Both also have a highly developed sense of humor and can laugh together at life's problems. You'll never bore each other . . . or anyone else who's around. You're each independent and capable of looking after yourself . . . Do you really NEED each other? No. But you *want* each other a lot.

CLOUDS: Someone has to look after the home (neither of you will be in it for long) and the budget, since neither cares to keep track of joint finances. Then, too, Sagittarius's flirtations may upset the normally free-wheeling Aquarian. Sagittarius may find Aquarius too much talk and no action!

WITH WATER SIGNS: They give you depth; you lighten their emotional load. You've got lots to give each other and lots of compromising to do, too!

CANCER-AQUARIUS

First Lady Nancy
and President Ronald Reagan
Frank Jamison and Eva Gabor
Natalie Wood and Robert Wagner

SMILING SUN: When Cancer's changing moods meet Aquarian unpredictability . . . WOW! Never a dull moment! Chances are you reached each other through your sense of humor (both of you have highly developed funnybones). Aquarius tickles Cancer's fantasy and together they can probe life's mysteries. Cancer will keep a cool eye on the budget and may even finance Aquarius's causes (they like to mother the world).

CLOUDS: Cancer is possessive, while Aquarius was born free. Cancer is home-loving, Aquarius is a traveler (in mind and spirit, if not in body). Cancer wants, more than anything else, a warm, loving nest . . . Aquarius has nary a shred of domesticity. Still, if other planets are in harmony, there's hope!

SCORPIO-AQUARIUS

Goldie Hawn and Burt Reynolds
in *Best Friends*
Sally Field and Burt Reynolds
Loretta Swit and Alan Alda in "Mash"

SMILING SUN: Aquarians' noble ideals appeal to the higher mind of Scorpio, as does their willingness to flaunt convention and stand behind their beliefs. There can be some fantastic sexual highs as Scorpio endeavors to live out your every fantasy — no matter how far out. Some Scorpios will even enjoy your unconventional eccentric side . . . and will understand your need to be alone, from time to time.

CLOUDS: Scorpios are intensely possessive, which freedom-loving Aquarius just can't understand (or condone). They spend lots of time trying to figure Aquarians out and then, as you suspected, gain control. Scorpio needs security; you need freedom . . . a tough combo to make work.

PISCES-AQUARIUS

Joanne Woodward and Paul Newman
"La Belle" Simone Levitt and Bill
Dinah Shore and Burt Reynolds
Jennifer Jones and Norton Simon

SMILING SUN: It's one of the zodiac miracles that there are so many long-lasting relationships between the detached Aquarians and the intensely emotional Pisceans. They continually fascinate each other (Aquarius gives perspective to Pisces) and both know intuitively what the other needs. Pisces is one of the few signs that can get really CLOSE to remote Aquarius.

CLOUDS: Piscean pessimism could pour cold water on Aquarian dreams of the perfect world. Aquarius may grow weary of bolstering Pisces's spirits and become bored with constantly professing undying love. Both of you are givers, so somebody *else* had better watch the cash flow. A beautiful bubble . . . can you weather the storm?

OTHER FAMOUS AQUARIUS PERSONALITIES

WOMEN

Fleur Cowles Meyer
Evangeline Adams
Tallulah Bankhead
Helen Gurley Brown
Carol Channing
Eva Gabor
Zsa Zsa Gabor
Claudine Longet
Marisa Berenson
Mia Farrow
Yoko Ono
Princess Caroline of Monaco
Vanessa Redgrave
Germaine Greer
Ayn Rand
Gertrude Stein
Lana Turner
Virginia Woolf
Farrah Fawcett
Morgan Fairchild
Linda Blair
Jeanne Moreau
Maria Tallchief
Angela Davis
Barbi Benton
Suzanne Pleshette
Jessica Walter
Ida Lupino
Betty Friedan
Dame Edith Evans
Gypsy Rose Lee
Carole King
Leontyne Price
Judith Anderson
Roberta Flack
Virginia Johnson
Kim Novak
Eileen Farrell
Bess Truman
Claire Bloom
Katherine Cornell
Marian Anderson
Cybill Shepherd

MEN

Clark Gable
President Ronald Reagan
President Abraham Lincoln
Burt Reynolds
Tom Selleck
John Travolta
Placido Domingo
Paul Newman
Lorenzo Lamas
Telly Savalas
Lord Byron
Harold Geneen
Edouard Manet
Robert Motherwell
Oral Roberts
Neil Diamond
John Belushi
Roger Vadim
Alan Alda
Mikhail Baryshnikov

John Forsythe
W. C. Fields
Norman Mailer
Eddie Cantor
Franz Schubert
Norman Rockwell
Charles Lindbergh
Adlai Stevenson
Norton Simon
François Truffaut
Louis Nizer
Rip Torn
Babe Ruth
Fabian
Claudio Arrau
Eubie Blake
Buster Crabbe
Jim Brown
Jack Lemmon
Gary Coleman
James Dean
Roger Mudd
Robert Wagner
Thomas Edison
Oliver Reed
Charles Darwin
Galileo Galilei
John Barrymore
Carl Bernstein
Sonny Bono
Edgar Bergen
Adolphe Menjou
Prince Andrew of England
Lee Marvin
Jack Palance
H. L. Hunt
James Hoffa
Jules Verne
James A. Michener
Tommy Smothers
James Joyce
President William Henry Harrison
Mark Spitz

CELEBRITY COUPLES AND ROMANTIC PAIRINGS

Clark Gable (Aquarius) and Lana Turner (Aquarius) in *Honky Tonk*
John Forsythe (Aquarius) and Joan Collins (Gemini) in "Dynasty"
Clark Gable (Aquarius) and Marilyn Monroe (Gemini) in *The Misfits*
Clark Gable (Aquarius) and Carole Lombard (Libra)
Peter Beard (Aquarius) and Cheryl Tiegs (Libra)
Roger Vadim (Aquarius) and Brigitte Bardot (Libra)
Bess Truman (Aquarius) and Harry S Truman (Taurus)
Farrah Fawcett (Aquarius) and Lee Majors (Taurus)
John Travolta (Aquarius) and Lily Tomlin (Virgo) in *Moment to Moment*
Clark Gable (Aquarius) and Ava Gardner (Capricorn) in *Mogambo*
Mikhail Baryshnikov (Aquarius) and Gelsey Kirkland (Capricorn)
Farrah Fawcett (Aquarius) and Ryan O'Neal (Aries)
Princess Caroline (Aquarius) and Philippe Junot (Aries)
Claire Bloom (Aquarius) and Rod Steiger (Aries)
Barbi Benton (Aquarius) and Hugh Hefner (Aries)
Cybill Shepherd (Aquarius) and Peter Bogdanovich (Leo)
Burt Reynolds (Aquarius) and Loni Anderson (Leo)

Helen Gurley Brown (Aquarius) and David Brown (Leo)
Placido Domingo (Aquarius) and Marta (Sagittarius)
Mia Farrow (Aquarius) and Woody Allen (Sagittarius)
Rip Torn (Aquarius) and Geraldine Page (Sagittarius)
Abraham Lincoln (Aquarius) and Mary Todd (Sagittarius)
Alan Alda (Aquarius) and Loretta Swit (Scorpio) in "Mash"
Burt Reynolds (Aquarius) and Sally Field (Scorpio)
Burt Reynolds (Aquarius) and Goldie Hawn (Scorpio) in *Best Friends*
Paul Newman (Aquarius) and Joanne Woodward (Pisces)
Bill Levitt (Aquarius) and "La Belle" Simone Levitt (Pisces)
Burt Reynolds (Aquarius) and Dinah Shore (Pisces)
Norton Simon (Aquarius) and Jennifer Jones (Pisces)
Eva Gabor (Aquarius) and Frank Jamison (Cancer)
Claudine Longet (Aquarius) and Andy Williams (Sagittarius)
Jeanne Moreau (Aquarius) and William Friedkin (Virgo)
Claire Bloom (Aquarius) and Philip Roth (Pisces)
President Ronald Reagan (Aquarius) and his Nancy (Cancer)
W. C. Fields (Aquarius) and Mae West (Leo) in *My Little Chickadee*
Fleur Cowles Meyer (Aquarius) and Tom Meyer (Leo)

LUCKY AQUARIUS PLACES TO BE

Arizona
Massachusetts
Kansas
Michigan
Sweden
Liechtenstein
Oregon

The element of Water stands for the emotions, feelings, intangibles, and mysteries of life. (Through water, life is sustained.) Through those signs that make up the Water element, we are all joined together on an emotional, nonverbal level. These Water people are mysterious types whose magic can hypnotize even the most determined realist. They are extremely intuitive and have uncanny perceptions about people, places, and situations. They are sensitive creatures who, like the elephant, never forget a favor or a slight.

The three Water signs of the zodiac — Cancer, Scorpio, and Pisces — have the potential for attaining the heights of mysticism and art or the depths of darkness and despair. Much depends on how (and if) they harness their emotions, perceptions, and talents.

Cancer, the first Water sign (June 22-July 22), is ruled by the Moon and, for this reason, Cancers are often referred to as Moon Children. (They do their best work at night!) This sign is symbolized by the crab (and they do retreat into their shell when their feelings are hurt!). The lesson in life that all Cancers have to learn is not to give in to their moods, which fluctuate with the phases of the Moon.

The Cancer woman is a great homemaker, a super hostess, and the "Mother of the World." (She can also balance the budget.) The Cancer man is a good provider (he's a whiz at business) and the most home-loving man in the zodiac. In fact, former President Gerald Ford and First Lady Nancy Reagan are excellent examples of the potential of the Cancer sign.

Scorpio, the second Water sign (October 24-November 21) is ruled jointly by Mars and Pluto, and is the sex sign of the zodiac. Its symbol is the Scorpion (or the Eagle). Scorpios' lesson in life is to learn to use their passion for sex and power constructively. The charismatic Scorpio woman (the late Princess Grace of Monaco) is intuitive, mysterious, sensual, and determined. The dynamic Scorpio man (like Richard Burton) has a fine, constructive mind, but a very jealous nature. He's possessive, intense, and powerful. Both males and females make exciting partners and you'll never be bored. Both desire fidelity in their mates (even though they may not always give it).

Pisces, the third Water sign (February 20-March 20), is ruled by Neptune and symbolized by two fish swimming in opposite directions. (They often feel pulled between the devil and the deep blue sea.) They are the dreamers of the zodiac and very creative. Their lesson to learn is to put their dreams to work, to be more practical, and to think for themselves. (They can sometimes be swayed by the opinions of others.) Pisceans must also learn not to procrastinate.

The Pisces woman (Elizabeth Taylor) is artistic and perceptive; she appreciates the beautiful things in life. Known for her allure and femininity, the Lorelei of the zodiac sometimes finds herself in romantic hot water! The Pisces man is sensitive, romantic, and creative (like Michael Caine). He has a fondness for liquids (great when they're oil or perfume; not great when they're alcoholic). Both males and females should swim toward partners who give them direction, a safe (relaxing) harbor, and emotional security.

Those influenced by the Water element should find harmony and tranquillity with Earth signs. Earth gives form and shape to Water (think of a sandy beach or a beautiful lake); Water makes the Earth bloom. It's a very creative combination. Earth signs are receptive to Water's talent and emotional depth. Usually Water will supply the waves of inspiration while Earth will supply the foundation. Problems usually arise when Earth smothers Water with too much practicality and materialism, or Water erodes Earth's sense of purpose, sidetracking it with tides of excess emotion. (Think of those storm-swept cliffs!)

Water and Fire are a vital, volatile combination, making powerful gusts of steamy energy. (And this steamboat really goes places. Of course, it can dehydrate or drown its passengers, too!) A combination of elements like this is always a challenge. Intuitive Water can cater to Fire's ego and need to take the spotlight without competing. Fire can give the somewhat lazy, procrastinating Water signs a burst of energy to get them going. When they both believe in each other's goals, this combination can be a winner — with

Fire promoting the talent of Water and Water happily reflecting Fire's glow.

Air and Water take much understanding to mix well. If each is willing to compromise to meet the other's needs, they can create miracles together. For instance, Water signs need emotional reassurance constantly (Air signs usually avoid emotions whenever possible). Air must learn to speak those words of love! In turn, Water signs must understand Air signs' fear of being closed in (curb that possessiveness!), their need to be free to explore their ideas. On the other hand, Water and Air can turn each other on creatively. Water will give depth to Air, Air will give perspective to Water (lift them out of their dark moods). There's much to give and receive here!

Some signs work better together for friendships, others for love affairs, others for marriage. But the point is that there are no particular ideal combinations of signs or elements. In fact, while researching this book, I met many couples who belonged to diverse elements, who loved each other because each gave the other something that was missing (and needed). Although many couples preferred their own element (and often the same sign — I found many Aries/Aries, Scorpio/Scorpio and Leo/Leo pairings), some of the most exciting and long-lasting partnerships were of disparate pairs. (Of course, their Moon, Venus, and Mars placements held the key to their harmony.) So, Scorpio/Gemini, Aries/Virgo and Pisces/Aquarius . . . there's a bright future in the stars when you understand and accept each other . . . Any zodiac combination can work together if you know the key! And I hope your Lovescope will help you find it!

10
CANCER (OR MOON CHILD) THE MOONSTRUCK LOVER

June 22-July 22

The first Water sign of the zodiac is ruled by the Moon, so Cancers are often referred to as "Moon Children." Like the Moon, Cancers go through many phases and many moods. They're caring souls who are sensitive, creative, and reflective. They must learn to swim with the tides of their emotions (or rise above them) . . . and so must everyone who loves them!

Their slogan is "I sense," their key word, "nurture." Cancer is the most nurturing and maternal sign of the zodiac (Rose Kennedy, Ann Landers, and "Dear Abby" Van Buren). Even the Cancerian man likes to "mother" his lady love. They're possessive, mystical, and secretive (they've usually got a secret love life worth writing about). Their home is their castle and maintaining harmony there or making it comfortable and beautiful for their loved ones is a major characteristic of their sign.

Cancers, like the Crab, their symbol, hang on to the things they love, be it possessions or people. (Cancers sometimes confuse the two!) So watch out, Gemini and Aquarius . . . two signs who don't like to be possessed. Cancerians also like to hang on to money. For this reason, they often accumulate great wealth in later years (both men and women of their sign have a shrewd business sense). Highly intuitive, Cancers have a knowledge that other signs do not possess. It is wisdom of the soul. They're sensitive and passionate, creatures to whom love is a fine art.

Like the Crab, Cancerians tend to have a tough self-protective shell and a soft inner body — with a heart of gold. (They'll pull right into that shell, too, whenever threatened or hurt.)

While the Moon affects all signs of the zodiac, it most particularly affects Cancers. They're especially vulnerable just before, during, and immediately after the full Moon, when they must not make any emotional decisions. Rather, they should wait until the time of the new Moon, or immediately thereafter.

Cancerians will never forget old friends, old loves, childhood experiences, or their mothers. They keep up family traditions and love antique furnishings and restoring beautiful old Victorian houses. They prefer the comfort of the home to the search for earthly success and pleasures. If they do work, however, their offices are most likely to be home or homelike. Still, they have a healthy respect for worldly knowledge and have an acute business sense. Maybe it's because they know how to use their intuition productively, to supply people with products and services they really need. They also have a keen sense of value and can be very shrewd about buying and selling, especially homes or family dwellings.

To them, the celebration of life comes through food. They're great shoppers, zeroing in on the best buys in town, you can expect them to know the best butcher and grocer by their first names.

Needless to say, they're happier married than single, as their instinct is to populate and raise children in a cozy, secure environment. Therefore, they must be careful to choose mates who not only appreciate their domestic qualities, but can also provide them with the emotional security and understanding they need to help wash away those darker lunar moods.

THE CANCER/GEMINI CUSP
(June 20-June 25)

This cusp has the sparkle of champagne . . . or it falls flat. Your life revolves around people and you're one of the zodiac's great communicators, with the wit and sociability of Gemini and the nurturing and "mothering" instinct of Cancer. You make everybody feel at home! Your keen intuition, strong emotions, and great way with words (you can sweet-talk your lover into anything!) could have you shine as a novelist, an interior designer, a host or hostess of a TV talk show.

THE CANCER/LEO CUSP
(July 21-26)

With Leo's theatrical flair for drama and Cancer's emotional depth, you're sure to take center stage, playing a starring role. You're proud, affectionate, warm, and witty, with a good sense of business. Open your heart to the world and it will put your name in lights. As the song goes, you have the Sun in the morning and the Moon at night. What a combination! . . . one that's sure to keep your audience applauding throughout a long run. Those of this cusp make great impresarios, politicians, parents, coaches, or teachers and excel in just about any career that provides an appreciative audience.

THE CANCER MAN

Here's a man who could talk you into a trip to the moon! He can be charm personified and extremely persuasive when he wants to sell you one of his imaginative new schemes. He intuitively knows just what you want and how to please you. And he's a very good provider — whether of cash, a cozy nest, or limitless affection!

On the other hand, once in that cozy nest, he's not easy to coax out or live with there. He's highly emotional, can be fussy and critical, and wants things done "*his way*." However, he's sympathetic, loves children (though he insists on discipline), and needs very much to be loved and appreciated. He's overly sensitive to ridicule, so never make fun of him, even in jest.

He appreciates thrift in a woman, so don't be extravagant. He's an expert on putting figures together, so don't let him catch you overspending (or overweight). He's conservative and prefers his woman to be well groomed, well mannered, and above reproach (as if he were taking you home to mother).

Since he's a Water sign, his favorite sports are sailing (a cruising sloop?), fishing, or skiing (snow is water, too!). He's also a good amateur photographer and will love taking photos of you. He's very jealous and possessive (flirtatious women make him feel insecure). So, focus all your attention on him! If you *can* and *do*, he'll shower you with tender affection and take care of you the way Mother never did!

HOW TO TAKE A TRIP TO THE MOON WITH YOUR CANCER MAN

- Give him lots of praise and moral support. Never criticize him in public. (Even in private, be sure to be constructive and diplomatic.)
- Create a relaxing tranquil atmosphere that he'll never want to leave . . . with good food, good wine, and good company.
- Water soothes him, so give him an aquarium filled with tropical fish, and make love on a waterbed.
- Join him on a fishing expedition or learn to sail . . . Cancer loves the sea.
- When upset, he'll retreat into his shell. Wait a while, then coax him out with a delicious meal in a beautiful comfortable setting.
- Don't overspend. Cancer likes to see his hard-earned cash accumulate.
- Though conservative types, Cancers will spend on a good investment . . . like a mink, diamond or real estate.
- Make friends with his mother, you'll be seeing (and hearing) a lot of her! Observe how she treats him for valuable clues.
- Let him take your photo in some interesting and revealing poses. Then turn out the lights . . .
- Baby him with a glass of warm milk at bedside. Then cover him with kisses and a relaxing message.
- Don't throw out his special treasures . . . like old tennis shoes, threadbare suits, battered hats (let *him* do it), or photographs of his grandparents (place them in a lovely family album).

HIS LESSONS TO LEARN

- Learn not to take criticism personally. You, too, can improve!
- Get out of the house and kick up your heels. Try something new!
- You're the zodiac pack rat, hoarding mementos from the past. Once a year, throw out those things that are past their prime.
- Don't cling to old loves, either . . . douse the torch when the affair is over.
- Don't confuse your lover with your mother! Both esteemed ladies have their rightful place in your life (sometimes as far away from each other as possible).
- You love to take care of your family . . . but give loved ones space and independence, or they'll flee the nest.
- Watch your weight. Cancer tends to put on weight with the years. Join a gym and cut your portions in half.
- Don't become so set in your ways that you can't (or won't) make changes for the better.

THE CANCER MOON MAIDEN

Intuitive Cancer ladies often wish on the Moon and sometimes reach for it. You're both protective and possessive of all your own (things and people). Your family comes first and you very rarely stray too far from them. Chances are that your most important relationship, no matter what your age, is with your mother.

You're happiest when you have an outlet for your maternal instincts, either with your own children, in caring for friends, or creating homes for others (as an architect or interior designer). You're blessed with emotional depth and a keen intuition . . . you can also be successful in the business world, particularly if it has to do with food or home products . . . or running a restaurant (you're a wonderful cook!).

Your biggest problem — and biggest asset — is your great sensitivity. This same depth of feelings gives you a marvelous creative talent (some can become award-winning actresses — Ginger Rogers) but a tendency to be too self-protective. You overreact to any real or imagined slight, withdrawing into your shell in a black mood. You'll also tend to feel sorry for yourself and complain (while others, observing your talent, accomplishments and hoard of cash, offer little sympathy!). But the positive you has enough discipline and persistence to reach the Moon!

You can also create a beautiful and comfortable home (complete with gourmet meals) for the man in your life . . . which could encourage him to settle down and forget those less domestic rivals.

ON WINNING A MOON CHILD

- She does her best work at night. So take her for a moonlight stroll and a dip in the pool. (She's at her creative best in water!)
- Give her compliments . . . she soaks them up like a sponge and you'll get the fringe benefits! Once possessed, you'll never get away (or want to).

- Cancer women are deeply emotional, especially during the full Moon. Always have a handkerchief and shoulder ready — and fresh sheets on the bed.
- She's patriotic and a fabulous cook — design her a red, white and blue kitchen!
- Money is one of her favorite topics. If you can earn it, she'll spend and invest it wisely.
- Victoriana suits this old-fashioned Moon Child. Make love in a canopy bed.
- Start a collection of antique silver, crystal, and china for her — she also loves antique satin and lace nightgowns and negligees. (Then help her remove them carefully later.)
- Give her sapphires, moonstones, and pearls . . . and she'll weave a spell around you from which you'll never want to escape.
- Give her a gift of time at a spa once or twice a year. She tends to put on weight and she'll reward you with even more devotion.

HER LESSONS TO LEARN

- You cling to the tried and true. Shake yourself free from time to time by trying a new fad, a new recipe, even a new philosophy.
- Force yourself to get out of your comfortable nest. Dash off to an exotic place for a weekend.
- Associate with friends who will keep you alert and on the move . . . the more interests you cultivate, the less likely you are to get bogged down in your emotions.
- You have a tendency to stick with those you have known for years . . . accept more invitations and meet new people.
- You complain a lot. Look for the positive side of life and let some sunshine in.
- Learn to tackle your problems head on, instead of withdrawing into your shell. The longer you avoid them, the longer they'll remain.
- Don't get too involved in others' problems. Help them to solve their own. (They will.)
- Mother, but don't smother!
- Don't let those pounds accumulate; enroll in a gym or sign up for an aerobics course.

YOUR CANCER SUN-CAST

With celebrity couples and romantic pairings . . . for better or for worse . . . from the stage, screen, television, and real life.

WITH OTHER WATER SIGNS: You'll either be the deepest soul mates . . . or drown each other!

CANCER-CANCER

Playwright Jean Kerr and
Critic Walter Kerr
Richard Rodgers and Oscar Hammerstein II

SMILING SUN: Get a good seat for many enchanted evenings. If they love you . . . you can't say no. You're both very sensitive and very loving. You both love domestic life and making a beautiful home for each other. Could make beautiful music together.

CLOUDS: You may want to wash this one right out of your hair after a few mutually moody spells. You both get carried away with the most minor disagreement and brood for days. Mother each other until the mood swings back in your favor.

SCORPIO-CANCER

Prince Charles and
Princess Diana

SMILING SUN: A match made in Heaven. Cancer's TLC soothes intense Scorpio, while their possessiveness gives you all the emotional security you need. A great match financially, too, as your flair for finance pairs with a Scorpio's discipline. It's hard to fault this one!

CLOUDS: Scorpio wants your all, while they always hold a little (sometimes a LOT) of themselves in reserve. Cancer can cling too much (which then becomes an irresistible challenge to break loose . . . Scorpio loves a challenge!). And when a black Scorpio mood collides with Cancer's lunar madness, watch out!

PISCES-CANCER

Johnny Cash and June Carter Cash
James Taylor and Carly Simon
Elizabeth Taylor and Michael Wilding

SMILING SUN: You love to take care of Pisces; they understand your emotional needs. You'll both ride the tides of passion (you'll keep an eye on the refrigerator and the cash!). Pisces could take you on a "trip to the Moon on gossamer wings," from which you both may never want to return.

CLOUDS: The Fish can be a bit slippery, when you dig in that possessive claw. And even nurturing Moon Children may get a bit tired of constantly tending their needs. When all the emotions start flowing, you may feel you're in over your head!

WITH AIR SIGNS: It could sparkle and bubble or be a whole lot of trouble!

GEMINI-CANCER

Jessica Tandy and Hume Cronyn
The Duchess of Windsor and
the Duke
Mary Wells and Harding Lawrence

SMILING SUN: Cancer appreciates the Gemini talent and potential: blended with your emotional appeal you could sway anyone! You give

Gemini depth; they give you the light touch that can help blow away your darker moods. A magic combination.

CLOUDS: You're looking for security, not continual stimulation . . . and Gemini may seem to have little substance to offer. They're not much help when a blue mood hits and you need tender loving care. This relationship takes a lot of work from you, a lot of play from Gemini.

LIBRA-CANCER

William Paley and his "best-dressed" wife, Babe

SMILING SUN: Beauty-loving Libra responds to your creative talent and is mystified by your wonderful intuitive powers. You know instinctively how to create the harmonious environment Librans need to thrive. You'll entertain exquisitely and your "mothering" approach could soothe Libra's nerves.

CLOUDS: You follow your emotions while Libra is forever trying to be impartial. Just when you need sympathy, Libra will take the opposite view, and when you need soothing words of love, they'll want to discuss the world situation. Lots of understanding on both parts could make this work, however.

AQUARIUS-CANCER

President Ronald Reagan and his wife, Nancy

SMILING SUN: An unlikely combination that often works beautifully. If your basic philosophies harmonize and you share a cause (you'd love to mother the world) this pairing could be a winner. You'll provide the personal touch and strong devotion Aquarius needs. You love their knowledge, intelligence and idealism; they love your intuition and practical sense.

CLOUDS: The deeply emotional Cancer could be looking for far more depth and intimacy than cool Aquarians can give. (They'd far rather be at a political rally than home cuddling with you!) If you can't join them, you'd better get used to evenings alone.

WITH EARTH SIGNS: A garden of roses . . . or mud flats! (Watch out for quicksand, too!)

TAURUS-CANCER

Rita Coolidge and Kris Kristofferson
Alice Faye and Phil Harris

SMILING SUN: Taurus steadies the Cancerian emotional ups and downs; you create the cozy home life Taurus loves. There's hardly ever a shortage of love or money in this combination. Sex is as romantic as a moonlit beach.

CLOUDS: Taurus likes love to flow smoothly and may not understand Cancer's fluctuating moods (no use advising them to wait for the next lunar phase). Cancer may find Taurus too stubborn and uncompromising. The Bull and the Crab may not suit each other's appetites.

VIRGO-CANCER Anne Bancroft and Mel Brooks

SMILING SUN: You're both caretakers who love tending each other's needs. Virgo's logical, practical approach to life jibes with yours (you'll use your intuition as well as logic). You're both beautifully organized and seem to steady each other . . . you calm their nerves, they steady your emotions. Your home will be a beautiful and comfortable place for the world to visit.

CLOUDS: Virgo can be overly critical . . . and any kind of criticism shakes Cancerians up. Petty bickering could send you into a lunar eclipse of gloom and doom. Virgo is not sensitive to your every mood . . . and will wonder why your're making such a fuss. Hmmmmm!

CAPRICORN-CANCER Diane and Prince Egon von Fürstenberg
Gwen Verdon and Bob Fosse
Chet Huntley and David Brinkley
Marlene Dietrich and Ernest Hemingway

SMILING SUN: You're two achievers who love to care for those you love. Capricorn gives Cancer the security you need, financially and emotionally. Sexually, tender Cancer will keep Capricorn contentedly at home. You'll both give each other helping hands!

CLOUDS: Capricorn has no patience with Cancerian moods: they're too busy to be bothered with that sort of thing. Cancer may crave affection . . . and seek it elsewhere. You both have your darker moods . . . hopefully not at the same time or you might just withdraw permanently!

WITH FIRE SIGNS: You'll reflect Fire's glory . . . making the blaze even more intense, or there'll be a drizzle, sizzle and fizzle!

ARIES-CANCER Marsha Mason and Neil Simon
Betty and Former President Gerald Ford
Cleopatra and Julius Caesar
Ali McGraw and Robert Evans

SMILING SUN: You give Aries stability and security . . . while they encourage your achievements and promote your creative ideas. You love their spark and energy; they lift you out of your soggy moods. You can make *them* stars.

CLOUDS: Restless Aries is not one to hang around the house, while you yearn for cozy evenings at home. Aries can be very selfish, while you are very self-protective. Chances are they'll never get inside your shell — completely.

LEO-CANCER Robert Taylor and
Barbara Stanwyck
Napoleon and Josephine
Eydie Gormé and Steve Lawrence

SMILING SUN: You'd love to make the Lion your favorite pet. Leos are distinguished, poised; and when they purrrrr . . . WOW! And so generous! Leo soaks up your tender loving care . . . and you'll shine by Leo's fire!

CLOUDS: Sunny Leos don't understand Cancer's lunar moods . . . it's a phase they'd rather not go through. They also don't understand that you need constant attention and to shine in your own special way. Leo needs its own territory and might feel a bit fenced in by Cancer. Explore this jungle thoroughly before committing yourselves.

SAGITTARIUS-CANCER

Noel Coward and Gertrude Lawrence
Liv Ullman and Ingmar Bergman

SMILING SUN: You bring out Sag's star quality with lots of loving attention, while jovial Sag jokes you out of many a bleak mood . . . and gets you up and out of the house, or else! You'll share many happy (and sexual) adventures together. Sag can be your best friend and lover.

CLOUDS: Sag loves to play games and take risks . . . neither appeals to Cancer. You are too cautious and self-protective for this daredevil, especially in the financial area. Cancer is a home lover . . . Sag hates to stay in any one place for long. This one takes a lot of patience.

OTHER FAMOUS MOON CHILDREN

WOMEN

Lindsay Wagner
Anne Morrow Lindbergh
Meryl Streep
Cyndy Garvey
Empress Josephine
Carly Simon
June Lockhart
Anna Moffo
Pearl Buck
Helen Keller
Ruth Warrick
Susan Hayward
Lena Horne
Princess Diana
Leslie Caron
Olivia de Havilland
Karen Black
Genevieve Bujold
Isabelle Adjani
Virginia Graham
"Dear Abby" Van Buren
Ann Landers

Rose Kennedy (Leo/Cancer cusp)
Gina Lollobrigida
Eva Marie Saint
Tokyo Rose
Julie Nixon Eisenhower
Barbara Cartland
Eunice Shriver
Polly Bergen
Ginger Rogers
Mary Baker Eddy
Diahann Carroll
Phyllis Diller
Barbara Stanwyck
Lucie Arnaz
Natalie Wood
George Sand
Nancy Reagan
Janet Leigh
Dorothy Kirsten
Jean Kerr
Shirley Eder

MEN

Sylvester Stallone
Kris Kristofferson
Bill Blass
Gower Champion
Bob Fosse
Joseph Papp
Erich Maria Remarque
John Dillinger
The Duke of Windsor
Dr. Alfred Kinsey
George Abbott
Claude Chabrol
Henry Ward Beecher
Jack Dempsey
Sidney Lumet
Richard Rodgers
Jean-Jacques Rousseau
Mel Brooks
Robert Evans
Stokeley Carmichael
Peter Paul Rubens
William Zeckendorf
Buddy Rich
Tab Hunter
Stavros Niarchos
Geraldo Rivera
George M. Cohan
George Sanders
Henry Cabot Lodge
Merv Griffin
Nelson Rockefeller
Roone Arledge
Steve Lawrence
Billy Eckstine
John D. Rockefeller
O. J. Simpson
David Brinkley
Max von Sydow
Marcel Proust
Yul Brynner
Milton Berle
Van Cliburn
Julius Caesar
Amedeo Modigliani
Oscar Hammerstein II
Harrison Ford
Ingmar Bergman
Former President Gerald Ford
Art Linkletter
Pete Rose
Donald Sutherland
James Cagney
Elliott Richardson
Ernest Hemingway
Oscar de la Renta (cusp Leo)
Phil Carey
Jason Robards
Alexander Calder
Haile Selassie
Harding Lawrence
Cat Stevens
Paul Anka
Arthur Treacher
Robert Sarnoff
President Calvin Coolidge
Senator Robert Dole (cusp Leo)
Richard J. Durrell (cusp Leo)

CELEBRITY COUPLES AND ROMANTIC PAIRINGS

Mel Brooks (Cancer) and Anne Bancroft (Virgo)
Rose Kennedy (Cancer) and Joseph Kennedy, Sr. (Virgo)
Bob Fosse (Cancer) and Gwen Verdon (Capricorn)
David Brinkley (Cancer) and Chet Huntley (Capricorn)
Ernest Hemingway (Cancer) and Marlene Dietrich (Capricorn)
Neil Simon (Cancer) and Marsha Mason (Aries)
Ginger Rogers (Cancer) and Fred Astaire (Taurus)
Julius Caesar (Cancer) and Cleopatra (Aries)

Robert Evans (Cancer) and Ali MacGraw (Aries)
Former President Gerald Ford (Cancer) and Betty (Aries)
Barbara Stanwyck (Cancer) and Robert Taylor (Leo)
Steve Lawrence (Cancer) and Eydie Gormé (Leo)
Josephine (Cancer) and Napoleon (Leo)
Gertrude Lawrence (Cancer) and Noel Coward (Sagittarius)
Ingmar Bergman (Cancer) and Liv Ullmann (Sagittarius)
Jean Kerr (Cancer) and Walter Kerr (Cancer)
Richard Rodgers (Cancer) and Oscar Hammerstein II (Cancer)
Princess Diana (Cancer) and Prince Charles (Scorpio)
June Carter Cash (Cancer) and Johnny Cash (Pisces)
Michael Wilding (Cancer) and Elizabeth Taylor (Pisces)
Carly Simon (Cancer) and James Taylor (Pisces)
Hume Cronyn (Cancer) and Jessica Tandy (Gemini)
The Duke of Windsor (Cancer) and his Duchess (Gemini)
Cyndy Garvey (Cancer) and Marvin Hamlisch (Gemini)
Harding Lawrence (Cancer) and Mary Wells Lawrence (Gemini)
Babe Paley (Cancer) and William S. Paley (Libra)
First Lady Nancy Reagan (Cancer) and President Ronald Reagan (Aquarius)
Kris Kristofferson (Cancer) and Rita Coolidge (Taurus)
Phil Harris (Cancer) and Alice Faye (Taurus)

LUCKY CANCER PLACES TO BE

Holland
New Hampshire
Idaho
New York City
Africa
Istanbul
Liberia
Scotland
Venice

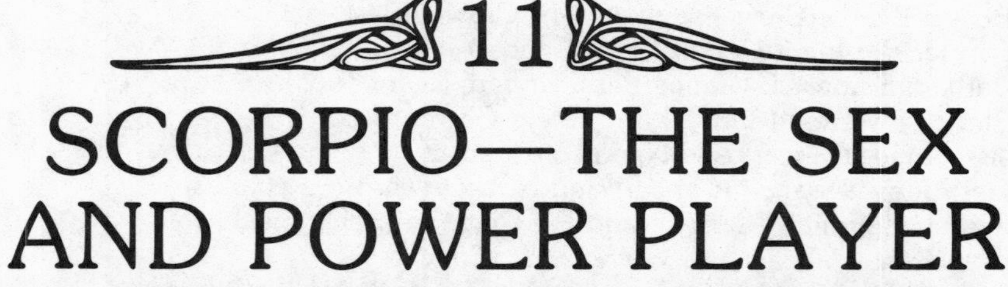

11 SCORPIO—THE SEX AND POWER PLAYER

October 24-November 21

Scorpio, known as the sex sign of the zodiac, is full of swirling passion and sexual magnetism. Symbolized by the earthy Scorpion and the soaring Eagle, Scorpios can be both heavenly and earthy at the same time, and they have a profound instinct for survival and reproduction. Secretive and intimate, they are self-directed creatures with a will of steel!

Ruled by Mars and Pluto jointly, their slogan is "I desire"; their key word is "dominate." Scorpios must be in control at all times and rarely reveal their secret thoughts. They can create, manipulate, and control you with a magician's touch.

Scorpios have intense personal magnetism (you'll know what I mean if you've ever been pinned to your seat by their riveting gaze). And they always know what you're thinking. There's practically no task they won't tackle if they're intrigued. And when they tackle *you* . . . you're in for a breathtaking time. (They say Count Dracula was a Scorpio. Hmmmm.) Exciting natives of this sign is easy. It's cooling them down that's a challenge. They are a vibrant living force, in a constant state of readiness, and will pursue their goals despite any obstacles that may stand in their way. Wow!

Scorpio sex symbols tend to be "still waters run deep" types. On the surface, they appear placid, but inside the waters boil. They love to keep you guessing, and one thing's sure . . . this is not a sign for a casual fling. They're possessive, jealous, and vengeful. On the other hand, maybe all that intensity is worth it! They never do anything halfway. Marie Antoinette, King Louis XVI's Scorpio queen, was such a serious pleasure-seeker that she literally lost her head!

This sign loves mystery more than any other. Scorpios can't resist a whodunit and will sleuth out your darkest secrets (but just try to get them to reveal theirs). They make marvelous scientists, doctors, and detectives. One reason they're so secretive is that they are also very emotionally vulnerable . . . no sign can suffer more acutely than Scorpio when truly hurt (they'll never forget or forgive for this reason!).

Scorpios may love on impulse, but they rarely marry without knowing *why* and *how* their mates will fit into their life's plan. (Every Scorpio has a life plan . . . but that's a secret!)

When they judge you worthy of their affections, no sign is more loyal, loving, or steadfast in times of trouble. They are the embodiment of truth and courage and have a spiritual and healing side that is very underrated.

Scorpio women are often cool, tailored types like Linda Evans, Jane Pauley, Katharine Hepburn, or the late Princess Grace of Monaco. The Scorpio man can be either walking dynamite (Billy Graham and Richard Burton) or controlled combustion (Dick Cavett or Roy Rogers). Scorpios marry for keeps (they do everything intensely) and make exciting, powerful mates. But better stock up on vitamins!

THE SCORPIO/LIBRA CUSP (October 22-27)

You mask an iron fist in a velvet glove. Your Libra charm and diplomacy covers deep feelings and a strong will. You can be airy and romantic, then switch to a deeply sensual side, giving a slightly mixed message to your lover: are you a flirt or someone to take seriously? But your way with words plus an innate strength of purpose propel you to the highest places. You're an inspiring leader with a gift for charming the masses (François Mitterrand, Johnny Carson).

THE SCORPIO/SAGITTARIUS CUSP (November 20-25)

Daring and outspoken, you are extremely independent and energetic, with a sharp Scorpio sting! You'll say what you think, regardless! You're a formidable opponent who never gives up. Your zany Sagittarius side can make you a great comic (Harpo Marx), while your Scorpio discipline and intensity can make you a winner in any contest (Billie Jean King, Charles de Gaulle). You're a potent combination of idealism and willpower that could soar above the crowd like an eagle or arrow!

THE SCORPIO MAN

The Scorpio man makes a very exciting partner. You will never be bored (but you may get tired). He has a fine constructive mind, but a very jealous nature. Like Caesar's wife, you'll have to be above reproach. He'll suspect you even though you're the soul of fidelity. He can never get enough love and affection (from you or anyone!).

Some men of this sign work tirelessly and often thanklessly for the benefit of the human race. Some are great surgeons and political leaders. You can be sure, no matter where they are placed, that matters of life and death absorb them (think of Picasso's *Guernica* and Billy Graham's concern with saving souls). Though Scorpio is considered the sex sign of the zodiac, don't always expect a spectacular lover . . . actually, this sign is just as concerned with power: getting it and using it . . . many of them make excellent hypnotists.

They love to exercise control and will try to dominate the woman in their life. (But if you give in too easily they get bored!) Scorpio wants a partner worthy of him, one he can respect. He'll test your mettle in many ways before he claims you, projecting a glacial calm outwardly. He's looking for a sensual woman who will be his alone, dress elegantly, go with him to offbeat islands, and dive at odd hours. You'll have to share his interests, but keep your *own* to intrigue him. If you can be both cool and caring, passionate and faithful, you might like to fly with this Eagle and escape the Scorpion sting!

HOW TO RAISE THE TEMPERATURE OF A DYNAMIC SCORPIO MAN

- Rendezvous in a haunted house!
- Tune in to his sexual fantasies . . . underneath that placid exterior are some wonderful surprises.
- Scorpio loves black. Wear it in every form . . . from black satin lingerie to black leather jeans . . . and don't forget those sheer black stockings!
- Scorpio turns on to schoolgirl white cottons, too (for the Humbert Humbert in him, the Lolita in you).
- Men of this sign are often workaholics. Soothe him with a jacuzzi for two . . . steer him away from escaping with drink or drugs. Learn how to give a professional massage and you'll both have fun!
- Appeal to his senses with Oriental incense and perfumes, rich tapestry colors and textures.
- He loves seafood . . . so find a good fish restaurant or Japanese sushi bar to enjoy. Caviar is another Scorpio soul-food.
- Keep him home nights with a sensuous bedroom and let him tuck you in!
- Don't be a "yes" woman. Keep him guessing. Don't tell all your secrets no matter how much he probes (and he's the Dick Tracy of lovers!).
- Explore the occult together; learn to read his tarot cards.
- Ask him to teach you all the mysteries of love and sex (even if you already know them!).

HIS LESSONS TO LEARN

- Work off your frustrations with exercise and sports . . . don't turn to drink or drugs!
- Even though you love to be in control, learn to let others take the reins once in a while. They'll be forever grateful.
- Don't be so demanding. Others may have their own standards to live up to.
- You overdo everything; allow yourself some private time to relax and refill.

- Your jealousy and possessiveness can make your partner feel secure . . . or want to bolt! Allow your love enough flexibility to develop her own interests . . . she'll be more interesting to you and herself.
- Don't ask fidelity of others when you don't give it yourself.

THE SCORPIO WOMAN

Whether she's a cool, controlled blonde (Grace Kelly or Linda Evans) or a smoldering brunette (Jaclyn Smith or Hedy Lamarr), you can be sure there is more to her than meets the eye! She's a woman of mystery who loves a good detective story or a scientific problem. Or maybe she'll probe the mysteries of life as a doctor or member of a religious order! One way or another, matters of life and death fascinate her. She's the best detective in the zodiac, so better not try to hide anything from her (though you'll have a tough time guessing what *she's* all about . . . and you may never really find out!). Interestingly, Grace Kelly's greatest hits were mystery stories (*Dial M for Murder, Rear Window, To Catch a Thief)!*

This enigmatic siren loves a challenge and is very discriminating about the man she selects as her mate or companion. Chances are, he'll be able to satisfy her sexual cravings and stand up to her considerable temper (Spencer Tracy and Katharine Hepburn). She is one of the zodiac's most spirited ladies and when there's a cause she believes in, she'll fight to the finish.

She never does anything halfway. Her intensity and need to control every situation can often be too much for a man. However, this same intensity makes her one of the most passionate and talented signs of the zodiac. If her mate will respect her privacy, laugh her out of her darker moods, match her passion in bed, and know when to keep her guessing, he'll have a loyal, devoted, fascinating mate for life!

HOW TO HAVE A GHOST OF A CHANCE WITH A SCORPIO GAL

- Make love in a perfumed bubble bath.
- When a black mood hits, take her for a weekend of scuba diving!
- Most Scorpio women love outdoor as well as indoor sports. Get in shape together. She may think of some interesting ways to use that gym equipment.
- Scorpio is a great organizer. Let her feel she is running your life.
- Give her black lace lingerie. She'll know what to do with it.
- Bring her a bouquet of honeysuckle; it's the Scorpio flower. And, some perfume with a honeysuckle base — she'll know where to put it!
- She can be the epitome of the femme fatale . . . help her reach her full potential . . . and she'll help you reach yours!
- Be honest. She'll respect you for telling the truth.
- Explore the occult with her. Buy her some tarot cards and let her bewitch you with her mystical talents.
- Challenge her powers of perception with your air of mystery.

HER LESSONS TO LEARN

- Stop being so mysterious and say what you really think . . . others will trust you more!
- Let go of your old grudges and concentrate on creating happiness now, not revenge!
- Take care of your health. Go to a spa to refresh and refill. You can over-indulge (even though you think you're indestructible!). Allow yourself time to recuperate from an eating, drinking, or sexual binge.
- You love to play games . . . often for high emotional stakes. Find an easier way to get your own way than manipulating others emotionally.
- When a self-destructive streak hits . . . head for the beach or the mountains. You need some private time alone to sort things out.
- Exercise regularly to work off some of those destructive feelings. Try a solitary sport, gymnastics or tap dancing.

YOUR SCORPIO SUN-CAST

With celebrity couples and romantic pairings . . . for better or for worse . . . from the stage, screen, televison, and real life.

WITH OTHER WATER SIGNS: You'll get along swimmingly . . . if the water isn't too deep. Too much emotion can sink you!

CANCER-SCORPIO

Princess Diana and
Prince Charles

SMILING SUN: A love written in the stars! Cancers love your intense passion . . . it makes them feel so secure. You love Cancers' sensitivity; their nurturing qualities soothe you. You'll spend a lot of time at home . . . in the bedroom. Wheeee!

CLOUDS: Both of you have bleak, black moods. Cancer tends to self-pity. Scorpio gets depressed. If your moods hit at the same time . . . you'll need a third party to get you out of the doldrums (and since both of you are insanely jealous, make sure your mediator doles out the emotional stroking equally!)

SCORPIO-SCORPIO

Dale Evans and Roy Rogers
The late Shah of Iran and
Empress Farah
Abigail and John Adams

SMILING SUN: A romance of historic proportions. You'll soar like eagles together. No couple understands each other like two Scorpios.

You'll satisfy each other's considerable demands sexually, stick together through thick and thin.

CLOUDS: You'll both struggle for control, openly and secretly, with neither giving in. That's part of the challenge . . . but it's also part of the problem. Neither forgives nor forgets . . . and that stings! You're both possessive, but don't like to be possessed.

PISCES-SCORPIO

Elizabeth Taylor and
Richard Burton

SMILING SUN: The two of you may never get out of bed; you have a hypnotic fascination for each other. Erotic, dreamy Pisces is quite enough for sexy Scorpio to handle. Both are extremely intuitive; you don't have to say a word (those eyes speak volumes). You seem to complement each other on every level.

CLOUDS: Pisces can be downright slippery Fish when you try to hook them (you can't!). Scorpio must dominate and control, and may think at first that vacillating Pisceans are an easy mark. Ha! Remember, the barracuda is also a fish.

WITH FIRE SIGNS: You see them as a challenge worthy of your mettle . . . or you see right *through* them!

ARIES-SCORPIO

Spencer Tracy and
Katharine Hepburn
Elaine May (cusp) and Mike Nichols
Ethel and Robert Kennedy
Brad Dillman and Suzy Parker

SMILING SUN: You're both endowed with Martian energy and love a sexy sparring partner. Here's someone who will match your power play . . . and you'll love every minute. You're both loyal and jealous . . . you'll never get bored.

CLOUDS: Self-centered Aries insists on taking the lead, while you manipulate behind the scenes. Arians will never understand your hidden depths . . . and what's more won't even *try*. When you sense that they're all surface and ego, you might want to douse their Fire fast.

LEO-SCORPIO

John Derek and
Linda Evans/Bo Derek
Dorothy Hamill and Dino Martin

SMILING SUN: An intense attraction as Leo tries to sweep you off your feet and you try to bowl Scorpio over. You'll live up to Leo's image, and you'll both be lords of the jungle together: Leo has creative leadership and authority, while Scorpio has power and intensity. A powerful pairing!

CLOUDS: Clashes between you two can be rip-roaring. Both of you are strong-willed and unyielding. Better be sure you agree on most things before you even contemplate this match. Leo loves to make a hit with the opposite sex, too . . . so control your jealous tendencies here.

SAGITTARIUS-SCORPIO

Tina and Ike Turner
Phil Donahue and Marlo Thomas
Garson Kanin and Ruth Gordon

SMILING SUN: Good-humored Sag jokes you out of your depressions, takes you off to the seashore! The Archer and the Eagle soar philosophically and metaphysically together . . . and create lots of steam in bed. You both love the outdoors and can find many interesting things to do under the stars.

CLOUDS: Sags can't quite fathom your intensity . . . and when they try to laugh it off — you fume! Too many "downers" and Sag will head for the airport! Sag is flirtatious, loves having many friends . . . which could easily arouse your jealousy. You're possessive. Try to tie this wanderer down and you could hang up the relationship for keeps.

WITH EARTH SIGNS: You two can have a very solid relationship and move mountains together . . . but keep those grudges buried!

TAURUS-SCORPIO

Candice Bergen and
Louis Malle
Tyrone Power and Linda Christian
Pierre and Marie Curie

SMILING SUN: Earthy Taurus and deep, intense Scorpio make passion flower! The Bulls have rock-steady emotions and are as dedicated and possessive as you are . . . they can match your stamina in bed. You both agree on money matters, too, and could build a fortune together.

CLOUDS: You're two stubborn signs — convinced you know best (better be sure you agree on most things before you get in too deep). Also, you're both set in your ways . . . each has to make adjustments, or else!

VIRGO-SCORPIO

Louis XVI and
Marie Antoinette

SMILING SUN: You plumb the depths of Virgo's reserve to uncover a smoldering sexpot! Nothing stays a virgin for long with Scorpio in hot pursuit. Virgos get a chance to live out their wildest fantasies . . . you can even top them with some naughty little secrets. Wheeee!

CLOUDS: Virgos are critical, but when you retaliate with a few stings, they fold their tents and "turn off" for weeks. When you're both playing it cool, it gets so cold that you just might not be able to thaw this one out again . . . but try . . .

CAPRICORN-SCORPIO

Cary Grant and
Barbara Hutton

SMILING SUN: Both of you are hard-working and ambitious. Together you can reach the top. Capricorns keep their eyes on practical goals, while you teach them to release their inhibitions and really let go in bed.

CLOUDS: Both of you are moody types. Hopefully, Saturn's dark clouds won't coincide with Scorpio's depressions, or watch out for a black-out. Both of you need time alone . . . and alone together. When ambition takes over, this relationship could be all work and no play.

WITH AIR SIGNS: Your sting could burst their bubbles . . . or you could find them very up-lifting.

GEMINI-SCORPIO

Ruth and Billy Graham
Prince Rainier and Princess Grace
Isadora Duncan and Auguste Rodin
Laurence Olivier and Vivien Leigh

SMILING SUN: Quicksilver Geminis are always a challenge for you to figure out. Just when you've got them pinned down (you think), they change completely. In bed, you both have a marvelous time! Their sparkling humor sends your blues away. Their innovative ideas on sex keep you flying high. Great companions and playmates.

CLOUDS: You want to give your soul . . . Gemini only wants your *head!* You're continually frustrated trying to control Geminis . . . they just laugh off your Scorpio stings and retaliate with a devastating slice of wit. Your moods get on their nerves. And their constant flirtations make you see GREEN . . . Not the easiest combination, and always a challenge.

LIBRA-SCORPIO

June Allyson and Dick Powell
Dwight and Mamie Eisenhower
Deborah Kerr and Burt Lancaster
in *From Here to Eternity*

SMILING SUN: You can turn Libra from sweet to sizzling in the flick of a Bic. Libra will leave most of the decisions to you, which suits you fine. You'll appreciate Libras' touch of class as well as their style and charm. They'll smooth over your rough edges and bring you out of your depressions into the social whirl.

CLOUDS: To Libra, flirting is merely entertainment. To Scorpio, it's serious business. You'll have to control your jealousy. Scorpio needs time alone; Libra feels abandoned when there are no friends around. Lots of compromises to be made here.

AQUARIUS-SCORPIO

John Forsythe and Linda Evans
in "Dynasty"
Clark Gable and Vivien Leigh
in *Gone with the Wind*

SMILING SUN: The chemistry is magic! Great-looking Aquarius has some far-out ideas in bed . . . and it won't take you long to get there. This Air sign's idealism appeals to your higher instincts. Here's someone to abandon yourself with!

CLOUDS: Possessive Scorpios don't like to share their love with anyone or anything . . . you have to be Aquarius's most worthy cause or it's *no go*. If Aquarians insist on pursuing outside interests regardless, you'll point them to the door . . . and they "frankly, won't give a damn!"

OTHER FAMOUS SCORPIO PERSONALITIES

WOMEN

Minnie Pearl
Barbara Cook
Bo Derek
Linda Evans
Helen Reddy
Jaclyn Smith
Elsa Lanchester
Edith Head
Pauline Trigère
Suzy Parker
Melba Moore
Kate Jackson
Grace Slick
Ruth Gordon
Georgia O'Keeffe
Jane Pauley
Grace Kelly
Barbara Bel Geddes
Dale Evans
Betsy Palmer
Marie Antoinette
Marie Curie
Loretta Swit
Elke Sommer
Vivien Leigh
Tatum O'Neal
Sally Field
Joni Mitchell
Joan Sutherland
Katharine Hepburn
Patti Page
June Havoc
Hedy Lamarr
Bibi Andersson
Abigail Adams
Stephanie Powers
Nadia Comeneci
Linda Christian
Jean Seberg
Mamie Eisenhower
Lauren Hutton
Brenda Vaccaro
Jody Foster
Eleanor Powell
Marlo Thomas
Goldie Hawn
Doris Duke (Sag cusp)
Indira Gandhi
Kaye Ballard
Petula Clark
Empress Farah of Iran
Barbara Hutton
Billie Jean King (Sag cusp)

MEN

Pablo Picasso
Billy Graham
The Shah of Iran
Roy Rogers
Johann Strauss
François Mitterrand
President Theodore Roosevelt
Evelyn Waugh
Henry Winkler
Richard Dreyfuss
Gordon Parks
Ezra Pound
John Keats
Jan Vermeer

Burt Lancaster
Richard Burton
President James Polk
President Warren Harding
Calvin Klein
Art Carney
Walter Cronkite
Bob Considine
Art Garfunkel
Spiro Agnew
Alain Delon
King Edward VII
Sargent Shriver
Kurt Vonnegut, Jr.
General George Patton
Charles Manson
Auguste Rodin
Oskar Werner
Robert Louis Stevenson
Claude Monet
Jawaharlal Nehru
Dick Powell
Prince Charles
Daniel Barenboim
Averell Harriman
Sam Waterston
Burgess Meredith
George S. Kaufman
Martin Luther
Alan Shepard
President James Garfield
Harpo Marx
Voltaire
Robert Vaughn
Alistair Cooke
Dick Cavett
Rock Hudson
Lee Strasberg
Dino Martin
Ed Asner
Charles de Gaulle (Sag cusp)

CELEBRITY COUPLES AND ROMANTIC PAIRINGS

Billy Graham (Scorpio) and Ruth (Gemini)
Dale Evans (Scorpio) and Roy Rogers (Scorpio)
The Shah of Iran (Scorpio) and Empress Farah (Scorpio)
Abigail Adams (Scorpio) and John Adams (Scorpio)
Prince Charles (Scorpio) and Princess Diana (Cancer)
Richard Burton (Scorpio) and Elizabeth Taylor (Pisces)
Katharine Hepburn (Scorpio) and Spencer Tracy (Aries)
Robert Kennedy (Scorpio) and Ethel Kennedy (Aries)
Suzy Parker (Scorpio) and Brad Dillman (Aries)
Mike Nichols (Scorpio) and Elaine May (Aries cusp)
Bo Derek (Scorpio) and John Derek (Leo)
Linda Evans (Scorpio) and John Derek (Leo)
Dino Martin (Scorpio) and Dorothy Hamill (Leo)
Ike Turner (Scorpio) and Tina Turner (Sagittarius)
Marlo Thomas (Scorpio) and Phil Donahue (Sagittarius)
Ruth Gordon (Scorpio) and Garson Kanin (Sagittarius)
Louis Malle (Scorpio) and Candice Bergen (Taurus)
Linda Christian (Scorpio) and Tyrone Power (Taurus)
Marie Curie (Scorpio) and Pierre Curie (Taurus)
Marie Antoinette (Scorpio) and Louis XVI (Virgo)
Barbara Hutton (Scorpio) and Cary Grant (Capricorn)
Princess Grace of Monaco (Scorpio) and Prince Rainier (Gemini)

Auguste Rodin (Scorpio) and Isadora Duncan (Gemini)
Vivien Leigh (Scorpio) and Laurence Olivier (Gemini)
Dick Powell (Scorpio) and June Allyson (Libra)
Mamie Eisenhower (Scorpio) and Dwight Eisenhower (Libra)
Burt Lancaster (Scorpio) and Deborah Kerr (Libra) in *From Here to Eternity*
Linda Evans (Scorpio) and John Forsythe (Aquarius) in "Dynasty"
Bo Derek (Scorpio) and Dudley Moore (Aries) in *10*
Vivien Leigh (Scorpio) and Clark Gable (Aquarius) in *Gone with the Wind*

LUCKY SCORPIO PLACES TO BE

Morocco
Catalonia
New Orleans
South Dakota
Norway
Israel
Brazil
Washington (state)
Bavaria
China
Panama
Oklahoma

12 PISCES—THE COSMIC CONNECTION

February 20-March 20

Pisces, the last Water sign, is one of the most mysterious signs of the zodiac. Those born between February 20 and March 20 have a bit of the devil and a lot of the deep blue sea in them.

The Pisces woman is a mermaid (Lorelei) sitting seductively on the rocks, luring men to their fate. The men of this sign are the poets of the zodiac. They dance to their own drummer, and are often very theatrical.

Pisces is ruled by Neptune, the planet of illusions. It is symbolized by two fish swimming in opposite directions . . . yet tied together. You Pisceans are of two minds about everything and easily influenced by the last person with whom you talked.

Pisces loves to hear (and tell) a sob story. You're the most sympathetic sign of the zodiac (the one the rest of us tell our problems and secrets to!). You love to be in love and *have* to be most of the time! You're mysterious and sensuous . . . you're usually the "other woman" or "other man" in a romantic triangle.

Piscean lovers are creative in every way. Their key word is "sympathize." Their slogan is "I perceive"; they are quick to perceive your every need. The Pisces man sometimes drifts with the tide. But, if the woman in his life provides emotional stability, there's no limit to where those Neptune tides can take them both.

More than any other sign, Pisces are what they make themselves. Therefore, they should be very sure they know what they want and where they want to go! With their fondness for introspection, they have all the tools for self-knowledge . . . they have foresight and a powerful imagination, and these can be helpful in achieving their goals (once they've made up their mind what they are!). Pisces are happiest when they are actively using their talents . . . an out-of-work Pisces is a very sad Fish!

Even if they never walk onto a stage, Pisceans have a fine dramatic sense (Elizabeth Taylor, Rex Harrison). They sometimes feel that they're "acting out" life instead of actually living it (a tendency they should control

©L+D DILLON 83

lest they venture too far into a fantasy world). Their ruler, Neptune, is known as the planet of misty illusion, which could allow them to delude themselves or create a state of vacillation and confusion. But illusion, when held in perspective, is essential to artistic endeavors. Pisces is the most artistic of the signs, and if Pisceans developed their talents to the fullest, they could excel in art (Renoir and Michelangelo), music (Handel and Chopin), the dance (Nijinsky and Nureyev), and literature (Tom Wolfe, Philip Roth and John Updike), as well as the theater.

Pisceans should select their working partners and their mates with extreme care . . . mates should be able to supply whatever Pisces lacks in the partnership. Usually this Water sign works best with an organized person who has drive and ambition, an arrangement that allows freedom to provide the creative spark. If Pisceans can find the sort of person who enhances them without trying to dominate or control the relationship (Pisces hate to be caught in a net and will either swim off or drown their sorrows!), they can make very loving, considerate, and successful mates!

THE PISCES/AQUARIUS CUSP (February 19-24)

One of the most talented cusps in the zodiac, you are blessed with the vision of Aquarius and the creative ability of Pisces . . . an interesting blend of sensitivity and objectivity. You're adventurous and highly original, sometimes prophetic! When Uranus and Neptune team up you can accomplish far-reaching goals. Your creativity is likely to favor the musical (Chopin, Segovia), poetic (Edna St. Vincent Millay), or artistic (Gloria Vanderbilt) world. Chances are you'll have several marriages before you find that special someone who understands you mentally and emotionally.

THE PISCES/ARIES CUSP (March 19-24)

A mixture of the driving force of Mars and the inventive visions of Neptune, this cusp will never be content just to dream. Arian determination will bolster Piscean confidence, while Pisces consideration will cool the Aries ego. You're a charmer with a theatrical bent (Joan Crawford), a blend of positives and negatives that's hard to pin down, both easygoing and energetic, mystical (Edgar Cayce), and everybody's ideal mate (Ozzie Nelson of "Ozzie and Harriet").

THE PISCES MAN

The Pisces man is magnetic and sensual. He likes his home and prefers to spend most of his time there. Ruled by the planet Neptune, he has an idealistic and spiritual side to his nature, which in some Pisceans makes for a kind of indolence. He is not the "doer" of the zodiac by any means. He's reflective and dreamy, often procrastinating. He's also not the best provider.

On the plus side, he's sociable, considerate, sympathetic, loving and attentive. He'll do anything to please you (he's the poet of the zodiac, remember!). If he can't provide much in material ways, he tries to make up for it by being a charming companion and good husband. He's artistic, fastidious and appreciates the best things in life. He loves good food (and wine). This, combined with a natural indolence, makes him tend to put on weight. The constructive partner will go to exercise class with him and cook healthful meals served in an appetizing way. Be sure there are a variety of beverages to drink (other than alcohol). Get a fruit or vegetable juicer!

He needs a woman who will encourage, not compete, with him though she may have to watch the cash flow. (Pisces are one of the big spenders, not the big savers, of the zodiac.) In love, he's creative and delightful. He'll sense how to please you and will just adore giving you the ultimate in pleasure. He is not, however, known for fidelity; should your relationship go through difficult times, he's almost sure to seek consolation elsewhere. Keep your lines of communication open at all times . . . or he may escape and withdraw mentally and physically. Accentuate the *positive* and you can keep this one afloat!

HOW TO FISH FOR A ROMANTIC PISCES MAN

- Bait him with a Betamax and some sexy film cassettes, then watch them together on a waterbed.
- Tell him your favorite fantasy . . . he'll make it come true.
- Help him keep his ideas afloat. He needs you to remind him how creative he is!
- Dress in colors of the sea: seafoam green, aqua, lily white . . . and he'll swim your way!
- Intoxicate him with perfume. But be careful with alcoholic beverages! These are liquids to keep Pisces *away* from!
- He's got exotic tastes in food and love! Inspire him with your culinary creativity.
- Take him skiing or ice-skating . . . he'll warm up to you fast.
- Set a dreamy mood with music. He's susceptible to sound waves! Then try some X-rated pillow talk.
- The way to Pisces's heart is through his feet. Give him a foot massage . . . and he'll get your message.
- Make love in a hot tub, under a waterfall, or in a vibrating shower.

HIS LESSONS TO LEARN

- Learn to swim with the tide . . . your intuition will tell you when the water's fine!
- You love to give of yourself . . . but make sure you have a good receiver. Don't waste your gifts or poetry on someone who doesn't appreciate them!

- Associate with people of action, "doers" who will engage your energies. Beware of negative people, energy drainers!
- Watch your fondness for liquids. Stay away from alcohol . . . buy her some eau de cologne and perfume instead!
- Get an exercise regime you can stick to . . . find the best gym and instructor in town and GO! (Women appreciate beautiful bodies too!)
- You tend to have a girl in every port. Learn to be discreet . . . or your fickleness could do you in!

THE PISCES WOMAN

You Pisces women wrap your extraordinary talent with a subtle air of illusion. You manage to get what (and whom) you want by hardly appearing to move a muscle (except maybe your eyelashes). You'll cleverly project an air of helpless femininity to lure that strong man across a crowded room, then train strenuously to run the next marathon!

Change is your keynote. You'll change wardrobes, residences, friends, jobs, and men many times. Usually you marry more than once (and, once hooked, you have been known to carry on some extracurricular activities. You enjoy solitary hobbies (except those engaged in at night) rather than team sports, and we'll find you at the ballet rather than a tennis match (unless, of course, you fall in love with a dashing tennis player; then you'd get into the racket fast!).

You need a strong sense of direction (or someone who can give it to you) to navigate the rougher waters of life. Usually you get comfort and rewards (financial and emotional) from developing your creative talents. You can be an extremely hard worker (Liza Minnelli) and you love to help the needy (especially if they're tall, dark and handsome).

You're in love with love and you make sex one of your special art forms: using beautiful lingerie, fragrances (Pisces rules perfumes), massage oils (you also rule petroleum!), and spirits (alcoholic and otherwise) to their best advantage. If you can finally settle for one man, you'll make him the wife/mistress of his dreams — an empathetic mate who understands his every mood, never competes, and creates a pool of tranquillity for him to swim around in!

HOW TO MAKE A PISCES YOUR LEADING LADY

- Surprise her with new ideas. She'll play your favorite role!
- Don't hold back . . . she needs oceans of affection.
- Surround her with water . . . aquariums, jacuzzis, and a house by the sea!
- Applaud her flights of fancy. You'll love some of her original ideas.
- If she's depressed, arrange for a trip to Bali or a cruise on the QE2.
- Fill her rooms with tuberoses and gardenias. They're her flowers and her fragrances.
- She loves to go barefoot, so tickle her toes . . . she'll dance for you!

- Pour your heart into a poem . . . and wrap it around a cabochon sapphire or a large aquamarine.
- Let her tend to your needs . . . she loves to make all of you feel good!

HER LESSONS TO LEARN

- Develop all your creative talents . . . they'll pull you through those rough times and give you the chance to indulge yourself in some of the finer things in life.
- Cultivate positive friends . . . you need people around you who look on the sunny side of life . . . who can give as well as take.
- Look for a partner who boosts *your* talents. It's too easy to fall for a strong man who uses your talents to further *his* goals.
- Stay away from dangerous alcoholic liquids . . . Even though your sign rules spirits, your system reacts badly to alcohol. It's better to work off your troubles in a gym than drown them in alcohol (you may only *preserve* them!).
- Get your finances under control. Find a good business manager and set up a savings plan together.
- Don't get so engrossed in your love life that you neglect your friends. You'll need shoulders to cry on from time to time.

YOUR PISCES SUN-CAST

With celebrity couples and romantic pairings . . . for better or for worse . . . from the stage, screen, television, and real life.

WITH OTHER WATER SIGNS: You're on each other's wave length . . . but be sure you don't drown in too much passion!

CANCER-PISCES

Carly Simon and James Taylor
June Carter Cash and Johnny Cash
George Sand and Frédéric Chopin
Anna Moffo and David Sarnoff

SMILING SUN: Lots of beautiful harmony here! Cancer keeps an eye on the cash flow and a protective eye on you! Cancer can turn your dreams into reality. You boost Cancers' tender ego, make the most of their creative sensual nature in bed. You both know how to show each other appreciation.

CLOUDS: This one can get a little soggy at times. Cancer's complaints bring you *down*. Both of you can get overly emotional, exaggerating the most trifling disagreements. Pisces's theatrics will drive Cancer right into a shell.

SCORPIO-PISCES

Richard Burton and
Elizabeth Taylor

SMILING SUN: A love that can break all conventions. Pisces swims happily in Scorpion depths. Endless fascination sexually — Scorpio never gets enough, and Pisces never gets drained. Once in love, you'll stay in each other's lives, married or not! You could make history together.

CLOUDS: Scorpio's possessive and power hungry. Pisces is a free-floater who tries to avoid the net. The more Scorpios dictate and try to control, the less chance they have of hooking the big Fish. Scorpio's stings could bring out the JAWS in Pisces. You could both drown in alcohol.

PISCES-PISCES

Rex Harrison and Elizabeth Taylor
in *Cleopatra*
Leo and Diane Dillon

SMILING SUN: Here's your psychic soulmate. Your sex life can be out of this world . . . pure poetry (but not too pure!). You'll protect each other's sensitive feelings yet communicate on all levels. Give and get back, for a change! You may never get out of bed!

CLOUDS: These slippery Fish could slide by each other romantically. This pairing often works better as friends and lovers than long term. Pisces needs variety, not more of the same! (Two Fish are enough; four Fish make turbulent emotional waters.) Somebody has to fight your battles for you, not swim away when the tides get rough!

WITH FIRE SIGNS: You could get into a lot of hot water together . . . or at least a steamy scene or two.

ARIES-PISCES

Leopold Stokowski
and Gloria Vanderbilt
Jean-Paul Belmondo and Ursula Andress
Dudley Moore and Liza Minnelli in *Arthur*
Oleg Cassini and Gene Tierney

SMILING SUN: Aries's energy and vitality are contagious. You can steam up the bedroom mirrors together. Aries sweeps you off your feet. You'll massage the gigantic Aries ego — and more sensitive parts. Could be love at first sight. You fascinate each other totally.

CLOUDS: Your feelings and Aries's pride are both vulnerable spots. And when Aries makes a typical thoughtless jibe, you'll retaliate with a deflating sting (you know just where to hurt this one, too). You're not as easy to dominate as you look . . . but Aries keeps trying.

LEO-PISCES

Geoffrey Holder
and Carmen de Lavallade
George Hamilton and Lynda Bird Johnson
John Derek and Ursula Andress
Sally Struthers and Rob Reiner
in "All in the Family"
William Powell and Jean Harlow

SMILING SUN: Leo gives Pisces confidence, while Pisces treats Leo royally. This could be a mutual admiration society — a great team. Leos love to make you look good (so they can show you off). You'll find Leo full of action as well as talk and you know just what to do with both!

CLOUDS: Neither of you is good at hanging onto cash. Better get a financial manager (or a good lawyer). Pisces's many moods baffle Leo, who likes to stay sunny side up. When the Lion roars, the Fish bites! There could be an ocean of fundamental differences between you!

SAGITTARIUS-PISCES

Frank Sinatra and Barbara
Betty Grable and Harry James
Louis Prima and Keely Smith

SMILING SUN: Here's a great one to play around with! Fun-loving Sag lightens and brightens your life with a great sense of humor, lots of get up and go. You'll work out together — in the bedroom — and may even carry it outdoors. A great traveling companion and fellow explorer!

CLOUDS: Emotionally, this could be too lightweight for you. Pisces needs a solid home base and Sag likes life on the road. You're both flirtatious and might not even stick together long enough to get jealous. Financially, high-risk Sags and freeloading Pisceans spell disaster! Try to stay friends.

WITH EARTH SIGNS: These loves help you get organized, put those dreams into action . . . but watch out for nets, they'd love to hook you permanently.

TAURUS-PISCES

Roberto Rossellini and Anna Magnani
James and Pamela Mason

SMILING SUN: Taurus gives you the moral and financial support you need . . . a solid base of security. You provide the romance and imagination. Both of you are stunningly sensual, physical beings who enjoy all the pleasures of life, together.

CLOUDS: Pisces needs excitement and might take some risks that try Taurean patience. You can also be extravagant with Taurus's hard-earned cash. Your innate restlessness may irritate the placid Bull. Taurus can get bossy, which sends the Fish swimming off in other directions.

VIRGO-PISCES

Sean Connery and Ursula Andress in *Dr. No*

SMILING SUN: Two opposites with a chemical attraction. You could be so good for each other. Cool, efficient Virgo gets you organized, takes care of you. Your warmth and devotion break down Virgo's reserve . . . what fun exploring all your fantasies together!

CLOUDS: Virgo's criticism can wound your tender feelings. And their puritanical streak could stifle your sex life. Your changeable nature stymies Virgo, who keeps trying to make you more efficient. A LOT of patience could make this work.

CAPRICORN-PISCES

Former President Richard M. Nixon and Pat
Tony Martin and Cyd Charisse

SMILING SUN: A great team! Capricorn gives Pisces something solid to hold on to. Pisces takes some of Cap's burdens away. This union seems to get better as time goes by. Sexually, you bring Capricorn much joy and make the worries of the world float away.

CLOUDS: Capricorns are devoted to work, money, and power. Their constant status-seeking could bore Pisces and make them swim off to more pleasurable waters. If Capricorn can respond to the arts and make creativity their mutual hobby, this union has a good chance to survive.

WITH AIR SIGNS: Just the loves to take you over the rainbow . . . but don't forget to bring a parachute!

GEMINI-PISCES

Martha and George Washington

SMILING SUN: There's sparkle aplenty here. Both of you are several people rolled into one. And the party's terrific: at least six of your multiple personalities will like each other, and several may even fall in love! You may get tired, but you won't get bored.

CLOUDS: After taking their flights of fantasy, creative Pisces and mental Gemini need some way to get down to earth. Finances will also be a problem for these naturally restless (and extravagant) types. Pisces's moods get on Gemini's nerves. And Gemini is walking insecurity for Pisces. Happy landings!

LIBRA-PISCES

George C. Scott and Trish Van Devere
Lotte Lenya and Kurt Weill
Montgomery Clift and Elizabeth Taylor in *Suddenly Last Summer*

SMILING SUN: It's easy for you two lovers of beauty to love each other! Your creativity and charm captivate each other. A good time is had by all as you dance from party to party, enjoying the finer things in life, including extra-sensual lovemaking. Both of you elevate sex to an art form!

CLOUDS: You both need shoring up and neither is ready to provide this service. Could be lots of scales and fish swinging and swimming about, making for utter confusion. And, since neither of you likes to make decisions, you may never make it to the preacher!

AQUARIUS-PISCES

Paul Newman and Joanne Woodward
Claire Bloom and Philip Roth
Bill and "La Belle" Simone Levitt

SMILING SUN: You're one of the few who can get really close to this detached sign. Aquarians pride themselves on being unemotional, but

Pisces understand how Aquarians care about their causes. Aquarians in turn gives Pisces perspective. And you love their far-out ideas in bed.

CLOUDS: Depth of feeling and emotional displays turn Pisces on and Aquarius off. This one could be short-circuited if Pisces gets too possessive and clingy . . . or if Aquarius spends too much time away from home. If Pisces has strong interests and lots in common mentally with Aquarius, this could work.

OTHER FAMOUS PISCES PERSONALITIES

WOMEN

Liza Minnelli
Elizabeth Taylor
Jennifer O'Neill
Gloria Vanderbilt
Joanne Woodward
Patty Hearst
Buffy Sainte-Marie
Nina Simone
Tricia Nixon Cox
Pat Nixon
Adelle Davis
Madeleine Carroll
Marian Anderson
Joan Bennett
Bernadette Peters
Dinah Shore
Ursula Andress
Jennifer Jones
Dominique Sanda
Karen Carpenter
Jean Harlow
Lee Radziwill
Paula Prentiss
Barbara McNair
Samantha Eggar
Elizabeth Barrett Browning
Cyd Charisse
Anna Magnani
Lynn Redgrave
Claire Trevor
Trish Van Devere
Keely Smith
Irene Pappas
Dorothy Schiff
Barbara Feldon
Marjorie Merriweather Post
Mercedes McCambridge
Lynda Bird Johnson Robb
Mollie Parnis
Sandy Duncan
Janet Guthrie
Barbara Sinatra
Carol Tonsing

MEN

Rex Harrison
Frédéric Chopin
David Niven
Michael Caine
Michelangelo
Robert Altman
Ansel Adams
Aleksei Kosygin
Edward Albert
Sam Peckinpah
Senator Ted Kennedy
Peter Fonda
Luis Buñuel
George Washington
Roy Cohn
John Foster Dulles
Enrico Caruso
Jean Renoir
George Harrison
Hubert Givenchy

Emanuel Ungaro
Kenzo
Vincente Minnelli
Fred Brisson
Linus Pauling
Albert Einstein
Mario Andretti
Tom Courtenay
Fats Domino
Tony Randall
Johnny Cash
Prince Edward of England
Prince Albert of Monaco
Lawrence Welk
Harold Wilson
Robert Lowell
Harry Winston
Robert Conrad
Tom Wolfe
John Fairchild
Rob Reiner
Anthony Armstrong-Jones
Maurice Ravel
Piet Mondrian
Sam Jaffe
Rudolf Nureyev
Waslaw Nijinsky
Valery Panov
James Taylor
Walter Schirra
Neil Sedaka
Frank Borman
Harry James
Edward Albee
Philip Roth
Peter Graves
Gianni Agnelli
President Andrew Jackson
Daniel Patrick Moynihan
Mike Mansfield
Neville Chamberlain
Nikolai Rimsky-Korsakov
Irving Wallace
Henrik Ibsen
John Erlichman
Ozzie Nelson
Bobby Orr
Nat King Cole

CELEBRITY COUPLES AND ROMANTIC PAIRINGS

Rex Harrison (Pisces) and Elizabeth Taylor (Pisces) in *Cleopatra*
Rex Harrison (Pisces) and Margaret Leighton (Pisces) in *Separate Tables*
James Taylor (Pisces) and Carly Simon (Cancer)
Johnny Cash (Pisces) and June Carter Cash (Cancer)
Frédéric Chopin (Pisces) and George Sand (Cancer)
David Sarnoff (Pisces) and Anna Moffo (Cancer)
Elizabeth Taylor (Pisces) and Richard Burton (Scorpio)
Gloria Vanderbilt (Pisces) and Leopold Stokowski (Aries)
Gloria Vanderbilt (Pisces) and Sidney Lumet (Cancer)
Carmen de Lavallade (Pisces) and Geoffrey Holder (Leo)
Lynda Bird Johnson (Pisces) and George Hamilton (Leo)
Ursula Andress (Pisces) and John Derek (Leo)
Ursula Andress (Pisces) and Jean-Paul Belmondo (Aries)
Rob Reiner (Pisces) and Sally Struthers (Leo) in "All in the Family"
Jean Harlow (Pisces) and William Powell (Leo)
Liza Minnelli (Pisces) and Dudley Moore (Aries) in *Arthur*
Gene Tierney (Pisces) and Oleg Cassini (Aries)
Harry James (Pisces) and Betty Grable (Sagittarius)

Keely Smith (Pisces) and Louis Prima (Sagittarius)
Barbara (Pisces) and Frank Sinatra (Sagittarius)
Anna Magnani (Pisces) and Roberto Rossellini (Taurus)
Pamela Mason (Pisces) and James Mason (Taurus)
Ursula Andress (Pisces) and Sean Connery (Virgo) in *Dr. No*
Patricia Nixon (Pisces) and Richard M. Nixon (Capricorn)
Cyd Charisse (Pisces) and Tony Martin (Capricorn)
George Washington (Pisces) and Martha (Gemini)
Trish Van Devere (Pisces) and George C. Scott (Libra)
Kurt Weill (Pisces) and Lotte Lenya (Libra)
Elizabeth Taylor (Pisces) and Montgomery Clift (Libra) in *Suddenly Last Summer*
Joanne Woodward (Pisces) and Paul Newman (Aquarius)
"La Belle" Simone Levitt (Pisces) and Bill Levitt (Aquarius)
Philip Roth (Pisces) and Claire Bloom (Aquarius)

LUCKY PISCES PLACES TO BE

Portugal
Nebraska
Normandy
Haiti
Alexandria, Egypt
Ohio
Flanders
Seville, Spain
Maine
Vermont
Saharan Africa
Hamburg, Germany

FEELING IT!

THE IMPORTANCE OF YOUR MOON

The Moon influences everything on earth — from the ebb and flow of the tides, to a woman's fertility cycle, to all the chemical fluids that constitute our physical selves.

The cycle of the Moon takes approximately twenty-eight days to pass through each of the twelve signs of the zodiac (as it circles the Earth), spending about 2 ½ days in each sign on its way.

According to astrology, the Moon governs our emotions, instincts, and imagination — our likes and dislikes as well as our habits and moods. It is our "subconscious" mind.

The symbol of the Moon is ☽ . Shaped like a cup, it represents all that is receptive in our nature. It rules our senses. I believe that the moon is a sensitive reflecting device which translates the energy from our personal star into a language our bodies can understand.

As the Sun is our ever-constant shining source of light during the daytime, the Moon is our nighttime *Mother,* lighting up the night and moving swiftly, reflecting our changing phases of behavior and personality. If we're happy, we repeat certain habits or feelings that bubble up from our subconscious, vanishing and changing as the Moon moves from one sign to another.

Since the Moon rules our emotions and defines our personality, it also influences our sexuality (determined by the sign in which it was placed on the day of our birth) and defines our tastes in romance and marriage. With couples who sustain a lasting romantic relationship, there is almost always a "lunar link," a harmonious contact between both Moons in their charts, one's Moon and the other's Sun or one's Moon, Mars, or Venus in the other's sign, or another sign that activates it for better or for worse.

To find out your lunar connection with the one you love, look up the month, day, and year of your birth in the ephemeris at the back of this chapter. Find out where your Moon is (and where your partner's lies), then read about your placements in this chapter to see what it means in setting the stage for your relationship.

The Moon in the same sign as your lover's is the best aspect for a meaningful and long-lasting relationship. Moons in the same element (Fire, Earth, Air, or Water) but different signs are another excellent aspect. You'll strongly support and complement one another. There's much harmony here. Moons in complementary elements (Fire with Air and Earth with Water) are favorable for friendship and emotional closeness, but may require a bit more give and take for you to really get to know each other.

Moons in contrasting elements (Fire and Water, Earth and Fire, Air and Earth, Air and Water) will attract you sexually, but will present a challenge, as you are attempting to blend two elements that are not really congenial. You will not instinctively understand each other and will both have to compromise to make each other happy. You'll have to make a greater effort to communicate your desires to make the relationship work. (Of course, much depends on your Sun, Mars, and Venus contacts, too.)

If your Moon is six signs away from your lover's Moon, it is said that these Moons are in opposition. This means the Moons are in complementary elements (Earth with Water, Fire with Air). However, there is a difference of purpose, a tug in the opposite direction. This can be resolved (or more likely *treated*) with good communication between you and efforts to understand and make adjustments on both sides.

Throughout history, the great queens and courtesans, from Cleopatra to Madame Pompadour and Josephine, have known the magic of a beautiful boudoir where dramas of life, love, and power (political and otherwise) take place! The most exciting boudoirs put their occupants in a receptive mood for romantic encounters, with the perfect colors, music, fragance, food, or wine — and other delightful temptations. Your Moon placement reveals the ambience that can put you (and your partner) in the right mood, and can give some valuable clues to setting the stage for romance.

Your Moon-ruled colors will compliment you when you make love, so be sure to use them in your bedroom, on the walls, in bed linens, upholstery, and your most intimate apparel. Your partner's Moon colors will put him or her in a relaxed, contented state, so be sure to blend in those as well. Extra touches (like mirrors, artwork, fabrics, and flowers) complete this total setting for love. And don't forget music and fragrance, also influenced by the Moon.

To create the perfect setting for your "lunar link," read on!

MOON IN ARIES

Your emotional nature is restless and impetuous — you fall in love too easily and out of it just as quickly. Your enthusiasms are as easily aroused as your temper. Watch out that this Moon, in a Fire sign ruled by Mars, doesn't make you too independent, domineering and self-willed. Stress the softer, more tender side of your nature, most particularly in the bedroom, and if you are a woman, wear a fragrance with a rose and jasmine note.

You love a challenge and will pursue what you want with determination, especially a love partner. You'll gravitate toward brilliant, assertive, impulsive, affectionate, and somewhat temperamental loves (with traits like yours) and the resulting romance could be a duel between experts. Win the love match by giving your partner a chance to gain some points. And cultivate tolerance, patience, moderation, and humility . . . or your emotional life will be a stormy one.

Setting the Stage

Set the stage for romance with your lucky color *red* (for passion) in all its varying hues, from hot pink to fire engine. Your home should be a bower of flowers — tulips, roses, anemones — all in varying shades of red, which is the keynote of your Moon nature. Use red accents throughout your home, especially in your boudoir and as accessories in your wardrobe.

A roaring fire in the fireplace (or at least a collection of candles), dramatic works of art, comfortable furniture (you'll go for baroque), and a cozy, warm ambience are best for you. For more Aries ambience, use red velvet, rough-textured tweeds, with the beat of Diana Ross, Aretha Franklin, or Ravel's *Bolero* in the air (and perhaps a bottle of red Bordeaux or burgundy nearby).

YOUR BEST BETS:

A partner with Moon in Aries: Here's a mutual admiration society with occasional fireworks. You'll love the excitement generated by this one.

An Aries/Leo Moon combination: The Leo Moon has a steady emotional nature with lots of star quality. You should harmonize . . . the Leo Moon will love your merry chase.

An Aries/Sagittarius Moon combination: You're both independent, idealistic types who won't smother each other . . . You'll seek the truth together!

ALSO GOOD:

An Aries/Gemini Moon combination: Gemini will love Arians' action and animation. Aries's drive will give Gemini powerful support.

An Aries/Aquarius Moon combination: A volatile combination, full of surprises. Not one to build your ego, but then again, you won't be bored!

YOU'LL HAVE TO WORK THESE OUT:

An Aries/Cancer Moon combination: Aries may find Cancer overly sensitive, too traditional, and possessive.

An Aries/Capricorn Moon combination: You're both interested in getting recognition and respect, not in giving it. You might starve each other! *An Aries/Scorpio Moon combination:* A real firecracker! Arguments galore, ending with lovemaking!

NEEDS MUCH UNDERSTANDING AND COMMUNICATION:

An Aries/Libra Moon combination: You both need separate territories in which to shine or operate, or this could be a real clash of egos and emotions.

NEUTRAL TERRITORY:

These Moons could go either way: Taurus, Virgo, Pisces.

MOON IN TAURUS

You are emotionally easygoing and practical. You want the solid comforts of luxurious living — the best of everything (and you usually get it). Sociable, affectionate, and resourceful, you love to travel (first class, of course) and entertain on a grand scale.

Outwardly you're calm and relaxed. You rarely show violent emotions. You're sentimental and romantic and like all the accoutrements of love: flowers, telegrams, soft music (Burt Bacharach, Barbra Streisand, Brahms, Glen Campbell, country music), well-chosen wines, gourmet meals, admiration, and *gifts*. The women are attracted to men who'll provide them with the pleasant surroundings to live happily ever after.

Setting the Stage

Your Moon-nature colors are like a Fragonard painting: powder blue, moss green, earth tones, and pink (no bright reds or the Bull will charge!). Your gemstone is the emerald. Your semiprecious stones are imperial jade, turquoise, malachite and lapis lazuli. You love all spring flowers, especially those that grow close to the earth, like forget-me-nots and the Cecil Bruner rose. You are an excellent gardener and will create an indoor garden wherever you live with lots of plants and flowers everywhere.

Your decor should be sensuous and lush with the textures of soft leathers, beautiful wood paneling, and collections of antique objects. You usually prefer a warm, traditional setting. You'll complete the ambience with a floral or citrus fragrance, or bowls of potpourri. Your *other* great tastes should be indulged with a hidden bedside refrigerator.

YOUR BEST BETS:

A partner with Moon in Taurus: You'll both enjoy sharing the best things in life, especially sensual and material pleasures and treasures.

A Taurus/Virgo Moon combination: An enriching relationship, in more ways than one. You'll organize and build a lasting union with lots of physical and material satisfactions.

A Taurus/Capricorn Moon combination: You'll satisfy each other's needs on many levels: physically, materially, and sensually. An ambitious pairing that's bound to succeed.

ALSO GOOD:

A Taurus/Cancer Moon combination: Taurus will give sensitive Cancer Moons the emotional security and stability they seek. An emotionally fulfilling combination.

A Taurus/Libra Moon combination: Both Venus-ruled, you'll work to please each other's esthetic sense and ideals.

A Taurus/Pisces Moon combination: You're good for one another. Material-minded Taurus and spiritual, idealistic Pisces can balance each other beautifully.

YOU'LL HAVE TO WORK THESE OUT:

A Taurus/Leo Moon combination: You're both stubborn and have different ideas about ruling the roost. Leo likes to spend money and take risks; Taurus likes to save and build. Not easy!

A Taurus/Aquarius Moon combination: Another stubborn pairing, with neither prepared to give in. Idealistic Aquarius and materialistic Taurus both like to have the final word.

NEEDS MUCH UNDERSTANDING AND COMMUNICATION:

A Taurus/Scorpio Moon combination: You're both possessive but don't like to be possessed. Neither of you adjusts easily. Might work if you have much in common to begin with and can work out who handles the money!

NEUTRAL TERRITORY:

These can go either way: Moons in Aries, Sagittarius, or Gemini.

MOON IN GEMINI

You have an emotional nature that fluctuates from the heights of ecstasy to the depths of dispair. There seem to be few placid periods in your emotional life. You must fight this tendency and try to keep your feelings on a more even keel.

You're clever, witty, perceptive, and more apt to enjoy a professional life than a domestic one. A lover seeking a home-loving mate would be wasting his time with you, since most of your inner satisfaction comes from pleasing your public.

You're flirtatious and pleasure-loving. If you want to preserve your marriage and keep the affections of your love partner, you'll have to ignore that fascinating charmer across the room.

Setting the Stage

Your decor will be in a constant state of change, whenever you get the urge for variety. You should choose a neutral background, perhaps in soft Windsor blue, off-white, gray, or yellow, which can blend with your eclectic mixture of art, furniture, and accessories. Polka dots and paisleys, as well as monochromatic color schemes, are also good for you. You need lots of mirrors to watch the goings-on, telephones to keep in touch, and a second home in a contrasting location to switch the scene from time to time.

Good background music for love: Cole Porter, Peggy Lee, Schumann, Grieg, Stravinsky, or the songs of Marvin Hamlisch. Perfume the air with scented candles, potpourri, and incense in airy abstract fragrances. Your flowers are the acacia and the camellia. The blue-white diamond is your gemstone; it reflects your many-faceted nature. Your minerals are the crystal and lapis lazuli.

YOUR BEST BETS:

A partner with Moon in Gemini: Here you'll have a meeting of the minds and interests with lots of happy talk. You'll keep each other fascinated for a long time.

A Gemini/Libra Moon combination: Mental communication is much favored. Neither of you like emotional dramas. A great *permanent* companionship.

A Gemini/Aquarius Moon combination: You'll never cease to fascinate each other. A great mental rapport with a total lack of possessiveness.

ALSO GOOD:

A Gemini/Aries Moon combination: Lots of action here to keep you intrigued. Energetic, pioneering Aries lets Gemini wander, and may even have some new ideas on how to get there.

A Gemini/Leo Moon combination: Neither of you likes to get bogged down in deep emotions. The dramatic Leo Moon and lighthearted Gemini keep it entertaining.

YOU'LL HAVE TO WORK THESE OUT:

A Gemini/Virgo Moon combination: On the emotional level, Gemini will find the Virgo Moon a bit too heavy-going. Great communication, though.

A Gemini/Pisces Moon combination: The Pisces Moon may be too emotional and clinging for you. You'll need other favorable planetary placements to help this one out.

NEEDS MUCH UNDERSTANDING AND COMMUNICATION:

A Gemini/Sagittarius Moon combination: You've got different philosophies and are attracted to different activities and types of people. You'll disagree on so many things. Can be lively but also nerve-wracking.

NEUTRAL TERRITORY:

These can go either way: Moons in Taurus, Cancer, Scorpio, Capricorn.

MOON IN CANCER

The Moon is "at home" in this sign.

You express yourself emotionally rather than intellectually and prefer conventional values and established institutions. A good marriage is one of your most important goals in life. You're sentimental, affectionate and devoted to your family. You may even work at home or in a home-like office, finding more comfort there than in a cold business environment.

You may have psychic powers and become rather mystic, sometimes "marrying" yourself to a church or a philosophy.

Although your nature is rather passive, you're capable of sudden bursts of enthusiasm, especially for causes involving social welfare or children in need. (This brings out your need to "mother" the world!)

Setting the Stage

You need a secure haven that is restful, relaxing, and inspiring, with lots of boxes, bureaus, and shelves to store your belongings, mementos, and old love letters. You like a rather dark room, with twinkling crystal, mirrors and candlelight. You may also have a shell collection, or an aquarium filled with exotic fish and sea treasures.

The moonstone, coral, and pearls become your Moon nature. Silvery white, sea-foam green, midnight blue, and shell coral are your special colors. Bedroom lighting should be dimmed to reflect luminescent skin (yours or your lover's). You'll probably prefer the many moods of artists like Chagall, Degas, or Modigliani, and romantic music from Rodgers and Hammerstein, Lena Horne, Carly Simon, Mahler or Van Cliburn. Create a sensuous bathroom with a jacuzzi or pulsating shower and lots of foaming milk baths and luxurious perfumed oils. Your flowers are all the lilies: calla lilies, water lilies and lily of the valley (which is also your fragrance) . . . and Sea Breeze for the men!

YOUR BEST BETS:

A partner with Moon in Cancer: Nurturing family life and each other is important to you both. Together you create a secure, cozy nest. Your many moods complement each other.

A Cancer/Scorpio Moon combination: You understand each other's deepest needs. There's plenty of emotional security here. Lots of privacy and sensual fulfillment, too.

A Cancer/Pisces Moon combination: A very sensitive pair who can intuitively fill each other's deepest needs. You create a great emotional closeness and sense of well-being.

ALSO GOOD:

A Cancer/Taurus Moon combination: Taurus gives this sensitive moon security and stability. Cancer saves, while Taurus accumulates.

A Cancer/Virgo Moon combination: Virgo keeps emotion in its proper tidy place, which gives Cancer a sense of security and order.

YOU'LL HAVE TO WORK THESE OUT:

A Cancer/Aries Moon combination: Aries can't stand a clinger. Cancer can't let go. Aries wants excitement. Cancer wants emotional security. And that's the problem.

A Cancer/Libra Moon combination: Cancer likes family; Libra likes social life. Cancer is emotional; Libra is mostly mental. Hard to find a balance here.

NEEDS MUCH UNDERSTANDING AND COMMUNICATION:

A Cancer/Capricorn Moon combination: Cancer gets emotional security from the home. Capricorn gets it from work. Better work at home!

NEUTRAL TERRITORY:

These can go either way: Moon in Sagittarius, Leo, Gemini, or Aquarius.

MOON IN LEO

Your concept of love is intensely romantic and very passionate. You take everything and everyone to "heart." You are instinctively attracted to all that is good, generous, and honorable in life. You are willing to make all sorts of sacrifices for those you love, but also expect a lot from *them*. Very often, you are attracted to someone weaker than you, who adores your ability to take command — a trait that may be more suited to business than marriage.

You don't want anyone else stealing your scenes, either, so better not fall in love with a flirt. This will only bring out your jealous side. Find someone who enjoys being smothered with love and dominated a little at the same time. Love can be greatly fulfilling if you have the right partner, a heartbreaking experience if not!

Setting the Stage

Your ambience should be worthy of royalty. Leopard skin, gold ormolu, antique French furniture (Louis XV and XVI style), and all that is opulent excites you. Twilight is your special time of day (perfect for a *cinq-à-sept* rendezvous), and your colors are those of the sunset: gold, yellow-orange, mauve, and coral. You'll have lots of framed photos of admirers, suitcases filled with love letters, a portrait of yourself (beautifully framed), and perhaps a disappearing video screen to watch vintage movies.

Your love themes are the great operas and hit Broadway and motion-picture show tunes. They make great background music for your love dramas. The bed is your stage on which to perform. It should have a canopy with draw curtains (and mirrored headboard), perhaps a fur bedspread, and a very firm mattress to protect your vulnerable back. Surround yourself with sunflowers, tiger lilies, or tea roses, and the scent of jasmine and rose. Your gemstones are the cabochon ruby and the canary diamond. Also lucky: corals and the tiger's eye.

YOUR BEST BETS:

A partner with Moon in Leo: You know just how to stroke each other's ego without scratching! Lots of warm generosity here and understanding. A great co-star . . . just learn to take turns in the spotlight.

A Leo/Aries Moon combination: The regal Leo Moon stabilizes the dynamic Aries Moon. You should shine brighter together. Lots of action here.

A Leo/Sagittarius Moon combination: You both love to have a good time and to be on the go. A good-humored combination.

ALSO GOOD:

A Leo/Libra Moon combination: You complement and appreciate each other. Leo plays to Libra's audience.

A Leo/Gemini Moon combination: Leo projects Gemini's ideas. Gemini sees life and love played on the "big screen."

A Leo/Pisces Moon combination: Pisces creativity sparks the Leo sense of drama. Leo's energy helps Pisces swim upstream.

YOU'LL HAVE TO WORK THESE OUT:

A Leo/Taurus Moon combination: You're both stubborn and motivated differently. And Taurus may not provide the cash for the glamour Leo needs, or be Leo's best audience.

A Leo/Scorpio Moon combination: You both want your own way and neither can really compromise. Might be a case of opposites attracting, then *colliding*.

NEEDS MUCH UNDERSTANDING AND COMMUNICATION:

A Leo/Aquarius Moon combination: It's the personal versus the impersonal. Aquarius won't buy Leo's star trip. You want more recognition than you'll get here.

NEUTRAL TERRITORY:

These could go either way: Moons in Cancer, Virgo, or Capricorn.

MOON IN VIRGO

You are highly discriminating and find it hard to give of yourself emotionally until your partner has measured up to your ideals. Then you do what is expected of you (and more!) Perfection in all things is your principal aim in life. You are critical of yourself and others and accept nothing that isn't top quality.

Try to relax your standards a bit. Nothing and no one is perfect. Learn to reach out to people, compromise sometimes, and show some sympathy and interest in other's affairs. Then you'll discover the rewards of a "special" relationship.

Setting the Stage

Your ambiance is an expert mix of the past and the present. You have an eye for the perfect detail from another era: hand-embroidered sheets, old laces, vintage china, and pure forms in pottery and glass. You enjoy uncluttered modern designs and natural fabrics (especially linen). Your home will be beautifully organized and systematized, with plenty of places to put things . . . often your collection of antique miniatures will be beautifully lit and displayed in cabinets.

Your colors are pure white, wheat, earth tones, gray, and navy. You probably have a special herb or organic garden with trellised vines. Hurricane lights, country naive paintings, Chinese export porcelain, cloissoné, and very detailed objects like Japanese Inro, beautifully bound books, Wedgwood pottery, and framed etchings are your special collectibles.

Surround yourself with the sound of the classics, string quartets, and Puccini operas, the smell of sandalwood or French-milled soaps, and violet, woodsy-mossy perfume. Your flowers are violets and bachelor's buttons, and your gemstone is the emerald; you also love sapphires and lapis lazuli.

YOUR BEST BETS:

A partner with Moon in Virgo: You'll be able to create the perfect setting to inspire each other and tune in to each other's fantasies.

A Virgo/Taurus Moon combination: Physical and material satisfaction contributes to your emotional security. Taurus sets a beautiful scene and Virgo takes care of the details.

A Virgo/Capricorn Moon combination: You're both achievers who will work to earn each other's respect and love.

ALSO GOOD:

A Virgo/Cancer Moon combination: Virgo makes the Cancer Moon feel very secure with attention to detail. Just watch the nitpicking.

A Virgo/Scorpio Moon combination: Scorpio warms up Virgo's cool emotional nature, while Virgo equalizes Scorpio's intensity and tidies up their sex life.

YOU'LL HAVE TO WORK THESE OUT:

A Virgo/Gemini Moon combination: It may be difficult to communicate your feelings: Gemini doesn't care about details and is a bit too flighty for your taste.

A Virgo/Sagittarius Moon combination: Virgos are a bit too precise for Sags. They, too, can't be bothered with details, or dealing with Virgo's critical tongue.

NEEDS MUCH UNDERSTANDING AND COMMUNICATION:

A Virgo/Pisces Moon combination: You're madly attracted to each other *but* it's hard to bring the Pisces moon down to earth. You never seem to agree on little things or to meet each other's emotional needs.

NEUTRAL TERRITORY:

These could go either way: Moons in Aries, Leo, Libra, or Aquarius.

MOON IN LIBRA

You're partnership-oriented and think of love and marriage as the best things in life, although you don't care very much for the domestic scene as such. You're emotionally well balanced and can make a success of any romantic liaison. You prefer such relationships to be traditional and conservative. Your occasional flirtations will be very circumspect.

You have a strong emotional response and some of you have a strong sex drive. If this is the case, be careful not to show your feelings to the world, only to the one you love. You must keep your passions in balance or your romantic life can swing precariously from one extreme to another. You need a stable partnership to be fully content.

Setting the Stage

You prefer a traditional background and will set the stage for love in shades of pink, from shell to shocking. (Males like the airy blues.) In decor, you are a purist, relating your art and furniture and accessories to the style and color of your favorite period. Your rooms will be symmetrical and beautifully proportioned, with nary a jarring note. Light will be strategically placed to flatter guests and your works of art. Everything will be coordinated, including the clothes you wear.

You respond to romantic music: Verdi, Liszt, Horowitz piano, Luciano Pavarotti, Yves Montand, and John Lennon. Lavender and roses in flower and scent bring out your sentimental personality. Your gemstone is the pink diamond. Also lucky for you: pink opals, pink jade, and rose quartz.

YOUR BEST BETS:

A partner with Moon in Libra: You both work for peace and harmony in beautiful surroundings. Should be smooth going.

A Libra/Gemini Moon combination: You communicate mentally and emotionally. Libra creates harmony for the restless Gemini moon. Gemini parties with Libra. Whee!

A Libra/Aquarius Moon combination: An Aquarius moon can stabilize your emotional needs and get you involved in community activities. Companionship can breed a lasting relationship.

ALSO GOOD:

A Libra/Leo Moon combination: A very sociable pairing. You'll enjoy the same lifestyle with lots of mutual admiration.

A Libra/Sagittarius Moon combination: Libra will keep it light and gay for casual Sags. And they'll bring out Librans' philosophical side, help them rise above those swaying emotions.

YOU'LL HAVE TO WORK THESE OUT:

A Libra/Cancer Moon combination: This can be too heavy on the emotions and confining to your social life. Cancer will want to tie you down. You'll want to flee the nest, look for fresh air.

A Libra/Capricorn Moon combination: Another heavy one. Libra will feel weighted down by Capricorn's serious approach to life.

NEEDS MUCH UNDERSTANDING AND COMMUNICATION:

A Libra/Aries Moon combination: Opposites attract, but this reckless Moon keeps you off balance. It's hard to work in tandem here, with one racing ahead and the other holding back.

NEUTRAL TERRITORY:

These Moons could go either way: Moon in Scorpio, Virgo, Pisces, or Taurus.

MOON IN SCORPIO

You're a femme fatale or Svengali with a power-packed sex drive that can drive you (and others) to extremes. Your lovers will either respond to your intensity or be frightened away by it. The one you marry will hopefully be someone whose passions can match yours!

On the other hand, you may choose to channel that same force and energy into your work. This placement really shines in the fields of medicine, religion, philosophy, and police work — you make a great detective (and you're sure to keep track of your loved one!).

Setting the Stage

Your bedroom should be a study in contrasts with darker colors (deep rose, wine, or navy) accentuated with purest white. You prefer subtle Old Master shades, oriental rugs, rich, heavy, dark carved woods in the Victorian or Renaissance style (gnarled woods are also Moon in Scorpio), and tapestry fabrics. Dolphins are a decorative theme, and claw feet indicate the Pan or "warlock" side of your nature. You love to put your favorite objects on carved pedestals. You may also have a collection of crystal objets d'art. Your artists are the symbolists, the pre-Raphaelites, Picasso; Oriental artwork and nudes delight you, too. You'll light with twinkling altar candles in varying sizes and shapes (and burn incense).

Your soul responds to powerful symphonic music, dramatic operas (*Carmen, Mefistofele, Don Giovanni*), and Simon and Garfunkel. Your bath will be an extension of your bedroom, with luxurious fabrics and accessories. A large bathtub with strategically placed jacuzzi jets is a must. Your fragrance should be an oriental blend with a honeysuckle base. Your flowers are the magnolia and the honeysuckle. The black pearl and bloodstone are your lucky talismans, and your gemstone is the deep blue sapphire.

YOUR BEST BETS:

A partner with Moon in Scorpio: The emotional rapport here is complete and intense. You'll be lasting soulmates. You'll share the deepest feelings together.

A Scorpio/Cancer Moon combination: You'll give each other security and communicate your deepest feelings. Your home will be a romantic haven.

A Scorpio/Pisces Moon combination: You're both sensitive and very protective of each other. Emotional closeness is needed and given.

ALSO GOOD:

A Scorpio/Virgo Moon combination: You'll do much for each other. Scorpio turns Virgos on and releases their inhibitions, while Virgo organizes Scorpio's emotional life.

A Scorpio/Capricorn Moon combination: Both persevere. (You'll keep working on this romance no matter what the obstacles!) You also admire each other's ability to achieve.

YOU'LL HAVE TO WORK THESE OUT:

A Scorpio/Leo Moon combination: Lots of steamy sex here, but something or someone has got to give. You're both very stubborn and like to be in control.

A Scorpio/Aquarius Moon combination: You need much more emotional and physical closeness than the Aquarius moon is able to deliver.

NEEDS MUCH UNDERSTANDING AND COMMUNICATION:

A Scorpio/Taurus Moon combination: Property disputes and territorial differences here. A tug of war!

NEUTRAL TERRITORY:

These could go either way: Moons in Sagittarius, Gemini, Libra, or Aries.

MOON IN SAGITTARIUS

You're eager to try all of life's experiences and make ambitious plans for exciting adventures. Not attracted to conventional domesticity, you can have a good marriage with someone who is a good sport and who thinks of you as an equal partner — one who will not cramp your style and who will understand your wanderlust.

Outdoor and sports-oriented, you're a born adventurer, not in *love,* but in *life* itself. Always on the go, you have hundreds of plans and projects, and the love in your life will have to accept them. When things get sticky or emotional, you'll leave 'em guessing (like O. Henry's story endings), crack a joke, or just leave 'em.

Setting the Stage

You enjoy a dramatic setting, with an emphasis on purple or red (or a combination of the two). Your ideal decor is a casual mix of modern and traditional. The Outdoor You may enjoy the English country look with dog or horse paintings and lots of saddle leather. Or you could go exotic and ethnic, surrounded by souvenirs and trophies from your travels to far-off lands. Your rooms should be very spacious with big walk-in fireplaces to gather around and lots of framed photos.

The bedside telephone is a must. (Just be sure you spend as much time talking to your live-in partner as to your long-distance friends.) All fabrics should be pet-proof, as you're sure to have a large hound around. You respond to the smell of fine old leather, to oriental blends, and to carnation. Your music ranges from Puccini to Frank Sinatra, Rudolf Friml, Gershwin, Noel Coward, and country music. The ruby is your gemstone. The turquoise is your signature talisman, and deep red carnations, holly, and poinsettias are your flowers.

YOUR BEST BETS:

A partner with Moon in Sagittarius: You'll understand each other emotionally and philosophically, and will give each other plenty of room to roam.

A Sagittarius/Aries Moon combination: You're both emotionally independent types who won't make too many demands on the other. You'll travel on the same plane.

A Sagittarius/Leo Moon combination: Sag will find a playful mate with the fun-loving Leo Moon. You'll laugh away the rough spots together! There's lots of action and attraction here.

ALSO GOOD:

A Sagittarius/Libra Moon combination: You both love to flirt and will understand this in each other. Librans love flattery — so Sags should toss a compliment their way from time to time.

A Sagittarius/Aquarius Moon combination: You'll soar mentally together and will rarely get too bogged down in emotional dramas.

YOU'LL HAVE TO WORK THESE OUT:

A Sagittarius/Virgo Moon combination: You're at odds with each other emotionally and mentally. Virgo can't see the forest; Sag can't see the trees.

A Sagittarius/Pisces Moon combination: Pisces needs deep emotional contact. Sagittarius would rather skim the surface. No oceans of emotions for you!

NEEDS MUCH UNDERSTANDING AND COMMUNICATION:

A Sagittarius/Gemini Moon combination: Lots of missed opportunities here. You'll both talk *at* each other (usually at the same time and in different languages). Learn to listen.

NEUTRAL TERRITORY:

These could go either way: Moons in Scorpio, Cancer, Taurus, or Capricorn.

MOON IN CAPRICORN

The Moon in this Earth sign makes you want to rise to the top and to compete in a man's world if you are a woman. You're capable of complete devotion and dedication when you love someone, yet you want to be an equal in the battle of the sexes. You have a very strong character and a strong drive to succeed.

Romance would be much easier for you if you would learn to look at the lighter side of love. Be a bit more capricious, whimsical, spontaneous. To help you break out of the "workaholic" mold, cultivate your marvelous sense of style, your green thumb, your love of animals, your talent in the kitchen, and your delightful dry sense of humor.

Setting the Stage

You have excellent taste and your background will be elegant, traditional, and influenced by medieval Spain or the Renaissance. Tapestries, unicorns, high canopy beds (with carved wood frames), crewel embroidery, pure linens trimmed with a monogram or crest, cathedral ceilings, and beautiful dark woods will appeal to you. You are very conscious of details and status symbols and locations.

On the walls: strong modern paintings, Matisse/Cezanne-style, mixed with Renaissance art. A glorious medieval candelabra could illuminate your background. Your colors are the dark tapestry tones, earth shades, black and white sparked with blood red. You'll enjoy medieval music, string quartets, Latin rhythms (tangos or flamenco guitars), the ballads of

Tony Martin, the country music of Dolly Parton, or, for a surprise, the sounds of David Bowie or the late Elvis Presley to stir your senses. Your flower, and special fragrance, is the geranium. Your talismans are the black and white onyx, Russian malachite, and imperial jade. The emerald is your gemstone.

YOUR BEST BETS:

A partner with Moon in Capricorn: You're both mentally in tune and can work to achieve emotional closeness. (You'll understand each other's priorities.)

A Capricorn/Taurus Moon combination: A great blending of complementary needs. You can work together for material and career success.

A Capricorn/Virgo Moon combination: You're both serious types who have similar motivations. A very productive pairing that gets down to business together.

ALSO GOOD:

A Capricorn/Scorpio Moon combination: You'll love the intensity and dedication of this sign. Scorpio brings out Cap's sensuality; Cap helps channel Scorpio's energy.

A Capricorn/Pisces Moon combination: You'll bring this Moon down to earth and give it direction. It will arouse your emotions . . . put romance into your life.

YOU'LL HAVE TO WORK THESE OUT:

A Capricorn/Libra Moon combination: Libra Moons are too indecisive and extravagant for Capricorn, who's too demanding and practical for them.

A Capricorn/Aries Moon combination: A very difficult combination. You both aim for success in different directions and constantly disagree. Neither builds the other's ego.

NEEDS MUCH UNDERSTANDING AND COMMUNICATION:

A Capricorn/Cancer Moon combination: Capricorn is a workaholic; the Cancer Moon, a stay-at-home. The only solution is to work at home and go to bed early.

NEUTRAL TERRITORY:

These could go either way: Moons in Sagittarius, Aquarius, Leo, or Gemini.

MOON IN AQUARIUS

The Moon is very stable in this sign. You have a warm, generous, and seductive aura. A true humanitarian, you are eager to help people and therefore a most endearing person. You're tolerant, understanding, and very pleasant to be with. You'll be happiest with someone who shares your concerns for mankind and who will appreciate your individuality. Very unpredictable and sometimes unreliable, you love to surprise people. (Not for you the conventional types who operate on schedule!)

Setting the Stage

You must have a feeling of space in your setting, either *outer,* with perhaps a geodesic dome, a glass roof, or way-out modern decor, or *inner,* with spiritual paintings and objects to meditate on. You're happiest in an uncluttered, modern, even futuristic environment of Grecian simplicity. You love to live on high floors where everything points to the sky.

Your colors are stark white, electric blue, or all the vivid psychedelics. You need big windows with a view (nothing closed in), rooms with spaces that flow one into the other, and the latest electronic gadgets (particularly a good telephone and intercom system for instant communication). Your bedroom will be unusual, clean and uncluttered, with perhaps a vibrating bed or one that disappears into the wall (your home should be full of unexpected surprises).

Shiny surfaces, patterned fabrics in dramatic abstract prints or plaids, and avant-garde art and music all help you live in the future — the Age of Aquarius. A clean, abstract fragrance in the air (no woodsy or floral notes) completes your mood.

You'll probably have a sophisticated built-in sound system with New Wave rock, jazz, Delius, Placido Domingo, Schubert, and Roberta Flack coming at you from all sides. Your gemstone is the geometric cut diamond in a simple setting, with the light blue sapphire and amethyst as your lucky talismans. Your flower is the white lilac or orchid.

YOUR BEST BETS:

A partner with Moon in Aquarius: Lots of common interests form the basis of your emotional rapport. Your shared ideals make this relationship long term.

An Aquarius/Libra Moon combination: Together you can harmonize beautifully. Libra provides the romantic melody. You provide the electronic beat.

An Aquarius/Gemini Moon combination: You're both "with-it" — gregarious and mentally oriented. Great rapport and communication can make this team a winner.

ALSO GOOD:

An Aquarius/Aries Moon combination: You're full of surprises for each other. Aquarians have to adjust to the Aries ego, and Aries must let Aquarians pursue their own interests. But Aries enthusiasm and energy can put Aquarian ideas into motion.

An Aquarius/Sagittarius Moon combination: You'll give each other plenty of space and even travel there together. Neither wants a clinging vine and neither gets one here.

YOU'LL HAVE TO WORK THESE OUT:

An Aquarius/Taurus Moon combination: Taureans can be too materialistic for Aquarius, who's too "far out" for them. You're both fixed in your ways. Ouch!

An Aquarius/Scorpio Moon combination: Scorpio's emotional intensity can drown high-flying Aquarian ideals. Get yourself a boat.

NEEDS MUCH UNDERSTANDING AND COMMUNICATION:

An Aquarius/Leo Moon combination: You want different things out of life. Leo demands attention. Aquarius won't take orders. Pretty hard to find common ground.

NEUTRAL TERRITORY

These could go either way: Moons in Capricorn, Pisces, Virgo, or Cancer.

MOON IN PISCES

You need lots of love and affection, which you're more than willing to give in return. You procrastinate and need a partner who will get you moving and laugh off your fits of depression. You're artistic, creative, intuitive, and very responsive to a romantic atmosphere. Your choice of a mate is very important, for this person can either bring out your natural talents and help you give them positive expression or leave you writing mournful sagas of unrequited love. You love home life and need a secure environment from which to depart on flights of fantasy. You're very sensitive and can also be very psychic.

Setting the Stage

You should have a house by the water to soothe your psyche, or perhaps an indoor pool, aquarium, indoor waterfall, and jacuzzi. You'll need lots of pillows and soft chairs you can sink into, beautiful thick pile rugs (to walk barefoot). Your furniture should be pet-proof to accommodate your adopted strays. Oriental motifs, Japanese screens, and low beds are important. So is a health-oriented kitchen with a juicer for healthful liquids (forget the home bar). You may also need a vaporizer to help fragile skin and breathing passages.

Your colors are all the sea shades and watercolors. Your flowers: tuberoses and gardenias. Enjoy their fragrances in incense and oil forms. Arrange your lighting in romantic, indirect pools of light. The walls might show off your talent for photography, watercolors, or seascapes. You'll also love Monet or Renoir prints. Your sounds should be all kinds of mood music, especially Handel (composer of *Water Music* for the royal barge on the Thames), Chopin, Nat King Cole, cool jazz, Nina Simone, Rimsky-Korsakov. Your gemstone is the blue cabochon sapphire, with pearls and aquamarines as your lucky talismans.

YOUR BEST BETS:

A partner with Moon in Pisces: You are true soulmates who can guess each other's thoughts and feelings and communicate without words.

A Pisces/Cancer Moon combination: Deep feelings are important to both of you. You'll guard each other's sensitive natures.

A Pisces/Scorpio Moon combination: Scorpio intensity and determination blends well with the other-worldly Pisces Moon, helping Pisces focus their emotions and talents.

ALSO GOOD:

A Pisces/Capricorn Moon combination: The Pisces romantic nature gives ballast to the workaholic Capricorn Moon. And they help your dreams materialize.

A Pisces/Taurus Moon combination: Pisces enjoy the Taurus Moon's sensuality and protectiveness, though they may feel "owned" and fenced-in. But you can work it out.

YOU'LL HAVE TO WORK THESE OUT:

A Pisces/Gemini Moon combination: Lots of frustrations and irritations here. Gemini wants to *talk* about love (and everything), while Pisces wants to *feel* it (and everything).

A Pisces/Sagittarius Moon combination: Pisces want total intimacy, to merge with their lover. Sag wants to be free at all costs. Somebody's going to lose out!

NEEDS MUCH UNDERSTANDING AND COMMUNICATION:

A Pisces/Virgo Moon combination: Virgo's a practical planner who may spoil many a Piscean reverie. You both want different things from love, and get no joy from giving in to each other.

NEUTRAL TERRITORY:

These could go either way: Moons in Aries, Leo, Aquarius, or Libra.

HOW TO FIND THE PLACEMENT OF YOUR MOON

The sign in which the Moon was located at the time of your birth is important in determining your emotional love nature. The following tables (ephemeris) will enable you to find the zodiac sign for your Moon's position (by degree) if your birthday took place between 1900 and 1989. (We're thinking ahead!) The time and degree given is for Greenwich Meridian Time.

Find the page on which your birth month is located, choose the year of your birth from the left hand column, then trace your finger across the page until you reach the day of your birth. If there is no symbol next to the number (degree) listed there, move your finger back a day or two until you find one. That symbol will indicate your Moon sign.

Now read and compare your Moon placement with that of your love partner.

SYMBOLS

The Love Planets

Sun	☉
Moon	☽
Venus	♀
Mars	♂

Signs of the Zodiac

Aries	♈	Libra	♎
Taurus	♉	Scorpio	♏
Gemini	♊	Sagittarius	♐
Cancer	♋	Capricorn	♑
Leo	♌	Aquarius	♒
Virgo	♍	Pisces	♓

January

	1st	2nd	3rd	4th	5th	6th	7th	8th	9th	10th	11th	12th	13th	14th	15th	16th
1900	01♑	16	01♒	16	01♓	15	00♈	14	28	11♉	24	07♊	20	03♋	15	27
1901	18♉	02♊	16	00♋	13	27	10♌	23	05♍	17	29	11♎	23	05♏	17	29
1902	02♎	14	26	08♏	19	01♐	13	25	07♑	20	02♒	15	28	11♓	25	08♈
1903	02♒	14	26	08♓	20	03♈	16	29	13♉	27	12♊	27	13♋	28	13♌	28
1904	08♊	22	07♋	22	07♌	22	07♍	22	06♎	19	03♏	16	28	11♐	23	06♑
1905	10♏	24	07♐	21	04♑	17	00♒	13	25	07♓	19	01♈	13	24	06♉	19
1906	21♓	03♈	15	27	09♉	21	03♊	15	28	10♋	23	06♌	19	03♍	16	00♎
1907	22♋	04♌	16	29	11♍	24	07♎	21	05♏	19	04♐	19	04♑	19	04♒	18
1908	29♏	13♐	28	13♑	29	13♒	28	13♓	27	11♈	24	07♉	20	02♊	14	26
1909	02♉	16	29	12♊	25	08♋	20	03♌	15	27	09♍	21	02♎	14	26	09♏
1910	11♍	23	05♎	17	29	11♏	23	05♐	17	00♑	13	27	10♒	24	08♓	23
1911	13♑	25	07♒	20	03♓	16	29	13♈	27	11♉	25	10♊	25	09♋	24	09♌
1912	19♉	03♊	18	04♋	19	04♌	19	04♍	18	02♎	15	28	10♏	22	05♐	16
1913	24♎	07♏	20	03♐	16	28	11♑	23	05♒	17	19	10♓	22	04♈	16	29
1914	01♓	13	25	06♈	18	00♉	12	25	07♊	20	04♋	18	02♌	16	00♍	15
1915	03♋	16	28	11♌	24	08♍	21	05♎	19	03♏	17	02♐	16	01♑	15	29
1916	10♏	25	10♐	25	10♑	25	10♒	25	09♓	22	05♈	18	01♉	13	25	07♊
1917	16♈	29	12♉	24	07♊	19	01♋	13	25	07♌	19	00♍	12	24	07♎	29
1918	20♌	02♍	14	26	08♎	20	02♏	16	27	11♐	24	08♑	22	07♒	22	06♓
1919	13♐	06♑	19	02♒	16	29	13♓	27	11♈	25	10♉	24	08♊	22	06♋	20
1920	02♉	16	02♊	16	01♋	16	00♌	15	29	13♍	26	09♎	21	03♏	15	27
1921	07♎	10	03♏	15	28	10♐	21	03♑	15	27	09♒	21	03♓	15	27	10♈
1922	10♒	22	04♓	16	28	10♈	22	04♉	17	00♊	14	28	13♋	28	13♌	28
1923	13♊	16	10♋	23	07♌	21	05♍	20	04♎	18	02♏	16	00♐	14	27	11♑
1924	23♎	08♏	22	07♐	22	07♑	21	05♒	19	03♓	16	28	11♈	23	05♉	26
1925	28♓	11♈	24	06♉	18	00♊	12	24	06♋	17	29	11♌	23	06♍	18	01♎
1926	00♌	12	24	06♍	18	00♎	12	25	07♏	21	05♐	19	04♑	19	04♒	19
1927	03♐	17	00♑	14	28	13♒	27	12♓	26	10♈	24	08♉	22	05♊	19	02♋
1928	16♈	00♉	14	29	13♊	27	12♋	26	09♌	23	05♍	18	00♎	12	24	06♏
1929	19♍	02♎	14	26	08♏	20	02♐	14	26	08♑	20	02♒	14	27	09♓	22
1930	20♑	02♒	14	26	08♓	20	02♈	15	28	11♉	25	09♊	24	09♋	25	10♌
1931	23♉	07♊	20	05♋	19	04♌	19	04♍	18	03♎	17	00♏	14	27	10♐	23
1932	08♎	22	06♏	21	05♐	19	03♑	16	00♒	13	25	08♓	20	02♈	14	26
1933	09♓	22	04♈	16	28	10♉	22	04♊	16	28	10♋	22	05♌	18	01♍	14
1934	11♋	23	04♌	16	28	11♍	23	06♎	19	02♏	16	01♐	15	00♑	16	01♒
1935	13♏	27	11♐	25	10♑	25	10♒	25	10♓	24	08♈	22	05♉	18	01♊	14
1936	01♈	15	29	13♉	27	10♊	24	07♋	20	03♌	15	27	10♍	21	03♎	15
1937	29♌	11♍	24	06♎	18	00♏	12	24	06♐	18	00♑	13	25	09♒	22	05♓
1938	01♑	13	25	07♒	19	02♓	14	27	10♈	24	08♉	22	06♊	21	06♋	21
1939	03♉	17	01♊	16	01♋	16	01♌	16	01♍	16	00♎	14	27	10♏	22	05♐
1940	23♍	07♎	21	05♏	18	02♐	14	28	10♑	23	05♒	17	29	11♓	23	05♈
1941	19♒	01♓	14	26	08♈	19	01♉	13	25	08♊	20	03♋	16	00♌	13	27
1942	21♊	03♋	15	28	10♌	23	06♍	19	02♎	15	29	13♏	28	13♐	28	22♑
1943	24♎	08♏	22	07♐	22	07♑	22	07♒	22	07♓	21	04♈	18	00♉	13	25
1944	15♓	29	13♈	27	10♉	23	06♊	19	01♋	13	26	07♌	19	01♍	13	25
1945	08♌	21	03♍	15	27	09♎	21	03♏	15	27	10♐	23	07♈	20	04♒	18
1946	11♐	23	06♑	18	01♒	14	27	10♓	24	08♈	22	06♉	20	04♊	19	03♋
1947	15♈	29	13♉	27	12♊	27	13♋	28	13♌	27	11♍	25	08♎	21	03♏	16
1948	07♍	21	05♎	19	02♏	15	27	09♐	22	04♑	16	28	09♒	21	03♓	15
1949	28♑	11♒	23	05♓	17	29	11♈	22	05♉	17	00♊	13	27	11♋	25	10♌
1950	01♊	13	26	09♋	22	05♌	19	02♍	16	00♎	14	28	12♏	26	11♐	25
1951	07♎	20	04♏	19	03♐	18	04♑	19	03♒	18	02♓	15	28	11♈	23	05♉
1952	28♒	12♓	26	10♈	23	05♉	18	00♊	12	24	06♋	18	00♌	12	24	05♍
1953	19♋	01♌	13	25	07♍	18	00♎	12	24	07♏	20	03♐	17	01♑	16	01♒
1954	21♏	03♐	16	29	12♑	26	10♒	24	08♓	22	06♈	21	05♉	19	03♊	16
1955	28♓	12♈	26	11♉	25	10♊	25	09♋	24	08♌	22	05♍	18	01♎	13	25
1956	19♌	03♍	17	01♎	14	26	09♏	21	03♐	15	26	08♑	20	02♒	14	26
1957	09♑	21	03♒	15	27	08♓	20	02♈	15	27	10♉	23	07♊	22	06♋	21
1958	10♉	23	06♊	19	03♋	17	01♌	16	00♍	15	29	13♎	27	11♏	25	08♐
1959	21♍	05♎	18	03♏	17	01♐	16♑	00	14	28♒	12	25♓	08	21♈	03	15
1960	10♒	24	08♓	21	04♈	17	29	11♉	23	05♊	16	28	10♋	22	05♌	17
1961	29♊	11♋	23	05♌	17	29	11♍	23	05♎	18	01♏	14	28	12♐	27	12♑
1962	00♏	13	26	09♐	23	08♑	22	07♒	22	06♓	21	05♈	19	03♉	16	00♊
1963	13♓	27	11♈	25	09♉	23	08♊	22	05♋	19	02♌	15	28	10♍	22	04♎
1964	00♌	14	28	11♍	24	07♎	19	01♏	13	25	06♐	18	00♑	13	25	07♒
1965	20♐	01♑	13	25	07♒	19	01♓	13	26	09♈	22	05♉	19	03♊	18	03♋
1966	20♈	03♉	16	29	13♊	28	13♋	28	18♌	28	13♍	27	11♎	25	08♏	21
1967	05♍	19	04♎	18	02♏	16	29	13♐	26	09♑	22	05♒	18	00♓	12	24
1968	20♑	04♒	18	01♓	14	27	09♈	21	02♉	14	26	08♊	20	03♋	15	28
1969	10♊	22	04♋	15	28	10♌	22	04♍	17	00♎	13	26	10♏	25	09♐	24
1970	10♎	23	06♏	20	04♐	19	04♑	19	04♒	19	04♓	18	03♈	16	29	12♉
1971	27♒	11♓	26	10♈	24	07♉	21	04♊	18	00♋	13	26	08♌	20	02♍	14
1972	11♋	25	08♌	21	04♍	16	28	10♎	22	04♏	16	28	10♐	23	06♑	19
1973	00♐	12	24	06♑	18	00♒	13	25	08♓	21	05♈	18	02♉	16	01♊	16
1974	01♈	14	27	11♉	25	09♊	24	09♋	25	10♌	25	09♍	24♉	07♎	20	03♏
1975	19♌	03♍	18	02♎	16	00♏	13	26	09♐	21	04♑	16	28	10♒	22	04♓
1976	01♑	15	28	11♒	24	06♓	18	00♈	12	23	05♉	17	00♊	13	26	09♋
1977	10♉	02♊	14	26	08♋	21	04♌	17	00♍	13	27	10♎	24	08♏	23	07♐
1978	22♍	05♎	18	01♏	16	00♐	15	00♑	16	01♒	16	00♓	14	28	11♈	24
1979	10♒	25	10♓	24	08♈	21	04♉	17	00♊	12	24	06♋	18	00♌	12	24
1980	23♊	06♋	19	01♌	14	26	08♍	19	01♎	13	25	07♏	20	03♐	16	00♑
1981	10♏	22	04♐	16	29	11♑	24	08♒	21	05♓	19	03♈	17	01♉	15	29
1982	13♓	26	09♈	23	07♉	22	06♊	21	06♋	21	06♌	20	04♍	18	01♎	14
1983	01♌	16	01♍	15	29♎	13	26♏	08	21♐	03	15	27♑	09	20♒	02	14
1984	14♐	26	09♑	21	03♒	15	27	09♓	21	03♈	15	27	10♉	23	06♊	20
1985	29♈	11♉	23	06♊	18	02♋	15	29	13♌	27	11♍	25	09♎	25	08♏	22
1986	05♍	18	01♎	15	29	13♏	28	12♐	27	12♑	26	11♒	25	08♓	21	04♈
1987	22♑	07♒	22	06♓	10	03♈	16	29	11♉	23	05♊	17	29	11♋	23	05♌
1988	05♊	17	29	12♋	24	06♌	16	29	11♍	23	05♎	17	00♏	13	26	10♐
1989	19♎	01♏	13	26	09♐	22	06♑	20	04♒	18	03♓	17	02♈	16	00♉	14

	17th	18th	19th	20th	21st	22nd	23rd	24th	25th	26th	27th	28th	29th	30th	31st
1900	09♌	21	03♍	15	27	09♎	21	03♏	16	29	12♐	26	10♑	24	09♒
1901	12♐	24	07♑	21	05♒	19	03♓	18	02♈	16	01♉	15	28	12♊	26♊
1902	22	06♉	20	04♊	19	04♋	18	03♌	17	00♍	14	27	09♎	22	04♏
1903	12♍	26	10♎	23	05♏	17	29	11♐	23	05♑	17	29	11♒	23	05♓
1904	18	00♒	12	23	05♓	17	29	11♈	23	06♉	19	02♊	16	00♋	15♋
1905	01♊	14	28	12♋	26	10♌	25	09♍	24	08♎	23	07♏	21	04♐	18♐
1906	14	28	12♏	27	11♐	25	10♑	24	07♒	21	04♓	16	29	11♈	23♈
1907	02♓	16	00♈	13	25	07♉	20	01♊	13	25	07♋	19	01♌	13	26♌
1908	08♋	20	02♌	14	25	07♍	19	02♎	14	27	10♏	23	07♐	21	06♑
1909	21	04♐	18	02♑	16	01♒	16	01♓	16	00♈	15	29	13♉	26	09♊
1910	07♈	21	05♉	19	03♊	17	01♋	14	28	11♌	24	06♍	19	01♎	13♎
1911	23	07♍	20	03♎	15	27	09♏	21	03♐	15	27	09♑	21	04♒	17♒
1912	28	10♑	22	04♒	16	28	10♓	22	05♈	18	01♉	14	28	12♊	27♊
1913	11♉	24	08♊	22	07♋	22	07♌	22	07♍	22	06♎	20	04♏	17	00♐
1914	29	13♎	27	11♏	25	09♐	22	06♑	19	02♒	14	27	09♓	21	02♈
1915	13♒	27	10♓	22	05♈	17	29	11♉	23	05♊	17	29	11♋	24	07♌
1916	19	00♋	12	24	06♌	18	01♍	13	26	09♎	22	06♏	20	04♐	19♐
1917	02♏	15	29	13♐	27	12♑	27	13♒	28	13♓	27	12♈	25	09♉	21♉
1918	12	05♈	20	04♉	17	01♊	14	27	09♋	22	04♌	16	29	10♍	22♍
1919	03♌	17	00♍	12	25	07♎	19	00♏	12	24	06♐	19	01♑	14	27♑
1920	08♐	20	02♑	14	27	09♒	22	05♓	28	01♈	14	28	12♉	26	10♊
1921	23	06♉	19	03♊	18	03♋	18	04♌	19	04♍	18	03♎	16	29	12♏
1922	13♍	28	12♎	26	09♏	22	05♐	18	00♑	13	25	07♒	19	01♓	13♓
1923	24	07♒	20	02♓	14	26	08♈	20	02♉	14	26	08♊	21	04♋	18♋
1924	28	10♊	22	05♋	17	00♌	13	26	09♍	23	06♎	20	04♏	18	03♐
1925	14	27	11♏	25	09♐	24	09♑	24	09♒	24	09♓	23	06♈	19	02♉
1926	04	19	03♈	17	00♉	14	26	09♊	21	03♋	15	27	09♌	21	03♍
1927	15	27	10♌	22	04♍	16	28	10♎	22	04♏	16	28	11♐	24	08♑
1928	18	00♐	12	24	07♑	20	03♒	17	00♓	14	28	13♈	27	11♉	25♉
1929	06♈	19	03♉	17	01♊	15	00♋	15	00♌	15	29	13♍	27	10♎	22♎
1930	25	10♍	24	08♎	22	05♏	17	00♐	12	24	06♑	17	29	11♒	23♒
1931	05♑	18	00♒	12	24	06♓	18	00♈	11	23	06♉	18	01♊	14	28♊
1932	07♉	19	02♊	14	27	10♋	24	08♌	22	06♍	20	05♎	19	03♏	17♏
1933	27	11♎	25	09♏	23	07♐	22	07♑	21	05♒	20	03♓	16	29	12♈
1934	16	01♓	15	29	12♈	25	08♉	20	02♊	14	26	08♋	10	01♌	13♌
1935	26	08♋	20	02♌	14	26	08♍	20	02♎	14	26	09♏	22	05♐	19♐
1936	27	09♏	22	04♐	17	00♑	14	2	13♒	27	12♓	27	11♈	26	10♉
1937	19	03♈	17	01♉	15	00♊	14	28	12♋	26	10♌	23	06♍	19	02♎
1938	06♌	21	05♍	19	03♎	15	28	10♏	22	04♐	16	28	09♑	21	04♒
1939	17	29	11♑	22	04♒	16	28	10♓	22	04♈	17	29	12♉	26	09♊
1940	17	29	11♉	24	07♊	20	04♋	19	04♌	19	04♍	19	03♎	18	02♏
1941	11♍	25	09♎	24	08♏	22	06♐	20	04♑	17	01♒	14	27	09♓	21♓
1942	27	12♒	26	09♓	22	05♈	18	00♉	12	24	06♊	17	29	12♋	24♋
1943	07♊	19	01♋	13	25	07♌	18	00♍	13	25	07♎	20	03♏	17	01♐
1944	07♎	19	01♏	14	27	11♐	25	10♑	24	09♒	25	10♓	24	09♈	23♈
1945	03♓	17	02♈	16	00♉	14	28	12♊	25	08♋	21	04♌	17	29	11♍
1946	18	02♌	16	29	12♍	25	08♎	20	02♏	14	25	07♐	19	01♑	14♑
1947	28	09♐	21	03♑	15	27	09♒	21	03♓	16	29	12♈	25	09♉	23♉
1948	27	09♈	22	04♉	18	01♊	15	00♋	15	00♌	16	01♍	16	00♎	15♎
1949	25	09♍	24	08♎	23	06♏	20	03♐	16	29	12♑	25	07♒	19	01♓
1950	09♑	23	06♒	19	02♓	15	27	09♈	21	03♉	15	27	09♊	21	04♋
1951	17	29	11♊	23	05♋	17	29	12♌	24	07♍	20	04♎	17	01♏	15♏
1952	18	00♎	12	25	09♏	22	06♐	21	06♑	21	06♒	22	06♓	21	05♈
1953	16	01♓	15	00♈	14	28	12♉	25	08♊	21	03♋	15	27	09♌	21♌
1954	00♋	13	27	09♌	22	05♍	17	29	11♎	23	04♏	16	29	11♐	24♐
1955	07♏	19	01♐	13	25	07♑	20	02♒	15	28	12♓	25	09♈	23	07♉
1956	08♓	21	04♈	17	00♉	14	28	12♊	27	12♌	27	12♌	27	11♍	26♍
1957	07♌	22	07♍	22	06♎	20	03♏	16	29	11♐	24	06♑	18	00♒	12♒
1958	21	04♑	17	00♒	12	25	07♓	19	00♈	12	24	06♉	18	01♊	14♊
1959	27	09♉	20	02♊	15	27	10♋	23	06♌	20	03♍	17	01♎	15	29♎
1960	29	12♍	25	08♎	22	05♏	19	04♐	18	03♑	18	03♒	18	02♓	16♓
1961	28	13♒	28	13♓	27	11♈	24	07♉	20	02♊	14	26	08♋	20	02♌
1962	13	25	08♋	20	03♌	15	27	08♍	20	02♎	14	26	08♏	21	04♐
1963	16	28	10♏	22	04♐	17	00♑	13	27	10♒	24	09♓	23	07♈	22♈
1964	20	03♓	17	00♈	14	28	12♉	26	10♊	25	09♋	24	08♌	22	06♍
1965	18	03♌	18	03♍	18	02♎	15	28	10♏	23	06♐	17	28	10♑	22♑
1966	04♐	16	29	11♑	23	05♒	17	29	10♓	22	04♈	16	29	11♉	24♉
1967	06♈	18	00♉	12	24	07♊	20	03♋	17	01♌	16	00♍	15	00♎	14♎
1968	12♌	25	08♍	22	06♎	20	04♏	18	02♐	16	01♑	15	29	13♒	26♒
1969	09♑	24	09♒	24	08♓	22	05♈	28	00♉	13	25	06♊	18	00♋	12♋
1970	25	07♊	19	01♋	13	25	07♌	19	01♍	13	25	07♎	19	02♏	15♏
1971	26	07♎	19	02♏	14	27	10♐	23	07♑	22	07♒	21	06♓	21	06♈
1972	02♒	16	00♓	14	28	12♈	26	11♉	25	09♊	23	06♋	20	03♌	16♌
1973	00♋	15	00♌	14	28	12♍	25	08♎	20	03♏	15	26	08♐	20	02♑
1974	16	28	10♐	22	04♑	15	27	09♒	21	03♓	15	28	10♈	23	06♉
1975	16	27	09♈	22	04♉	17	00♊	13	28	12♋	27	12♌	27	13♍	28♍
1976	23	07♌	21	06♍	20	05♎	19	03♏	17	01♐	14	28	11♑	24	07♒
1977	22	06♑	21	05♒	19	02♓	15	28	10♈	22	04♉	16	28	10♊	22♊
1978	06♉	18	00♊	12	24	06♋	17	29	12♌	24	06♍	19	02♎	15	28♎
1979	06♍	18	00♎	12	24	07♏	20	04♐	18	03♑	18	03♒	18	04♓	19♓
1980	14	28	13♒	27	12♓	27	11♈	25	09♉	23	06♊	19	02♋	15	27♋
1981	14♊	28	12♋	25	09♌	22	05♍	17	00♎	12	24	06♏	17	29	12♐
1982	26	08♏	20	02♐	14	26	08♑	20	02♒	14	27	10♓	23	06♈	20♈
1983	26	08♓	20	03♈	15	28	11♉	25	09♊	24	09♋	24	09♌	24	09♍
1984	04♋	18	03♌	18	04♍	18	03♎	17	01♏	15	28	11♐	23	06♑	18♑
1985	05♐	19	03♑	16	29	12♒	25	07♓	29	01♈	13	15	07♉	19	01♊
1986	16	28	10♉	22	03♊	15	27	10♋	22	05♌	18	01♍	15	28	12♎
1987	17	29	11♍	24	06♎	19	03♏	16	00♐	15	00♑	15	00♒	15	00♓
1988	24	09♑	24	10♒	25	10♓	24	09♈	22	06♉	19	02♊	14	26	08♋
1989	27	11♊	24	07♋	20	03♌	15	27	09♍	21	03♎	15	27	09♏	21♏

February

	1st	2nd	3rd	4th	5th	6th	7th	8th	9th	10th	11th	12th	13th	14th	15th	16th
1900	25♒	10♓	25	10♈	24	08♉	21	04♊	17	00♋	12	24	06♌	18	00♍	12
1901	09♋	22	05♌	18	01♍	13	25	07♎	19	01♏	13	25	07♐	19	02♑	15
1902	16♍	27	09♐	21	03♑	16	28	11♒	24	08♓	21	05♈	19	03♉	17	01♊
1903	18♓	00♈	13	16	09♉	23	07♊	21	06♋	21	06♌	21	06♍	20	04♎	18
1904	00♌	16	01♍	16	01♎	15	29	12♏	25	08♐	20	03♑	15	27	09♒	20
1905	01♑	14	26	09♒	21	03♓	15	27	09♈	21	02♉	15	27	09♊	22	06♋
1906	05♉	17	29	11♊	23	06♋	18	01♌	15	28	12♍	26	11♎	25	09♏	24
1907	08♍	21	04♎	18	01♏	15	29	13♐	28	13♑	27	12♒	26	10♓	24	07♈
1908	21♑	06♒	21	07♓	21	06♈	20	03♉	16	29	11♊	23	05♋	17	29	10♌
1909	22♊	04♋	17	29	11♌	23	05♍	17	29	11♎	23	05♏	17	00♐	13	26
1910	25♎	07♏	18	00♐	13	25	08♑	21	05♒	19	04♓	18	03♈	17	02♉	16
1911	00♓	13	26	10♈	23	07♉	21	05♊	20	04♋	18	03♌	17	01♍	14	28
1912	12♋	27	12♌	27	12♍	25	10♎	24	06♏	29	01♐	13	25	07♑	19	01♒
1913	13♐	25	08♑	20	02♒	14	26	07♓	19	01♈	13	25	07♉	20	03♊	16
1914	14♈	26	08♉	20	02♊	15	28	12♋	26	10♌	25	09♍	24	09♎	24	08♏
1915	20♌	04♍	18	02♎	16	00♏	14	28	12♐	26	10♑	24	08♒	21	05♓	18
1916	03♑	18	03♒	18	02♓	16	00♈	14	26	09♉	21	03♊	15	27	09♋	21
1917	04♊	16	28	10♋	22	04♌	16	27	09♍	21	04♎	16	28	11♏	24	08♐
1918	04♎	16	28	10♏	23	05♐	18	02♑	16	00♒	15	00♓	15	00♈	15	00♉
1919	11♒	25	09♓	24	08♈	22	06♉	20	04♊	18	02♋	15	29	12♌	25	08♍
1920	25♊	09♋	24	09♌	23	07♍	20	04♎	16	29	11♏	23	05♐	17	28	10♑
1921	24♏	07♐	18	00♑	12	24	06♒	18	00♓	12	24	07♈	19	02♉	16	29
1922	24♓	06♈	18	00♉	13	25	09♊	22	06♋	21	06♌	21	07♍	22	07♎	21
1923	02♌	16	01♍	15	00♎	14	29	13♏	27	10♐	24	07♑	20	03♒	16	28
1924	17♐	01♑	16	00♒	14	27	10♓	23	06♈	18	00♉	12	24	06♊	18	00♋
1925	15♉	27	09♊	21	02♋	14	26	08♌	20	03♍	15	28	11♎	24	07♏	21
1926	14♍	26	09♎	21	03♏	16	29	13♐	27	12♑	27	12♒	27	12♓	27	12♈
1927	22♑	07♒	21	06♓	21	06♈	21	05♉	19	02♊	16	29	11♋	24	06♌	18
1928	09♊	23	07♋	21	04♌	17	01♍	13	26	08♎	20	02♏	14	26	08♐	20
1929	05♏	17	29	10♐	22	04♑	16	28	11♒	23	06♓	19	02♈	16	29	13♉
1930	05♓	17	29	12♈	24	07♉	20	04♊	18	03♋	18	03♌	18	03♍	18	03♎
1931	13♋	27	12♌	28	13♍	28	12♎	27	10♏	24	07♐	20	02♑	15	27	09♒
1932	01♐	15	29	12♑	25	08♒	21	04♓	16	28	10♈	22	03♉	15	27	09♊
1933	24♈	06♉	18	00♊	12	24	06♋	18	01♌	14	27	10♍	24	08♎	21	06♏
1934	25♌	08♍	20	03♎	16	29	12♏	26	10♐	24	09♑	24	09♒	24	08♓	23
1935	03♑	18	03♒	18	03♓	19	03♈	18	02♉	15	28	11♊	23	05♋	17	29
1936	23♉	07♊	20	03♋	16	29	11♌	24	06♍	18	00♎	12	23	05♏	17	00♐
1937	14♎	26	08♏	20	01♐	13	26	08♑	21	04♒	17	01♓	15	29	14♈	28
1938	16♒	28	11♓	24	07♈	21	04♉	18	02♊	16	00♋	15	00♌	14	29	13♍
1939	24♊	09♋	24	09♌	24	10♍	24	09♎	23	06♏	19	01♐	14	26	08♑	19
1940	15♏	29	12♐	25	07♑	20	02♒	14	26	08♓	20	02♈	13	25	07♉	19
1941	03♈	15	27	09♉	21	03♊	15	28	11♋	24	08♌	22	06♍	21	05♎	20
1942	07♌	19	02♍	15	29	12♎	26	10♏	24	08♐	23	07♑	21	06♒	20	04♓
1943	15♐	00♑	15	00♒	15	00♓	15	29	13♈	26	09♉	22	04♊	16	28	10♋
1944	07♉	20	03♊	16	28	10♋	22	04♌	16	28	10♍	22	04♎	16	28	10♏
1945	23♍	05♎	17	29	11♏	23	05♐	18	01♑	14	28	12♒	27	12♓	27	12♈
1946	27♑	10♒	23	07♓	20	04♈	18	03♎	17	01♊	15	29	13♋	27	10♌	24
1947	07♊	21	06♋	21	06♌	21	05♍	19	03♎	16	29	12♏	24	06♐	18	29
1948	28♎	11♏	24	07♐	19	01♑	13	25	06♒	18	00♓	12	24	06♈	19	01♉
1949	13♓	25	07♈	19	01♉	13	25	08♊	21	04♋	19	03♌	18	03♍	18	03♎
1950	17♋	00♌	14	28	12♍	26	11♎	25	09♏	23	07♐	21	05♑	18	02♒	15
1951	29♏	13♐	28	12♑	27	12♒	26	10♓	23	06♈	19	01♉	13	25	07♊	19
1952	19♈	02♉	15	27	09♊	21	03♋	15	27	09♌	20	03♍	15	27	09♎	22
1953	03♍	15	27	09♎	21	03♏	15	28	11♐	25	09♑	24	09♒	24	09♓	24
1954	07♑	20	04♒	29	03♓	18	02♈	17	01♉	16	00♊	13	25	10♋	23♓	06♌
1955	21♉	05♊	20	04♋	18	02♌	16	00♍	13	26	09♎	21	03♏	15	27	09♐
1956	09♎	22	05♏	17	29	11♐	23	05♑	17	29	11♒	23	05♓	18	01♈	14
1957	23♒	05♓	17	29	11♈	23	06♉	19	02♊	16	00♋	14	29	15♌	00♍	15
1958	27♊	11♋	25	10♌	24	09♍	24	09♎	24	08♏	21	05♐	18	01♑	14	26
1959	14♏	28	12♐	26	10♑	23	07♒	20	03♓	16	29	11♈	23	05♉	16	28
1960	29♓	12♈	25	07♉	19	01♊	13	25	07♋	19	01♌	13	26	09♍	22	05♎
1961	14♌	26	08♍	20	02♎	14	27	10♏	23	07♐	21	06♑	21	06♒	21	06♓
1962	17♐	01♑	15	00♒	15	00♓	15	00♈	15	29	13♉	27	10♊	23	05♋	17
1963	06♉	20	04♊	18	01♋	15	28	11♌	23	06♍	18	00♎	12	24	06♏	18
1964	19♍	02♎	15	27	09♏	21	03♐	14	26	08♑	21	03♒	16	29	13♓	27♒
1965	04♒	16	28	10♓	23	05♈	18	01♉	15	29	13♊	27	12♋	26	11♌	26
1966	08♊	21	06♋	21	06♌	21	06♍	22	06♎	21	05♏	18	01♐	13	26	08♑
1967	28♎	12♏	26	10♐	23	06♑	29	01♒	14	26	08♓	20	02♈	14	26	08♉
1968	09♓	22	04♈	16	28	10♉	22	04♊	16	28	11♋	24	07♌	20	04♍	18
1969	24♋	06♌	19	01♍	14	27	10♎	23	07♏	21	05♐	19	03♑	18	03♒	17
1970	28♏	12♐	27	12♑	27	12♒	27	12♓	27	11♈	25	08♉	21	04♓	16	28
1971	20♈	04♉	18	01♊	14	27	10♋	22	05♌	17	29	10♍	22	04♎	16	28
1972	29♌	12♍	24	06♎	18	00♏	12	24	06♐	18	01♑	14	27	11♒	25	09♓
1973	14♑	26	09♒	22	05♓	18	01♈	15	29	13♉	27	11♊	25	10♋	24	08♌
1974	20♉	04♊	18	03♋	17	03♌	18	03♍	17	02♎	16	29	12♏	24	07♐	19
1975	12♎	26	10♏	23	06♐	18	01♑	13	25	07♒	19	01♓	12	24	06♈	18
1976	19♒	02♓	14	26	08♈	20	01♉	13	25	08♊	20	03♋	17	01♌	15	00♍
1977	04♋	17	29	13♌	26	10♍	23	07♎	21	05♏	19	04♐	18	02♑	16	00♒
1978	11♏	25	10♐	24	09♑	24	09♒	24	08♓	22	06♈	19	02♉	14	26	08♊
1979	03♈	17	02♉	14	27	09♊	21	03♋	15	27	09♌	21	03♍	15	27	09♎
1980	10♌	22	04♍	16	28	09♎	21	03♏	15	28	11♐	24	07♑	22	06♒	21
1981	24♐	07♑	20	03♒	17	00♓	15	29	13♈	28	12♉	26	10♊	24	08♋	21
1982	04♉	17	02♊	16	01♋	15	00♌	14	28	12♍	26	09♎	22	04♏	16	28
1983	24♍	08♎	21	05♏	17	00♐	12	24	06♑	17	29	11♒	23	05♓	17	00♈
1984	00♒	12	24	06♓	18	29	11♈	23	06♉	18	01♊	14	28	12♋	26	11♌
1985	13♊	26	09♋	23	07♌	22	06♍	21	06♎	20	04♏	18	02♐	16	29	12♑
1986	26♎	10♏	24	08♐	22	07♑	21	05♒	19	03♓	16	29	11♈	24	06♉	18
1987	14♓	28	12♈	25	07♉	20	02♊	14	26	07♋	19	01♌	13	25	08♍	21
1988	21♋	02♌	14	26	8♍	20	02♎	14	26	09♏	21	05♐	19	03♑	17	02♒
1989	03♐	16	00♑	14	28	12♒	17	12♓	27	12♈	26	10♉	24	08♊	21	04♋

	17th	18th	19th	20th	21st	22nd	23rd	24th	25th	26th	27th	28th	29th
1900	24	06♎	18	00♏	12	24	07♐	10	04♑	18	02♒	17♒	
1901	29	13♒	28	12♓	27	12♈	27	11♉	25	09♊	23	06♋	
1902	15	29	13♋	27	11♌	25	09♍	22	05♎	17	29	11♏	
1903	01♏	13	26	08♐	20	02♑	13	25	07♒	29	02♓	14♓	
1904	02♌	14	26	08♍	20	02♎	15	28	11♏	25	09♐	24	08♑
1905	29	04♌	18	03♍	18	03♎	18	03♏	17	01♐	14	28♐	
1906	08♐	22	06♑	19	03♒	16	29	12♓	24	07♈	19	01♉	
1907	21	03♉	16	28	10♊	21	03♋	15	27	09♌	22	05♍	
1908	22	04♍	16	29	11♎	24	06♏	19	03♐	16	00♑	15	29♑
1909	10♑	24	09♒	24	09♓	24	09♈	24	09♉	22	06♊	29♊	
1910	00♊	14	27	11♋	24	07♌	20	02♍	15	29	09♎	21♎	
1911	11♎	23	05♏	17	29	11♐	23	05♑	17	29	12♒	25♒	
1912	13	25	07♓	19	02♈	15	28	11♉	24	08♊	22	06♋	21♋
1913	00♋	15	00♌	15	00♍	15	00♎	15	29	13♏	27	10♐	
1914	22	06♐	19	02♑	15	28	11♒	23	05♓	17	29	11♈	
1915	00♈	13	25	07♉	19	00♊	12	24	07♋	19	02♌	15♌	
1916	03♌	15	27	10♍	23	06♎	19	03♏	17	00♐	15	29	13♑
1917	22	06♑	20	05♒	21	06♓	21	06♈	20	04♉	17	00♊	
1918	14	28	11♊	24	06♋	19	01♌	13	25	07♍	19	01♎	
1919	20	03♎	15	27	08♏	20	02♐	14	26	09♑	22	05♒	
1920	23	05♒	18	01♓	14	27	11♈	25	09♉	23	07♊	21	05♋
1921	13♊	27	12♋	27	12♌	27	12♍	26	10♎	24	07♏	20♏	
1922	05♏	19	02♐	15	27	10♑	22	04♒	16	28	09♓	21♓	
1923	10♓	22	02♈	16	28	10♉	22	04♊	16	29	12♋	26♋	
1924	13	25	08♌	21	05♍	18	02♎	17	01♏	15	29	14♐	28♐
1925	05♐	19	04♑	18	03♒	18	02♓	16	00♈	14	27	10♉	
1926	26	10♉	23	06♊	18	00♋	12	24	06♌	18	00♍	11♍	
1927	00♍	12	24	06♎	18	00♏	12	24	06♐	19	02♑	16♑	
1928	02♑	15	28	11♒	25	10♓	24	09♈	23	07♉	22	06♊	20♊
1929	27	11♊	25	10♋	24	09♌	23	07♍	21	04♎	17	00♏	
1930	17	00♏	13	26	08♐	20	02♑	14	26	08♒	20	02♓	
1931	21	03♓	15	26	08♈	20	02♉	14	27	10♊	23	07♋	
1932	22	05♋	18	02♌	16	00♍	15	00♎	15	14♏	28	12♐	
1933	20	04♐	18	02♑	16	00♒	14	28	11♓	24	07♈	20♈	
1934	07♈	20	03♉	16	28	10♊	22	04♋	16	28	10♌	22♌	
1935	11♌	23	05♍	17	28	11♎	23	05♏	18	01♐	14	28♐	
1936	12	25	08♑	22	06♒	21	06♓	21	06♈	21	06♉	20	04♊
1937	12♉	26	10♊	24	08♋	22	05♌	19	02♍	15	27	10♎	
1938	27	10♎	23	06♏	18	00♐	12	24	06♑	18	00♒	12♒	
1939	01♒	13	25	07♓	19	01♈	14	26	09♉	22	05♊	19♊	
1940	02♊	15	28	12♋	27	12♌	27	12♍	27	12♎	27	11♏	25♏
1941	04♏	19	03♐	16	00♑	14	27	10♒	23	05♓	17	00♈	
1942	17	00♈	13	25	08♉	20	02♊	13	25	07♋	20	02♌	
1943	21	03♌	15	27	10♍	22	05♎	17	00♏	14	27	11♐	
1944	23	06♐	19	03♑	38	02♒	17	03♓	18	03♈	18	02♉	16♉
1945	26	11♉	25	09♊	22	05♋	18	01♌	13	25	07♍	20♍	
1946	07♍	20	03♎	15	27	09♏	21	03♐	15	27	09♑	22♑	
1947	11♑	23	05♒	18	00♓	13	26	09♈	22	06♉	19	03♊	
1948	14	27	10♊	24	08♋	23	08♌	24	09♍	24	09♎	23	07♏
1949	18	03♏	17	00♐	13	26	09♑	22	04♒	16	28	10♓	
1950	28	10♓	23	05♈	17	29	11♉	23	04♊	17	29	12♋	
1951	01♋	13	25	08♌	21	13♍	17	00♎	14	27	11♏	25♏	
1952	05♏	18	02♐	16	00♑	15	00♒	15	30	14♓	29	13♈	27♈
1953	09♈	24	08♉	21	05♊	18	00♋	12	24	06♌	18	00♍	
1954	18	01♍	13	25	07♎	19	01♏	13	24	07♐	19	02♑	
1955	21	03♑	15	28	11♒	24	07♓	21	05♈	20	04♉	18♉	
1956	27	10♉	24	08♊	22	06♋	21	06♌	20	05♍	19	03♎	17♎
1957	00♎	15	29	12♏	26	08♐	21	03♑	15	27	09♒	20♒	
1958	09♒	21	03♓	15	27	09♈	21	02♉	14	27	09♊	22♊	
1959	10♊	22	05♋	18	01♌	14	28	12♍	27	11♎	26	10♏	
1960	19	02♏	16	00♐	14	29	13♑	27	12♒	26	10♓	24	07♈
1961	21	05♈	19	03♉	16	29	11♊	23	05♋	17	29	11♌	
1962	29	11♌	23	05♍	17	29	11♎	23	05♏	17	00♐	13♐	
1963	00♐	12	25	08♑	21	05♒	19	03♓	18	03♈	17	02♉	
1964	10♈	24	08♉	23	07♊	21	05♋	19	03♌	17	00♍	14	27♍
1965	11♍	26	10♎	23	06♏	19	01♐	13	25	07♑	19	00♒	
1966	20	02♒	14	26	07♓	19	01♈	13	25	08♉	20	03♊	
1967	20	02♊	14	27	11♋	25	09♌	24	09♍	24	09♎	24♎	
1968	02♎	16	01♏	15	29	13♐	27	11♑	25	08♒	21	05♓	17♓
1969	02♓	16	00♈	13	26	08♉	21	03♊	15	26	08♋	20♋	
1970	10♋	22	04♌	16	28	10♍	22	04♎	16	29	12♏	25♏	
1971	10♏	22	05♐	18	01♑	15	00♒	14	29	15♓	00♈	15♈	
1972	24	08♈	23	07♉	22	06♊	19	03♋	16	29	12♌	25	07♍
1973	22	06♍	20	03♎	16	28	10♏	22	04♐	16	28	10♑	
1974	00♑	12	24	06♒	18	00♓	12	25	07♈	20	03♉	16♉	
1975	00♉	13	25	08♊	22	06♋	20	05♌	20	06♍	21	06♎	
1976	15	00♎	15	29	14♏	28	11♐	25	08♑	21	03♒	16	28♒
1977	13	27	10♓	23	06♈	18	00♉	12	24	06♊	17	29♊	
1978	20	02♋	14	26	08♌	20	03♍	16	28	11♎	25	08♏	
1979	21	04♏	16	00♐	13	27	12♑	26	11♒	26	12♓	26♓	
1980	06♓	21	06♈	21	05♉	19	03♊	16	29	12♋	24	07♌	19♌
1981	04♌	17	00♍	13	25	08♎	20	02♏	13	25	07♐	19♐	
1982	10♐	22	04♑	16	28	10♒	23	06♓	19	03♈	16	00♉	
1983	12	25	08♉	21	05♊	19	03♋	17	02♌	17	02♍	17♍	
1984	27	12♍	27	12♎	27	11♏	24	07♐	20	03♑	15	27	09♒
1985	25	08♒	21	03♓	16	28	10♈	12	03♉	15	27	09♊	
1986	29	11♊	23	05♋	28	00♌	13	27	10♍	24	08♎	22♎	
1987	03♎	16	29	13♏	27	10♐	25	09♑	24	09♒	23	08♓	
1988	18	03♓	18	03♈	17	01♉	15	28	11♊	23	05♋	18	09♋
1989	17	29	12♌	24	06♍	18	29	11♎	23	05♏	17	27♏	

March

	1st	2nd	3rd	4th	5th	6th	7th	8th	9th	10th	11th	12th	13th	14th	15th	16th
1900	03♈2	18	03♈	18	03♉	17	01♊	14	26	09♋	21	03♌	15	27	09♍	21
1901	19♋	02♌	15	27	09♍	22	04♎	16	27	09♏	21	03♐	15	27	10♑	23
1902	23♏	05♐	17	29	11♑	24	06♒	19	03♓	16	00♈	15	29	13♉	28	12♊
1903	27♓	10♈	23	06♉	20	03♊	17	02♋	16	00♌	15	00♍	14	28	12♎	25
1904	24♌	09♍	24	09♎	23	07♏	21	04♐	17	29	12♑	24	06♒	17	20	11♓
1905	11♑	23	06♒	18	00♓	12	24	06♈	17	29	11♉	23	05♊	18	01♋	14
1906	13♉	25	07♊	19	01♋	13	26	09♌	23	07♍	21	06♎	20	05♏	10	04♐
1907	18♏	01♎	14	28	12♏	26	10♐	24	08♑	23	07♒	21	05♓	19	01♈	15
1908	14♒	29	14♓	29	14♈	28	11♉	25	07♊	20	02♋	14	25	07♌	19	01♍
1909	02♋	14	26	08♌	20	02♍	14	26	08♎	20	02♏	14	26	09♐	21	05♑
1910	03♏	15	26	08♐	21	03♑	16	29	13♒	27	12♓	27	12♈	27	12♉	26
1911	09♓	22	06♈	20	04♉	18	02♊	16	00♋	15	28	12♌	26	10♍	23	06♎
1912	06♌	21	05♍	20	04♎	18	01♏	14	27	09♐	21	03♑	15	27	09♒	21
1913	22♐	05♑	17	29	11♒	23	04♓	16	28	10♈	22	04♉	17	00♊	13	26
1914	23♈	04♉	16	28	11♊	23	06♋	20	04♌	18	03♍	18	03♐	18	03♑	18
1915	29♌	13♍	27	11♎	26	10♏	25	09♐	23	07♑	21	04♒	17	00♓	13	26
1916	28♑	12♒	26	10♓	24	08♈	21	04♉	17	29	11♊	23	05♋	17	29	11♌
1917	13♊	25	07♋	19	01♌	12	24	06♍	18	01♎	13	25	08♏	21	04♐	18
1918	13♎	25	07♏	19	01♐	14	27	10♑	24	08♒	23	08♓	25	09♈	24	09♉
1919	19♒	04♓	18	03♈	18	02♉	17	01♊	15	29	12♋	26	09♌	21	04♍	16
1920	29♋	03♌	18	01♍	15	28	12♎	24	07♏	19	01♐	13	24	06♑	18	01♒
1921	03♐	15	27	09♑	21	03♒	15	27	09♓	21	04♈	16	29	13♉	26	09♊
1922	03♈	15	27	09♉	22	04♊	18	01♋	15	29	14♌	29	14♍	00♎	15	29
1923	10♌	24	09♍	24	09♎	24	09♏	23	07♐	21	04♑	17	00♒	13	25	07♓
1924	12♑	25	09♒	22	06♓	19	01♈	14	26	08♉	20	02♊	14	26	08♋	20
1925	23♉	05♊	17	29	11♋	22	04♌	16	29	11♍	24	07♎	21	04♏	18	02♐
1926	23♍	06♎	18	00♏	13	26	09♐	23	06♑	21	05♒	20	05♓	20	05♈	20
1927	00♒	15	29	15♓	00♈	15	00♉	15	29	12♊	25	08♋	21	03♌	15	27
1928	03♋	17	00♌	13	26	09♍	22	04♎	16	28	10♏	22	04♐	16	28	10♑
1929	12♏	25	06♐	18	00♑	12	24	06♒	19	02♓	15	28	12♈	25	10♉	24
1930	14♓	26	09♈	21	04♉	17	00♊	14	28	12♋	27	12♌	26	11♍	16	10♎
1931	21♋	05♌	20	06♍	21	06♎	21	05♏	20	03♐	16	29	12♑	24	06♒	18
1932	26♐	09♑	22	05♒	17	00♓	12	24	06♈	18	00♉	12	24	06♊	18	00♋
1933	02♉	14	26	08♊	20	02♋	14	26	09♌	22	05♍	19	03♎	17	02♏	16
1934	04♍	17	29	12♎	26	09♏	23	06♐	20	05♑	19	03♒	18	02♓	17	01♈
1935	12♑	26	11♒	26	11♓	27	12♈	26	10♉	24	07♊	20	02♋	14	26	08♌
1936	17♊	00♋	13	26	08♌	20	02♍	14	26	08♎	20	02♏	14	26	08♐	21
1937	22♎	04♍	16	27	09♐	21	03♑	16	29	12♒	26	10♓	24	09♈	23	08♉
1938	25♒	07♓	21	04♈	17	01♉	15	29	13♊	27	11♋	25	09♌	24	08♍	21
1939	03♋	17	02♌	17	02♍	18	02♎	17	01♏	14	27	10♐	22	04♑	16	28
1940	08♐	21	04♑	17	29	11♒	23	05♓	17	29	10♈	22	04♉	16	29	11♊
1941	12♈	23	05♉	17	29	11♊	23	06♋	19	02♌	16	00♍	15	00♎	15	29
1942	15♌	28	11♍	25	09♎	23	07♏	21	05♐	19	04♑	18	02♒	15	29	12♓
1943	25♐	10♑	24	09♒	23	08♓	23	07♈	21	04♉	17	00♊	12	24	06♋	18
1944	29♉	12♊	25	07♋	29	01♌	13	25	07♍	19	01♎	13	25	07♏	20	02♐
1945	02♎	13	25	07♏	19	01♐	13	26	09♑	22	06♒	20	05♓	20	06♈	21
1946	05♒	18	02♓	16	00♈	14	29	13♉	28	12♊	26	10♋	23	07♌	20	03♍
1947	17♊	01♋	16	00♌	15	29	13♍	27	11♎	24	07♏	20	02♐	14	26	07♑
1948	20♏	03♐	15	28	10♑	21	03♒	15	27	09♓	21	03♈	16	28	11♉	24
1949	22♓	04♈	15	27	09♉	21	04♊	16	29	13♋	27	11♌	26	11♍	27	12♎
1950	25♋	08♌	22	06♍	21	06♎	20	05♏	20	04♐	18	02♑	15	28	11♒	24
1951	10♐	24	08♑	22	06♒	20	04♓	18	01♈	14	27	09♉	21	03♊	15	27
1952	10♉	23	05♊	18	00♋	12	23	05♌	17	29	11♍	25	06♎	19	02♏	15
1953	12♍	24	06♎	18	00♏	12	25	07♐	10	04♑	18	02♒	17	02♓	17	02♈
1954	15♑	28	12♒	27	12♓	27	12♈	27	11♉	26	10♊	24	07♋	20	03♌	15
1955	02♊	16	00♋	14	28	12♌	25	08♍	21	04♎	17	29	11♏	23	05♐	17
1956	00♏	13	25	07♐	19	01♑	13	25	07♒	19	01♓	14	27	10♈	24	07♉
1957	01♓	14	26	08♈	21	03♉	16	28	12♊	25	09♋	23	08♌	23	08♍	23
1958	05♋	19	03♌	17	03♍	18	03♎	18	03♏	17	01♐	15	28	11♑	24	06♒
1959	24♏	09♐	23	06♑	20	03♒	16	29	12♓	24	07♈	19	01♉	13	24	06♊
1960	20♈	02♉	15	27	09♊	21	03♋	15	27	09♌	22	04♍	18	01♎	15	29
1961	22♌	04♍	17	29	11♎	24	07♏	20	03♐	17	01♑	15	00♒	14	29	14♓
1962	26♐	09♑	24	08♒	23	08♓	23	09♈	24	08♉	22	06♊	19	02♋	14	27
1963	17♉	01♊	15	28	12♋	25	07♌	20	02♍	15	27	09♎	21	03♏	14	26
1964	10♎	22	05♏	17	29	10♐	22	04♑	16	29	11♒	24	08♓	22	06♈	20
1965	12♒	25	07♓	20	02♈	15	28	12♉	25	09♊	23	07♋	21	06♌	20	05♍
1966	17♊	00♋	14	29	14♌	29	14♍	00♎	15	29	13♏	27	10♐	22	05♑	17
1967	08♏	23	06♐	20	03♑	16	28	11♒	23	05♓	17	29	11♈	23	04♉	16
1968	00♈	12	24	06♉	18	00♊	12	24	06♋	19	01♌	15	28	12♍	27	11♎
1969	02♌	15	27	10♍	23	06♎	20	04♏	17	01♐	15	00♑	14	28	12♒	27
1970	08♐	22	06♑	21	05♒	20	05♓	20	05♈	19	03♉	17	00♊	12	25	07♋
1971	00♉	14	28	11♊	24	07♋	19	02♌	14	25	07♍	29	01♎	13	25	07♏
1972	20♍	02♎	14	26	08♏	20	02♐	14	26	09♑	21	05♒	18	03♓	17	02♈
1973	22♑	05♒	17	00♓	14	27	11♈	25	10♉	24	08♊	22	06♋	20	04♌	18
1974	00♊	14	28	12♋	27	11♌	26	11♍	25	10♎	23	07♍	20	02♐	15	27
1975	21♎	05♏	19	02♐	15	28	10♑	22	04♒	16	28	09♓	21	03♈	15	28
1976	10♓	22	04♈	16	28	10♉	22	04♊	16	28	11♋	25	09♌	23	08♍	23
1977	12♋	24	07♌	21	05♍	19	03♎	17	02♏	16	00♐	14	29	12♑	26	10♒
1978	22♏	06♐	10	04♑	19	03♒	18	02♓	16	00♈	14	27	09♉	22	04♊	16
1979	11♈	25	09♉	22	04♊	18	00♋	12	24	06♌	18	00♍	12	24	06♎	18
1980	01♍	12	24	06♎	18	00♏	12	24	06♐	19	02♑	16	00♒	14	29	14♓
1981	02♑	14	27	11♒	25	09♓	23	08♈	23	08♉	22	07♊	21	05♋	18	01♌
1982	14♉	28	13♊	27	11♋	25	09♌	23	07♍	20	04♎	17	29	12♏	24	06♐
1983	02♎	16	00♏	13	26	08♐	20	02♑	14	26	08♒	20	02♓	14	26	09♈
1984	21♒	03♓	15	26	08♈	10	02♉	15	27	10♊	23	06♋	10	05♌	20	05♍
1985	21♊	04♋	17	01♌	15	00♏	15	00♎	15	00♏	14	29	13♐	26	09♑	22
1986	07♏	21	05♐	19	03♑	16	01♒	14	28	11♓	24	07♈	19	01♉	13	25
1987	22♓	06♈	10	03♉	15	28	10♊	22	04♋	16	28	10♌	22	04♍	17	00♎
1988	11♌	23	05♍	17	29	11♎	23	06♏	18	01♐	14	28	12♑	26	11♒	26
1989	12♐	25	08♑	22	06♒	20	05♓	20	05♈	21	05♉	20	04♊	18	01♋	14

	17th	18th	19th	20th	21st	22nd	23rd	24th	25th	26th	27th	28th	29th	30th	31st
1900	03♎	15	27	09♏	21	04♐	16	00♑	13	27	11♒	26	11♓	26	11♈
1901	07♒	12	06♓	21	06♉	21	06♉	21	05♊	19	03♋	16	29	12♌	24♌
1902	26	10♋	24	08♌	21	04♍	17	00♎	13	25	07♏	19	01♐	13	25♐
1903	08♍	21	04♐	16	28	10♑	22	03♒	16	28	10♓	23	06♈	19	03♉
1904	23	05♈	17	29	12♉	25	08♊	21	05♋	19	03♌	18	02♍	17	02♎
1905	28	12♌	26	11♍	26	12♎	27	12♏	26	10♐	24	06♑	20	03♒	15♒
1906	19	02♑	16	29	13♒	25	08♓	21	03♈	15	27	09♉	21	03♊	15♊
1907	28	11♉	23	05♊	17	29	11♋	23	05♌	17	00♍	13	26	10♎	24♎
1908	13	15	08♎	20	03♏	16	00♐	13	27	11♑	25	09♒	24	08♓	23♓
1909	18	02♒	17	02♓	17	03♈	18	03♉	17	01♊	15	28	11♋	23	05♌
1910	10♊	24	08♋	21	04♌	16	29	11♍	24	06♎	18	29	11♏	23	05♐
1911	18	01♏	13	25	07♐	19	01♑	13	25	07♒	20	03♓	17	01♈	15♈
1912	03♓	16	28	11♈	24	08♉	21	05♊	19	03♋	17	01♌	16	00♍	14♍
1913	10♋	24	08♌	23	08♍	23	08♎	23	08♏	22	05♐	18	01♑	13	26♑
1914	02♐	16	29	12♑	25	08♒	20	02♓	14	26	08♈	19	01♉	13	25♉
1915	08♈	21	03♉	15	27	08♊	20	02♋	15	27	10♌	23	07♍	21	05♎
1916	23	06♍	19	02♎	15	29	13♏	27	11♐	26	10♑	24	08♒	22	06♓
1917	01♑	15	00♒	14	29	14♓	29	14♈	28	12♉	25	08♊	21	03♋	15♋
1918	23	07♊	20	03♋	16	28	10♌	22	04♍	16	28	10♎	22	04♏	16♏
1919	29	11♎	23	05♏	17	28	10♐	22	04♑	17	00♒	13	27	12♓	26♓
1920	13	26	09♓	23	07♈	21	05♉	19	03♊	18	02♋	16	00♌	14	27♌
1921	23	07♋	22	06♌	21	06♍	20	04♎	18	02♏	15	28	11♐	23	05♑
1922	14♏	27	11♐	24	06♑	19	01♒	13	25	06♓	19	00♈	12	24	06♉
1923	19	01♈	13	25	06♉	18	00♊	12	25	07♋	20	04♌	18	02♍	17♍
1924	03♌	16	29	13♍	27	12♎	26	11♏	26	10♐	24	08♑	22	06♒	19♒
1925	16	00♑	14	28	13♒	27	11♓	25	09♈	22	05♉	18	00♊	13	25♊
1926	04♉	18	01♊	14	27	09♋	21	03♌	14	26	08♍	20	02♎	15	26♎
1927	09♍	21	03♎	15	27	09♏	21	03♐	15	28	11♑	25	08♒	23	08♓
1928	23	06♒	19	03♓	18	03♈	18	03♉	17	02♊	16	00♋	14	27	10♌
1929	08♊	22	06♋	20	05♌	18	02♍	16	29	13♎	25	08♏	20	02♐	14♐
1930	24	08♏	21	04♐	16	29	11♑	23	04♒	16	28	10♓	23	05♈	18♈
1931	00♓	12	23	05♈	17	29	11♉	24	06♊	19	02♋	16	00♌	14	29♌
1932	13	26	10♌	24	08♍	23	08♎	23	09♏	23	08♐	22	06♑	19	02♒
1933	01♐	15	29	13♑	27	10♒	24	07♓	20	03♈	15	28	10♉	22	04♊
1934	14	28	11♉	24	06♊	18	00♋	12	24	06♌	18	00♍	13	25	08♎
1935	20	02♍	13	25	08♎	20	02♏	15	28	11♐	24	08♑	21	06♒	20♒
1936	03♑	17	00♒	14	29	14♓	29	15♈	00♉	15	29	13♊	27	10♋	23♋
1937	23	07♊	21	05♋	19	02♌	15	28	11♍	23	06♎	18	00♏	12	24♏
1938	05♎	18	01♏	14	26	08♐	20	02♑	14	26	08♒	20	03♓	16	29♓
1939	10♒	22	04♓	16	28	11♈	23	06♉	19	02♊	16	29	13♋	28	12♌
1940	24	07♋	21	05♌	20	05♍	20	05♎	20	05♐	20	04♐	17	01♑	13♑
1941	14♏	29	13♐	27	11♑	24	07♒	19	02♓	14	26	08♈	20	02♉	14♉
1942	25	08♈	21	03♉	15	28	09♊	21	03♋	15	27	10♌	23	06♍	19♍
1943	00♌	12	24	06♍	18	01♎	14	27	10♏	24	08♐	22	06♑	20	04♒
1944	15	29	13♑	27	11♒	26	11♓	26	11♈	26	10♉	24	08♊	21	04♋
1945	06♉	20	05♊	19	02♋	15	28	10♌	22	04♍	16	28	10♎	22	04♏
1946	16	29	11♎	23	05♏	17	29	11♐	23	05♑	17	00♒	12	26	10♓
1947	19	01♒	13	26	09♓	22	05♈	18	02♉	16	00♊	14	28	12♋	26♋
1948	07♊	20	04♋	18	03♌	17	02♍	17	02♎	17	01♏	15	28	11♐	24♐
1949	27	11♏	26	10♐	23	06♑	19	01♒	13	25	07♓	19	01♈	12	24♈
1950	07♓	19	01♈	13	25	07♉	29	01♊	13	25	07♋	20	03♌	16	00♍
1951	09♋	21	03♌	16	29	12♍	25	09♎	23	08♏	22	06♐	21	05♑	19♑
1952	29	12♐	26	10♑	25	09♒	24	08♓	23	07♈	21	05♉	18	01♊	13♊
1953	17	02♉	16	00♊	14	27	09♋	21	03♌	15	27	09♍	21	03♎	15♎
1954	27	09♍	22	04♎	15	27	09♏	21	03♐	15	27	10♑	23	06♒	20♒
1955	28	11♑	23	05♒	18	02♓	16	00♈	15	29	14♉	28	13♊	27	11♋
1956	21	05♊	19	03♋	17	01♌	15	00♍	14	28	12♎	25	08♏	21	03♐
1957	08♎	23	07♏	21	04♐	17	29	11♑	23	05♒	17	29	11♓	23	05♈
1958	18	00♓	12	24	06♈	18	29	11♉	23	05♊	18	01♋	14	27	11♌
1959	18	00♋	13	26	09♌	22	06♍	21	05♎	20	00♏	20	05♐	19	09♑
1960	13♏	27	11♐	25	09♑	24	08♒	21	05♓	19	02♈	15	28	10♉	23♉
1961	29	13♈	27	11♉	24	07♊	19	01♋	13	25	07♌	19	01♍	13	25♍
1962	09♌	20	02♍	14	26	08♎	20	02♏	14	26	09♐	22	05♑	19	03♒
1963	08♐	20	03♑	16	29	12♒	26	11♓	26	11♈	26	11♉	26	11♊	25♊
1964	05♉	19	03♊	18	02♋	16	29	13♌	26	10♍	23	05♎	18	00♏	13♏
1965	19	04♎	17	01♏	14	27	09♐	21	03♑	15	27	08♒	21	03♓	15♓
1966	29	11♒	22	04♓	16	28	10♈	23	05♉	17	00♊	13	26	10♋	24♋
1967	28	11♊	23	06♋	19	03♌	17	02♍	17	02♎	17	03♏	17	02♐	16♐
1968	26	11♏	25	10♐	24	08♑	22	05♒	18	01♓	14	26	08♈	21	03♉
1969	10♓	24	08♈	21	04♉	16	28	10♊	22	04♋	16	28	10♌	23	05♍
1970	19	01♌	12	24	06♍	18	01♎	13	26	09♏	22	05♐	19	02♑	16♑
1971	19	01♐	14	27	10♑	24	08♒	23	08♓	23	08♈	23	08♉	23	07♊
1972	17	02♉	17	02♊	16	00♋	13	26	09♌	22	04♍	17	29	11♎	23♎
1973	01♍	15	28	11♎	24	06♏	18	00♐	12	24	06♑	18	00♒	12	25♒
1974	09♑	20	02♒	14	26	08♓	21	04♈	17	00♉	13	27	11♊	24	08♋
1975	10♉	22	05♊	18	01♋	15	29	14♌	29	14♍	29	14♎	29	13♏	27♏
1976	09♎	24	09♏	23	07♐	21	05♑	18	00♒	13	25	07♓	19	01♈	13♈
1977	23	06♓	19	01♈	14	25	08♉	20	02♊	13	25	07♋	20	02♌	15♌
1978	28	10♋	22	04♌	16	29	11♍	24	07♎	21	05♏	19	03♐	17	01♑
1979	01♏	13	26	10♐	23	07♑	21	06♒	20	05♓	20	05♈	19	03♉	17♉
1980	29	14♈	29	14♉	28	12♊	26	09♋	21	04♌	16	28	09♍	21	03♎
1981	14	27	09♍	22	04♎	16	28	10♏	22	04♐	15	28	10♑	22	05♒
1982	18	00♑	11	23	06♒	18	01♓	14	28	12♈	26	10♉	25	09♊	24♊
1983	22	05♉	18	02♊	15	29	13♋	27	12♌	26	11♍	25	10♎	24	07♏
1984	20	05♎	20	05♏	19	03♐	16	29	12♑	24	06♒	18	00♓	12	23♓
1985	05♒	18	00♓	12	24	06♈	18	00♉	12	24	05♊	18	00♋	13	26♋
1986	07♊	19	01♋	13	25	08♌	21	05♍	19	03♎	17	02♏	17	01♐	16♐
1987	13	26	10♏	23	07♐	21	06♑	20	04♒	18	03♓	17	01♈	14	27♈
1988	11♓	26	11♈	25	09♉	23	06♊	19	02♋	14	26	08♌	20	02♍	13♍
1989	26	09♌	21	03♍	15	26	08♎	20	02♏	14	26	08♐	21	04♑	17♑

April

	1st	2nd	3rd	4th	5th	6th	7th	8th	9th	10th	11th	12th	13th	14th	15th	16th
1900	26♈	11♉	25	09♊	22	05♋	18	00♌	12	24	06♍	18	29	11♎	24	06♏
1901	06♍	19	02♎	12	24	06♏	18	00♐	12	24	06♑	19	02♒	16	00♓	14
1902	07♑	19	01♒	14	27	11♓	25	09♈	23	08♉	23	08♊	22	07♋	21	04♌
1903	16♉	00♊	14	28	13♋	27	11♌	25	09♍	23	07♎	20	03♏	16	29	11♐
1904	17♎	01♏	15	29	12♐	25	08♑	20	02♒	14	26	08♓	19	01♈	14	26
1905	27♒	09♓	21	03♈	14	26	08♉	20	02♊	15	27	10♋	23	07♌	20	05♍
1906	27♊	09♋	21	04♌	17	01♍	15	29	14♎	29	14♏	29	14♐	29	13♑	26
1907	08♏	22	07♐	21	05♑	19	03♒	17	01♓	14	28	11♈	24	07♉	19	01♊
1908	08♈	22	06♉	19	03♊	15	28	10♋	22	03♌	15	27	09♍	21	04♎	17
1909	17♌	29	11♍	23	05♎	17	29	11♏	23	06♐	18	01♑	14	28	12♒	26
1910	17♐	29	11♑	24	08♒	21	05♓	20	05♈	20	05♉	21	05♊	20	04♋	17
1911	29♈	14♉	28	13♊	27	11♋	25	09♌	23	06♍	19	02♎	14	27	09♏	21
1912	29♍	12♎	26	09♏	22	05♐	17	29	11♑	23	05♒	17	29	11♓	24	07♈
1913	08♒	19	01♓	13	25	07♈	19	01♉	14	27	10♊	23	06♋	20	04♌	18
1914	07♊	20	02♋	15	28	12♌	26	11♍	26	11♎	26	1♏	26	11♐	25	09♑
1915	20♎	05♏	20	05♐	20	04♑	18	01♒	14	27	10♓	23	05♈	17	29	11♉
1916	19♓	03♈	16	29	12♉	15	07♊	19	01♋	13	25	06♌	19	01♍	14	27
1917	27♋	09♌	21	03♍	15	27	09♎	22	05♍	18	01♐	15	28	12♑	26	10♒
1918	28♏	10♐	23	06♑	19	03♒	17	02♓	16	02♈	17	02♉	17	02♊	15	29
1919	11♈	27	12♉	26	11♊	25	09♋	22	06♌	18	01♍	13	26	08♎	20	02♏
1920	11♍	24	07♎	20	02♏	15	27	09♐	20	02♑	14	26	08♒	21	04♓	17
1921	17♑	29	11♒	23	05♓	17	00♈	13	26	09♉	23	06♊	20	04♋	18	03♌
1922	19♉	01♊	14	27	11♋	25	09♌	23	08♍	23	08♎	23	07♏	22	06♐	29
1923	02♎	17	02♏	17	02♐	17	00♑	14	27	10♒	22	04♓	16	28	10♈	22
1924	01♓	15	28	10♈	22	04♉	16	28	10♊	22	04♋	16	28	11♌	24	07♍
1925	07♋	18	00♌	12	24	07♍	20	03♎	16	00♏	14	28	13♐	27	11♑	25
1926	10♏	23	06♐	29	03♑	17	01♒	15	29	14♓	29	14♈	28	12♉	26	09♊
1927	23♓	08♈	23	09♉	23	08♊	21	05♋	17	00♌	12	24	06♍	18	00♎	12
1928	23♌	06♍	18	01♎	13	25	07♏	19	00♐	12	24	06♑	18	01♒	14	28
1929	26♐	08♑	20	02♒	14	27	10♓	23	07♈	21	05♉	20	04♊	10	03♋	17
1930	01♉	14	27	11♊	25	09♋	23	07♌	22	06♍	20	05♎	19	02♏	16	29
1931	14♍	29	14♎	29	14♏	28	12♐	25	08♑	20	03♒	15	27	08♓	20	02♈
1932	15♒	27	09♓	21	03♈	15	27	09♉	20	02♊	14	27	09♋	22	05♌	18
1933	16♊	28	10♋	22	04♌	17	00♍	13	27	11♎	26	11♏	26	11♐	25	10♑
1934	22♎	05♏	19	03♐	17	01♑	16	00♒	14	28	12♓	26	09♈	23	06♉	19
1935	05♓	20	05♈	20	04♉	18	02♊	15	28	10♋	23	05♌	16	28	10♍	22
1936	05♌	17	29	11♍	23	05♎	17	29	11♏	23	05♐	17	00♑	13	26	09♒
1937	06♐	17	29	11♑	24	07♒	20	04♓	18	02♈	17	02♉	17	02♊	17	01♋
1938	13♈	27	11♉	25	09♊	24	08♋	22	06♌	20	04♍	17	01♎	14	27	09♏
1939	27♌	11♍	26	10♎	25	08♏	22	05♐	18	00♑	12	24	06♒	18	00♓	12
1940	26♑	08♒	20	02♓	14	25	07♈	19	01♉	13	26	08♊	21	04♋	17	01♌
1941	25♉	07♊	19	02♋	14	27	10♌	24	08♍	23	08♎	23	08♏	23	08♐	23
1942	03♎	17	02♏	17	01♐	16	00♑	14	28	12♒	25	09♓	22	04♈	17	29
1943	19♒	03♓	17	01♈	15	29	23♉	25	08♊	20	02♋	14	26	08♌	19	02♍
1944	16♋	28	10♌	22	04♍	15	27	09♎	22	04♏	17	29	12♐	26	09♑	23
1945	16♏	28	10♐	22	05♑	18	01♒	15	29	13♓	28	14♈	29	14♉	29	14♊
1946	24♓	08♈	24	08♉	23	08♊	22	06♋	20	04♌	17	00♍	13	25	08♎	20
1947	10♌	25	08♍	22	06♎	19	02♏	15	27	10♐	22	03♑	15	27	09♒	21
1948	06♑	18	00♒	12	24	06♓	18	00♈	12	25	08♉	21	04♊	17	01♋	15
1949	06♉	18	01♊	13	26	09♋	22	06♌	20	05♍	20	05♎	20	05♏	20	04♐
1950	14♍	29	14♎	29	14♏	29	14♐	28	12♑	25	09♒	21	04♓	16	28	10♈
1951	03♒	27	00♓	14	27	10♈	22	05♉	17	29	11♊	23	05♋	17	29♌	11
1952	26♊	08♋	10	01♌	13	25	07♍	10	02♎	15	28	12♏	25	09♐	23	07♑
1953	27♎	09♏	22	04♐	17	00♑	14	28	12♒	26	11♓	26	11♈	25	10♉	25
1954	05♓	20	05♈	20	05♉	20	04♊	19	03♋	17	29	12♌	24	07♍	19	01♎
1955	25♋	08♌	22	05♍	18	00♎	13	25	07♏	19	01♐	13	25	07♑	19	01♒
1956	15♐	27	09♑	21	03♒	15	27	10♓	23	06♈	19	03♉	17	01♊	15	29
1957	17♈	00♉	13	25	09♊	22	05♋	19	03♌	18	02♍	17	02♎	16	01♏	15
1958	26♌	11♍	26	11♎	26	11♏	26	10♐	24	07♑	20	03♒	15	27	09♓	21
1959	17♑	00♒	13	26	09♓	21	03♈	15	27	09♉	21	03♊	15	27	09♋	21
1960	05♊	17	29	11♋	22	05♌	17	29	12♍	26	09♎	24	08♏	22	07♐	22
1961	08♎	21	04♏	17	00♐	14	28	12♑	26	10♒	24	09♓	23	07♈	21	05♉
1962	17♒	02♓	16	02♈	17	02♉	16	01♊	14	28	11♋	23	05♌	17	29	11♍
1963	08♋	22	04♌	17	29	12♍	24	06♎	18	29	11♏	23	05♐	17	29	12♑
1964	25♏	07♐	18	00♑	12	24	07♒	19	02♓	16	00♈	14	29	14♉	29	14♊
1965	28♓	11♈	25	08♉	22	06♊	20	04♋	18	02♌	16	01♍	15	29	12♎	26
1966	08♌	23	08♍	23	08♎	23	07♏	21	05♐	18	01♑	13	25	07♒	19	01♓
1967	29♐	13♑	25	08♒	20	02♓	14	26	08♈	20	02♉	13	25	07♊	20	02♋
1968	14♉	26	08♊	20	02♋	14	27	09♌	23	06♍	20	05♎	20	05♏	20	05♐
1969	18♍	02♎	15	29	13♏	28	12♐	26	11♑	25	09♒	23	06♓	20	03♈	16
1970	01♒	15	29	14♓	29	13♈	27	11♉	25	08♊	20	03♋	15	27	09♌	21
1971	20♊	03♋	16	28	11♌	22	04♍	16	28	10♎	22	04♏	16	28	11♐	24
1972	05♏	16	28	10♐	22	04♑	17	00♒	13	27	11♓	25	10♈	26	11♉	26
1973	08♓	22	06♈	20	05♉	20	04♊	19	03♋	17	01♌	15	28	11♍	24	07♎
1974	23♋	04♌	21	06♍	20	04♎	18	02♏	15	28	10♐	22	05♑	16	28	10♒
1975	11♐	24	06♑	29	01♒	13	24	06♓	18	00♈	12	24	07♉	19	02♊	15
1976	25♈	07♉	18	00♊	12	25	07♋	20	04♌	17	02♍	16	01♎	17	02♏	17
1977	29♌	13♍	27	11♎	26	11♏	26	10♐	25	09♑	23	07♒	20	03♓	16	28
1978	15♑	29	14♒	28	11♓	25	09♈	22	05♉	17	00♊	12	24	06♋	18	00♌
1979	01♊	14	26	09♋	21	02♌	14	26	08♍	20	02♎	15	27	10♏	23	07♐
1980	15♎	27	09♏	21	03♐	16	29	12♑	25	09♒	23	07♓	22	07♈	22	08♉
1981	19♒	03♓	17	02♈	17	02♉	17	02♊	17	01♋	15	28	11♌	24	06♍	19
1982	08♋	22	05♌	29	03♍	16	29	12♎	25	08♏	20	02♐	14	26	08♑	19
1983	21♏	04♐	16	28	10♑	22	04♒	16	28	10♓	22	05♈	18	01♉	15	25
1984	05♈	17	00♉	12	24	07♊	20	03♋	16	00♌	14	29	14♍	29	14♎	28
1985	09♌	23	08♍	23	08♎	23	08♏	23	08♐	22	06♑	19	02♒	15	27	09♓
1986	00♑	14	28	11♒	25	08♓	20	03♈	15	28	10♉	22	04♊	15	27	09♋
1987	10♉	23	06♊	18	00♋	12	24	05♌	18	00♍	12	25	08♎	22	05♏	29
1988	25♍	08♎	20	02♏	15	28	11♐	25	08♑	22	06♒	21	05♓	20	05♈	19
1989	00♒	14	29	13♓	28	14♈	29	14♉	29	13♊	27	10♋	23	05♌	18	00♍

	17th	18th	19th	20th	21st	22nd	23rd	24th	25th	26th	27th	28th	29th	30th
1900	18	01♐	13	26	10♑	23	07♒	21	06♓	20	05♈	20	05♉	19♉
1901	29	14♈	29	14♉	29	14♊	28	14♋	25	08♌	21	03♍	16	28♍
1902	18	01♍	14	27	09♎	22	04♍	16	28	10♐	21	03♑	15	27♑
1903	24	06♑	17	29	11♒	23	06♓	18	01♈	14	28	12♉	26	10♊
1904	09♉	22	05♊	18	02♋	15	29	13♌	28	12♍	26	11♎	25	09♏
1905	19	04♎	20	05♏	20	06♐	19	03♑	16	29	12♒	24	06♓	18♓
1906	10♒	23	05♓	18	00♈	12	24	06♉	18	00♊	12	24	05♋	18♋
1907	13	25	07♋	19	01♌	13	25	08♍	21	04♎	18	03♏	16	02♐
1908	00♏	13	26	10♐	24	08♑	22	06♒	20	04♓	18	02♈	17	01♉
1909	11♓	26	11♈	26	11♉	25	09♊	23	06♋	19	02♌	14	26	08♍
1910	01♌	14	26	08♍	21	03♎	15	26	08♏	20	02♐	14	26	08♑
1911	03♐	15	27	09♑	21	03♒	15	28	11♓	15	09♈	23	08♉	23♉
1912	10	04♉	17	01♊	15	00♋	14	28	12♌	26	10♍	24	08♎	21♎
1913	03♍	17	02♎	17	01♏	15	29	13♐	27	09♑	22	04♒	16	28♒
1914	22	04♒	17	29	11♓	23	05♈	16	28	10♉	22	04♊	17	29♊
1915	23	05♊	17	29	11♋	23	05♌	18	01♍	15	29	14♎	29	14♏
1916	10♎	24	09♏	23	07♐	22	06♑	21	05♒	19	02♓	16	29	12♈
1917	24	09♓	23	08♈	22	06♉	20	03♊	16	29	11♋	23	05♌	17♌
1918	12♋	25	07♌	19	01♍	13	25	07♎	19	01♏	13	25	08♐	20♐
1919	13	25	07♐	19	01♑	13	26	09♒	22	06♓	20	05♈	20	05♉
1920	01♈	15	29	14♉	29	13♊	28	13♋	27	11♌	24	08♍	21	04♎
1921	17	01♍	15	29	13♎	27	10♏	23	06♐	19	01♑	13	25	07♒
1922	02♑	15	27	09♒	21	03♓	15	27	09♈	21	03♉	16	28	11♊
1923	03♉	15	27	09♊	22	04♋	17	00♌	13	27	11♍	25	10♎	25♎
1924	21	05♎	20	05♏	20	05♐	20	05♑	19	03♒	16	29	12♓	25♓
1925	09♒	23	07♓	21	04♈	17	01♉	13	26	08♊	21	03♋	14	26♋
1926	22	05♋	17	29	11♌	23	04♍	16	29	11♈	23	06♏	19	03♐
1927	24	06♏	18	00♐	12	25	08♑	21	04♒	18	02♓	17	02♈	17♈
1928	12♓	26	11♈	26	11♉	26	11♊	26	10♋	24	07♌	20	03♍	15
1929	01♌	15	29	12♍	26	09♎	21	04♏	16	28	10♐	22	04♑	16
1930	12♐	24	07♑	19	01♒	12	24	06♓	19	01♈	14	27	10♉	24♉
1931	24	26	08♉	21	03♊	16	29	12♋	26	10♌	24	08♍	23	08♎
1932	02♍	17	01♎	16	02♏	17	02♐	17	01♑	15	28	11♒	24	06♓
1933	24	07♒	21	04♓	17	29	12♈	24	06♉	18	00♊	12	24	06♋
1934	02♊	14	26	08♋	20	02♌	14	26	08♍	21	04♎	17	01♏	15♏
1935	04♎	16	29	12♏	25	08♐	21	04♑	18	02♒	16	00♓	15	29♓
1936	23	08♓	22	08♈	23	08♉	23	08♊	22	06♋	19	02♌	14	26♌
1937	15	29	12♌	25	08♍	20	03♎	15	27	09♏	21	02♐	14	26♐
1938	22	04♐	16	28	10♑	21	03♒	16	28	11♓	24	07♈	21	05♉
1939	24	07♈	19	02♉	15	29	12♊	26	10♋	24	08♌	23	07♍	21♍
1940	15	29	14♍	29	14♎	29	13♏	28	12♐	26	09♑	22	04♒	17♒
1941	07♑	20	04♒	16	29	11♓	23	05♈	17	29	11♉	22	04♊	16♊
1942	12♎	24	06♊	18	29	11♋	23	05♌	18	01♍	14	27	11♎	26♎
1943	14	26	09♎	23	06♏	20	04♐	18	03♑	17	01♒	15	29	13♓
1944	07♒	21	05♓	20	05♈	19	04♉	18	02♊	16	29	12♋	24	06♌
1945	28	11♋	24	07♌	29	01♍	14	25	07♎	19	01♏	13	25	07♐
1946	02♏	14	26	08♐	19	01♑	13	25	08♒	21	04♓	18	02♈	17♈
1947	04♓	17	00♈	13	27	11♉	26	10♊	24	09♋	23	07♌	21	05♍
1948	29	13♌	27	12♍	26	11♎	25	09♏	23	06♐	19	01♑	14	26♑
1949	18	02♑	15	27	10♒	22	04♓	16	28	09♈	21	03♉	15	28♉
1950	22	04♉	16	28	09♊	21	04♋	16	28	11♌	25	08♍	23	07♎
1951	24	06♍	20	03♎	18	02♏	17	02♐	16	01♑	16	00♒	14	27♒
1952	21	06♒	20	04♓	18	02♈	16	29	13♉	26	09♊	21	04♋	16♋
1953	08♊	22	05♋	18	00♌	12	24	05♍	17	29	11♎	23	06♏	18♏
1954	12	24	06♏	18	00♐	12	24	07♑	19	02♒	16	29	14♓	28♓
1955	13	26	10♓	24	08♈	23	08♉	23	08♊	23	07♋	21	05♌	19♌
1956	14♋	28	12♌	26	10♍	23	07♎	20	03♏	16	29	11♐	23	06♑
1957	29	12♐	25	07♑	19	02♒	13	25	07♓	19	01♈	14	26	09♉
1958	03♈	15	26	08♉	20	03♊	15	28	10♋	24	07♌	21	05♍	20♍
1959	04♌	17	00♍	14	29	13♎	29	14♏	29	14♐	29	13♑	27	10♒
1960	06♑	20	04♒	18	02♓	15	28	11♈	24	06♉	19	01♊	13	25♊
1961	19	02♊	15	27	09♋	21	03♌	15	27	09♍	21	03♎	16	29♎
1962	23	05♎	17	29	11♏	23	06♐	19	02♑	15	29	13♒	27	11♓
1963	24	07♒	21	05♓	19	04♈	19	05♉	20	05♊	20	04♋	18	01♌
1964	28	12♋	26	10♌	23	06♍	19	02♎	15	27	09♏	21	03♐	15♐
1965	09♏	22	04♐	17	29	11♑	23	04♒	16	28	11♓	23	06♈	20♈
1966	13	25	07♈	19	02♉	14	27	10♊	23	07♋	21	05♌	19	03♍
1967	15	28	12♌	26	11♍	25	10♎	26	11♏	26	10♐	24	08♑	21♑
1968	20	04♑	18	02♒	15	28	11♓	23	05♈	17	29	11♉	23	05♊
1969	29	12♉	24	06♊	18	00♋	12	24	06♌	18	01♍	13	26	10♎
1970	02♍	14	27	09♎	22	06♏	18	02♐	15	29	13♑	27	11♒	26♒
1971	07♑	20	04♒	18	02♓	16	01♈	15	01♉	16	01♊	15	29	12♋
1972	11♊	26	09♋	23	06♌	19	01♍	14	26	08♎	20	02♏	13	25♏
1973	20	02♏	14	16	08♐	20	02♑	14	26	08♒	20	03♓	16	00♈
1974	22	04♓	17	29	12♈	26	09♉	23	07♊	21	05♋	19	04♌	18♌
1975	28	12♋	25	09♌	24	08♍	23	08♎	22	07♏	21	05♐	19	02♑
1976	02♐	16	00♑	14	27	10♒	22	04♓	16	28	10♈	22	04♉	16♉
1977	10♈	22	04♉	16	28	10♊	22	04♋	16	28	11♌	24	07♍	21♍
1978	12	24	06♍	19	02♎	16	00♏	14	28	13♐	27	12♑	26	10♒
1979	20	04♑	18	02♒	16	00♓	15	29	13♈	27	11♉	25	08♊	21♊
1980	22	07♊	21	04♋	17	00♌	12	24	06♍	18	00♎	12	24	06♏
1981	01♎	13	26	07♏	19	00♐	12	24	06♑	19	01♒	14	27	11♓
1982	01♒	14	26	09♓	22	06♈	20	05♉	20	05♊	19	04♋	18	02♌
1983	12♊	26	10♋	24	08♌	22	06♍	21	05♎	19	02♏	16	29	11♐
1984	13♏	27	11♐	25	07♑	20	02♒	14	26	08♓	20	02♈	14	26♈
1985	21	03♈	15	27	09♉	21	02♊	15	27	09♋	22	05♌	18	02♍
1986	21	04♌	16	29	13♍	27	11♎	26	11♏	26	11♐	25	10♑	24♑
1987	04♐	18	02♑	17	01♒	15	29	13♓	26	10♈	23	06♉	19	01♊
1988	03♉	17	01♊	14	27	10♋	22	04♌	16	28	10♍	22	04♎	16♎
1980	12	23	05♎	17	29	11♏	23	07♐	18	00♑	13	26	10♒	24♒

May

	1st	2nd	3rd	4th	5th	6th	7th	8th	9th	10th	11th	12th	13th	14th	15th	16th
1900	03♊	17	00♋	13	26	08♌	20	02♍	14	26	08♎	20	02♏	15	27	24♐
1901	09♎	21	03♏	15	27	09♐	21	03♑	16	28	12♒	25	09♓	23	08♈	24
1902	10♒	22	05♓	19	03♈	17	02♉	17	02♓	17	02♋	16	01♌	15	28	11♍
1903	25♊	09♋	24	08♌	22	06♍	19	03♎	16	29	12♏	25	07♐	20	02♑	23
1904	23♏	07♐	20	03♑	16	28	10♒	22	04♓	16	28	10♈	22	05♉	18	24♊
1905	29♓	11♈	23	05♉	17	29	12♊	24	07♋	20	03♌	17	00♍	14	29	13♎
1906	00♌	13	26	09♍	23	07♎	22	08♏	23	08♐	23	08♑	22	06♒	19	02♓
1907	17♐	01♑	16	00♒	14	28	11♓	24	07♈	20	08♉	15	28	10♊	22	04♋
1908	14♉	27	10♊	23	05♋	18	29	11♌	23	05♍	17	30	12♎	25	08♏	24
1909	20♍	01♎	13	25	08♏	20	03♐	15	28	11♑	25	08♒	22	06♓	21	05♈
1910	21♑	03♒	17	00♓	14	29	13♈	29	14♉	29	14♊	28	13♋	26	10♌	23
1911	08♊	23	07♋	22	06♌	20	03♍	16	29	11♎	24	06♏	18	00♐	12	23
1912	05♏	18	00♐	13	25	07♑	19	01♒	13	25	07♓	19	02♈	15	28	12♉
1913	09♓	21	03♈	15	28	10♉	23	06♊	20	03♋	17	01♌	15	29	13♍	27
1914	12♋	25	08♌	21	05♍	20	04♎	19	04♏	19	04♐	19	03♑	17	00♒	13
1915	29♏	14♐	29	14♑	28	11♒	24	07♓	20	02♈	14	26	08♉	20	02♊	14
1916	25♈	08♉	21	03♊	15	27	09♋	21	03♌	14	27	09♍	22	05♎	19	03♏
1917	29♌	11♍	23	05♎	18	01♏	14	27	11♐	25	09♑	23	07♒	21	05♓	19
1918	03♑	16	29	13♒	27	11♓	26	11♈	26	11♉	25	10♊	24	07♋	20	03♌
1919	20♉	05♊	20	04♋	18	02♌	15	28	10♍	23	05♎	17	29	10♏	22	04♐
1920	16♎	29	11♏	23	05♐	17	29	11♑	22	04♒	17	29	12♓	25	09♈	23
1921	19♒	01♓	13	25	08♈	21	04♉	18	02♊	17	01♋	15	29	14♌	28	12♍
1922	24♊	08♋	21	05♌	19	03♍	18	02♎	17	01♏	16	00♐	14	27	10♑	23
1923	11♏	26	11♐	25	09♑	23	06♒	19	01♓	13	25	07♈	19	00♉	12	24
1924	07♈	19	01♉	13	25	07♊	19	01♋	13	25	07♌	19	02♍	16	29	13♎
1925	08♌	20	02♍	15	28	11♎	25	09♏	23	08♐	22	07♑	22	06♒	20	04♓
1926	16♐	00♑	14	27	11♒	26	10♓	24	08♈	23	07♉	21	04♊	17	00♋	13
1927	02♉	17	01♊	16	00♋	13	26	09♌	21	03♍	15	27	09♎	21	03♏	15
1928	28♍	10♎	22	04♏	15	27	09♐	21	03♑	15	27	10♒	23	06♓	20	05♈
1929	28♑	10♒	22	05♓	18	01♈	15	29	14♉	29	14♊	28	13♋	28	12♌	26
1930	07♊	21	05♋	20	04♌	18	02♍	16	00♎	14	28	11♏	24	07♐	20	02♑
1931	23♎	07♏	22	06♐	20	03♑	16	29	11♒	23	05♓	17	29	10♈	22	05♉
1932	18♓	00♈	12	24	06♉	17	29	11♊	24	06♋	18	01♌	14	28	11♍	26
1933	18♋	00♌	12	25	08♍	21	05♎	20	04♏	20	05♐	20	05♑	20	04♒	18
1934	29♏	13♐	28	12♑	26	11♒	25	08♓	22	06♈	19	02♉	15	28	10♊	22
1935	14♈	28	12♉	26	10♊	23	06♋	18	01♌	13	24	06♍	18	00♎	12	25
1936	08♍	20	02♎	14	26	08♏	20	02♐	14	27	10♑	23	06♒	19	03♓	17
1937	08♑	20	03♒	15	28	12♓	26	11♈	25	11♉	26	11♊	26	10♋	25	08♌
1938	20♉	05♊	19	04♋	18	03♌	17	00♍	14	27	10♎	23	06♏	18	00♐	12
1939	05♎	19	03♏	17	00♐	13	26	08♑	20	02♒	14	26	08♓	20	02♈	15
1940	29♒	10♓	22	04♈	16	28	10♉	22	05♊	18	01♋	14	28	11♌	25	09♍
1941	29♊	11♋	23	06♌	19	03♍	17	01♎	16	01♏	16	02♐	17	01♑	16	29
1942	11♏	26	11♐	26	10♑	25	09♒	22	06♓	19	01♈	14	26	08♉	20	02♊
1943	27♓	10♈	24	07♉	20	03♊	16	28	10♋	22	04♌	15	27	09♍	22	04♎
1944	18♌	00♍	12	24	06♎	18	00♏	13	26	09♐	22	06♑	20	03♒	17	02♓
1945	19♐	02♑	14	27	10♒	24	08♓	23	07♈	22	07♉	23	07♊	22	06♋	20
1946	02♉	17	02♊	17	02♋	16	00♌	14	27	10♍	22	05♎	17	29	11♏	23
1947	19♍	02♎	15	28	11♏	23	06♐	18	00♑	11	23	05♒	17	29	12♓	25
1948	08♒	20	02♓	14	26	08♈	21	03♉	16	00♊	14	27	11♋	26	10♌	24
1949	10♊	23	06♋	19	02♌	16	00♍	14	29	14♎	28	13♏	28	12♐	26	10♌
1950	22♎	07♏	23	08♐	23	07♑	21	05♒	18	01♓	13	25	07♈	19	01♉	13
1951	10♓	23	06♈	19	01♉	13	26	08♊	20	01♋	13	25	07♌	19	02♍	15
1952	17♋	09♌	21	03♍	15	28	10♎	23	07♏	21	05♐	19	04♑	18	02♒	17
1953	01♐	14	27	11♑	24	08♒	22	06♓	21	05♈	20	04♉	19	03♊	17	00♋
1954	13♈	28	14♉	29	14♊	28	12♋	25	08♌	21	03♍	16	27	09♎	21	03♏
1955	02♍	15	27	10♎	22	04♏	16	28	10♐	21	03♑	15	27	10♒	22	05♓
1956	17♑	29	11♒	23	05♓	18	01♈	14	28	12♉	26	10♊	25	10♋	24	09♌
1957	22♉	05♊	19	02♋	16	00♌	14	29	13♍	27	11♎	26	09♏	23	07♐	20
1958	04♎	19	04♏	19	04♐	18	02♑	16	29	11♒	24	06♓	18	00♈	11	23
1959	23♒	06♓	18	00♈	12	24	06♉	18	00♊	12	24	06♋	18	00♌	13	26
1960	07♋	19	01♌	13	25	07♍	20	04♎	18	02♏	17	01♐	16	01♑	16	01♒
1961	13♏	26	10♐	24	09♑	23	07♒	21	06♓	19	03♈	17	00♉	14	27	10♊
1962	26♓	10♈	25	10♉	25	09♊	23	06♋	19	01♌	13	25	07♍	19	01♎	13
1963	14♌	26	09♍	21	03♎	15	26	08♏	20	02♐	14	26	09♑	21	02♒	17
1964	27♐	09♑	20	02♒	15	28	11♓	24	08♈	23	07♉	23	08♊	23	08♋	22
1965	03♉	17	02♊	16	00♋	15	29	13♌	27	11♍	25	08♎	22	05♏	18	00♐
1966	18♍	02♎	17	01♏	15	29	13♐	26	08♑	21	03♒	15	27	09♓	21	03♈
1967	04♒	17	29	11♓	23	05♈	17	28	10♉	22	05♊	17	29	12♋	25	09♌
1968	17♊	29	11♋	23	05♌	18	01♍	15	29	13♎	28	13♏	28	14♐	29	13♑
1969	24♎	08♏	23	07♐	22	07♑	21	06♒	20	03♓	17	00♈	13	26	08♉	20
1970	10♓	24	08♈	22	08♉	19	03♊	16	28	11♋	23	05♌	17	28	10♍	22
1971	25♋	07♌	19	01♍	13	25	06♎	18	00♏	13	25	08♐	21	04♑	17	00♒
1972	07♐	19	01♑	14	26	09♒	22	06♓	20	04♈	19	04♉	19	05♊	20	04♋
1973	14♈	29	14♉	29	14♊	29	13♋	27	11♉	25	08♍	21	04♎	17	29	11♏
1974	02♍	16	00♎	13	27	10♏	23	06♐	18	00♑	12	24	08♒	18	00♓	12
1975	14♑	27	09♒	21	03♓	15	26	09♈	21	03♉	16	29	12♊	25	08♋	22
1976	27♉	10♊	22	04♋	17	00♌	13	27	11♍	25	10♎	25	10♏	25	10♐	24
1977	05♎	19	04♏	19	05♐	20	04♑	19	03♒	17	00♓	13	25	07♈	19	01♉
1978	24♒	08♓	22	05♈	18	01♉	13	26	08♊	20	02♋	14	26	08♌	20	02♍
1979	04♋	16	29	10♌	22	04♍	16	28	10♎	23	06♏	19	03♐	16	00♑	15
1980	18♏	00♐	13	26	09♑	22	05♒	19	03♓	17	01♈	16	01♉	16	01♊	15
1981	25♓	10♈	25	10♉	26	11♊	26	10♋	24	07♌	21	03♍	16	28	10♎	22
1982	16♌	00♍	13	26	09♎	21	04♏	16	28	10♐	22	04♑	16	28	10♒	22
1983	24♐	06♑	18	00♒	12	24	06♓	18	00♈	13	26	10♉	24	08♊	22	06♋
1984	09♉	21	04♊	17	00♋	13	27	11♌	25	09♍	24	08♎	23	07♏	21	05♐
1985	16♍	01♎	16	01♏	16	01♐	16	01♑	15	28	11♒	24	06♓	18	00♈	12
1986	08♒	22	05♓	16	00♈	12	24	07♉	18	00♊	12	24	06♋	18	00♌	12
1987	14♊	26	08♋	20	01♌	13	25	08♍	20	03♎	16	00♏	14	28	13♐	28
1988	29♎	11♏	25	08♐	22	05♑	19	03♒	17	01♓	16	00♈	14	28	12♉	26
1989	08♓	22	07♈	22	07♉	22	07♊	21	05♋	18	01♌	14	26	08♍	20	02♎

	17th	18th	19th	20th	21st	22nd	23rd	24th	25th	26th	27th	28th	29th	30th	31st
1900	23	07♑	20	04♒	18	02♓	16	00♈	15	29	14♉	28	12♊	25	08♋
1901	07♉	23	08♊	22	07♋	21	04♌	17	00♍	12	24	06♎	18	00♏	12♏
1902	24	06♎	19	01♏	13	25	06♐	18	00♑	12	24	06♒	19	01♓	14♓
1903	26	07♒	19	01♓	14	26	09♈	22	06♉	20	05♊	19	04♋	19	04♌
1904	14	28	12♋	26	10♌	24	08♍	23	07♎	21	05♏	18	02♐	15	28♐
1905	28	13♏	28	13♐	27	11♑	24	07♒	20	02♓	14	26	08♈	20	02♉
1906	15	27	09♈	21	03♉	15	27	09♊	21	03♋	15	27	09♌	22	05♍
1907	15	27	09♌	21	03♍	16	29	13♎	27	11♏	26	11♐	26	11♑	26♑
1908	06♐	20	04♑	18	02♒	17	01♓	15	29	13♈	26	10♉	23	06♊	19♊
1909	20	05♉	19	04♊	17	01♋	14	27	10♌	22	04♍	16	28	10♎	22♎
1910	05♍	18	00♎	12	23	05♏	17	29	11♐	23	05♑	18	00♒	13	26♒
1911	05♑	17	29	11♒	24	07♓	20	03♈	17	01♉	16	01♊	16	02♋	17♋
1912	26	11♊	25	10♋	24	09♌	23	07♍	21	05♎	18	01♏	14	26	09♐
1913	12♎	26	10♏	24	08♐	21	04♑	17	00♒	12	24	06♓	17	29	11♈
1914	26	08♓	20	02♈	13	25	07♉	19	01♊	14	20	09♋	22	05♌	18♌
1915	26	08♋	20	02♌	14	27	10♍	24	08♎	22	07♎	22	08♐	23	08♑
1916	17	02♐	17	02♑	16	01♒	15	29	13♓	26	09♈	22	05♉	17	00♊
1917	04♈	18	01♉	15	28	12♊	24	07♋	19	01♌	13	25	07♍	19	01♎
1918	15	27	09♍	21	03♎	15	27	09♏	22	04♐	17	00♑	13	26	10♒
1919	16	28	10♑	22	05♒	18	01♓	15	29	13♈	28	13♉	28	13♊	28♊
1920	08♉	23	08♊	23	08♋	22	07♌	21	04♍	18	01♎	13	26	08♏	20♏
1921	26	09♎	23	06♏	19	09♐	14	27	09♑	21	03♒	15	27	09♓	21♓
1922	05♒	17	29	11♓	23	05♈	17	29	12♉	24	07♊	21	04♋	18	02♌
1923	06♊	19	01♋	14	26	09♌	23	06♍	20	05♎	19	04♏	19	04♐	19♐
1924	28	13♏	29	14♐	29	14♑	28	12♒	26	09♓	22	04♈	16	28	10♉
1925	17	01♈	14	27	10♉	22	05♊	17	29	11♋	23	04♌	16	28	10♍
1926	25	07♌	19	01♍	12	24	07♎	19	02♏	15	28	12♐	26	10♑	24♑
1927	27	09♐	22	05♑	18	01♒	15	28	12♓	27	11♈	26	11♉	25	10♊
1928	19	04♉	19	05♊	20	04♋	19	03♌	16	29	12♍	25	07♎	19	01♏
1929	09♍	23	05♎	18	01♏	13	25	07♐	19	01♑	13	24	06♒	18	01♓
1930	14	26	08♒	20	02♓	14	26	09♈	22	05♉	18	02♊	17	01♋	16♋
1931	17	00♊	13	26	09♋	23	07♌	21	05♍	19	03♎	17	02♏	16	00♐
1932	10♎	25	10♏	26	10♐	25	10♑	24	07♒	20	03♓	15	27	09♈	21♈
1933	01♓	14	27	09♈	21	03♉	15	27	09♊	21	03♋	15	27	09♌	21♌
1934	04♋	16	28	10♌	22	04♍	16	29	12♎	25	09♏	23	08♐	23	07♑
1935	08♏	21	04♐	17	01♑	15	29	13♒	27	11♓	25	10♈	24	08♉	21♉
1936	02♈	17	02♉	16	01♊	16	00♋	14	27	10♌	22	05♍	17	29	11♎
1937	22	05♍	17	00♎	12	24	06♏	18	29	11♐	23	05♑	17	29	12♒
1938	24	06♑	18	00♒	12	24	06♓	19	02♈	15	29	14♉	28	13♊	28♊
1939	28	11♉	24	08♊	22	06♋	21	05♌	20	04♍	18	02♎	16	29	12♏
1940	24	08♎	23	07♏	22	06♐	20	04♑	17	00♒	12	25	07♓	19	00♈
1941	13♒	26	08♓	20	02♈	14	26	08♉	19	01♊	13	25	08♋	20	03♌
1942	14	26	08♋	20	02♌	14	26	09♍	22	06♎	20	04♏	19	04♐	20♐
1943	18	01♏	15	29	14♐	28	13♑	27	12♒	26	10♓	24	07♈	21	04♉
1944	16	29	11♈	24	06♉	18	00♊	12	24	06♋	18	00♌	12	25	08♍
1945	03♌	16	28	10♍	22	04♎	16	28	10♏	22	04♐	16	29	11♑	24♑
1946	05♐	16	28	10♑	22	04♒	17	00♓	13	27	11♈	25	10♉	25	10♊
1947	08♈	21	05♉	20	05♊	19	04♋	19	04♌	18	02♍	16	29	12♎	25♎
1948	08♍	22	06♎	20	04♏	18	01♐	14	27	09♑	22	04♒	16	28	10♓
1949	23	06♒	18	00♓	12	24	06♈	18	00♉	12	24	07♊	19	02♋	16♋
1950	25	07♊	18	01♋	13	25	08♌	21	04♍	18	02♎	16	01♏	16	01♐
1951	28	11♎	26	10♏	25	10♐	26	11♑	25	10♒	24	07♓	20	03♈	16♈
1952	01♓	15	28	12♈	25	09♉	22	04♊	17	29	12♋	24	05♌	17	29♌
1953	13	25	08♌	20	02♍	14	25	07♎	19	02♏	14	27	10♐	24	07♑
1954	15	27	09♐	21	04♑	16	29	12♒	25	09♓	23	08♈	22	07♉	22♉
1955	18	02♈	17	01♉	16	01♊	17	02♋	16	01♌	15	28	11♍	24	07♎
1956	23	07♍	20	04♎	17	00♏	13	25	07♐	19	01♑	13	25	07♒	19♒
1957	03♑	15	27	09♒	21	03♓	15	27	09♈	22	04♉	17	01♊	14	28♊
1958	05♉	17	29	12♊	24	07♋	20	04♌	17	01♍	15	00♎	14	29	13♏
1959	09♍	23	07♎	22	07♏	22	07♐	22	07♑	22	06♒	19	02♓	15	27♓
1960	15	29	12♓	25	08♈	21	03♉	15	28	10♊	22	03♋	15	27	09♌
1961	23	05♋	17	29	11♌	23	05♍	17	29	11♎	24	08♏	21	05♐	20♐
1962	25	07♏	20	03♐	16	29	12♑	26	10♒	23	07♓	22	06♈	20	05♉
1963	00♓	14	28	13♈	28	13♉	28	13♊	28	12♋	26	10♌	22	05♍	17♍
1964	06♌	20	03♍	16	29	12♎	24	06♏	18	00♐	12	24	05♑	17	29♑
1965	13	25	07♑	19	01♒	12	24	06♓	19	01♈	14	28	12♉	26	10♊
1966	15	28	10♉	23	06♊	20	04♋	17	01♌	17	00♍	14	28	12♎	26♎
1967	22	06♍	20	05♎	19	04♏	19	04♐	18	02♑	16	00♒	13	25	08♓
1968	28	11♒	25	08♓	20	02♈	14	26	08♉	20	02♊	14	26	08♋	20♋
1969	03♊	15	27	09♋	21	02♌	14	26	09♍	21	04♎	18	02♏	16	01♐
1970	05♎	17	00♏	13	27	11♐	25	10♑	24	08♒	22	07♓	21	04♈	18♈
1971	14	28	12♓	26	11♈	26	10♉	25	09♊	23	07♋	20	03♌	15	27♌
1972	18	02♌	15	28	10♍	23	05♎	17	29	10♏	22	04♐	16	28	11♑
1973	23	06♐	17	29	11♑	22	04♒	17	29	12♓	25	09♈	23	07♉	22♉
1974	25	07♈	20	04♉	18	02♊	16	01♋	15	00♌	14	29	13♍	27	10♎
1975	06♌	20	04♍	19	03♎	17	02♏	16	00♐	13	26	09♑	22	05♒	17♒
1976	09♑	22	06♒	18	01♓	13	25	07♈	19	00♉	12	24	06♊	19	01♋
1977	13	25	07♊	19	01♋	13	25	07♌	20	02♍	16	29	13♎	28	13♏
1978	14	27	10♎	24	08♏	22	07♐	22	07♑	22	07♒	21	05♓	19	02♈
1979	29	13♒	27	11♓	25	09♈	23	07♉	20	04♊	17	00♋	12	24	06♌
1980	29	13♋	26	08♌	21	03♍	15	26	08♎	20	02♏	14	27	09♐	22♐
1981	04♏	16	27	09♐	21	03♑	16	28	11♒	23	07♓	20	04♈	19	04♉
1982	04♓	17	01♈	14	29	13♉	28	13♊	28	13♋	28	12♌	26	10♍	23♍
1983	21	05♌	19	03♍	17	01♎	15	28	11♏	24	07♐	20	02♑	14	26♑
1984	19	02♑	15	28	10♒	22	04♓	16	28	10♈	22	05♉	17	00♊	13♊
1985	24	06♉	18	30	12♊	24	06♋	19	02♌	15	28	12♍	26	11♎	25♎
1986	25	08♍	21	05♎	19	04♏	19	04♐	19	04♑	19	04♒	18	01♓	14♓
1987	13♑	27	12♒	26	10♓	23	06♈	20	02♉	15	27	10♊	22	04♋	16♋
1988	09♊	22	05♋	18	00♌	12	24	06♍	18	00♎	12	24	07♏	20	03♐
1989	14	26	08♏	20	02♐	15	27	10♑	23	07♒	20	04♓	18	02♈	17♈

June

	1st	2nd	3rd	4th	5th	6th	7th	8th	9th	10th	11th	12th	13th	14th	15th	16th
1900	21♋	04♌	16	28	10♍	22	04♎	16	28	10♏	23	06♐	19	03♑	16	00♒
1901	24♏	06♐	18	00♑	13	25	08♒	22	05♓	19	03♈	17	02♉	17	01♊	16
1902	27♓	11♈	25	10♉	25	10♊	25	11♋	25	10♌	24	08♍	21	03♎	16	28
1903	18♌	03♍	16	00♎	13	26	09♏	21	04♐	16	28	10♑	22	04♒	16	28
1904	11♑	24	06♒	18	00♓	12	24	05♈	18	00♉	13	26	10♊	24	08♋	22
1905	14♉	26	08♊	21	04♋	17	00♌	13	27	11♍	25	09♎	23	08♏	23	07♐
1906	18♍	02♎	16	01♏	16	01♐	17	02♑	16	01♒	15	28	11♓	24	06♈	18
1907	10♒	24	08♓	21	05♈	17	00♉	12	25	07♊	19	00♋	12	24	06♌	18
1908	01♋	13	26	07♌	19	01♍	13	25	07♎	20	03♏	16	00♐	14	29	13♑
1909	04♏	16	29	12♐	25	08♑	21	05♒	19	03♓	17	02♈	16	00♉	14	28
1910	10♓	24	08♈	23	07♉	22	07♊	22	07♋	21	05♌	18	01♍	14	26	08♎
1911	01♌	16	29	13♍	26	08♎	21	03♏	15	27	09♐	20	02♑	14	26	08♒
1912	21♐	03♑	15	27	09♒	21	03♓	15	27	10♈	23	06♉	20	05♊	19	04♋
1913	23♈	06♉	19	02♊	15	29	13♋	27	11♌	26	10♍	24	08♎	22	06♏	20
1914	02♍	15	00♎	14	29	13♏	28	13♐	27	11♑	25	08♒	21	04♓	16	28
1915	22♑	07♒	20	04♓	16	29	11♈	23	05♉	17	29	11♊	23	05♋	17	29
1916	12♊	24	06♋	17	29	11♌	24	05♍	17	00♎	13	27	11♏	25	10♐	25
1917	13♎	26	09♏	22	06♐	20	04♑	19	03♒	18	02♓	16	00♈	14	28	11♉
1918	24♒	08♓	22	06♈	21	05♉	20	04♊	18	02♋	15	28	11♌	23	05♍	18
1919	13♋	27	11♌	24	07♍	19	02♎	14	25	07♏	19	01♐	13	25	07♑	20
1920	02♐	14	26	07♑	19	01♒	13	26	08♓	21	04♈	18	02♉	16	01♊	16
1921	03♈	16	29	12♉	26	11♊	25	10♋	25	10♌	24	09♍	23	06♎	20	03♏
1922	16♌	00♍	14	28	13♎	27	11♏	25	08♐	22	05♑	18	01♒	13	25	07♓
1923	03♑	18	01♒	14	27	09♓	22	03♈	15	27	09♉	21	03♊	15	28	11♋
1924	22♉	04♊	16	28	10♋	22	04♌	16	29	11♍	25	08♎	22	07♏	22	07♐
1925	23♍	06♎	19	03♏	17	02♐	17	02♑	17	01♒	16	00♓	14	28	11♈	24
1926	08♒	22	07♓	21	05♈	19	03♉	16	00♊	13	26	08♋	21	03♌	15	27
1927	24♊	08♋	21	04♌	17	29	11♍	23	05♎	17	29	11♏	23	06♐	18	01♑
1928	12♏	24	06♐	18	00♑	12	24	07♒	20	03♓	16	00♈	14	28	13♉	28
1929	13♓	26	10♈	23	08♉	22	07♊	22	07♋	22	07♌	22	06♍	19	02♎	15
1930	00♌	15	29	13♍	27	11♎	24	07♏	20	03♐	16	28	11♑	23	05♒	17
1931	14♐	28	11♑	24	07♒	19	01♓	13	25	07♈	18	01♉	13	26	09♊	22
1932	02♉	14	25	08♊	21	03♋	16	28	11♌	24	08♍	22	06♎	20	04♏	29
1933	04♍	17	00♎	14	28	13♏	28	13♐	29	14♑	28	13♒	27	10♓	23	06♈
1934	22♑	07♒	21	05♓	19	03♈	16	29	12♉	24	07♊	19	01♋	13	25	06♌
1935	05♊	18	01♋	14	26	08♌	20	02♍	14	26	08♎	20	03♏	16	29	13♐
1936	22♎	04♏	16	29	11♐	24	06♑	19	03♒	16	00♓	14	28	12♈	27	11♉
1937	25♒	08♓	21	05♈	19	04♉	19	04♊	19	04♋	19	03♌	17	01♍	14	26
1938	13♋	28	13♌	27	11♍	24	07♎	20	03♏	15	27	09♐	21	03♑	15	26
1939	26♏	09♐	21	04♑	16	28	10♒	22	04♓	16	28	10♈	23	06♉	19	03♊
1940	12♈	24	06♉	19	01♊	14	27	11♋	24	08♌	22	06♍	20	04♎	19	03♏
1941	16♌	29	13♍	26	11♎	25	10♏	25	10♐	25	10♑	24	08♒	21	04♓	17
1942	05♑	20	04♒	18	02♓	15	28	11♈	23	05♉	17	29	11♊	23	05♋	17
1943	17♉	29	12♊	24	06♋	18	00♌	12	24	05♍	18	00♎	13	26	09♏	23
1944	21♍	05♎	19	04♏	19	04♐	19	03♑	18	02♒	16	00♓	13	26	08♈	21
1945	07♒	21	04♋	18	03♈	17	02♉	16	01♊	16	00♋	14	28	11♌	24	06♍
1946	25♊	10♋	25	09♌	23	06♍	19	02♎	14	26	08♏	20	02♐	13	25	07♑
1947	08♏	20	02♐	14	26	08♑	20	02♒	14	26	08♓	20	03♈	16	00♉	14
1948	21♓	04♈	16	29	12♉	25	09♊	23	07♋	22	06♌	21	05♍	19	03♎	17
1949	29♋	13♌	27	11♍	25	09♎	23	08♏	22	06♐	20	04♑	18	01♒	14	26
1950	16♐	01♑	16	00♒	14	27	10♓	22	04♈	16	28	10♉	22	03♊	15	28
1951	28♈	10♉	22	04♊	16	28	10♋	22	04♌	16	28	11♍	23	06♎	20	04♏
1952	11♍	23	06♎	18	02♏	15	29	14♐	28	13♑	18	13♒	27	11♓	25	09♈
1953	21♑	05♒	19	03♓	17	01♈	15	00♉	14	28	11♊	25	08♋	21	03♌	16
1954	07♊	22	06♋	20	04♌	17	29	12♍	24	06♎	18	00♏	12	24	06♐	18
1955	19♎	01♏	13	25	07♐	18	00♑	12	24	06♒	19	01♓	14	28	11♈	25
1956	01♓	13	26	09♈	22	06♉	20	04♊	19	04♋	19	04♌	19	03♍	17	01♎
1957	12♋	27	11♌	25	10♍	24	08♎	22	05♏	19	02♐	15	28	11♑	23	05♒
1958	28♏	12♐	26	10♑	24	07♒	19	02♓	14	26	08♈	20	01♉	13	26	08♊
1959	09♈	20	03♉	15	27	09♊	21	03♋	15	27	10♌	23	06♍	19	03♎	17
1960	21♌	03♍	16	29	12♎	26	10♏	26	10♐	25	10♑	26	10♒	25	09♓	22
1961	04♑	19	03♒	18	02♓	16	00♈	13	27	10♉	23	06♊	19	01♋	13	25
1962	19♉	03♊	17	01♋	14	27	09♌	21	03♍	15	27	09♎	21	03♏	16	28
1963	29♍	11♎	23	05♏	17	29	11♐	23	06♑	18	01♒	14	27	11♓	24	08♈
1964	11♒	24	06♓	19	03♈	17	01♉	16	01♊	16	01♋	16	01♌	15	29	13♍
1965	25♊	10♋	25	09♌	24	08♍	22	05♎	19	02♏	14	27	09♐	21	03♑	15
1966	10♏	24	08♐	21	04♑	16	29	11♒	23	05♓	17	29	11♈	23	06♉	18
1967	20♓	01♈	13	25	07♉	19	01♊	14	26	09♋	22	05♌	19	03♍	17	01♎
1968	02♌	15	27	10♍	24	08♎	22	07♏	22	07♐	22	07♑	22	06♒	20	04♓
1969	16♐	01♑	16	01♒	16	00♓	14	27	10♈	23	05♉	17	00♊	12	24	06♋
1970	02♉	15	28	11♊	24	07♋	19	01♌	13	25	06♍	18	00♎	13	25	08♏
1971	09♍	21	03♎	15	27	09♏	21	04♐	17	00♑	14	27	11♒	25	09♓	23
1972	23♑	06♒	19	02♓	15	29	14♈	28	13♉	28	13♊	28	12♋	27	10♌	24
1973	07♊	22	07♋	22	07♌	21	05♍	18	01♎	14	26	08♏	20	02♐	14	26
1974	23♎	06♏	19	02♐	14	27	09♑	21	02♒	14	26	08♓	20	03♈	15	29
1975	29♒	11♓	23	04♈	17	29	11♉	24	07♊	21	04♋	18	03♌	17	01♍	15
1976	14♋	27	10♌	24	07♍	21	05♎	20	04♏	19	04♐	18	03♑	17	00♒	14
1977	28♏	13♐	28	13♑	28	12♒	26	09♓	22	04♈	17	29	10♉	22	04♊	16
1978	15♈	27	10♉	22	05♊	17	29	11♋	23	04♌	16	28	10♍	23	05♎	19
1979	18♌	00♍	12	24	06♎	18	01♏	14	28	12♐	26	10♑	25	09♒	24	08♓
1980	05♑	19	02♒	16	29	13♓	27	12♈	26	11♉	25	09♊	23	07♋	21	04♌
1981	19♉	04♊	19	04♋	19	03♌	16	29	12♍	24	07♎	19	01♏	12	24	06♐
1982	06♎	19	01♏	13	25	07♐	19	01♑	13	24	06♒	18	01♓	13	26	09♈
1983	08♒	20	02♓	14	26	08♈	21	04♉	18	02♊	16	01♋	16	01♌	15	00♍
1984	26♊	10♋	24	07♌	22	06♍	20	04♎	18	03♏	17	00♐	14	27	11♑	23
1985	10♏	25	10♐	24	09♑	23	06♒	19	02♓	15	27	09♈	21	02♉	14	26
1986	27♓	09♈	22	04♉	15	27	09♊	21	03♋	15	27	09♌	21	04♍	17	00♎
1987	28♋	10♌	22	04♍	16	28	11♎	24	08♏	22	07♐	22	07♑	22	07♒	22
1988	17♐	01♑	15	00♒	14	28	12♓	27	11♈	24	08♉	22	05♊	18	01♋	14
1989	01♉	16	01♊	15	29	13♋	27	09♌	22	04♍	16	28	10♎	22	04♏	16

	17th	18th	19th	20th	21st	22nd	23rd	24th	25th	26th	27th	28th	29th	30th
1900	14	29	13♓	27	11♈	25	09♉	23	07♊	20	04♋	17	29	12♌
1901	00♋	15	29	12♌	25	08♍	21	03♎	15	26	08♏	20	02♐	14♐
1902	10♏	22	03♐	15	27	09♑	21	03♒	16	28	11♓	24	07♈	21♈
1903	10♓	22	04♈	17	00♉	14	28	13♊	28	13♋	29	14♌	28	13♍
1904	06♌	21	05♍	19	03♎	17	01♏	15	28	11♐	24	07♑	20	02♒
1905	21	05♑	19	02♒	15	28	10♓	22	04♈	16	28	10♉	22	04♊
1906	00♉	12	24	06♊	18	00♋	12	24	06♌	19	02♍	15	28	12♎
1907	00♍	12	25	08♎	21	05♏	19	04♐	19	04♑	19	04♒	19	04♓
1908	28	13♒	27	12♓	26	10♈	23	07♉	20	03♊	15	28	10♋	22♋
1909	12♊	26	09♋	22	05♌	18	00♍	12	24	06♎	18	00♏	12	24♏
1910	20	02♏	14	26	08♐	20	02♑	14	27	10♒	23	07♓	20	04♈
1911	20	03♓	16	29	12♈	26	10♉	25	10♊	25	10♋	25	10♌	24♌
1912	19	04♌	19	04♍	18	01♎	15	28	11♏	23	06♐	18	00♑	12♑
1913	03♐	17	00♑	13	25	08♒	20	02♓	13	25	07♈	19	01♉	14♉
1914	10♈	22	03♉	15	28	10♊	23	05♋	18	02♌	15	29	12♍	26♍
1915	11♌	24	07♍	20	03♎	17	01♏	16	01♐	16	01♑	16	01♒	15♒
1916	11♑	26	10♒	25	09♓	23	06♈	19	02♉	14	27	09♊	21	03♋
1917	25	08♊	20	03♋	15	27	09♌	21	03♍	15	27	09♎	21	04♏
1918	29	11♎	23	05♏	18	00♐	13	26	09♑	23	06♒	20	05♓	29♓
1919	02♒	15	28	11♓	25	09♈	23	08♉	22	07♊	22	07♋	21	05♌
1920	01♋	16	01♊	16	00♍	14	27	10♎	23	05♏	17	29	11♐	23♐
1921	16	28	11♐	23	05♑	17	29	11♒	23	05♓	17	29	11♈	24♈
1922	19	01♈	13	25	07♉	20	03♊	16	00♋	14	28	12♌	27	11♍
1923	23	07♌	20	03♍	17	01♎	15	29	14♏	28	13♐	28	12♑	26♑
1924	22	07♑	22	07♒	21	05♓	18	01♈	13	25	07♉	19	01♊	13♊
1925	07♉	19	02♊	14	26	08♋	19	01♌	13	25	07♍	19	01♎	14♎
1926	08♍	20	02♎	15	27	10♏	23	07♐	20	05♑	19	04♒	18	03♓
1927	14	28	11♒	25	09♓	23	08♈	22	06♉	20	05♊	19	02♋	16♋
1928	13♊	28	13♋	27	11♌	25	08♍	21	03♎	15	27	09♏	21	03♐
1929	28	10♏	22	04♐	16	28	09♑	21	03♒	15	27	10♓	22	05♈
1930	28	10♓	22	04♈	17	00♉	13	27	11♊	25	10♋	25	10♌	25♌
1931	05♋	19	03♌	17	02♍	16	00♎	14	28	12♏	26	10♐	23	06♑
1932	04♐	19	03♑	18	02♒	15	28	11♓	23	05♈	17	29	11♉	23♉
1933	18	00♉	12	24	06♊	18	00♋	12	24	06♌	18	01♍	13	26♍
1934	18	00♍	12	24	07♎	20	03♏	17	01♐	16	01♑	16	01♒	16♒
1935	26	10♑	25	09♒	24	08♓	22	06♈	20	04♉	18	01♊	14	27♊
1936	26	10♊	24	08♋	22	05♌	18	00♍	13	25	07♎	19	01♏	13♏
1937	09♎	21	03♏	15	26	08♐	20	02♑	14	26	09♒	22	05♓	18♓
1938	08♒	20	03♓	15	28	11♈	24	08♉	22	07♊	22	07♋	22	07♌
1939	17	01♋	16	01♌	15	00♍	15	29	12♎	26	09♏	22	05♐	18♐
1940	17	01♐	15	29	12♑	25	08♒	20	03♓	15	26	08♈	20	02♉
1941	29	11♈	23	04♉	16	28	10♊	22	05♋	17	00♌	13	26	10♍
1942	29	11♌	23	05♍	18	01♎	15	28	13♏	28	13♐	28	13♑	28♑
1943	08♐	22	07♑	22	07♒	22	06♓	20	04♈	18	01♉	14	26	09♊
1944	09♉	23	06♊	19	02♋	15	28	10♌	22	04♍	16	28	10♎	22♎
1945	18	00♎	12	24	06♏	18	00♐	13	25	08♑	21	04♒	18	01♓
1946	19	01♒	14	26	09♓	23	06♈	20	04♉	19	04♊	19	04♋	19♋
1947	28	13♊	28	13♋	28	13♌	28	12♍	26	09♎	22	05♏	17	29♏
1948	01♏	14	27	10♐	23	05♑	18	00♒	12	24	06♓	18	00♈	12♈
1949	08♓	20	02♈	14	26	08♉	20	02♊	15	28	12♋	25	09♌	23♌
1950	10♋	22	05♌	18	01♍	14	28	12♎	26	10♏	25	10♐	25	09♑
1951	19	04♐	19	04♑	19	04♒	19	03♓	17	00♈	13	25	08♉	20♉
1952	22	05♉	18	01♊	14	26	08♋	20	02♌	14	26	07♍	19	01♎
1953	28	10♍	21	03♎	15	27	10♏	23	06♐	19	03♑	17	01♒	15♒
1954	01♑	13	26	09♒	22	06♓	20	04♈	18	02♉	17	02♊	16	00♋
1955	10♉	25	10♊	25	10♋	25	09♌	24	07♍	20	03♎	16	28	10♏
1956	14	27	09♏	22	04♐	16	28	10♑	22	04♒	16	28	10♓	22♓
1957	17	29	11♓	23	05♈	17	00♉	12	26	09♊	23	07♋	22	07♌
1958	21	04♋	17	01♌	14	28	12♍	26	10♎	24	09♏	23	07♐	21♐
1959	01♏	16	01♐	16	01♑	16	00♒	14	28	11♓	24	06♈	18	00♉
1960	05♈	18	00♉	13	25	07♊	19	00♋	12	24	06♌	18	00♍	12♍
1961	07♌	19	01♍	13	25	07♎	19	02♏	16	29	14♐	28	13♑	28♑
1962	11♐	25	08♑	22	06♒	20	04♓	18	03♈	17	01♉	15	29	13♊
1963	23	08♉	22	07♊	22	06♋	20	04♌	18	01♍	13	26	08♎	20♎
1964	26	09♎	21	03♏	15	27	09♐	21	02♑	14	26	08♒	21	03♓
1965	27	09♒	21	03♓	15	27	10♈	23	06♉	20	04♊	29	04♋	19♋
1966	01♊	15	29	13♋	27	12♌	26	11♍	25	09♎	23	07♏	20	04♐
1967	15	29	14♏	28	12♐	27	11♑	24	08♒	21	03♓	16	28	09♈
1968	17	29	11♈	23	05♉	17	29	11♊	23	05♋	17	29	12♌	24♌
1969	17	29	11♌	23	05♍	17	00♎	13	26	10♏	25	09♐	25	10♑
1970	22	06♐	20	04♑	19	04♒	18	03♓	17	01♈	15	29	12♉	25♌
1971	07♈	21	06♉	20	04♊	18	01♋	15	28	10♌	23	05♍	17	29♍
1972	06♍	19	01♎	13	25	07♏	19	01♐	13	25	07♑	20	03♒	16♒
1973	08♑	19	01♒	13	26	08♓	21	04♈	18	01♉	16	01♊	16	01♋
1974	12♉	26	10♊	25	10♋	25	10♌	25	09♍	23	07♎	20	03♏	16♏
1975	00♎	14	28	12♏	25	09♐	22	05♑	18	00♒	13	25	07♓	19♓
1976	26	09♓	21	03♈	15	27	09♉	21	03♊	15	28	11♋	24	07♌
1977	28	10♋	22	04♌	17	29	12♍	25	09♎	23	07♏	21	06♐	21♐
1978	02♏	16	01♐	16	01♑	16	01♒	16	01♓	15	28	12♈	25	07♉
1979	22	06♈	20	03♉	17	00♊	13	26	08♋	21	03♌	15	26	08♍
1980	16	29	11♍	23	04♎	16	28	10♏	23	05♐	18	01♑	15	28♑
1981	18	00♑	13	25	08♒	20	03♓	17	00♈	14	29	13♉	28	13♊
1982	23	07♉	22	07♊	22	07♋	22	07♌	21	06♍	29	03♎	15	28♎
1983	14	28	12♎	25	08♏	21	04♐	16	28	11♑	23	04♒	16	28♒
1984	06♒	18	00♓	12	24	06♈	18	00♉	13	25	08♊	21	05♋	19♋
1985	08♊	20	03♋	16	29	12♌	25	09♍	23	07♎	21	05♏	20	04♐
1986	14	28	12♏	27	12♐	28	13♑	28	12♒	27	10♓	23	06♈	18♈
1987	06♓	20	03♈	17	29	12♉	24	07♊	19	01♋	13	25	06♌	18♌
1988	26	08♌	20	02♍	14	26	08♎	20	02♏	15	28	12♐	26	10♑
1989	28	11♐	24	07♑	20	03♒	17	01♓	16	29	13♈	27	12♉	26♉

July

	1st	2nd	3rd	4th	5th	6th	7th	8th	9th	10th	11th	12th	13th	14th	15th	16th
1900	24♌	06♍	18	00♎	12	23	06♏	18	01♐	14	28	11♑	26	10♒	25	09♓
1901	27♐	09♑	22	05♒	19	02♓	16	00♈	14	28	12♉	26	11♊	25	09♋	23
1902	05♉	19	04♊	19	04♋	19	04♌	18	03♍	16	29	12♎	24	07♏	19	00♐
1903	26♍	10♎	23	06♏	18	01♐	13	25	07♑	19	01♒	13	25	06♓	19	01♈
1904	14♒	26	08♓	20	02♈	13	26	08♉	21	04♊	18	02♋	17	01♌	16	01♍
1905	17♊	01♋	13	26	10♌	24	03♍	22	06♎	20	04♏	18	03♐	17	01♑	14
1906	26♎	11♏	25	10♐	25	10♑	25	09♒	23	06♓	19	02♈	14	27	09♉	20
1907	18♓	01♈	14	27	09♉	22	04♊	16	27	09♋	21	03♌	15	27	09♍	21
1908	04♌	16	28	09♍	21	03♎	16	28	11♏	25	08♐	22	07♑	22	07♒	22
1909	07♐	20	03♑	17	01♒	15	00♓	14	28	13♈	27	11♉	25	08♊	22	05♋
1910	18♈	03♉	17	02♊	16	01♋	15	29	13♌	26	09♍	22	04♎	16	28	10♏
1911	08♍	22	05♎	17	00♏	12	24	06♐	17	29	11♑	23	05♒	28	00♓	13
1912	24♑	06♒	18	00♓	12	24	06♈	18	01♉	15	29	13♊	28	13♋	28	13♌
1913	27♉	10♊	24	08♋	22	07♌	22	06♍	21	05♎	19	03♏	16	00♐	13	26
1914	10♎	25	09♏	23	08♐	22	06♑	20	03♒	16	29	12♓	24	06♈	18	00♉
1915	29♒	12♓	25	08♈	20	02♉	14	26	08♊	20	02♋	14	26	08♌	21	04♍
1916	14♋	26	08♌	20	02♍	14	26	09♎	22	06♏	20	04♐	19	04♑	19	04♒
1917	17♏	01♐	14	29	13♑	28	13♒	28	12♓	27	11♈	25	08♉	22	02♊	17
1918	03♈	17	01♉	16	29	13♊	27	10♋	23	06♌	19	01♍	13	25	07♎	19
1919	19♌	02♍	15	28	10♎	22	04♏	16	27	09♐	21	04♑	16	29	12♒	25
1920	04♑	16	28	10♒	23	05♓	17	00♈	13	27	11♉	25	10♊	24	10♋	26
1921	07♉	21	05♊	19	04♋	19	04♌	19	04♍	19	03♎	16	00♏	13	25	08♐
1922	25♍	09♎	23	07♏	21	05♐	18	01♑	14	27	09♒	21	03♓	15	27	09♈
1923	09♒	22	05♓	17	00♈	12	23	05♉	17	29	11♊	24	07♋	20	03♌	16
1924	25♊	07♋	19	01♌	13	26	08♍	21	05♎	18	02♏	16	01♐	16	01♑	16
1925	28♎	11♏	25	10♐	25	10♑	25	10♒	25	10♓	24	08♈	21	04♉	16	29
1926	17♓	02♈	16	00♉	13	26	09♊	22	05♋	17	29	11♌	23	05♍	17	29
1927	29♋	12♌	25	07♍	19	01♎	13	25	07♏	19	01♐	14	27	10♑	23	07♒
1928	15♐	27	09♑	21	04♒	17	00♓	13	27	10♈	24	09♉	23	07♊	22	07♋
1929	18♈	02♉	16	01♊	15	01♋	16	01♌	16	01♍	15	28	12♎	24	07♏	19
1930	10♍	24	08♎	21	04♍	17	00♐	13	25	07♑	29	01♒	13	25	07♓	29
1931	19♑	02♒	15	27	09♓	21	03♈	14	26	09♉	21	04♊	17	00♋	14	28
1932	05♊	17	29	12♋	25	08♌	21	05♍	18	02♎	16	00♏	15	29	14♐	28
1933	09♎	23	07♏	22	07♐	22	07♑	22	07♒	21	05♓	19	02♈	15	27	09♉
1934	01♓	15	29	13♈	26	09♉	21	04♊	16	28	10♋	22	03♌	15	27	09♍
1935	10♋	22	04♌	17	28	10♍	22	04♎	16	28	1♏	24	07♐	21	05♑	19
1936	25♏	07♐	20	02♑	16	29	13♒	26	11♓	25	09♈	23	07♉	22	06♊	19
1937	01♈	15	29	14♉	28	13♊	28	13♋	27	11♌	25	09♍	22	05♎	17	29
1938	22♌	06♍	20	04♎	17	00♏	12	24	06♐	18	00♑	12	24	05♒	17	00♓
1939	00♑	12	25	07♒	18	00♓	12	24	06♈	18	01♉	14	27	11♊	25	10♋
1940	14♉	27	10♊	23	06♋	20	04♌	18	03♍	17	01♎	15	29	13♏	27	11♐
1941	23♍	07♎	21	05♏	20	04♐	19	04♑	18	02♒	16	29	12♓	25	07♈	19
1942	13♒	27	11♓	25	07♈	20	02♉	14	26	08♊	20	02♋	14	26	08♌	20
1943	21♊	03♋	15	27	09♌	20	02♍	14	26	08♎	21	04♏	18	02♐	16	01♑
1944	04♏	17	00♐	13	27	11♑	25	10♒	24	09♓	23	08♈	22	06♉	19	03♊
1945	15♓	29	13♈	28	12♉	26	11♊	25	09♋	22	06♌	19	02♍	14	26	06♎
1946	03♌	18	01♍	15	28	10♎	23	05♏	17	28	10♐	22	04♑	16	28	11♒
1947	11♐	23	05♑	17	29	10♒	22	05♓	17	29	12♈	25	08♉	22	07♊	21
1948	24♈	07♉	20	03♊	17	01♋	16	01♌	16	01♍	15	00♎	14	28	11♏	24
1949	07♍	22	06♎	20	04♏	18	02♐	16	29	13♑	26	09♒	22	04♓	16	28
1950	24♑	08♒	22	05♓	18	00♈	12	24	06♉	18	00♊	12	24	06♋	19	02♌
1951	02♊	13	25	07♋	19	01♌	13	25	07♍	20	03♎	16	29	13♏	28	12♐
1952	14♎	27	10♏	23	08♐	22	07♑	22	07♒	22	07♓	21	05♈	19	02♉	15
1953	29♒	14♓	28	12♈	26	10♉	24	08♊	21	04♋	17	29	12♌	24	06♍	18
1954	14♋	28	12♌	25	07♍	20	02♎	14	26	08♏	20	02♐	14	27	09♑	22
1955	22♏	04♐	15	27	09♑	21	03♒	16	28	11♓	24	08♈	21	05♉	19	04♊
1956	04♈	17	00♉	14	28	13♊	27	13♋	28	13♌	28	13♍	27	10♎	24	06♏
1957	21♌	06♍	20	05♎	19	02♏	16	29	12♐	24	07♑	19	02♒	14	26	08♓
1958	05♑	19	02♒	15	27	10♓	22	04♈	16	27	09♉	21	04♊	16	29	13♋
1959	12♉	24	05♊	17	29	12♋	24	07♌	20	03♍	16	29	13♎	27	11♏	25
1960	25♍	08♎	21	05♏	19	03♐	18	04♑	19	04♒	19	03♓	18	01♈	14	27
1961	13♒	28	12♓	26	10♈	24	07♉	20	03♊	16	28	10♋	22	04♌	16	28
1962	26♊	09♋	22	05♌	17	29	11♍	23	05♎	17	29	11♏	24	06♐	20	03♑
1963	02♏	13	25	07♐	20	02♑	15	28	11♒	24	07♓	21	05♈	19	04♉	18
1964	16♓	29	12♈	26	10♉	25	10♊	25	10♋	25	09♌	24	08♍	21	05♎	17
1965	04♌	19	04♍	18	02♎	15	29	11♏	24	06♐	18	00♑	12	24	06♒	18
1966	17♐	00♑	12	25	07♒	19	01♓	13	25	07♈	19	01♉	13	26	10♊	23
1967	21♈	03♉	15	27	09♊	22	05♋	18	02♌	16	29	13♍	28	12♎	26	10♏
1968	07♍	21	04♎	18	02♏	16	01♐	16	01♑	15	00♒	14	28	12♓	25	07♈
1969	25♑	10♒	25	09♓	23	07♈	20	02♉	15	27	09♊	21	03♋	14	25	08♌
1970	08♊	20	03♋	15	27	09♌	21	03♍	15	26	09♎	21	03♏	16	00♐	28
1971	11♎	23	05♏	17	00♐	12	26	09♑	23	07♒	21	05♓	20	04♈	18	02♉
1972	29♒	12♓	26	10♈	24	08♉	23	07♊	22	06♋	21	05♌	18	02♍	14	27
1973	16♋	01♌	15	00♍	14	27	10♎	23	06♏	17	29	11♐	23	05♑	16	28
1974	29♏	11♐	23	05♑	17	29	11♒	23	05♓	17	29	11♈	24	07♉	20	04♊
1975	00♈	12	24	07♉	19	02♊	16	29	13♋	28	12♌	27	12♍	26	11♎	25
1976	21♌	04♍	18	02♎	16	00♏	15	29	13♐	27	11♑	25	09♒	22	04♓	17
1977	07♑	22	06♒	21	04♓	18	01♈	13	25	07♉	19	01♊	13	25	07♋	19
1978	20♉	02♊	14	26	08♋	20	01♌	13	25	07♍	19	02♎	14	27	11♏	25
1979	20♍	02♎	14	26	09♏	22	06♐	20	04♑	19	04♒	19	04♓	18	02♈	17
1980	12♒	26	10♓	24	09♈	23	07♉	21	05♊	19	02♋	16	29	12♌	24	07♍
1981	28♊	12♋	27	11♌	24	07♍	20	03♎	15	27	09♏	21	03♐	15	27	09♑
1982	10♏	22	04♐	16	28	10♑	22	03♒	15	28	10♓	23	06♈	19	02♉	16
1983	10♓	22	04♈	17	29	13♉	26	10♊	25	10♋	25	10♌	25	10♍	24	08♎
1984	03♌	18	02♍	17	01♎	15	29	13♏	27	10♐	23	06♑	19	02♒	14	26
1985	19♐	03♑	17	01♒	14	28	10♓	23	05♈	17	29	10♉	22	04♊	17	29
1986	01♉	12	24	06♊	18	00♋	12	24	06♌	19	01♍	14	27	10♎	24	08♏
1987	00♍	12	24	07♎	20	03♏	16	01♐	15	00♑	16	01♒	16	01♓	15	30
1988	25♑	10♒	24	09♓	23	07♈	21	05♉	18	02♊	15	27	10♋	22	04♌	16
1989	10♊	24	08♋	21	05♌	17	00♍	12	24	06♎	18	00♏	12	24	07♐	19

	17th	18th	19th	20th	21st	22nd	23rd	24th	25th	26th	27th	28th	29th	30th	31st
1900	24	08 ♈	22	06 ♉	20	04 ♊	17	00 ♋	13	25	08 ♌	20	02 ♍	14	26 ♍
1901	07 ♌	20	03 ♍	16	29	11 ♎	23	04 ♏	16	28	10 ♐	22	05 ♑	18	01 ♒
1902	12	24	06 ♑	18	00 ♒	13	25	08 ♓	21	04 ♈	17	01 ♉	15	29	13 ♊
1903	13	26	09 ♉	23	07 ♊	22	07 ♋	22	07 ♌	22	07 ♍	22	06 ♎	19	03 ♏
1904	16	00 ♎	14	28	12 ♏	25	08 ♐	21	04 ♑	16	28	11 ♒	23	04 ♓	16 ♓
1905	28	11 ♒	23	06 ♓	18	00 ♈	12	24	06 ♉	18	00 ♊	12	25	08 ♋	22 ♋
1906	02 ♊	14	26	08 ♋	21	03 ♌	16	29	12 ♍	25	09 ♎	23	07 ♏	21	05 ♐
1907	04 ♎	17	00 ♏	14	28	13 ♐	28	13 ♑	28	13 ♒	28	12 ♓	26	10 ♈	23 ♈
1908	07 ♓	22	06 ♈	20	04 ♉	17	00 ♊	12	25	07 ♋	19	01 ♌	13	24	06 ♍
1909	18	01 ♌	13	26	08 ♍	20	02 ♎	14	26	08 ♏	20	02 ♐	15	28	12 ♑
1910	22	04 ♐	16	28	11 ♑	23	07 ♒	20	04 ♓	17	01 ♈	15	29	13 ♉	28 ♉
1911	25	08 ♈	22	06 ♉	20	04 ♊	19	04 ♋	19	04 ♌	18	03 ♍	17	00 ♎	13 ♎
1912	28	13 ♍	27	11 ♎	25	08 ♏	20	03 ♐	15	27	09 ♑	21	03 ♒	15	27 ♒
1913	09 ♑	21	04 ♒	16	28	10 ♓	22	03 ♈	15	27	09 ♉	22	05 ♊	18	02 ♋
1914	12	24	06 ♊	18	01 ♋	14	27	11 ♌	25	09 ♍	23	07 ♎	21	06 ♏	20 ♏
1915	17	00 ♎	13	27	11 ♏	26	10 ♐	25	10 ♑	25	09 ♒	23	07 ♓	20	03 ♈
1916	19	04 ♓	18	02 ♈	16	29	11 ♉	24	06 ♊	18	00 ♋	11	23	05 ♌	17 ♌
1917	00 ♋	12	24	06 ♌	18	00 ♍	11	23	05 ♎	17	00 ♏	12	25	09 ♐	23 ♐
1918	01 ♏	13	25	08 ♐	21	04 ♑	18	02 ♒	16	00 ♓	15	00 ♈	14	28	12 ♉
1919	08 ♓	22	06 ♈	20	04 ♉	18	02 ♊	17	01 ♋	15	00 ♌	13	27	10 ♍	23 ♍
1920	10 ♌	25	09 ♍	23	06 ♎	19	02 ♏	14	26	08 ♐	19	01 ♑	13	25	07 ♒
1921	20	02 ♑	14	26	08 ♒	20	02 ♓	14	26	08 ♈	20	03 ♉	16	29	13 ♊
1922	21	03 ♉	15	28	11 ♊	24	08 ♋	23	07 ♌	22	07 ♍	21	06 ♎	20	04 ♏
1923	00 ♍	14	28	12 ♎	26	10 ♏	24	09 ♐	23	07 ♑	21	04 ♒	17	00 ♓	13 ♓
1924	01 ♒	15	29	13 ♓	26	09 ♈	22	04 ♉	16	28	10 ♊	21	03 ♋	15	28 ♋
1925	11 ♊	23	05 ♋	16	28	10 ♌	22	04 ♍	16	28	11 ♎	24	07 ♏	20	04 ♐
1926	11 ♎	23	05 ♏	18	01 ♐	15	29	13 ♑	28	13 ♒	28	13 ♓	28	12 ♈	26 ♈
1927	21	06 ♓	20	04 ♈	19	03 ♉	17	01 ♊	15	28	11 ♋	25	08 ♌	20	03 ♍
1928	21	05 ♌	19	03 ♍	16	29	11 ♎	24	06 ♏	17	29	11 ♐	23	05 ♑	18 ♑
1929	01 ♐	13	25	07 ♑	18	00 ♒	12	25	07 ♓	19	02 ♈	15	28	12 ♉	26 ♉
1930	01 ♈	13	25	08 ♉	21	05 ♊	19	04 ♋	19	04 ♌	19	04 ♍	19	04 ♎	18 ♎
1931	13 ♌	27	12 ♍	26	11 ♎	25	09 ♏	23	06 ♐	19	03 ♑	16	28	11 ♒	23 ♒
1932	12 ♑	26	10 ♒	23	06 ♓	19	01 ♈	13	25	07 ♉	19	01 ♊	13	25	08 ♋
1933	21	03 ♊	15	27	09 ♋	21	03 ♌	15	28	10 ♍	23	06 ♎	20	03 ♏	17 ♏
1934	21	03 ♎	16	29	12 ♏	26	10 ♐	25	09 ♑	25	10 ♒	25	10 ♓	24	08 ♈
1935	04 ♒	19	04 ♓	18	03 ♈	17	01 ♉	15	28	11 ♊	24	06 ♋	19	01 ♌	13 ♌
1936	03 ♋	17	00 ♌	13	26	08 ♍	21	03 ♎	15	27	08 ♏	20	03 ♐	15	28 ♐
1937	11 ♏	23	05 ♐	17	29	11 ♑	23	06 ♒	18	02 ♓	15	28	12 ♈	26	10 ♉
1938	12	24	07 ♈	20	03 ♉	17	01 ♊	15	00 ♋	15	01 ♌	16	01 ♍	15	29 ♍
1939	25	10 ♌	25	10 ♍	25	09 ♎	23	06 ♏	19	02 ♐	15	27	09 ♑	21	03 ♒
1940	24	08 ♑	21	04 ♒	16	29	11 ♓	23	04 ♈	16	28	10 ♉	22	05 ♊	18 ♊
1941	01 ♉	13	24	06 ♊	19	01 ♋	14	26	09 ♌	23	06 ♍	20	04 ♎	18	02 ♏
1942	03 ♍	15	28	11 ♎	24	08 ♏	22	07 ♐	22	07 ♑	22	07 ♒	21	06 ♓	19 ♓
1943	16	01 ♒	16	01 ♓	16	00 ♈	14	27	10 ♉	23	06 ♊	18	00 ♋	12	24 ♋
1944	16	29	11 ♋	24	06 ♌	18	00 ♍	12	24	06 ♎	18	00 ♏	12	25	08 ♐
1945	20	02 ♏	14	26	08 ♐	21	04 ♑	17	00 ♒	14	28	12 ♓	26	10 ♈	24 ♈
1946	23	06 ♓	20	03 ♈	16	00 ♉	14	29	13 ♊	28	13 ♋	27	12 ♌	26	10 ♍
1947	06 ♋	22	07 ♌	22	07 ♍	21	05 ♎	18	01 ♏	14	26	08 ♐	20	02 ♑	14 ♑
1948	07 ♐	20	02 ♑	14	26	09 ♒	20	02 ♓	14	26	08 ♈	20	02 ♉	15	28 ♉
1949	10 ♈	22	04 ♉	16	28	11 ♊	24	07 ♋	21	05 ♌	19	03 ♍	18	02 ♎	17 ♎
1950	15	28	11 ♍	25	08 ♎	22	06 ♏	21	05 ♐	19	04 ♑	18	02 ♒	16	00 ♓
1951	27	13 ♑	28	13 ♒	27	12 ♓	25	09 ♈	22	04 ♉	16	28	10 ♊	22	04 ♋
1952	28	11 ♊	23	05 ♋	17	29	11 ♌	22	04 ♍	16	28	10 ♎	23	05 ♏	18 ♏
1953	29	11 ♎	23	05 ♏	18	01 ♐	14	27	11 ♑	25	10 ♒	25	09 ♓	24	09 ♈
1954	05 ♒	19	03 ♓	17	01 ♈	15	29	13 ♉	27	12 ♊	26	10 ♋	23	07 ♌	20 ♌
1955	19	04 ♋	18	03 ♌	18	02 ♍	16	29	12 ♎	24	06 ♏	18	00 ♐	12	24 ♐
1956	19	01 ♐	13	25	07 ♑	19	01 ♒	13	25	07 ♓	19	01 ♈	14	26	10 ♉
1957	20	01 ♈	13	25	08 ♉	21	04 ♊	17	01 ♋	16	01 ♌	16	01 ♍	16	01 ♎
1958	26	10 ♌	24	09 ♍	23	07 ♎	21	05 ♏	19	03 ♐	17	01 ♑	14	27	10 ♒
1959	10 ♐	25	09 ♑	24	08 ♒	22	06 ♓	19	02 ♈	14	26	08 ♉	20	02 ♊	14 ♊
1960	09 ♉	22	04 ♊	16	27	09 ♋	21	03 ♌	15	27	09 ♍	22	05 ♎	17	01 ♏
1961	09 ♍	21	03 ♎	15	28	11 ♏	24	08 ♐	22	07 ♑	22	07 ♒	22	07 ♓	22 ♓
1962	17	01 ♒	16	00 ♓	15	29	14 ♈	28	12 ♉	26	09 ♊	22	05 ♋	18	01 ♌
1963	02 ♊	17	01 ♋	15	29	12 ♌	26	09 ♍	21	04 ♎	16	28	10 ♏	21	03 ♐
1964	00 ♏	12	24	06 ♐	17	29	12 ♑	23	05 ♒	18	00 ♓	13	26	09 ♈	23 ♈
1965	00 ♓	12	24	06 ♈	19	02 ♉	15	28	12 ♊	27	12 ♋	27	12 ♌	28	13 ♍
1966	07 ♋	22	07 ♌	22	06 ♍	21	06 ♎	20	04 ♏	17	01 ♐	14	26	09 ♑	21 ♑
1967	24	08 ♐	22	06 ♑	19	03 ♒	16	29	11 ♓	23	05 ♈	17	29	11 ♉	23 ♉
1968	20	02 ♉	14	25	07 ♊	19	01 ♋	13	26	09 ♌	21	04 ♍	18	01 ♎	14 ♎
1969	20	02 ♍	14	27	09 ♎	22	06 ♏	19	04 ♐	18	03 ♑	18	04 ♒	19	03 ♓
1970	28	13 ♑	28	13 ♒	28	13 ♓	27	12 ♈	25	09 ♉	22	05 ♊	18	00 ♋	12 ♋
1971	16	00 ♊	14	27	11 ♋	23	06 ♌	19	01 ♍	13	25	07 ♎	19	01 ♏	13 ♏
1972	09 ♎	21	03 ♏	15	27	09 ♐	21	04 ♑	16	29	12 ♒	25	09 ♓	23	07 ♈
1973	10 ♒	23	05 ♓	18	01 ♈	14	27	11 ♉	25	10 ♊	24	09 ♋	24	09 ♌	24 ♌
1974	19	03 ♋	18	03 ♌	19	04 ♍	19	03 ♎	17	00 ♏	13	26	08 ♐	20	02 ♑
1975	08 ♏	22	05 ♐	18	01 ♑	14	26	09 ♒	21	03 ♓	15	27	09 ♈	21	03 ♉
1976	29	11 ♈	23	05 ♉	17	29	11 ♊	23	06 ♋	19	03 ♌	16	00 ♍	15	29 ♍
1977	01 ♌	14	26	09 ♍	22	06 ♎	19	03 ♏	17	01 ♐	16	01 ♑	15	00 ♒	15 ♒
1978	09 ♐	24	09 ♑	25	10 ♒	25	10 ♓	24	08 ♈	21	04 ♉	16	29	11 ♊	23 ♊
1979	00 ♉	14	27	10 ♊	22	05 ♋	17	29	11 ♌	23	05 ♍	17	28	10 ♎	22 ♎
1980	19	01 ♎	12	24	06 ♏	18	01 ♐	13	26	10 ♑	23	07 ♒	22	06 ♓	21 ♓
1981	22	04 ♒	17	00 ♓	14	27	11 ♈	25	09 ♉	24	08 ♊	23	07 ♋	21	05 ♌
1982	01 ♊	15	00 ♋	15	00 ♌	15	00 ♍	14	28	11 ♎	24	07 ♏	19	01 ♐	13 ♐
1983	22	05 ♏	18	01 ♐	13	25	07 ♑	19	01 ♒	13	25	07 ♓	19	01 ♈	13 ♈
1984	08 ♓	20	02 ♈	14	26	08 ♉	20	03 ♊	16	00 ♋	14	28	13 ♌	27	12 ♍
1985	12 ♋	25	08 ♌	22	06 ♍	19	04 ♎	18	02 ♏	16	00 ♐	14	28	12 ♑	26 ♑
1986	22	06 ♐	21	06 ♑	21	06 ♒	21	05 ♓	18	02 ♈	14	27	09 ♉	21	03 ♊
1987	13 ♈	26	09 ♉	22	04 ♊	16	28	10 ♋	22	04 ♌	15	27	09 ♍	21	04 ♎
1988	28	10 ♍	22	04 ♎	16	28	10 ♏	23	06 ♐	20	04 ♑	19	04 ♒	19	04 ♓
1989	02 ♑	16	29	13 ♒	27	11 ♓	26	10 ♈	24	08 ♉	22	06 ♊	20	04 ♋	17 ♋

August

	1st	2nd	3rd	4th	5th	6th	7th	8th	9th	10th	11th	12th	13th	14th	15th	16th
1900	08♎	20	02♏	14	26	09♐	22	06♑	20	04♒	19	04♓	19	04♈	18	03♉
1901	15♒	28	12♓	26	11♈	25	09♉	23	07♊	21	05♋	19	02♌	16	29	12♍
1902	28♊	13♋	28	12♌	27	11♍	24	08♎	20	03♏	15	27	09♐	21	02♑	14
1903	15♏	28	10♐	22	04♑	16	28	10♒	22	04♓	16	28	10♈	23	05♉	19
1904	28♓	10♈	22	04♉	16	29	12♊	26	10♋	25	10♌	25	10♍	25	10♎	24
1905	05♌	19	04♍	18	02♎	17	01♏	15	29	13♐	27	10♑	24	07♒	19	02♓
1906	20♐	04♑	19	03♒	17	01♓	14	27	10♈	22	05♉	17	28	10♊	22	04♋
1907	06♉	18	01♊	13	24	06♋	18	00♌	12	24	06♍	18	01♎	14	27	10♏
1908	18♍	00♎	12	24	07♏	20	03♐	17	01♑	15	00♒	15	01♓	16	01♈	15
1909	26♑	10♒	25	10♓	24	09♈	24	08♉	22	05♊	19	02♋	14	27	10♌	22
1910	12♊	26	10♋	24	08♌	21	04♍	17	00♎	12	24	06♏	18	00♐	12	24
1911	26♎	08♏	20	02♐	14	26	08♑	20	02♒	14	27	10♓	22	05♈	19	02♉
1912	09♓	21	03♈	15	28	10♉	24	07♊	22	06♋	21	07♌	22	07♍	22	06♎
1913	16♋	01♌	16	01♍	16	01♎	15	29	13♏	27	10♐	23	06♑	18	00♒	13
1914	04♐	18	02♑	15	29	12♒	25	07♓	20	02♈	14	26	08♉	19	01♊	14
1915	16♈	28	10♉	22	04♊	16	28	10♋	22	05♌	17	00♍	13	27	10♎	24
1916	29♌	11♍	23	06♎	19	02♏	15	29	13♐	28	12♑	27	12♒	27	12♓	27
1917	07♑	22	07♒	22	07♓	22	07♈	21	05♉	18	01♊	14	27	09♋	21	03♌
1918	26♉	10♊	23	06♋	19	02♌	15	27	10♍	22	04♎	15	27	09♏	21	03♐
1919	06♎	18	00♏	12	24	05♐	17	00♑	12	25	08♒	21	05♓	18	02♈	17
1920	20♒	02♓	15	27	10♈	23	07♉	21	05♊	19	04♋	19	03♌	18	03♍	17
1921	27♊	12♋	27	13♌	28	13♍	28	12♎	26	09♏	22	05♐	17	29	11♑	23
1922	18♏	01♐	15	28	11♑	23	06♒	18	00♓	12	24	05♈	17	29	11♉	23
1923	25♓	07♈	19	01♉	13	25	07♊	20	02♋	15	28	12♌	26	10♍	24	08♎
1924	10♌	23	05♍	18	02♎	15	29	13♏	27	11♐	26	10♑	25	09♒	23	07♓
1925	19♐	03♑	18	04♒	19	04♓	18	03♈	16	00♉	13	25	08♊	20	02♋	13
1926	10♉	23	06♊	19	02♋	14	26	08♌	20	02♍	13	25	07♎	19	01♏	14
1927	15♍	27	09♎	21	03♏	15	27	09♐	22	05♑	18	02♒	16	01♓	15	00♈
1928	00♒	13	26	10♓	23	07♈	21	05♉	19	03♊	18	02♋	16	00♌	14	28
1929	10♊	24	09♋	24	09♌	24	09♍	23	07♎	20	03♏	15	28	10♐	21	03♑
1930	01♏	14	27	10♐	22	04♑	16	28	10♒	22	04♓	16	28	10♈	22	04♎
1931	05♓	17	29	11♈	23	04♉	17	29	12♊	25	09♋	23	07♌	22	07♍	22
1932	21♋	04♌	17	01♍	15	29	13♎	27	11♏	26	10♐	24	08♑	22	05♒	19
1933	02♐	16	01♑	16	01♒	15	29	13♓	27	10♈	23	05♉	18	00♊	11	23
1934	22♈	05♉	18	01♊	13	25	07♋	19	00♌	12	24	06♍	18	00♎	13	25
1935	25♌	07♍	19	01♎	12	24	07♏	19	02♐	15	29	13♑	27	12♒	27	13♓
1936	11♑	24	08♒	22	06♓	21	05♈	20	04♉	18	02♊	16	00♋	13	26	09♌
1937	24♉	08♊	23	07♋	21	06♌	20	04♍	17	00♎	13	25	07♏	19	01♐	13
1938	13♎	26	09♏	21	03♐	15	27	09♑	20	02♒	14	27	09♓	21	04♈	17
1939	15♒	27	09♓	21	03♈	15	27	10♉	22	06♊	19	03♋	18	03♌	18	04♍
1940	01♋	15	29	13♌	28	12♍	27	12♎	26	10♏	24	08♐	21	04♑	17	00♒
1941	16♏	00♐	14	29	13♑	27	11♒	24	07♓	20	02♈	15	27	09♉	21	02♊
1942	03♈	16	29	11♉	23	05♊	17	29	11♋	23	05♌	17	29	12♍	25	08♎
1943	06♌	17	29	11♍	23	05♎	18	00♏	13	27	10♐	25	09♑	24	09♒	24
1944	21♐	05♑	19	04♒	19	04♓	19	03♈	18	02♉	16	00♊	13	26	08♋	21
1945	09♉	23	07♊	21	04♋	18	01♌	14	27	10♍	22	04♎	16	28	10♏	22
1946	23♍	06♎	19	01♏	13	25	07♐	18	00♑	12	25	07♒	20	03♓	16	00♈
1947	26♑	08♒	20	02♓	14	26	09♈	22	05♉	18	02♊	16	00♋	15	00♌	15
1948	11♊	25	10♋	24	09♌	25	10♍	25	10♎	24	08♏	21	04♐	17	29	11♑
1949	01♏	15	29	12♐	26	09♑	22	05♒	18	00♓	12	24	06♈	18	00♉	12
1950	13♓	26	08♈	20	02♉	14	26	08♊	20	02♋	15	28	11♌	24	07♍	21
1951	16♋	28	10♌	22	05♍	17	00♎	13	26	09♏	23	08♐	22	07♑	22	06♒
1952	02♐	16	00♑	15	00♒	16	01♓	16	00♈	15	29	12♉	25	08♊	20	02♋
1953	23♈	07♉	21	04♊	18	01♋	13	26	08♌	20	02♍	14	26	08♎	20	02♏
1954	03♍	15	28	10♎	22	04♏	16	28	10♐	22	05♑	17	01♒	14	28	12♓
1955	06♑	18	00♒	13	25	08♓	21	05♈	18	02♉	16	00♊	14	28	13♋	27
1956	23♉	07♊	21	06♋	21	06♌	21	06♍	21	05♎	19	03♏	15	28	10♐	22
1957	15♎	29	13♏	26	09♐	21	04♑	16	28	11♒	23	04♓	16	28	10♈	22
1958	23♒	06♓	18	00♈	12	24	05♉	17	29	12♊	24	08♋	21	05♌	19	04♍
1959	26♊	08♋	20	03♌	16	29	13♍	26	10♎	24	08♏	22	06♐	20	05♑	19
1960	14♏	28	13♐	27	12♑	27	12♒	27	12♓	26	10♈	23	06♉	18	00♊	12
1961	05♈	20	04♉	17	00♊	13	25	07♋	19	01♌	13	25	06♍	18	00♎	12
1962	13♌	25	08♍	19	01♎	13	25	07♏	19	02♐	14	28	11♑	25	10♒	24
1963	15♐	28	10♑	23	06♒	20	04♓	18	02♈	16	00♉	15	29	13♊	27	11♋
1964	06♉	20	05♊	19	04♋	18	03♌	18	02♍	16	00♎	13	26	08♏	20	02♐
1965	27♍	11♎	25	08♏	21	03♐	15	27	09♑	21	03♒	15	27	09♓	21	03♈
1966	04♒	16	28	10♓	21	03♈	15	27	09♉	22	05♊	18	01♋	16	00♌	15
1967	05♊	18	00♋	13	27	11♌	25	09♍	24	08♎	23	07♏	21	05♐	19	02♑
1968	28♎	12♏	26	11♐	25	10♑	24	09♒	23	06♓	20	03♈	15	28	10♉	22
1969	18♓	02♈	15	28	11♉	23	06♊	18	00♋	11	23	05♌	17	29	11♍	24
1970	24♋	06♌	18	00♍	11	23	05♎	17	00♏	12	25	08♐	22	06♑	21	06♒
1971	25♏	07♐	20	04♑	17	01♒	16	00♓	15	00♈	14	29	13♉	27	11♊	24
1972	21♈	05♉	19	03♊	18	02♋	16	00♌	13	27	10♍	22	05♎	17	29	11♏
1973	08♍	22	06♎	19	01♏	14	26	08♐	19	01♑	13	25	07♒	19	02♓	15
1974	14♑	26	08♒	20	02♓	14	26	08♈	20	03♉	16	29	13♊	27	12♋	27
1975	15♉	27	10♊	24	07♋	22	06♌	21	06♍	22	06♎	21	05♏	19	02♐	15
1976	13♎	27	11♏	25	09♐	23	07♑	21	04♒	17	00♓	13	25	07♈	19	01♉
1977	29♒	12♓	26	09♈	21	03♉	15	27	09♊	21	03♋	15	27	10♌	23	06♍
1978	05♋	17	28	10♌	22	04♍	16	29	11♎	24	07♏	21	04♐	19	03♑	18
1979	05♏	17	01♐	14	28	13♑	27	12♒	28	13♓	28	12♈	26	10♉	24	07♊
1980	05♈	19	04♉	18	02♊	15	29	12♋	25	08♌	20	03♍	15	27	09♎	20
1981	19♌	02♍	15	28	11♎	23	05♏	17	29	11♐	23	05♑	17	00♒	13	26
1982	25♐	07♑	18	00♒	12	25	07♓	20	03♈	16	29	13♉	26	10♊	25	09♋
1983	26♈	08♉	21	05♊	19	03♋	18	03♌	18	03♍	19	03♎	18	01♏	15	28
1984	27♍	12♎	26	10♏	24	07♐	20	03♑	16	28	11♒	23	05♓	17	29	11♈
1985	09♒	23	06♓	18	01♈	13	25	07♉	18	00♊	12	25	07♋	20	03♌	17
1986	15♊	26	08♋	21	03♌	15	28	11♍	24	07♎	21	04♏	18	02♐	17	01♑
1987	16♎	29	12♏	26	10♐	24	09♑	24	09♒	24	09♓	24	08♈	22	05♉	18
1988	19♓	03♈	18	02♉	15	29	12♊	24	07♋	19	01♌	13	25	07♍	19	01♎
1989	00♌	13	26	08♍	20	02♎	14	26	08♏	20	02♐	14	27	10♑	24	08♒

	17th	18th	19th	20th	21st	22nd	23rd	24th	25th	26th	27th	28th	29th	30th	31st
1900	17	01♊	14	27	10♋	22	05♌	17	29	11♍	23	05♎	17	28	10♏
1901	24	07♎	19	01♏	12	24	06♐	18	00♑	13	26	09♒	23	07♓	22♓
1902	27	09♒	22	04♓	17	01♈	14	28	11♉	25	09♊	24	08♋	22	07♊
1903	02♊	16	01♋	15	00♌	16	01♍	16	00♎	14	28	11♏	24	07♐	19♐
1904	08♏	22	05♐	18	01♑	13	25	08♒	19	01♓	13	25	07♈	19	01♉
1905	14	26	08♈	20	02♉	14	26	08♊	20	03♋	16	00♌	14	28	13♍
1906	17	29	12♌	25	08♍	22	05♎	19	04♏	18	02♐	16	00♑	14	28♑
1907	24	08♐	22	07♑	21	06♒	21	06♓	20	04♈	18	01♉	14	27	09♊
1908	00♉	13	26	09♊	22	04♋	16	28	10♌	21	03♍	15	27	09♎	21♎
1909	04♍	16	28	10♎	22	04♏	16	28	10♐	23	06♑	20	04♒	18	03♓
1910	06♑	19	02♒	15	29	13♓	27	12♈	26	10♉	24	08♊	22	06♋	20♋
1911	16	00♊	14	28	13♋	28	12♌	27	11♍	25	08♎	21	04♏	16	29♏
1912	20	04♏	17	00♐	12	24	06♑	18	00♒	12	24	06♓	18	00♈	12♈
1913	25	07♓	18	00♈	12	24	06♉	18	01♊	13	27	11♋	25	09♌	24♌
1914	26	09♋	22	06♌	20	04♍	18	03♎	18	02♏	16	01♐	15	28	12♑
1915	08♏	22	06♐	21	05♑	19	04♒	18	01♓	15	28	11♈	24	06♉	18♉
1916	11♈	24	07♉	20	02♊	14	26	08♋	20	02♌	14	26	08♍	20	03♎
1917	15	27	08♍	20	02♎	14	26	09♏	21	04♐	17	01♑	15	00♒	15♒
1918	16	29	12♑	26	10♒	25	10♓	25	10♈	24	09♉	23	07♊	20	03♋
1919	01♉	15	29	13♊	27	11♋	25	09♌	22	05♍	19	02♎	14	26	08♏
1920	01♎	14	27	10♏	22	04♐	16	28	10♑	22	04♒	16	29	11♓	24♓
1921	05♒	17	29	11♓	23	05♈	17	29	12♉	25	08♊	22	07♋	21	06♌
1922	06♊	19	03♋	16	01♌	16	01♍	16	01♎	16	00♏	14	28	12♐	25♐
1923	23	07♏	21	05♐	19	03♑	17	00♒	13	26	09♓	21	03♈	15	27♈
1924	21	04♈	17	00♉	12	24	06♊	18	00♋	12	24	06♌	19	02♍	15♍
1925	25	07♌	19	01♍	13	25	08♎	21	03♏	17	00♐	14	28	13♑	27♑
1926	26	10♐	23	07♑	21	06♒	21	06♓	22	07♈	21	06♉	20	03♊	16♊
1927	15	29	14♉	28	11♊	25	08♋	21	04♌	17	29	11♍	23	05♎	17♎
1928	11♍	24	07♎	19	02♏	14	25	07♐	19	01♑	13	26	09♒	22	05♓
1929	15	27	09♒	21	04♓	16	29	21♈	25	08♉	22	06♊	20	04♋	19♋
1930	17	00♊	14	28	12♋	27	12♌	27	13♍	28	12♎	27	10♏	24	06♐
1931	06♎	21	05♏	19	03♐	16	00♑	12	25	07♒	20	02♓	14	26	07♈
1932	02♓	14	27	09♈	21	03♉	15	27	09♊	21	03♋	16	29	12♌	26♌
1933	05♋	17	29	12♌	24	07♍	20	03♎	17	00♏	14	28	12♐	27	11♑
1934	08♏	22	05♐	19	03♑	18	03♒	18	03♓	18	03♈	17	01♉	14	27♉
1935	28	13♈	27	11♉	25	08♊	21	04♋	16	28	10♌	22	04♍	16	27♍
1936	22	04♍	17	29	11♎	23	05♏	16	28	21♐	23	06♑	19	02♒	16♒
1937	25	07♑	19	02♒	14	28	11♓	25	09♈	23	07♉	21	05♊	19	03♋
1938	00♉	13	27	11♊	25	09♋	24	09♌	24	09♍	23	07♎	21	04♏	17♏
1939	19	04♎	18	02♏	16	29	12♐	24	06♑	18	00♒	12	24	06♓	18♓
1940	13	25	07♓	19	01♈	13	24	06♉	18	00♊	13	26	09♋	23	07♌
1941	14	27	09♋	22	05♌	18	02♍	16	00♎	14	28	13♏	27	11♐	25♐
1942	21	05♏	19	03♐	17	01♑	16	01♒	15	00♓	14	27	11♈	24	07♉
1943	09♓	24	09♈	23	06♉	20	02♊	15	27	09♋	21	03♌	14	26	08♍
1944	03♌	15	27	09♍	21	03♎	14	26	08♏	21	03♐	16	29	13♑	27♑
1945	04♐	16	29	12♑	25	08♒	22	07♓	21	06♈	21	05♉	20	04♊	18♊
1946	13	27	11♉	25	09♊	24	08♋	22	06♌	20	04♍	18	01♎	14	27♎
1947	00♍	15	29	13♎	27	10♏	23	05♐	17	29	11♑	22	04♒	16	28♒
1948	23	05♒	17	29	11♓	23	05♈	17	29	11♉	24	07♊	20	04♋	18♋
1949	24	06♊	19	02♋	15	29	13♌	28	13♍	27	12♎	27	11♏	25	09♐
1950	05♎	19	03♏	17	02♐	16	00♑	14	28	12♒	25	08♓	21	04♈	16♈
1951	21	06♓	20	03♈	17	00♉	12	25	07♊	19	01♋	12	24	06♌	19♌
1952	14	26	08♌	19	01♍	13	25	07♎	20	02♏	15	28	11♐	25	09♑
1953	14	26	09♐	22	05♑	19	03♒	18	03♓	18	03♈	18	03♉	17	01♊
1954	27	11♈	26	10♉	24	08♊	22	06♋	19	03♌	16	29	11♍	24	06♎
1955	12♌	26	10♍	24	07♎	20	02♏	15	30	08♐	20	02♑	14	26	09♒
1956	04♑	16	28	10♒	22	04♓	16	28	11♈	23	06♉	19	03♊	17	01♋
1957	04♉	16	29	12♊	26	10♋	24	09♌	24	09♍	25	10♎	24	08♏	22♏
1958	18	03♎	18	02♏	16	00♐	14	27	11♑	24	07♒	19	02♓	14	26♓
1959	03♒	17	01♓	14	27	10♈	22	04♉	16	28	10♊	22	04♋	16	29♋
1960	24	06♋	18	00♌	12	24	06♍	19	02♎	14	28	11♏	25	09♐	23♐
1961	24	07♏	20	03♐	17	01♑	15	00♒	15	00♓	15	00♈	15	29	13♉
1962	09♊	24	09♈	24	08♉	22	06♊	19	02♋	15	28	10♌	22	04♍	16♍
1963	24	08♌	21	04♍	17	29	12♎	24	06♏	18	29	11♐	23	06♑	18♑
1964	14	26	08♑	20	02♒	14	27	10♓	23	06♈	20	03♉	17	01♊	15♊
1965	16	28	11♉	24	08♊	22	06♋	21	06♌	21	06♍	21	06♎	20	04♏
1966	00♏	16	01♐	15	00♏	14	27	11♐	23	06♑	18	01♒	13	25	07♓
1967	16	29	12♒	25	07♓	19	02♈	14	25	07♉	19	01♊	13	26	08♋
1968	04♊	15	27	10♋	22	04♌	17	00♍	14	27	11♎	25	09♏	23	07♐
1969	06♎	19	02♏	16	29	13♐	28	12♑	27	12♒	27	12♓	26	10♈	24♈
1970	21	06♓	22	06♈	21	05♉	18	02♊	14	27	09♋	21	03♍	15	27♌
1971	07♋	20	03♌	15	27	09♍	21	03♎	15	27	09♏	21	03♐	16	28♐
1972	23	05♐	17	29	12♑	24	07♒	21	04♓	18	03♈	17	01♉	16	00♊
1973	28	11♈	24	08♉	22	06♊	20	04♋	19	03♌	18	02♍	16	00♎	14♎
1974	12♌	27	12♍	27	12♎	26	09♏	22	05♐	17	29	11♑	23	05♒	17♒
1975	28	11♑	23	06♒	18	00♓	12	24	05♈	17	29	11♉	23	06♊	19♊
1976	12	25	07♊	19	01♋	14	28	11♌	25	10♍	24	09♎	23	08♏	22♏
1977	19	02♎	16	00♏	14	28	12♐	26	11♑	25	09♒	23	07♓	21	04♈
1978	03♒	18	03♓	18	02♈	16	29	12♉	25	07♊	20	02♋	13	25	07♌
1979	19	02♋	14	26	08♌	20	02♍	14	25	07♎	19	01♏	14	26	09♐
1980	02♏	14	26	09♐	21	04♑	18	02♒	16	00♓	15	00♈	15	00♉	14♉
1981	10♓	24	08♈	22	06♉	20	05♊	19	03♋	17	01♌	14	28	11♍	24♍
1982	24	09♌	24	08♍	22	06♎	20	03♏	15	27	09♐	21	03♑	15	27♑
1983	10♐	22	05♑	16	28	10♒	22	04♓	16	28	10♈	22	05♉	18	01♊
1984	22	04♉	16	29	11♊	24	08♋	22	06♌	21	06♍	21	06♎	21	06♏
1985	01♍	15	00♎	14	28	13♏	27	11♐	25	08♑	22	05♒	18	01♓	14♓
1986	16	00♒	15	29	13♓	26	10♈	22	05♉	17	29	11♊	23	05♋	17♋
1987	01♊	13	25	07♋	19	01♌	12	24	06♍	18	01♎	13	26	09♏	22♏
1988	12	24	07♏	19	02♐	15	28	13♑	27	12♒	27	12♓	27	12♈	27♈
1989	22	06♓	21	06♈	20	05♉	19	03♊	17	01♋	14	27	09♌	22	04♍

September

	1st	2nd	3rd	4th	5th	6th	7th	8th	9th	10th	11th	12th	13th	14th	15th	16th
1900	22♏	05♐	17	00♑	14	28	12♒	27	12♓	28	13♈	28	12♉	27	10♊	24
1901	06♈	21	05♉	20	04♊	18	02♋	15	29	12♌	25	08♍	20	03♎	15	27
1902	21♌	05♍	19	02♎	16	28	11♏	23	05♐	17	29	10♑	23	05♒	17	00♓
1903	01♑	13	25	07♒	18	00♓	13	25	07♈	20	03♉	16	29	12♊	26	10♋
1904	13♉	25	08♊	21	05♋	19	03♌	18	03♍	18	03♎	18	03♏	17	01♐	15
1905	27♍	12♎	27	12♏	26	10♐	24	07♑	20	03♒	16	28	11♓	23	05♈	17
1906	12♒	26	09♓	22	05♈	18	00♉	13	25	06♊	18	00♋	12	25	07♌	20
1907	21♊	03♋	15	26	08♌	20	03♍	15	28	11♎	24	07♏	21	05♐	19	03♑
1908	02♏	16	29	12♐	26	10♑	24	09♒	24	09♓	24	09♈	24	08♉	22	05♊
1909	19♓	04♈	19	04♉	18	02♊	15	29	12♋	24	07♌	19	01♍	13	25	07♎
1910	04♌	17	00♍	13	26	08♎	20	02♏	14	26	08♐	20	02♑	14	27	10♒
1911	10♐	22	04♑	16	28	10♒	23	06♓	19	02♈	15	29	13♉	27	11♊	25
1912	25♈	07♉	20	04♊	17	10♋	16	00♌	15	00♍	15	00♎	14	28	12♏	25
1913	09♍	25	10♎	24	09♏	23	07♐	20	03♑	15	28	10♒	22	03♓	15	27
1914	25♑	08♒	21	03♓	16	28	10♈	22	04♉	16	28	10♊	22	04♋	17	00♌
1915	00♊	12	24	06♋	18	00♌	13	26	09♍	23	06♎	21	05♏	19	03♐	18
1916	16♎	29	12♏	25	09♐	23	07♑	22	06♒	21	06♓	20	05♈	19	02♉	15
1917	00♊	15	01♈	16	00♉	14	28	11♊	23	06♋	18	00♌	12	24	05♍	17
1918	16♋	29	12♌	24	06♍	18	00♎	12	24	06♏	18	00♐	12	24	07♑	20
1919	20♏	01♐	13	25	07♑	20	03♒	16	00♓	14	28	12♈	27	11♉	26	10♊
1920	07♈	20	04♉	17	01♊	15	29	14♋	28	13♌	27	11♍	25	09♎	22	05♏
1921	21♌	06♍	21	06♎	21	04♏	18	01♐	14	26	08♑	20	02♒	14	26	08♓
1922	08♑	20	02♒	15	27	09♓	20	02♈	14	26	08♉	20	02♊	15	28	11♋
1923	09♉	21	03♊	15	27	10♋	23	06♌	20	04♍	19	03♎	18	03♏	17	02♐
1924	28♍	12♎	25	09♏	24	08♐	22	06♑	20	04♒	18	02♓	16	29	12♈	25
1925	12♒	27	12♓	26	11♈	25	08♉	21	04♊	16	28	10♋	22	04♌	22	28
1926	29♊	11♋	23	05♌	17	29	11♍	22	04♎	16	28	11♏	23	06♐	19	02♑
1927	29♎	11♏	23	05♐	17	00♑	13	26	10♒	24	09♓	24	09♈	24	09♉	24
1928	19♓	03♈	18	02♉	16	00♊	14	28	12♋	26	10♌	23	07♍	20	03♎	15
1929	04♌	18	03♍	17	01♎	15	28	11♏	24	06♐	18	00♑	11	23	05♒	18
1930	19♐	01♑	13	28	07♒	19	01♓	13	25	07♈	19	01♉	14	27	10♊	23
1931	19♈	01♉	13	25	07♊	20	03♋	17	01♌	15	00♍	15	00♎	15	00♏	15
1932	10♍	24	09♎	23	08♏	22	07♐	21	5♑	18	02♒	15	28	10♓	23	05♈
1933	25♑	10♒	24	08♓	22	05♈	18	01♉	13	25	08♊	19	01♋	13	25	07♌
1934	09♊	22	04♋	15	27	09♌	21	03♍	15	27	10♎	22	05♏	18	02♐	15
1935	09♎	21	03♏	16	28	11♐	24	07♑	21	06♒	21	06♓	21	06♈	21	06♉
1936	01♊	15	00♈	15	00♉	15	29	13♊	27	10♋	23	06♌	18	01♍	13	25
1937	17♋	01♌	15	29	12♍	25	08♎	21	03♏	15	27	09♐	21	03♑	15	27
1938	29♏	11♐	23	05♑	17	29	11♒	23	05♓	18	01♈	14	27	10♉	24	07♊
1939	00♈	12	25	06♉	19	02♊	15	28	12♋	27	12♌	27	12♍	27	12♎	27
1940	22♌	06♍	21	06♎	21	06♏	20	04♐	18	01♑	14	27	09♒	22	04♓	16
1941	09♑	23	06♒	20	03♓	16	28	11♈	23	05♉	17	28	10♊	22	05♋	17
1942	19♉	01♊	13	25	07♋	19	01♌	13	26	08♍	21	04♎	18	02♏	16	00♐
1943	20♍	02♎	15	27	10♏	23	06♐	20	04♑	18	03♒	18	03♓	18	02♈	17
1944	12♒	27	12♓	27	12♈	27	12♉	26	10♊	23	05♋	18	00♌	12	24	06♍
1945	01♋	15	28	11♌	23	06♍	18	01♎	13	25	07♏	18	00♐	12	24	07♑
1946	09♏	21	03♐	15	26	08♑	20	03♒	15	29	12♓	26	09♈	24	08♉	22
1947	11♓	23	06♈	19	02♉	15	28	12♊	26	10♋	25	09♌	24	09♍	23	08♎
1948	03♌	18	03♍	18	04♎	18	03♏	17	00♐	13	26	08♑	20	03♒	14	26
1949	23♐	06♑	19	02♒	14	27	09♓	21	03♈	15	26	08♉	20	02♊	14	27
1950	28♈	10♉	22	04♊	16	28	10♋	23	06♌	19	02♍	16	00♎	15	29	14♏
1951	01♍	14	27	10♎	23	06♏	20	04♐	18	02♑	17	01♒	16	00♓	14	28
1952	24♑	09♒	24	09♓	24	09♈	23	07♉	21	04♊	16	29	11♋	23	05♌	16
1953	15♊	28	10♋	23	05♌	17	29	11♍	23	05♎	17	28	10♏	23	05♐	17
1954	18♎	00♏	12	24	06♐	18	00♑	12	25	09♒	23	07♓	21	06♈	21	06♉
1955	21♒	04♓	17	01♈	15	29	13♉	27	11♊	25	09♋	23	07♌	21	05♍	19
1956	15♋	00♌	15	00♍	15	29	14♎	28	11♏	24	06♐	19	01♑	13	24	06♒
1957	05♐	18	01♑	13	26	08♒	20	01♓	13	25	07♈	19	01♉	13	26	08♊
1958	08♈	20	02♉	14	25	08♊	20	03♋	16	29	13♌	27	12♍	27	12♎	26
1959	12♌	25	08♍	22	06♎	20	04♏	19	03♐	17	01♑	15	29	13♒	26	09♓
1960	07♑	22	06♒	21	06♓	20	04♈	17	01♉	14	26	08♊	20	02♋	14	26
1961	26♉	09♊	22	04♋	16	28	10♌	22	03♍	15	27	09♎	22	04♏	17	00♐
1962	28♍	10♎	22	04♏	16	28	10♐	23	06♑	19	03♒	18	03♓	18	03♈	18
1963	01♒	15	29	13♓	27	12♈	26	11♉	25	10♊	24	07♋	21	04♌	17	00♍
1964	29♊	14♋	28	12♌	26	10♍	24	08♎	21	04♏	16	28	10♐	22	04♑	16
1965	17♏	00♐	12	24	06♑	18	00♒	12	24	06♓	18	00♈	13	25	08♉	21
1966	18♊	00♈	12	24	06♉	18	01♊	13	26	10♋	24	09♌	24	09♍	24	09♎
1967	22♋	05♌	19	04♍	18	03♎	18	03♏	17	01♐	15	29	13♑	26	09♒	21
1968	22♐	06♑	20	04♒	18	02♓	15	28	11♈	23	06♉	18	00♊	11	23	06♋
1969	07♉	19	02♊	14	26	08♋	20	02♌	14	26	08♍	21	03♎	16	29	13♏
1970	09♍	20	02♎	14	26	09♏	21	04♐	18	01♑	15	00♒	15	00♓	15	00♈
1971	12♑	25	10♒	24	09♓	24	09♈	24	09♉	23	07♊	21	04♋	17	00♌	12
1972	14♊	28	12♋	26	09♌	22	05♍	18	01♎	13	25	07♏	19	01♐	13	25
1973	27♎	09♏	22	04♐	16	28	09♑	21	03♒	16	28	11♓	24	07♈	21	05♉
1974	29♒	11♓	23	05♈	18	00♉	13	26	09♊	23	07♋	21	06♌	21	06♍	21
1975	02♋	16	00♌	15	00♍	15	00♎	15	00♏	15	29	12♐	25	08♑	20	03♒
1976	06♐	20	04♑	17	00♒	13	26	09♓	21	03♈	15	27	09♉	21	03♊	15
1977	17♈	29	11♉	23	05♊	17	29	11♋	23	06♌	18	01♍	15	28	12♎	26
1978	19♌	01♍	13	26	08♎	21	04♏	17	01♐	15	29	13♑	28	12♒	27	12♓
1979	23♐	07♑	21	06♒	21	06♓	21	06♈	21	05♉	19	03♊	16	29	11♋	23
1980	28♉	12♊	26	09♋	22	05♌	17	29	11♍	23	05♎	17	29	11♏	23	05♐
1981	06♎	19	01♏	13	25	07♐	19	01♑	13	25	08♒	21	05♓	19	03♈	18
1982	09♒	21	04♓	16	29	12♈	26	09♉	23	07♊	21	05♋	19	04♌	18	03♍
1983	14♊	28	12♋	27	11♌	27	12♍	27	12♎	26	10♏	23	06♐	19	01♑	13
1984	20♏	04♐	17	00♑	13	25	08♒	20	02♓	14	26	08♈	19	01♉	13	25
1985	27♊	09♈	21	03♉	15	26	08♊	20	03♋	15	28	02♌	25	10♍	24	09♎
1986	29♋	11♌	24	07♍	20	04♎	17	01♏	15	29	13♐	27	12♑	26	10♒	24
1987	06♐	19	04♑	18	03♒	18	03♓	18	02♈	16	00♉	13	26	09♊	21	03♋
1988	11♉	25	08♊	21	04♋	16	28	09♌	21	03♍	16	28	09♎	21	03♏	16
1989	17♍	29	11♎	22	04♏	16	28	10♐	23	05♑	18	02♒	16	00♓	15	00♈

	17th	18th	19th	20th	21st	22nd	23rd	24th	25th	26th	27th	28th	29th	30th
1900	07♋	19	02♌	14	26	08♍	10	02♎	14	26	07♏	19	01♐	14♐
1901	09♏	20	02♐	14	26	08♑	21	04♒	18	01♓	16	00♈	15	00♉
1902	13	27	10♈	24	08♉	22	06♊	20	05♋	19	03♌	17	01♍	14♍
1903	25	10♌	24	09♍	24	08♎	22	06♏	19	02♐	15	27	09♑	21♑
1904	28	10♑	22	05♒	17	28	10♓	22	04♈	16	28	10♉	22	05♊
1905	28	10♉	22	04♊	16	29	11♋	24	08♌	22	06♍	21	06♎	21♎
1906	03♍	17	01♎	15	00♏	14	29	13♐	27	11♑	25	09♒	22	05♓
1907	17	01♒	16	00♓	14	29	13♈	26	09♉	22	05♊	17	29	11♋
1908	18	01♋	13	25	07♌	18	00♍	12	24	06♎	18	01♏	13	26♏
1909	19	01♏	12	24	07♐	19	02♑	15	28	12♒	27	12♓	17	12♈
1910	24	08♊	22	07♈	21	06♉	21	05♊	19	03♋	17	00♌	14	27♌
1911	09♋	23	08♌	22	06♍	20	03♎	16	29	12♏	24	06♐	18	00♑
1912	08♐	20	03♑	15	27	08♒	20	02♓	14	27	09♈	22	04♉	17♉
1913	09♈	21	03♉	15	27	10♊	23	06♋	19	03♌	18	03♍	18	03♎
1914	14	18	12♍	27	12♎	27	12♏	27	11♐	25	09♑	22	05♒	10♒
1915	02♑	16	00♒	13	27	10♓	24	07♈	19	02♉	14	26	08♊	20♊
1916	28	11♊	23	05♋	16	28	10♌	22	04♍	17	29	12♎	25	09♏
1917	29	11♎	23	06♏	18	01♐	14	27	10♑	24	09♒	24	09♓	24♓
1918	04♒	18	03♓	18	03♈	19	04♉	18	03♊	17	00♋	13	26	09♌
1919	24	08♋	22	05♌	18	02♍	14	27	10♎	22	04♏	16	28	10♐
1920	18	00♐	12	24	06♑	18	00♒	12	24	07♓	20	03♈	17	00♉
1921	20	02♈	14	27	09♉	22	05♊	19	02♋	16	01♌	15	00♍	15♍
1922	25	09♌	24	09♍	24	09♎	24	09♏	24	08♐	21	04♑	17	29♑
1923	16	00♑	14	27	10♒	23	05♓	18	00♈	12	24	06♉	18	29♉
1924	07♉	20	02♊	14	26	07♋	19	02♌	14	27	10♍	23	07♎	21♎
1925	10♍	22	05♎	17	00♏	14	27	11♐	25	09♑	23	07♒	21	06♓
1926	16	00♒	14	29	15♓	00♈	15	00♉	14	28	12♊	25	08♋	20♋
1927	08♊	22	05♋	18	01♌	14	26	08♍	20	02♎	14	26	08♏	20♏
1928	27	10♏	21	03♐	15	27	09♑	21	04♒	17	00♓	14	28	12♈
1929	00♊	13	25	09♈	22	05♉	19	03♊	17	01♋	15	29	14♌	28♌
1930	07♋	21	06♌	21	06♍	21	06♎	20	05♏	19	02♐	15	28	10♑
1931	29	13♐	26	09♑	22	05♒	17	29	11♓	23	04♈	16	28	10♉
1932	17	29	11♉	23	05♊	17	29	11♋	24	07♌	20	04♍	18	03♎
1933	20	03♍	16	29	13♎	27	11♏	25	09♐	23	08♑	22	06♒	20♒
1934	29	13♑	28	12♒	27	12♓	26	11♈	25	09♉	22	05♊	18	00♋
1935	20	04♊	17	00♋	13	25	07♌	19	01♍	13	25	06♎	18	00♏
1936	07♎	19	01♏	13	25	07♐	19	01♑	14	27	10♒	24	09♓	24♓
1937	10♒	23	06♓	20	04♈	18	03♉	17	01♊	16	00♋	14	28	11♌
1938	21	05♋	20	04♌	19	03♍	18	02♎	16	29	12♏	25	07♐	19♐
1939	11♏	24	08♐	21	03♑	15	27	09♒	21	03♓	15	27	09♈	21♈
1940	28	09♈	21	03♉	15	27	09♊	22	04♋	18	01♌	15	00♍	15♍
1941	00♌	13	26	10♍	25	09♎	24	08♏	23	08♐	22	06♑	20	03♒
1942	14	28	12♑	26	10♒	25	08♓	22	06♈	19	02♉	15	27	08♊
1943	01♉	15	28	11♊	23	05♋	17	29	11♌	23	05♍	17	29	11♎
1944	18	00♎	11	23	05♏	18	00♐	12	25	08♑	22	06♒	20	05♓
1945	19	03♒	16	01♓	15	00♈	15	00♉	15	00♊	14	28	12♋	25♋
1946	06♊	20	04♋	18	02♌	16	00♍	13	26	09♎	22	05♏	17	29♏
1947	22	05♏	18	01♐	13	25	07♑	19	01♒	13	25	07♓	19	02♈
1948	08♊	20	02♈	14	26	08♉	21	03♊	16	00♋	13	27	12♌	27♌
1949	10♋	23	07♌	21	06♍	21	06♎	21	06♏	21	06♐	19	03♑	16♑
1950	28	13♐	27	11♑	24	08♒	21	04♓	17	00♈	12	24	06♉	18♉
1951	12♈	25	08♉	20	00♊	15	27	09♋	20	02♌	15	27	09♍	22♍
1952	28	10♍	22	04♎	17	29	12♏	25	08♐	21	05♑	19	03♒	18♒
1953	00♑	14	27	12♒	26	11♓	27	12♈	27	12♉	27	11♊	24	07♋
1954	21	05♊	19	03♋	16	29	12♌	25	08♍	20	02♎	15	27	08♏
1955	02♎	15	28	10♏	22	04♐	16	28	10♑	22	04♒	17	29	13♓
1956	18	00♓	12	25	08♈	20	03♉	16	00♊	13	27	11♋	25	10♌
1957	21	05♋	19	03♌	18	03♍	18	03♎	18	03♏	17	01♐	14	27♐
1958	12♏	26	11♐	24	08♑	21	04♒	16	29	11♓	23	05♈	17	29♈
1959	22	05♈	18	00♉	12	24	06♊	18	00♋	12	24	07♌	20	03♍
1960	08♌	20	03♍	15	28	11♎	24	08♏	22	05♐	20	04♑	18	02♒
1961	13	26	10♑	24	09♒	24	08♓	23	08♈	23	07♉	21	05♊	18♊
1962	03♉	18	02♊	16	29	12♋	25	07♌	19	01♍	13	25	07♎	19♎
1963	13	25	08♎	20	02♏	14	26	07♐	19	01♑	14	26	09♒	23♒
1964	28	10♒	22	05♓	18	02♈	16	00♉	14	28	12♊	26	10♋	24♋
1965	04♊	18	02♋	16	00♌	15	00♍	15	29	14♎	28	12♏	25	08♐
1966	24	09♏	23	07♐	20	03♑	15	28	10♒	22	04♓	15	27	09♈
1967	04♓	16	28	10♈	22	04♉	16	27	09♊	21	04♋	17	00♌	13♌
1968	17	00♌	12	26	09♍	23	07♎	21	05♏	20	04♐	18	03♑	18♑
1969	26	10♐	24	08♑	23	07♒	21	06♓	21	04♈	18	01♉	15	27♉
1970	15	29	13♉	27	11♊	23	06♋	18	00♌	12	24	05♍	17	29♍
1971	24	06♍	18	00♎	12	24	06♏	18	00♐	12	24	07♑	20	04♒
1972	07♑	19	02♒	15	29	13♓	27	12♈	27	12♉	26	11♊	25	09♋
1973	19	03♊	17	01♋	15	29	13♌	27	11♍	25	09♎	22	05♏	17♏
1974	05♎	20	04♏	18	01♐	13	26	08♑	20	02♒	13	25	07♓	20♓
1975	15	27	09♓	21	02♈	14	26	08♉	20	02♊	15	28	11♋	25♋
1976	27	09♋	22	06♌	19	04♍	18	03♎	18	03♏	18	02♐	17	01♑
1977	10♏	24	09♐	23	07♑	21	05♒	19	03♓	16	29	12♈	25	07♉
1978	26	10♈	24	07♉	21	03♊	16	28	10♋	22	03♌	15	27	10♍
1979	05♌	17	29	11♍	22	04♎	16	29	11♏	23	06♐	19	03♑	16♑
1980	17	00♑	13	26	10♒	24	08♓	23	09♈	24	09♉	24	08♊	22♊
1981	02♉	17	01♊	16	00♋	14	27	11♌	24	07♍	20	02♎	15	27♎
1982	17	01♎	14	28	11♏	23	05♐	17	29	11♑	23	05♒	17	29♒
1983	25	07♒	19	01♓	13	25	07♈	19	02♉	15	28	11♊	24	08♋
1984	08♊	20	03♋	16	00♌	15	29	14♍	00♎	15	00♏	15	29	13♐
1985	24	09♏	23	04♐	22	05♑	19	02♒	15	28	11♓	23	05♈	17♈
1986	08♓	21	05♈	18	00♉	13	25	07♊	19	01♋	13	25	07♌	19♌
1987	15	27	09♌	21	03♍	15	27	10♎	23	06♏	19	02♐	16	00♑
1988	28	11♐	24	08♑	21	06♒	20	05♓	20	06♈	21	05♉	20	04♊
1989	15	00♉	15	29	14♊	27	11♋	24	07♌	19	01♍	13	25	07♎

October

	1st	2nd	3rd	4th	5th	6th	7th	8th	9th	10th	11th	12th	13th	14th	15th	16th
1900	26♐	09♑	23	06♒	21	05♓	21	06♈	21	06♉	21	05♊	19	03♋	16	29
1901	15♉	00♊	14	28	12♋	26	09♌	22	05♍	17	29	11♎	23	05♏	17	29
1902	28♍	11♎	24	06♏	19	01♐	13	25	06♑	18	00♒	13	25	08♓	21	05♈
1903	03♒	15	27♓	09♓	21	04♈	16	29	12♉	26	09♊	23	07♋	21	05♌	20
1904	18♊	01♋	14	28	12♌	27	12♍	27	12♎	27	11♏	26	10♐	23	06♑	19
1905	06♏	21	06♐	20	04♑	17	00♒	13	25	08♓	20	02♈	13	25	07♉	19
1906	18♊	01♈	14	26	09♉	21	03♊	14	26	08♋	20	02♌	15	28	11♍	25
1907	23♋	04♌	16	29	11♍	24	07♎	20	04♏	17	01♐	15	29	14♑	28	12♒
1908	09♐	22	06♑	19	04♒	18	03♓	18	03♈	17	02♉	16	00♊	13	26	09♋
1909	27♈	12♉	27	11♊	25	08♋	21	04♌	16	28	10♍	22	04♎	16	28	10♏
1910	09♍	22	04♎	17	29	11♏	22	04♐	16	28	10♑	22	05♒	18	02♓	16
1911	12♑	24	06♒	18	01♓	14	27	11♈	25	09♉	23	07♊	22	06♋	20	04♌
1912	01♊	14	28	12♋	26	10♌	25	09♍	24	08♎	22	06♏	20	03♐	16	29
1913	18♎	03♏	18	02♐	16	29	12♑	24	07♒	19	00♓	12	24	06♈	18	00♉
1914	00♓	13	25	07♈	19	01♉	12	24	06♊	18	00♋	13	25	08♌	22	06♍
1915	02♋	14	26	08♌	21	04♍	17	01♎	15	00♏	15	29	14♐	28	13♑	26
1916	22♏	06♐	20	04♑	18	02♒	16	01♓	15	29	13♈	27	10♉	23	06♊	18
1917	09♈	24	08♉	22	06♊	19	02♋	14	27	09♌	20	02♍	14	26	08♎	20
1918	21♌	03♍	15	27	09♎	21	03♏	15	26	08♐	21	03♑	16	29	13♒	27
1919	21♐	03♑	15	28	11♒	24	08♓	22	06♈	21	06♉	21	06♊	20	04♋	18
1920	14♉	28	12♊	26	10♋	25	09♌	23	07♍	21	04♎	17	00♏	13	26	08♐
1921	00♎	14	29	12♏	26	09♐	22	04♑	16	28	10♒	22	04♓	16	28	11♈
1922	12♒	24	06♓	17	29	11♈	23	05♉	17	29	12♊	24	07♋	20	04♌	18
1923	11♊	23	06♋	18	01♌	14	28	12♍	27	12♎	27	12♏	27	12♐	26	10♑
1924	05♏	20	04♐	19	03♑	17	01♒	15	28	12♓	25	08♈	21	03♉	16	28
1925	20♓	05♈	19	03♉	16	29	12♊	24	06♋	18	00♌	12	24	06♍	18	01♎
1926	02♌	14	26	07♍	19	01♎	13	25	08♏	20	03♐	16	29	12♑	25	09♒
1927	02♐	14	26	08♑	21	04♒	18	03♓	17	03♈	18	03♉	18	03♊	17	01♋
1928	27♈	12♉	26	11♊	25	09♋	23	07♌	20	03♍	16	29	11♎	24	06♏	18
1929	12♍	26	10♎	23	06♏	19	01♐	14	26	08♑	19	01♒	13	26	08♓	21
1930	22♑	04♒	16	28	10♓	22	04♈	16	28	11♉	24	07♊	20	04♋	18	02♌
1931	22♉	04♊	16	29	12♋	26	09♌	24	08♍	23	08♎	24	09♏	24	08♐	22
1932	18♎	03♏	18	03♐	17	01♑	15	29	12♒	25	07♓	20	02♈	14	26	08♉
1933	03♓	17	00♈	13	26	09♉	21	03♊	15	27	09♋	21	03♌	15	28	11♍
1934	12♋	24	06♌	17	29	11♍	24	06♎	19	02♏	15	29	12♐	26	10♑	24
1935	13♏	25	08♐	20	03♑	17	00♒	15	29	14♓	29	14♈	00♉	14	29	13♊
1936	09♈	24	09♉	24	09♊	23	07♋	20	03♌	16	28	10♍	22	04♎	16	28
1937	25♌	08♍	21	04♎	17	29	11♏	23	05♐	17	29	11♑	23	05♒	18	01♓
1938	01♑	13	25	07♒	19	01♓	14	27	10♈	23	06♉	20	04♊	18	02♋	16
1939	03♉	16	29	12♊	25	08♋	22	07♌	21	06♍	21	06♎	20	05♏	19	03♐
1940	00♎	15	00♏	15	00♐	14	28	11♑	24	06♒	19	01♓	13	25	06♈	18
1941	16♒	29	12♓	25	07♈	19	01♉	13	25	07♊	19	01♋	13	25	08♌	21
1942	21♊	03♋	15	27	09♌	21	04♍	17	00♎	13	27	11♏	26	10♐	25	09♑
1943	24♎	07♏	20	03♐	17	01♑	14	29	13♒	27	12♓	26	11♈	25	09♉	23
1944	20♓	06♈	21	06♉	21	05♊	18	02♋	15	27	09♌	21	03♍	15	27	08♎
1945	08♌	20	03♍	15	27	09♎	21	03♏	15	27	09♐	21	03♑	15	28	11♒
1946	11♐	22	04♑	16	28	11♓	23	07♓	20	04♈	18	03♉	18	02♊	17	01♋
1947	15♈	28	12♉	25	09♊	23	07♋	21	05♌	19	04♍	18	02♎	16	00♏	13
1948	12♍	27	12♎	26	11♏	25	09♐	22	05♑	17	29	11♒	23	05♓	17	29
1949	29♑	11♒	24	06♓	18	00♈	12	23	05♉	17	29	11♊	23	06♋	19	02♌
1950	00♊	12	24	06♋	18	01♌	14	27	10♍	24	09♎	24	09♏	23	08♐	23
1951	06♎	19	03♏	17	01♐	15	29	13♑	28	12♒	26	09♓	23	07♈	20	03♉
1952	03♓	17	02♈	17	01♉	15	29	12♊	25	07♋	19	01♌	13	25	07♍	18
1953	20♋	02♌	14	26	08♍	20	02♎	14	26	08♏	20	02♐	14	27	10♑	23
1954	20♏	02♐	14	26	08♑	21	03♒	17	01♓	15	00♈	15	00♉	15	00♊	15
1955	26♓	10♈	24	09♉	23	07♊	22	06♋	20	04♌	17	01♍	15	28	11♎	24
1956	24♌	09♍	23	08♎	22	06♏	19	02♐	14	27	09♑	21	02♒	14	26	08♓
1957	10♑	22	05♒	16	28	10♓	22	04♈	16	28	10♉	23	05♊	18	01♋	15
1958	10♉	22	04♊	16	28	11♋	24	07♌	21	06♍	20	05♎	21	06♏	21	06♐
1959	17♍	01♎	15	00♏	14	29	14♐	28	12♑	26	10♒	23	06♓	19	01♈	14
1960	16♒	01♓	15	28	12♈	26	09♉	22	04♊	16	28	10♋	22	04♌	16	28
1961	00♋	13	25	07♌	18	00♍	12	24	06♎	18	01♏	14	27	10♐	23	07♑
1962	01♏	13	25	07♐	19	02♑	15	28	12♒	26	11♓	26	11♈	27	12♉	27
1963	07♓	21	06♈	21	06♉	21	06♊	20	04♋	18	01♌	14	27	10♍	22	04♎
1964	08♌	22	06♍	20	03♎	16	29	12♏	24	06♐	18	00♑	12	23	05♒	18
1965	20♐	02♑	14	26	08♒	20	02♓	14	26	09♈	22	05♉	18	01♊	15	29
1966	21♈	03♉	15	28	10♊	23	06♋	19	03♌	18	02♍	17	02♎	17	02♏	17
1967	27♌	12♍	27	12♎	27	12♏	27	11♐	25	09♑	23	06♒	18	01♓	13	25
1968	01♒	14	28	11♓	24	07♈	19	01♉	14	26	08♊	19	01♋	13	25	08♌
1969	10♊	22	04♋	16	28	10♌	22	04♍	16	29	12♎	25	09♏	23	07♐	21
1970	11♎	24	06♏	19	01♐	14	28	11♑	25	09♒	24	08♓	23	08♈	23	07♉
1971	18♒	02♓	17	02♈	18	03♉	18	03♊	17	01♋	14	27	09♌	21	03♍	15
1972	23♋	06♌	19	02♍	15	27	09♎	22	04♏	16	28	09♐	21	03♑	15	27
1973	00♐	12	24	05♑	17	29	11♒	24	06♓	19	03♈	16	00♉	15	29	13♊
1974	02♈	14	27	10♉	23	06♊	20	03♋	17	01♌	16	00♍	15	29	14♎	29
1975	09♌	23	08♍	23	09♎	24	09♏	23	07♐	21	04♑	17	29	12♒	24	06♓
1976	14♑	27	10♒	23	06♓	18	00♈	12	24	06♉	18	29	11♊	23	05♋	18
1977	19♉	01♊	13	25	07♋	19	01♌	14	26	09♍	23	07♎	21	05♏	20	05♐
1978	22♍	05♎	18	01♏	14	28	12♐	25	10♑	24	08♒	22	07♓	21	05♈	19
1979	00♒	15	29	14♓	29	14♈	29	14♉	28	11♊	25	07♋	20	02♌	14	26
1980	06♋	19	02♌	14	26	08♍	20	02♎	14	26	08♏	20	02♐	14	26	09♑
1981	09♏	21	03♐	15	27	09♑	21	03♒	16	29	13♓	27	12♈	27	12♉	27
1982	12♓	25	08♈	22	06♉	20	04♊	18	02♋	16	00♌	14	28	12♍	26	09♎
1983	22♋	06♌	21	06♍	20	05♎	20	04♏	18	02♐	15	27	09♑	22	03♒	15
1984	27♐	10♑	22	05♒	17	29	11♓	23	05♈	16	28	10♉	22	04♊	17	00♋
1985	19♈	11♉	23	05♊	16	29	11♋	23	06♌	20	04♍	18	02♎	17	03♏	18
1986	02♍	15	29	13♎	27	11♏	25	10♐	24	08♑	23	07♒	20	04♓	17	00♈
1987	14♑	28	13♒	27	12♓	26	10♈	24	08♉	21	04♊	17	29	11♋	23	05♌
1988	17♊	00♋	13	25	07♌	19	01♍	13	25	06♎	18	01♏	13	25	08♐	21
1989	19♎	01♏	13	25	07♐	19	01♑	14	27	10♒	24	08♓	23	08♈	23	09♉

	17th	18th	19th	20th	21st	22nd	23rd	24th	25th	26th	27th	28th	29th	30th	31st
1900	11♌	23	05♍	17	29	11♎	23	04♏	16	29	11♐	23	06♑	19	02♒
1901	11♐	23	05♑	17	29	12♒	26	09♓	24	08♈	23	09♉	24	09♊	24♊
1902	19	03♉	18	02♊	17	01♋	16	00♌	14	27	11♍	24	07♎	20	02♏
1903	04♍	18	03♎	17	00♏	14	27	10♐	23	05♑	17	29	11♒	23	05♓
1904	01♒	13	25	07♓	19	01♈	13	25	07♉	19	02♊	15	28	11♋	24♋
1905	01♊	13	25	08♋	20	03♌	16	00♍	14	29	14♎	29	15♏	00♐	15♐
1906	09♎	24	09♏	24	09♐	23	08♑	22	06♒	19	02♓	15	28	10♈	23♈
1907	26	10♓	24	08♈	21	04♉	17	00♊	13	25	07♋	19	00♌	12	24♌
1908	21	03♌	15	27	09♍	21	03♎	15	27	10♏	23	06♐	19	03♑	16♑
1909	21	04♐	16	28	11♑	24	07♒	21	05♓	20	05♈	20	06♉	21	05♊
1910	00♈	15	00♉	15	00♊	15	29	13♋	27	11♌	24	06♍	19	01♎	13♎
1911	18	02♍	16	29	12♎	25	08♏	20	02♐	14	26	08♑	20	02♒	14♒
1912	11♑	23	05♒	17	28	10♓	23	05♈	18	00♉	14	27	11♊	25	08♋
1913	12	24	07♊	19	02♋	16	29	13♌	27	12♍	25	11♎	26	11♏	25♏
1914	20	05♎	20	06♏	21	06♐	21	05♑	19	02♒	15	27	10♓	22	04♈
1915	10♒	24	07♓	20	03♈	15	28	10♉	22	04♊	16	28	10♋	22	04♌
1916	01♋	12	24	06♌	18	00♍	12	25	08♎	21	05♏	18	02♐	17	01♑
1917	03♏	15	28	11♐	24	07♑	21	05♒	19	03♓	18	03♈	17	02♉	16♉
1918	11♓	26	11♈	27	12♉	27	12♊	26	09♋	23	05♌	18	00♍	12	24♍
1919	02♌	15	28	11♍	24	06♎	19	01♏	13	24	06♐	18	00♑	12	24♑
1920	20	02♑	14	26	08♒	20	02♓	15	28	11♈	25	09♉	23	08♊	24♊
1921	23	06♉	19	02♊	16	29	13♋	27	11♌	26	10♍	24	09♎	23	07♏
1922	02♍	17	02♎	17	02♏	17	02♐	16	00♑	13	26	08♒	20	02♓	14♓
1923	24	07♒	20	02♓	15	27	09♈	21	03♉	14	26	08♊	20	02♋	14♋
1924	10♊	22	04♋	15	27	09♌	22	05♍	18	01♎	15	00♏	15	29	14♐
1925	13	27	10♏	24	07♐	21	05♑	19	03♒	18	02♓	16	00♈	14	28♈
1926	24	08♓	23	08♈	23	08♉	23	07♊	20	03♋	16	28	10♌	22	04♍
1927	15	28	11♌	23	05♍	17	29	11♎	23	05♏	17	29	11♐	23	05♑
1928	00♐	11	23	05♑	17	29	12♒	25	08♓	22	06♈	21	06♉	21	06♊
1929	04♈	17	01♉	15	29	13♊	27	12♋	26	10♌	24	08♍	22	05♎	19♎
1930	16	00♍	15	00♎	14	29	13♏	26	10♐	23	06♑	18	00	12	24♒
1931	05♑	19	01♒	14	26	08♓	20	01♈	13	25	07♉	19	01♊	14	26♊
1932	20	01♊	13	25	07♋	20	02♌	15	28	12♍	26	11♎	26	11♏	27♏
1933	24	07♎	21	06♏	20♐	05♐	20	04♑	18	03♒	16	00♓	13	26	09♈
1934	08♒	22	07♓	21	05♈	19	03♉	17	00♊	13	26	08♋	20	02♌	13♌
1935	26	09♋	22	04♌	16	28	09♍	21	03♎	15	27	10♏	22	05♐	17♐
1936	10♏	22	04♐	16	28	10♑	23	05♒	19	03♓	17	02♈	17	02♉	18♉
1937	14	28	12♈	27	12♉	27	11♊	26	10♋	24	08♌	22	05♍	18	01♎
1938	00♌	15	29	13♍	27	11♎	24	07♏	20	03♐	15	22	09♑	21	03♒
1939	16	29	11♑	24	06♈	18	29	11♓	23	05♈	18	00♉	13	25	09♊
1940	00♉	12	24	06♊	18	01♋	14	27	10♌	24	08♍	23	08♎	23	08♏
1941	04♍	18	03♎	17	02♏	18	03♐	18	02♑	16	00♒	13	26	09♓	22♓
1942	23	07♒	21	05♓	18	01♈	15	27	10♉	23	05♊	17	29	11♋	23♋
1943	06♊	19	01♋	13	25	07♌	19	01♍	13	25	07♎	20	03♏	16	00♐
1944	20	03♏	15	27	09♐	22	05♑	18	02♒	15	00♓	14	29	14♈	29♈
1945	25	09♊	23	08♈	23	09♉	24	09♊	23	08♋	21	04♌	17	00♍	12♍
1946	15	29	13♌	26	10♍	23	06♎	18	01♏	13	25	07♐	19	00♑	12♑
1947	26	08♐	21	03♑	15	27	09♒	21	03♓	15	28	11♈	24	07♉	21♉
1948	11♈	23	05♉	18	00♊	13	27	10♋	24	08♌	22	06♍	21	05♎	20♎
1949	16	00♍	14	29	14♎	29	14♏	29	14♐	28	12♑	25	08♒	21	03♓
1950	07♑	21	05♒	18	01♓	14	26	09♈	21	03♉	15	27	09♊	21	02♋
1951	16	28	11♊	23	05♋	16	28	10♌	22	05♍	17	00♎	14	28	12♏
1952	01♎	13	26	09♏	22	05♐	18	02♑	16	00♒	14	28	12♓	27	11♈
1953	07♒	21	05♓	10	05♈	20	05♉	20	05♊	19	03♋	16	29	11♌	23♌
1954	29	13♋	26	09♌	22	05♍	17	29	11♎	23	05♏	17	29	11♐	23♐
1955	06♏	18	00♐	12	24	06♑	18	00♒	12	24	07♓	21	04♈	18	03♉
1956	21	03♈	16	29	13♉	26	10♊	24	08♋	22	06♌	21	05♍	19	03♎
1957	28	12♌	27	12♍	26	11♎	26	11♏	25	09♐	23	06♑	18	01♒	13♒
1958	20	04♑	17	01♒	13	26	08♓	20	02♈	14	26	07♉	19	01♊	13♊
1959	26	08♉	20	02♊	14	26	08♋	20	02♌	15	27	11♍	24	09♎	23♎
1960	11♍	23	06♎	20	03♏	18	02♐	16	00♑	15	29	13♒	27	11♓	24♓
1961	20	04♒	19	03♓	18	02♈	17	01♉	15	29	13♊	26	08♋	21	03♌
1962	11♊	25	08♋	21	04♌	16	28	10♍	22	04♎	16	28	10♏	22	04♐
1963	17	29	10♏	22	04♐	16	28	10♑	22	05♒	17	01♓	15	29	14♈
1964	00♓	13	27	10♈	24	09♉	23	08♊	23	07♋	21	05♌	19	03♍	16♍
1965	13♋	27	11♌	25	10♍	24	08♎	22	06♏	20	03♐	15	28	10♑	22♑
1966	01♐	15	28	11♑	24	06♒	18	00♓	12	24	06♈	18	00♉	12	25♉
1967	07♈	19	01♉	12	24	06♊	18	00♋	13	25	08♌	22	06♑	20	05♎
1968	20	03♍	17	01♎	15	00♏	14	29	14♐	29	13♑	27	11♒	25	08♓
1969	05♑	19	03♒	18	02♓	16	29	13♈	26	10♉	23	05♊	18	00♋	12♋
1970	22	05♊	19	02♋	14	26	08♌	20	02♍	14	26	08♎	20	03♏	15♏
1971	27	09♎	21	03♏	15	27	09♐	21	04♑	16	29	13♒	27	11♓	26♓
1972	10♒	23	07♓	21	05♈	20	05♉	21	06♊	21	05♋	19	03♌	16	29♌
1973	27	12♋	26	10♌	24	07♍	21	04♎	17	00♏	13	25	08♐	20	01♑
1974	12♏	26	09♐	21	04♑	16	28	10♒	22	04♓	16	28	10♈	23	06♉
1975	17	29	11♈	23	05♉	17	00♊	12	25	08♋	21	04♌	18	03♍	17♍
1976	01♌	14	28	12♍	26	11♎	26	11♏	26	11♐	26	10♑	24	07♒	20♒
1977	19	04♑	18	02♒	16	29	12♓	25	08♈	21	03♉	15	27	09♊	21♊
1978	02♉	15	28	11♊	23	06♋	18	29	11♌	23	05♍	18	00♎	13	26♎
1979	07♍	19	01♎	13	25	08♏	20	03♐	16	29	13♑	26	10♒	24	09♓
1980	21	05♒	18	02♓	17	02♈	17	02♉	17	02♊	17	01♋	15	28	11♌
1981	11♊	26	10♋	24	08♌	21	04♍	16	29	11♎	24	06♏	18	00♐	11♐
1982	23	06♏	19	01♐	13	25	07♑	19	01♒	13	25	07♓	20	03♈	17♈
1983	27	09♓	21	03♈	16	29	11♉	24	08♊	21	05♋	19	03♌	17	01♍
1984	12	26	09♌	24	08♍	23	08♎	23	08♏	23	07♐	21	05♑	18	01♒
1985	03♐	17	02♑	15	29	12♒	25	08♓	20	02♈	14	26	08♉	20	01♊
1986	13	26	09♉	21	03♊	15	27	09♋	20	03♌	15	27	10♍	23	07♎
1987	17	29	11♍	23	06♎	19	02♏	15	29	13♐	27	11♑	25	09♒	23♒
1988	04♑	17	01♒	15	00♓	14	29	14♈	29	13♉	28	12♊	25	09♋	21♋
1989	24	09♊	23	07♋	20	03♌	16	28	10♍	22	04♎	16	28	10♏	22♏

November

	1st	2nd	3rd	4th	5th	6th	7th	8th	9th	10th	11th	12th	13th	14th	15th	16th
1900	16♒	00♓	14	29	14♈	29	14♉	29	13♊	27	11♋	24	07♌	19	02♍	14
1901	08♋	22	06♌	19	02♍	14	26	08♎	20	02♏	14	26	08♐	19	01♑	14
1902	15♏	27	09♐	21	03♑	14	26	08♒	21	03♓	16	29	13♈	27	11♉	26
1903	17♓	29	12♈	25	08♉	22	06♊	20	04♋	18	02♌	16	01♍	15	28	12♎
1904	08♌	22	06♍	21	05♎	20	05♏	19	04♐	18	01♑	14	27	09♒	21	03♓
1905	29♐	13♑	27	10♒	22	05♓	17	29	10♈	22	04♉	16	28	10♊	22	05♋
1906	05♉	17	29	11♊	23	05♋	16	28	11♌	23	06♍	19	03♎	17	02♏	17
1907	06♍	19	02♎	15	29	13♏	27	11♐	26	10♑	24	09♒	23	07♓	20	04♈
1908	00♒	14	28	13♓	27	12♈	26	10♉	24	08♊	21	04♋	17	29	11♌	23
1909	20♊	04♋	17	00♌	13	25	07♍	19	01♎	13	25	06♏	18	01♐	13	25
1910	25♎	07♏	19	01♐	13	25	06♑	19	01♒	14	27	10♓	24	08♈	23	08♉
1911	26♒	09♓	22	05♈	19	03♉	18	02♊	17	02♋	16	01♌	15	29	12♍	26
1912	23♋	07♌	21	05♍	19	03♎	17	01♏	15	28	11♐	24	06♑	19	01♒	13
1913	10♐	24	07♑	20	03♒	15	27	09♓	21	02♈	14	26	09♉	21	04♊	16
1914	16♈	27	09♉	21	03♊	15	27	09♋	22	04♌	17	01♍	15	29	13♎	28
1915	16♌	29	12♍	25	09♎	24	08♏	23	09♐	24	08♑	23	07♒	21	04♓	17
1916	15♑	29	13♒	27	11♓	25	09♈	22	06♉	19	01♊	14	26	08♋	20	02♌
1917	00♊	14	27	10♋	23	05♌	17	29	10♍	22	04♎	16	29	11♏	24	07♐
1918	06♎	18	00♏	12	24	06♐	18	00♑	13	25	09♒	22	06♓	20	05♈	20
1919	06♒	19	02♓	16	00♈	14	29	14♉	29	15♊	29	14♋	28	12♌	25	08♍
1920	07♋	21	06♌	20	03♍	17	00♎	14	26	09♏	22	04♐	16	28	10♑	22
1921	20♏	04♐	17	00♑	12	24	06♒	18	00♓	12	24	06♈	19	01♉	15	28
1922	26♊	08♈	20	02♉	14	26	09♊	21	04♋	17	01♌	14	28	12♍	26	11♎
1923	27♋	10♌	23	06♍	20	05♎	20	05♏	20	05♐	21	05♑	19	03♒	16	29
1924	29♐	14♑	28	12♒	25	09♓	22	04♈	17	00♉	12	24	06♊	18	00♋	12
1925	11♉	24	07♊	20	02♋	14	26	08♌	20	01♍	14	26	09♎	22	05♏	19
1926	16♍	28	10♎	22	04♏	17	00♐	12	26	09♑	22	06♒	20	04♓	18	03♈
1927	18♑	00♒	14	27	11♓	26	11♈	26	11♉	26	11♊	26	10♋	24	07♌	20
1928	21♊	05♋	19	03♌	17	00♍	13	26	08♎	20	03♏	15	26	08♐	20	02♑
1929	02♏	14	27	09♐	22	04♑	15	27	09♒	21	03♓	16	29	12♈	25	09♉
1930	06♓	18	00♈	12	24	07♉	20	03♊	17	01♋	14	28	13♌	27	11♍	25
1931	09♋	22	05♌	19	03♍	17	02♎	17	02♏	17	02♐	16	00♑	14	27	10♒
1932	12♐	27	11♑	25	08♒	21	04♓	17	29	11♈	23	05♉	17	28	10♊	22
1933	22♈	05♉	17	29	12♊	24	05♋	17	29	11♌	23	06♍	18	02♎	15	00♏
1934	25♌	07♍	19	02♎	14	28	11♏	25	08♐	22	07♑	21	05♒	19	03♓	17
1935	00♑	13	27	11♒	25	09♓	23	08♈	23	08♉	22	07♊	21	04♋	17	00♌
1936	03♊	18	02♋	16	29	12♌	25	07♍	19	01♎	13	25	07♏	19	01♐	13
1937	13♎	26	08♏	20	02♐	13	25	07♑	19	01♒	13	26	09♓	22	06♈	20
1938	15♒	27	09♓	22	05♈	18	01♉	15	29	14♊	28	13♋	27	12♌	26	10♍
1939	22♊	05♋	19	03♌	17	01♍	16	00♎	14	29	13♏	27	10♐	24	07♑	19
1940	23♏	08♐	22	06♑	20	03♒	15	28	10♓	22	03♈	15	27	09♉	21	03♊
1941	04♈	16	28	10♉	22	04♊	15	27	09♋	21	04♌	16	29	13♍	26	11♎
1942	05♌	17	29	11♍	24	08♎	22	06♏	20	05♐	20	05♑	19	04♒	18	02♓
1943	14♐	27	11♑	25	09♒	23	08♓	22	06♈	20	04♉	17	01♊	14	27	09♋
1944	14♉	29	13♊	27	10♋	23	05♌	18	00♍	11	23	05♎	17	29	11♏	24
1945	24♍	06♎	18	00♏	12	24	06♐	18	00♑	12	24	07♒	20	03♓	17	02♈
1946	24♑	06♒	19	01♓	14	28	12♈	27	11♉	26	11♊	26	11♋	25	10♌	23
1947	05♊	19	03♋	18	02♌	16	00♍	14	28	12♎	25	08♏	21	04♐	16	29
1948	05♏	19	03♐	16	00♑	13	25	07♒	19	01♓	13	25	07♈	19	01♉	14
1949	15♓	27	09♈	20	02♉	14	26	08♊	20	03♋	16	28	12♌	25	09♍	23
1950	14♋	27	09♌	22	05♍	18	02♎	17	02♏	17	02♐	17	02♑	17	01♒	15
1951	26♏	11♐	25	10♑	24	08♒	22	06♓	20	03♈	16	29	12♉	24	07♊	19
1952	25♈	09♉	23	07♊	20	03♋	15	27	09♌	21	03♍	14	25	09♎	21	04♏
1953	05♍	17	29	10♎	22	04♏	17	29	11♐	24	07♑	20	03♒	17	01♓	15
1954	05♑	17	29	12♒	25	09♓	23	08♈	23	08♉	23	08♊	23	08♋	22	06♌
1955	18♉	02♊	17	02♋	16	00♌	14	28	11♍	25	07♎	20	02♏	15	27	09♐
1956	17♎	00♏	14	27	10♐	22	04♑	16	28	10♒	22	04♓	16	29	11♈	24
1957	25♒	07♓	19	01♈	12	25	07♉	19	02♊	15	28	12♋	25	09♌	23	07♍
1958	25♊	08♋	20	03♌	17	00♍	14	29	14♎	29	14♏	29	14♐	28	13♑	26
1959	08♏	23	08♐	23	08♑	22	06♒	20	03♓	16	28	11♈	23	05♉	17	29
1960	08♈	21	04♉	17	00♊	12	24	06♋	18	00♌	12	24	06♍	18	01♎	14
1961	15♌	26	08♍	20	02♎	14	27	10♏	23	06♐	20	04♑	17	01♒	15	29
1962	16♐	29	12♑	25	08♒	21	05♓	20	05♈	20	05♉	20	05♊	19	03♋	17
1963	29♈	14♉	00♊	15	29	14♋	28	11♌	24	07♍	19	01♎	14	26	07♏	19
1964	29♍	12♎	25	08♏	20	02♐	14	26	08♑	20	01♒	13	26	08♓	21	04♈
1965	04♒	16	28	10♓	22	05♈	17	00♉	14	27	11♊	25	09♋	23	08♌	22
1966	07♊	20	03♋	16	00♌	14	28	12♍	27	11♎	26	11♏	25	09♐	23	06♑
1967	20♎	05♏	20	05♐	20	04♑	18	02♒	15	28	10♓	22	04♈	16	28	09♉
1968	21♓	03♈	16	28	10♉	22	04♊	16	28	10♋	22	04♌	16	28	11♍	25
1969	24♋	06♌	18	30	12♍	24	07♎	20	04♏	18	02♐	17	01♑	16	00♒	14
1970	28♏	11♐	25	08♑	22	06♒	20	04♓	18	03♈	17	01♉	16	00♊	13	27
1971	11♈	26	11♉	26	11♊	25	09♋	22	05♌	18	00♍	12	24	06♎	18	00♏
1972	12♍	24	06♎	19	01♏	13	24	06♐	18	00♑	12	24	06♒	19	02♓	15
1973	13♑	25	07♒	19	01♓	14	27	11♈	25	09♉	23	08♊	23	08♋	22	06♌
1974	19♉	03♊	16	00♋	14	28	12♌	26	11♍	25	09♎	23	07♏	20	04♐	16
1975	02♎	17	02♏	17	01♐	15	29	12♑	25	08♒	20	02♓	14	26	08♈	20
1976	03♓	15	27	09♈	21	03♉	15	26	08♊	20	02♋	15	27	10♌	23	06♍
1977	03♋	15	27	09♌	21	04♍	17	01♎	15	29	14♏	29	14♐	29	14♑	28
1978	10♏	24	08♐	22	06♑	21	05♒	19	02♓	17	01♈	14	28	11♉	24	07♊
1979	23♓	08♈	23	07♉	22	06♊	19	03♋	15	28	10♌	22	04♍	16	27	09♎
1980	23♌	05♍	17	29	11♎	23	05♏	17	29	11♐	23	06♑	18	01♒	14	28
1981	23♐	05♑	17	29	11♒	24	07♓	21	05♈	20	05♉	20	05♊	20	05♋	20
1982	01♉	15	29	14♊	28	13♋	27	11♌	25	09♍	22	06♎	19	02♏	15	27
1983	15♍	00♎	14	28	12♏	26	09♐	22	05♑	17	29	11♒	23	05♓	17	29
1984	13♒	26	08♓	19	01♈	13	25	07♉	19	01♊	14	27	09♋	23	06♌	20
1985	13♊	25	07♋	20	02♌	15	28	12♍	26	11♎	25	11♏	26	11♐	26	10♑
1986	21♎	05♏	20	05♐	20	05♑	19	03♒	17	01♓	14	27	10♈	23	06♉	17
1987	08♓	22	05♈	19	03♉	16	29	12♊	25	07♋	19	01♌	13	25	07♍	19
1988	04♌	16	28	09♍	21	03♎	15	27	09♏	22	05♐	18	01♑	14	28	12♒
1989	04♐	16	28	10♑	23	06♒	19	03♓	17	01♈	16	01♉	17	02♊	17	01♋

	17th	18th	19th	20th	21st	22nd	23rd	24th	25th	26th	27th	28th	29th	30th
1900	25	07♎	19	01♏	13	25	08♐	20	03♑	16	29	13♒	26	10♓
1901	26	08♒	21	04♓	18	02♈	17	01♉	17	02♊	17	02♋	17	01♌
1902	11♊	26	11♋	26	10♌	24	08♍	21	04♎	17	29	11♏	24	05♐
1903	26	09♏	22	05♐	18	01♑	13	25	07♒	19	01♓	12	25	07♈
1904	15	27	09♈	21	03♉	16	28	11♊	24	08♋	23	05♌	19	03♍
1905	17	00♌	12	26	09♍	23	08♎	22	07♏	23	08♐	23	07♑	21♑
1906	02♐	18	03♑	17	02♒	16	29	12♓	25	07♈	20	02♉	14	26♉
1907	17	00♉	13	26	08♊	21	03♋	15	27	08♌	20	02♍	14	27♎
1908	05♍	17	29	11♎	23	06♏	19	02♐	15	29	13♑	27	11♒	25♒
1909	08♑	21	04♒	17	01♓	15	29	14♈	29	14♉	29	13♊	27	11♋
1910	23	08♊	23	08♋	23♌	07♌	20	03♍	16	28	10♎	22	04♏	16♏
1911	09♎	21	04♏	16	29	11♐	23	04♑	16	28	10♒	22	04♓	17♓
1912	24	06♓	18	00♈	13	26	09♉	22	06♊	20	05♋	19	03♌	18♌
1913	29	13♋	26	10♌	23	07♍	21	06♎	20	05♏	19	04♐	18	02♑
1914	14♏	29	14♐	29	13♑	27	11♒	24	06♓	19	01♈	13	24	06♉
1915	00♈	12	25	07♉	19	01♊	13	25	07♋	18	00♌	12	25	07♍
1916	14	26	08♍	20	03♎	16	29	13♏	27	11♐	26	11♑	25	10♒
1917	21	04♑	18	01♒	15	29	14♓	28	12♈	27	11♉	25	09♊	22♊
1918	05♉	20	05♊	20	04♋	18	01♌	14	26	09♍	21	03♎	15	26♎
1919	21	03♎	16	28	09♏	21	03♐	15	27	09♑	21	03♒	15	28♒
1920	04♒	16	28	10♓	23	06♈	19	03♉	17	02♊	17	02♋	17	02♌
1921	12♊	26	10♋	24	08♌	22	06♍	20	04♎	18	02♏	16	29	12♐
1922	26	11♏	25	10♐	24	08♑	21	04♒	16	29	11♓	22	04♈	16♈
1923	12♓	24	06♈	18	00♉	11	23	05♊	17	29	11♋	24	06♌	19♌
1924	24	06♌	18	00♍	13	26	09♎	23	08♏	23	08♐	23	08♑	23♑
1925	03♐	17	02♑	16	00♒	14	29	13♓	26	10♈	24	07♉	20	03♊
1926	17	02♉	16	01♊	14	28	11♋	24	06♌	18	00♍	12	24	06♎
1927	02♍	14	26	08♎	20	02♏	14	26	08♐	20	02♑	15	27	10♒
1928	14	26	08♒	20	03♓	16	00♈	14	29	13♉	29	14♊	29	14♋
1929	24	08♊	23	08♋	22	07♌	21	05♍	19	02♎	15	28	11♏	23♏
1930	09♎	23	07♏	21	05♐	18	01♑	13	26	08♒	20	02♓	14	25♓
1931	22	04♓	16	28	10♈	22	04♉	16	28	10♊	23	06♋	19	02♌
1932	04♋	16	29	11♌	24	07♍	21	05♎	19	04♏	19	05♐	20	05♑
1933	14	29	14♐	29	14♑	29	13♒	27	10♓	23	06♈	19	02♉	14♉
1934	01♈	15	29	12♉	25	08♊	21	03♋	16	28	09♌	21	03♍	15♍
1935	12	24	06♍	18	00♎	12	24	06♏	18	01♐	14	27	10♑	24♑
1936	25	07♑	19	02♒	15	28	12♓	25	11♈	25	11♉	26	11♊	25♊
1937	05♉	20	05♊	20	05♋	20	04♌	18	02♍	15	28	10♎	23	05♏
1938	23	07♎	20	03♏	16	28	11♐	23	05♑	17	29	11♒	23	05♓
1939	02♒	14	26	07♓	19	01♈	13	26	08♉	21	04♊	18	02♋	16♋
1940	15	28	11♋	24	07♌	20	04♍	18	02♎	17	02♏	16	01♐	16♐
1941	25	10♏	26	11♐	26	11♑	26	09♒	23	06♓	18	01♈	13	25♈
1942	15	28	11♈	24	07♉	19	01♊	13	25	07♋	19	01♌	13	25♌
1943	21	03♌	15	27	09♍	21	03♎	15	28	12♏	25	09♐	23	07♑
1944	06♐	19	02♑	15	29	12♒	26	10♓	24	09♈	23	08♉	22	07♊
1945	16	02♉	17	02♊	17	02♋	16	00♌	13	26	09♍	21	03♎	15♎
1946	07♍	20	03♎	15	27	10♏	22	04♐	15	27	09♑	21	03♒	15♒
1947	11♑	23	05♒	16	28	10♓	23	05♈	18	02♉	15	00♊	14	29♊
1948	27	10♊	23	07♋	21	07♌	18	03♍	17	01♎	15	29	13♏	27♏
1949	08♎	22	07♏	22	07♐	22	06♑	20	04♒	17	29	11♓	23	05♈
1950	28	11♓	24	06♈	18	00♉	12	24	06♊	17	29	11♋	23	06♌
1951	01♋	13	24	06♌	18	00♍	13	25	08♎	22	06♏	20	05♐	20♐
1952	17	01♐	15	29	13♑	27	11♒	25	09♓	23	07♈	21	05♉	16♉
1953	29	14♈	29	14♉	18	13♊	27	11♋	24	07♌	19	01♍	13	25♍
1954	19	02♍	14	26	09♎	20	02♏	14	26	08♐	20	02♑	14	26♑
1955	21	02♑	14	26	08♒	20	03♓	15	29	12♈	26	11♉	26	11♊
1956	08♉	22	06♊	20	04♋	19	03♌	17	02♍	16	29	13♎	26	10♏
1957	21	06♎	20	05♏	19	03♐	17	00♑	13	26	09♒	21	03♓	15♓
1958	09♒	22	05♓	17	29	11♈	22	04♉	16	28	10♊	22	05♋	17♋
1959	11♊	23	04♋	16	28	11♌	23	06♍	19	03♎	17	01♏	16	01♐
1960	28	12♏	26	11♐	26	11♑	25	10♒	24	08♓	21	05♈	18	01♉
1961	13♓	28	12♈	26	10♉	24	04♊	21	04♋	16	28	11♌	22	04♍
1962	00♌	12	25	07♍	19	01♎	12	24	06♏	18	01♐	13	26	09♑
1963	01♐	13	25	07♑	19	01♒	14	26	10♓	23	08♈	22	07♉	22♉
1964	18	03♉	17	02♊	17	02♋	17	01♌	16	29	13♍	26	09♎	22♎
1965	06♍	20	04♎	18	01♏	15	28	11♐	23	06♑	18	00♒	12	24♒
1966	19	02♒	14	27	09♓	20	02♈	14	26	08♉	21	03♊	16	00♋
1967	21	03♊	15	27	10♋	22	05♌	18	01♍	15	29	13♎	28	13♏
1968	09♎	23	07♏	22	08♐	23	08♑	23	07♒	21	05♓	18	00♈	13♈
1969	28	12♓	26	09♈	22	06♉	18	01♊	14	26	08♋	20	02♌	14♌
1970	09♋	22	04♌	16	28	10♍	22	04♎	26	28	11♏	24	07♐	21♐
1971	12	24	06♐	18	01♑	13	26	09♒	23	07♓	21	05♈	20	04♉
1972	29	13♈	28	13♉	29	14♋	29	14♋	28	12♌	25	08♍	21	03♎
1973	20	04♍	18	01♎	14	27	09♏	22	04♐	16	28	10♑	22	03♒
1974	29	12♑	24	06♒	18	29	11♓	23	06♈	18	01♉	14	28	12♊
1975	02♉	14	26	09♊	22	05♋	18	01♌	15	29	13♍	27	12♎	26♎
1976	20	05♎	19	04♏	19	05♐	20	04♑	19	03♒	16	29	12♓	24♓
1977	12♒	26	09♓	22	05♈	18	00♉	12	24	06♊	18	00♋	12	24♋
1978	19	01♋	14	25	07♌	19	01♍	13	25	08♎	21	04♏	18	02♐
1979	22	04♏	17	00♐	13	25	10♑	23	07♒	21	05♓	19	03♈	18♈
1980	11♓	26	10♈	25	10♉	25	10♊	25	09♋	23	06♌	19	02♍	14♍
1981	04♌	17	01♍	14	26	08♎	21	03♏	15	27	08♐	20	02♑	14♑
1982	09♐	21	03♑	15	27	09♒	21	03♓	15	28	11♈	25	09♉	23♉
1983	12♈	24	07♉	20	04♊	17	01♋	15	29	14♌	28	12♍	26	10♎
1984	04♍	16	02♎	17	02♏	16	01♐	15	29	13♑	26	09	22	04♓
1985	25	08♒	22	04♓	17	29	11♈	23	05♉	17	28	10♊	22	04♋
1986	29	11♊	23	05♋	17	29	11♌	23	05♍	18	01♎	15	29	13♏
1987	01♎	14	27	10♏	24	08♐	23	07♑	22	06♒	20	04♓	18	02♈
1988	26	10♓	24	08♈	23	07♉	22	06♊	20	03♋	16	29	11♌	24♌
1989	15	29	12♌	25	07♍	19	01♎	13	25	07♏	19	01♐	13	25♐

December

	1st	2nd	3rd	4th	5th	6th	7th	8th	9th	10th	11th	12th	13th	14th	15th	16th
1900	25♓	09♈	23	08♉	23	07♊	21	05♋	19	02♌	15	27	10♍	22	04♎	15
1901	15♌	28	11♍	23	05♎	17	29	11♏	23	05♐	16	28	11♑	23	05♒	18
1902	17♐	29	11♑	23	05♒	17	29	11♓	24	07♈	21	05♉	19	04♊	29	05♋
1903	20♈	03♉	16	00♊	14	29	14♋	28	13♌	27	11♍	25	09♎	22	06♏	19
1904	17♍	01♎	15	00♏	14	28	12♐	26	09♑	22	05♒	17	29	11♓	23	05♈
1905	05♒	18	01♓	13	25	07♈	19	01♉	13	25	07♊	19	01♋	14	27	10♌
1906	08♊	20	01♋	13	25	07♌	19	02♍	15	28	11♎	26	10♏	25	10♐	26
1907	10♎	23	07♏	21	05♐	20	05♑	20	04♒	19	03♓	17	01♈	14	27	10♉
1908	09♓	23	08♈	22	06♉	19	03♊	16	29	12♋	24	07♌	19	01♍	13	24
1909	25♋	08♌	21	03♍	15	27	09♎	21	03♏	15	27	09♐	22	05♑	18	01♒
1910	28♏	10♐	22	04♑	16	28	10♒	23	06♓	19	03♈	17	01♉	16	01♊	16
1911	00♈	13	27	11♉	26	11♊	26	11♋	26	11♌	25	09♍	23	06♎	18	01♏
1912	02♍	16	00♎	14	27	10♏	24	07♐	19	02♑	14	27	09♒	20	02♓	14
1913	15♑	28	11♒	23	05♓	17	29	10♈	22	04♉	17	29	12♊	26	09♋	23
1914	18♉	00♊	12	24	07♋	19	02♌	14	27	11♍	24	08♎	23	07♏	22	07♐
1915	20♍	03♎	17	02♏	16	02♐	17	02♑	17	02♒	16	00♓	14	27	09♈	22
1916	24♒	08♓	22	05♈	19	02♉	15	28	10♊	22	05♋	17	28	10♌	22	04♍
1917	05♋	18	00♌	12	24	06♍	18	00♎	12	24	07♏	20	03♐	16	00♑	14
1918	08♏	20	02♐	15	27	10♑	23	06♒	19	02♓	16	00♈	15	29	14♉	28
1919	11♓	24	08♈	22	07♉	22	07♊	23	08♋	23	07♌	21	04♍	17	00♎	12
1920	16♌	00♍	14	27	10♎	23	06♏	18	00♐	13	25	06♑	18	00♒	12	24
1921	25♐	08♑	20	02♒	14	26	08♓	20	02♈	14	26	09♉	23	06♊	20	05♋
1922	28♈	10♉	22	05♊	18	01♋	14	28	11♌	25	09♍	23	07♎	21	05♏	20
1923	02♍	15	29	13♎	28	13♏	28	13♐	29	13♑	28	11♒	25	08♓	20	02♈
1924	08♒	22	05♓	19	02♈	14	27	09♉	21	03♊	15	27	09♋	21	02♌	14
1925	15♊	28	10♋	22	04♌	16	27	09♍	21	04♎	16	29	13♏	27	11♐	26
1926	18♎	00♏	13	25	08♐	22	05♑	19	03♒	17	01♓	15	29	13♈	28	12♉
1927	24♒	07♓	21	05♈	20	05♉	19	04♊	19	04♋	18	01♌	15	28	10♍	23
1928	29♋	13♌	27	10♍	23	05♎	18	00♏	12	23	05♐	17	29	11♑	23	05♒
1929	06♐	18	00♑	12	24	05♒	17	29	11♓	24	06♈	20	03♉	17	01♊	16
1930	08♈	20	02♉	15	29	12♊	26	10♋	25	09♌	24	08♍	22	06♎	20	03♏
1931	16♌	29	13♍	27	12♎	26	11♏	25	10♐	24	08♑	22	05♒	18	00♓	12
1932	20♑	04♒	17	01♓	13	26	08♈	20	02♉	13	25	07♊	19	01♋	13	26
1933	26♉	08♊	20	02♋	14	26	07♌	19	02♍	14	27	10♎	23	08♏	22	07♐
1934	27♍	10♎	22	06♏	19	03♐	17	02♑	16	01♒	15	00♓	14	28	12♈	25
1935	08♒	21	05♓	19	04♈	18	02♉	17	01♊	15	28	12♋	25	07♌	20	02♍
1936	10♋	24	08♌	21	03♍	16	28	10♎	22	04♏	16	27	09♐	22	04♑	16
1937	17♏	28	10♐	22	04♑	16	28	10♒	22	05♓	17	01♈	14	28	13♉	28
1938	17♓	29	12♈	26	09♉	23	08♊	23	08♋	23	07♌	22	06♍	20	04♎	17
1939	00♌	14	28	12♍	26	10♎	24	08♏	22	05♐	19	02♑	15	27	09♒	21
1940	00♑	14	28	11♒	24	06♓	18	00♈	12	23	05♉	17	29	12♊	25	07♋
1941	07♉	19	00♊	12	24	06♋	18	01♌	13	26	09♍	22	05♎	19	04♏	19
1942	07♍	19	02♎	16	29	14♏	29	14♐	29	14♑	29	14♒	28	12♓	25	08♈
1943	22♑	06♒	20	04♓	18	02♈	16	00♉	13	26	10♊	22	05♋	17	29	11♌
1944	21♊	04♋	18	01♌	13	25	07♍	19	01♎	13	25	07♏	20	02♐	15	28
1945	27♎	09♏	21	03♐	15	27	09♑	21	04♒	17	00♓	13	27	11♈	26	10♉
1946	27♒	10♓	23	06♈	20	04♉	19	04♊	19	05♋	20	05♌	19	03♍	16	29
1947	13♋	28	13♌	27	11♍	25	08♎	22	05♏	18	00♐	13	25	07♑	19	01♒
1948	11♐	24	08♑	20	03♒	15	27	09♓	21	03♈	15	27	09♉	22	05♊	19
1949	17♈	29	11♉	23	05♊	17	00♋	13	25	09♌	22	05♍	19	03♎	17	02♏
1950	18♌	01♍	14	27	11♎	25	10♏	25	10♐	26	11♑	26	10♒	24	07♓	20
1951	05♑	20	05♒	19	03♓	17	00♈	13	26	08♉	21	03♊	15	27	09♋	21
1952	02♊	15	28	10♋	23	05♌	17	29	10♍	22	04♎	17	29	12♏	26	09♐
1953	07♎	19	01♏	13	25	08♐	21	04♑	17	00♒	14	27	11♓	25	10♈	24
1954	09♒	22	05♓	18	02♈	16	01♉	16	01♊	16	01♋	16	00♌	14	27	10♍
1955	26♊	11♋	26	10♌	24	08♍	21	04♎	17	00♏	12	24	06♐	18	29	11♑
1956	23♏	05♐	18	00♑	12	24	06♒	18	00♓	12	24	06♈	19	02♉	16	29
1957	27♓	08♈	20	03♉	15	28	11♊	24	08♋	22	06♌	20	04♍	18	02♎	16
1958	00♌	13	27	10♍	24	08♎	23	07♏	22	07♐	22	06♑	20	04♒	18	00♓
1959	17♐	02♑	17	02♒	16	29	13♓	25	08♈	20	02♉	14	26	08♊	20	01♋
1960	13♉	26	08♊	20	03♋	15	26	08♌	20	02♍	14	26	09♎	22	06♏	20
1961	16♍	28	10♎	22	05♏	18	02♐	15	29	13♑	28	12♒	26	10♓	24	08♈
1962	22♑	05♒	18	02♓	16	00♈	14	29	14♉	28	13♊	27	11♋	27	07♌	20
1963	08♊	23	08♋	22	06♌	20	03♍	16	28	10♎	23	04♏	16	28	10♐	22
1964	04♏	17	29	11♐	23	04♑	16	28	10♒	22	04♓	17	29	13♈	26	10♉
1965	06♓	18	00♈	12	25	08♉	22	06♊	20	04♋	19	04♌	18	03♍	17	01♎
1966	13♋	27	10♌	24	08♍	23	07♎	21	05♏	19	03♐	17	01♑	14	27	10♒
1967	28♏	13♐	28	13♑	27	10♒	23	06♓	19	01♈	13	24	06♉	18	00♊	12
1968	25♈	07♉	19	01♊	13	25	07♋	19	00♌	13	25	07♍	20	03♎	17	01♏
1969	25♌	07♍	20	02♎	15	28	12♏	26	11♐	26	11♑	26	10♒	25	09♓	23
1970	05♑	19	03♒	17	01♓	15	29	13♈	27	11♉	25	08♊	22	05♋	17	00♌
1971	19♉	04♊	19	03♋	17	00♌	13	26	08♍	20	02♎	14	26	08♏	20	02♐
1972	16♎	28	10♏	21	03♐	15	27	09♑	21	03♒	16	28	11♓	24	08♈	22
1973	15♒	27	09♓	22	05♈	18	02♉	17	01♊	16	01♋	17	02♌	16	00♍	14
1974	26♊	10♋	24	09♌	23	07♍	22	05♎	19	03♏	16	29	12♐	25	07♑	20
1975	11♏	25	09♐	23	07♑	20	03♒	16	28	10♓	22	04♈	16	28	10♉	22
1976	06♈	18	00♉	11	23	05♊	17	29	12♋	24	07♌	20	03♍	16	00♎	14
1977	06♌	18	00♍	13	25	09♎	23	07♏	22	07♐	22	08♑	23	07♒	22	06♓
1978	17♐	02♑	16	01♒	15	00♓	14	27	11♈	24	07♉	20	03♊	15	28	10♋
1979	02♉	16	00♊	14	27	10♋	23	06♌	18	00♍	12	23	05♎	17	29	12♏
1980	26♍	08♎	20	01♏	13	25	08♐	20	03♑	15	28	11♒	24	08♓	22	06♈
1981	26♑	08♒	20	03♓	16	00♈	14	28	13♉	28	13♊	28	14♋	28	13♌	26
1982	08♊	23	08♋	22	07♌	22	06♍	19	03♎	16	29	11♏	24	06♐	18	00♑
1983	24♎	08♏	21	05♐	18	00♑	13	25	07♒	19	01♓	13	25	07♈	19	02♉
1984	16♓	28	10♈	21	03♉	15	28	10♊	23	06♋	19	03♌	16	00♍	14	28
1985	17♋	29	12♌	24	08♍	21	05♎	19	04♏	19	04♐	19	04♑	19	03♒	17
1986	17♏	13♐	29	14♑	29	13♒	27	11♓	24	07♈	20	02♉	14	26	08♊	20
1987	16♈	29	12♉	25	08♊	21	03♋	15	27	09♌	21	03♍	15	27	09♎	22
1988	05♍	17	29	11♎	23	05♏	18	01♐	14	27	11♑	25	09♒	23	07♓	21
1989	08♑	20	03♒	16	29	13♓	26	11♈	25	10♉	25	10♊	25	09♋	23	07♌

	17th	18th	19th	20th	21st	22nd	23rd	24th	25th	26th	27th	28th	29th	30th	31st
1900	27	09♏	21	04♐	16	29	12♑	26	09♒	23	07♓	21	05♈	20	04♉
1901	01♓	14	28	12♈	26	10♉	25	10♊	25	10♋	25	09♌	23	06♍	19♍
1902	20	05♌	20	04♍	17	01♎	14	26	08♏	20	02♐	14	26	08♑	20♑
1903	01♐	14	27	09♑	21	03♒	15	27	09♓	20	02♈	15	27	10♉	24♉
1904	17	29	11♉	24	07♊	20	03♋	17	01♌	15	29	14♍	28	12♎	26♎
1905	23	06♍	19	03♎	17	02♏	17	01♐	16	01♑	15	29	13♒	26	09♓
1906	11♑	26	10♒	24	08♓	21	04♈	17	29	11♉	23	05♊	17	28	10♋
1907	23	05♊	17	29	11♋	23	05♌	17	28	10♍	23	05♎	18	01♏	15♏
1908	06♎	19	01♏	14	27	10♐	24	08♑	22	07♒	21	06♓	20	04♈	18♈
1909	14	28	12♓	26	10♈	24	09♉	23	07♊	21	05♋	19	03♌	16	29♌
1910	01♋	16	01♌	15	29	12♍	25	07♎	19	01♏	13	25	07♐	18	00♑
1911	13	25	07♐	19	01♑	13	25	07♒	19	01♓	13	26	08♈	21	05♉
1912	26	08♈	21	03♉	17	00♊	14	29	14♋	28	13♌	28	12♍	27	10♎
1913	06♌	20	04♍	18	02♎	16	00♏	15	29	13♐	26	10♑	23	06♒	18♒
1914	22	07♑	21	05♒	19	02♓	15	27	09♈	21	03♉	15	27	09♊	21♊
1915	04♉	16	28	10♊	22	04♋	15	27	09♌	21	04♍	16	29	12♎	26♎
1916	16	28	11♎	24	07♏	21	05♐	20	04♑	19	04♒	19	04♓	18	02♈
1917	28	12♒	17	10♓	25	09♈	23	07♉	20	04♊	17	00♋	13	26	08♌
1918	13♊	27	12♋	25	09♌	22	04♍	17	29	11♎	23	05♏	16	28	11♐
1919	25	06♏	18	00♐	12	24	06♑	18	00♒	12	25	08♓	21	04♈	18♈
1920	06♓	18	01♈	14	27	11♉	25	10♊	25	10♋	26	11♌	25	10♍	24♍
1921	19	04♌	19	03♍	17	01♎	15	29	12♏	25	08♐	21	04♑	16	28♑
1922	04♐	18	02♑	16	29	12♒	24	06♓	18	00♈	12	24	06♉	18	01♊
1923	14	26	08♉	20	02♊	14	26	08♋	21	03♌	16	29	12♍	26	09♎
1924	26	09♍	21	04♎	18	02♏	16	01♐	16	01♑	17	02♒	16	01♓	14♓
1925	11♑	25	10♒	25	09♓	23	07♈	20	04♉	17	29	12♊	24	06♋	18♋
1926	25	09♊	23	06♋	19	01♌	14	26	08♍	20	02♎	14	26	08♏	21♏
1927	05♎	16	28	10♏	22	04♐	16	29	11♑	24	07♒	21	04♓	18	02♈
1928	17	00♓	12	25	09♈	23	07♉	22	07♊	22	07♋	22	07♌	21	05♍
1929	01♋	17	02♌	17	01♍	15	29	12♎	25	08♏	20	02♐	15	27	08♑
1930	17	00♐	13	26	09♑	21	04♒	16	28	10♓	21	03♈	15	28	10♉
1931	24	06♈	18	00♉	12	24	06♊	19	02♋	15	29	12♌	26	10♍	24♍
1932	08♌	21	04♍	17	00♎	14	28	13♏	28	13♐	28	13♑	27	12♒	25♒
1933	22	08♑	23	08♒	22	06♓	20	03♈	16	29	11♉	23	05♊	17	29♊
1934	08♉	21	04♊	17	29	12♋	24	06♌	17	29	11♍	23	05♎	17	00♏
1935	14	26	07♎	19	02♏	14	26	09♐	23	06♑	20	04♒	18	02♓	16♓
1936	29	12♒	25	09♓	22	06♈	20	05♉	19	04♊	19	03♋	18	02♌	15♌
1937	13♊	28	13♋	28	13♌	27	11♍	24	07♎	19	02♏	14	25	07♐	19♐
1938	00♏	13	25	07♐	20	02♑	14	26	07♒	19	01♓	13	25	08♈	20♈
1939	03♓	15	27	09♈	21	03♉	16	29	13♊	27	11♋	25	10♌	24	08♍
1940	21	04♌	17	01♍	15	29	13♎	27	11♏	26	10♐	24	08♑	22	06♒
1941	04♐	19	04♑	19	04♒	18	01♓	15	27	10♈	22	04♉	15	27	09♊
1942	21	04♉	16	28	10♊	22	04♋	16	28	10♌	21	03♍	16	28	11♎
1943	23	05♍	17	29	11♎	23	06♏	19	03♐	17	02♑	16	01♒	16	01♓
1944	12♑	25	09♒	23	07♓	21	05♈	19	03♉	18	02♊	15	29	12♋	26♋
1945	25	10♊	25	10♋	24	08♌	21	05♍	17	00♎	12	24	06♏	17	29♏
1946	12♎	25	07♏	19	01♐	12	24	06♑	18	00♒	12	24	06♓	19	02♈
1947	13	25	06♓	10	01♈	13	26	09♉	23	07♊	22	07♋	22	07♌	22♌
1948	02♋	16	01♌	15	29	14♍	28	12♎	26	09♏	23	07♐	20	03♑	16♑
1949	16	01♐	16	00♑	17	28	12♒	25	07♓	19	01♈	13	25	07♉	19♉
1950	03♈	15	27	09♉	21	03♊	14	26	08♋	20	03♌	15	28	10♍	23♍
1951	03♌	15	27	09♍	21	03♎	16	00♏	14	28	13♐	18	13♑	29	14♒
1952	23	08♑	22	07♒	21	06♓	20	04♈	18	01♉	15	28	11♊	24	06♋
1953	08♉	23	07♊	21	05♋	18	01♌	14	27	09♍	21	03♎	15	27	09♏
1954	23	05♎	17	29	11♏	23	05♐	17	29	11♑	23	06♒	19	02♓	15♓
1955	23	05♒	17	29	11♓	24	07♈	21	04♉	19	04♊	19	04♋	19	04♌
1956	14♊	28	13♋	28	13♌	28	12♍	26	10♎	23	06♏	19	02♐	14	27♐
1957	00♏	14	28	12♐	26	08♑	21	04♒	16	29	11♓	23	04♈	16	28♈
1958	13	25	07♈	19	01♉	12	24	07♊	19	01♋	14	27	10♌	24	07♍
1959	13	25	08♌	20	02♍	15	28	12♎	25	10♏	24	09♐	25	10♑	25♑
1960	04♐	19	04♑	20	05♒	19	04♓	18	01♈	15	28	10♉	23	05♊	17♊
1961	22	06♉	20	03♊	16	29	12♋	24	06♌	18	00♍	12	24	06♎	18♎
1962	03♍	15	27	09♎	20	02♏	14	27	09♐	22	05♑	18	01♒	15	29♒
1963	04♑	16	28	11♒	23	06♓	20	03♈	17	01♉	16	01♊	16	01♋	15♋
1964	25	10♊	25	10♋	25	10♌	25	09♍	23	06♎	19	01♏	14	26	08♐
1965	14	28	11♏	24	07♐	19	02♑	14	26	08♒	20	02♓	14	26	08♈
1966	22	04♓	16	28	10♈	22	04♉	16	29	12♊	25	09♋	23	07♌	21♌
1967	24	07♋	19	02♌	15	28	12♍	25	09♎	23	08♏	22	07♐	21	06♑
1968	16	00♐	16	01♑	16	01♒	16	00♓	14	27	10♈	22	04♉	16	28♉
1969	06♈	19	02♉	15	28	10♊	22	04♋	16	28	10♌	22	04♍	16	28♍
1970	12	24	06♍	18	29	11♎	24	06♏	19	02♐	16	29	14♑	28	13♒
1971	15	27	10♑	23	06♒	20	03♓	17	01♈	15	00♉	14	29	13♊	27♊
1972	07♉	22	07♊	22	07♋	22	06♌	20	07♍	17	00♎	12	24	06♏	18♏
1973	28	11♎	24	06♏	19	01♐	13	25	07♑	18	00♒	12	24	06♓	18♓
1974	02♒	14	25	07♓	19	01♈	13	26	09♉	22	06♊	20	04♋	19	04♌
1975	05♊	18	01♋	14	28	12♌	26	10♍	24	08♎	22	06♏	20	04♐	18♐
1976	28	13♏	28	13♐	28	12♑	27	11♒	24	07♓	20	02♈	14	26	08♉
1977	19	02♈	15	27	09♉	21	03♊	15	27	09♋	21	03♌	15	27	09♍
1978	22	04♌	15	27	09♍	21	03♎	16	29	12♏	26	10♐	25	10♑	25♑
1979	25	08♐	22	05♑	19	04♒	18	02♓	16	00♈	14	28	12♉	26	09♊
1980	20	05♉	19	04♊	19	03♋	17	01♌	14	27	10♍	22	04♎	16	28♎
1981	10♍	23	05♎	18	00♏	12	24	05♐	17	29	11♑	23	05♒	17	00♓
1982	12	24	05♒	17	29	11♓	23	06♈	19	03♉	16	01♊	16	01♋	16♋
1983	15	28	12♊	26	10♋	25	09♌	24	09♍	23	07♎	21	04♏	18	01♐
1984	13♎	27	11♏	25	10♐	24	07♑	21	04♒	17	29	12♓	24	06♈	17♈
1985	00♓	13	26	08♈	20	02♉	13	25	07♊	19	01♋	13	26	09♌	22♌
1986	02♋	14	26	08♌	20	02♍	14	27	10♎	23	07♏	21	06♐	21	07♑
1987	05♏	18	02♐	17	01♑	16	01♒	16	01♓	15	29	13♈	26	09♉	22♉
1988	05♈	19	03♉	17	01♊	15	28	11♋	24	07♌	19	01♍	13	25	07♎
1989	20	03♍	15	28	10♎	21	03♏	15	27	09♐	22	04♑	17	00♒	13♒

14 GETTING IT!

THE LOVE PLANET VENUS

Venus is beauty . . . it symbolizes harmony and radiance of a rare and elusive quality: beauty itself. It is refinement and delicacy, softness and charm. In astrology, it indicates grace, balance, and the esthetic sense. Where Venus is, we see beauty, a gentle drawing of energy and the need for satisfaction and completion. It is a special touch that finishes off rough edges.

The late Jacqueline Susann gave me her gold ring with the Venus symbol ♀ (a variation of the Egyptian *ankh*) at a party for the filming of the movie based on her book *The Love Machine*. (The ring was also pictured on the cover of the book.) Jackie, a Leo like me, advised: "Don't take it off! It will bring you long life and fertility." (How true. Three months later, I was pregnant with my darling Sonny!) Jackie was given a duplicate ring by our hostess, inset with a diamond, but, alas, it did not have the same effect on her.

Venus is the planet of sensitivity and affection and it is always the place for that other elusive phenomenon: love. Its ideal is the flame of spiritual love, as exemplified by Aphrodite, goddess of love and the sweetness and power of personal beauty.

Venus also can reveal much about living with others harmoniously. You may have wondered why one couple always quarrels and never seems to get along, while another couple exudes positive harmony and companionship. Or, why it is that some couples spend their time playing the "I can't live with him (her) and I can't live without him (her)" game. (Elizabeth Taylor and Richard Burton come to mind.)

The answer lies in their stars, particularly in the position of their Venus and how the two placements act and interact with each other. Venus in a chart reveals the way love is *received* (and if your partner can really please you), which is one of the most important keys to an understanding relationship.

The best way to work out problems in your love relationship is to find the placement of your Venus, then check to see how it acts and reacts to the four planets (Sun, Moon, Venus and Mars) in your partner's chart.*

HERE ARE THE ASPECTS TO LOOK FOR: (Note: these aspects apply to all of the love planets.)

THE SUN: Venus in the same sign (easy)

in the same element (easy)

in a complementary element (easy) (Fire with Air, Earth with Water)

in a conflicting element (difficult) (Fire or Air with Earth or Water)

six signs apart (difficult) (Aries/Libra, Taurus/Scorpio, Gemini/Sagittarius, Cancer/Capricorn, Leo/Aquarius, Virgo/Pisces)

THE MOON: Since the Moon deals with feelings, aspects will indicate whether your partnership will result in hurt feelings or elevated ones, deep feelings or the superficial.

MARS: Our partner's Mars on our Venus gives it action, makes it come alive for good or otherwise. This contact can be sexual or argumentative or both!

VENUS: This aspect shows the capacity for harmony, mutual esthetic appreciation, friendship, or the opposite.

VENUS ASPECTING THE SUN

Venus is passive (and reactive); the Sun is active. There can be an interchange of strong affection and a great emotional link between two people with compatible placements of these two planets.

The expression of love, affection, pleasure, and encouragement that Venus has to offer is met with a warm, ego-flattering response from the Sun person. The Sun person will be bolstered by the supportiveness and tenderness of the Venus person. Passion and glowing love from both parties are the usual result.

This interchange greatly reinforces a positive self-image in the Sun person. The Venus person can become a great social asset in the relationship. The Venus half of the partnership can "set the stage" for the Sun person to shine.

*To find these inter-aspects, consult the ephemeris tables at the end of each chapter; then set them up on the Lovescope Chart in the back of the book.

If, however, there are difficult aspects, which happens when the two planets are six signs apart or in conflicting elements, the relationship will be less harmonious. The Active Sun may try to dominate the Passive Venus and may not understand or comply with the tastes of the Venus person. Here, the Sun person is the "doer" and must compromise and make the effort to understand the partner. Venus in turn must learn tolerance for the Sun's "will."

VENUS ASPECTING THE MOON

One partner's Venus aspecting the other's Moon compatibly can be an interchange of quiet, passive harmony. Since both planets are reactive, this contact is not as energetic as the chemistry between Venus and Mars. Instead, emotional reactions become important.

A good aspect can have a soothing, tranquilizing effect, bringing about contentment and a mutual sensitivity to each other's needs and feelings. In a married partnership, there will be a wonderful expression of mutual affection. Venus persons will draw out the true feelings of Moon persons and will "tune in" to their subconscious. Sometimes they will draw out emotions that the Moon person didn't suspect were there. The Moon person will create an aura, an atmosphere that appeals to the esthetic sense of the Venus person.

Conflicting Moon and Venus aspects call for some velvet gloves. The Venus person can unwittingly wound the Moon person's feelings; or emotions will stay on the surface, never really becoming deep and meaningful. Their tastes will be different and they will unintentionally rub each other the wrong way, literally and figuratively.

VENUS ASPECTING MARS

Here's the hottest aspect in the zodiac! One partner's Mars on the other's Venus makes love come alive. Even a difficult placement (planets six signs apart or in conflicting elements) can create a sexy "chemistry" and a strong physical attraction. Arguments will stimulate sexual urges and you'll head for the bedroom after a fight. Good aspects will mean smooth harmony. No sexy sparring matches, but the Mars person will know just how to please the Venus person.

Again, Venus is passive (and reactive); Mars is *very* active. The Mars partner will try to dominate the relationship, while the Venus partner will try to create harmony. The "danger" is that this aspect can lead to over emphasis of the physical side of love (particularly by the Venus person). Mars will exploit Venus's attitiude of compromise to the fullest . . . to get their way in bed! With a deep and total commitment to each other, you can work out your difficulties in other areas while sparring in the "arena" of the boudoir . . . and have much pleasure in doing so!

VENUS ASPECTING VENUS

Venus represents the basic ability to receive and react to love. In its highest form, it is gentleness, kindness, and sensitivity. When your natal

Venus interchanges compatibly with that of your partner, there will be harmony and genuine friendship. You are both "turned on" by the same things. You understand what the other wants.

You'll also complement each other socially. For instance, if one of you is gregarious and likes to mix with people while the other is quiet and retiring, you will seek the middle ground when you're together. The communicator will talk less, while the quieter one will blossom into a more successful socializer. There is a balance here that can usually overcome any other difficult aspects between the two charts.

On the other hand, if Venus in your sign conflicts with your partner's Venus, you will have different tastes and will need to make an effort to understand what pleases the other. You'll get on each other's nerves for seemingly insignificant reasons: little things like a way of dressing, a gesture, a habit, a way of speaking.

VENUS IN ARIES

Your erogenous zone is the head, and the skin on your scalp has all kinds of delicious sensual possibilities. A scalp massage, gentle brushing or combing of the hair, or the running of fingers through it is an instant turn-on (though you're not too keen on hair-pulling). Your ears, too, are extremely sensitive to sweet words, hot breath and ear-otic tickling with the tongue. Women with this placement love the gentle friction of a man's moustache or beard in sensitive places (caution: *not* stubble!). Men often feel that growing beards and moustaches adds to their sexual potential. Butterfly kisses done with fluttering eyelashes are more subtle sensations to enjoy. Women particularly love to receive the "Love Facial" described under Venus in Capricorn.

This placement indicates a preference for being active in love . . . for "getting physical" (from the song of the same name!). You like plenty of movement in bed, changing positions often and unleashing your passion. You're not the silent type. You'll voice your approval loudly (and may entertain the neighbors).

You like to conquer and be conquered, so why not take up the martial arts with your lover as a prelude to other activities? You love words of praise, for your performance and your physical attributes, spoken ardently and *loudly*.

VENUS IN TAURUS

All your senses are highly developed and highly exploitable. You like long, slow lovemaking, taking the time to explore all avenues of sensual pleasure. You like to vocalize your passion and hear sweet sounds and loving words from your mate. Your skin is particularly sensitive. You love to be touched everywhere, especially around the neck and throat area with your lover's tongue. You also love to be hugged and kissed throughout the night, but you don't like to leave bed once you're in it. You *do* get hungry and thirsty after a long lovemaking session, so it's a good idea to have some delicious taste sensations nearby — in a small refrigerator beside the bed.

You adore to luxuriate in satin sheets, freshly laundered linen bedding, or on a hairy chest (if you're female). The air should be perfumed to mix erotically with the earthy fragrance of sex.

You prefer to make love with the lights ON, so you can enjoy the view of your loved one. (So turn some flattering pink lights on the subject.) You enjoy an ambience of luxury and relaxation, where ALL of your senses are stimulated at once! You need the feeling of privacy with plenty of time, nothing rushed, ever. This is not the placement for a "quickie" or love in a tawdry setting. You want the full treatment, preferably preceded by a delicious meal, the best wine, sweet words, and beautiful music.

VENUS IN GEMINI

You have a wild imagination and would prefer to have *two* lovers at the same time. (Lacking this, you'll *imagine* the other one!) Yours is the mental approach to sex and, to win you, your lover must, above all, be *interesting* and articulate. You'll experiment with many different types of gadgets and lovers. (Some of you may even try those of the same sex.)

The palm of your hand is your erogenous zone. A wise lover will know just how to tickle your fantasy there. A successful love partner must also pique your curiosity, be creative and inventive, *never* telling or showing you everything . . . always hinting that there is more to be seen and heard. Once they reveal all, Venus in Gemini will speed off to new sights and sounds.

Here, Venus is turned on by original places to make love . . . in a car, an airplane (you're charter members of the mile-high club), a train, or during a coffee break at the office. (It's even more exciting if there is a possibility that someone might walk in and discover your tryst.)

Infidelity is a problem. It often gets you in trouble. So be especially careful to seek a liberated and understanding mate, if you marry at all.

You keep in constant touch with your loved ones by telephone and love to make and receive erotic calls at all times of the day or night.

VENUS IN CANCER

You love the feeling of being totally possessed by your lover. And you dream about making love under the light of a full moon. During this time, you feel secure and emotionally "at home" — as if you belong to your partner.

You are gifted with great intuition and you can detect any false note in lovemaking. You prefer making love in your own bed, where you can relax without interruption. Some like to make love under the covers (burrowed underneath like the crab), on a boat or on the beach, with the sea lapping at their toes.

You like to "mother" your lovers and need to feel needed. Men with this placement are apt to have a Pygmalion complex and like to initiate their lover into the mysteries of sex. For this reason, you may choose a lover who is younger, and less experienced than you. The female loves lacy lingerie and sleepwear. She does her best work at night!

The breast is your sexually sensitive instant turn-on and to please you, your lover should pay attention to this area. You love to lie in bed late at night un-covering your lover's innermost thoughts and feelings (there should be a large picture window with the moon shining through). Photography is a talent that could give you erotic pleasure. Take colorful instant Polaroids of your lover at his or her sexual best to gaze at when they're not present. (How about keeping them locked in a beautiful Victorian album?)

VENUS IN LEO

Words of praise can raise Venus in Leo's temperature fast. You never tire of hearing sweet nothings and like to confirm the applause in a strategically placed bedroom mirror.

The boudoir is your personal stage to strut and shine. You *must* have the right setting for your amorous encounters (see Moon signs) or you'll be uncomfortable and unresponsive. The buildup to the bedroom is especially important and should begin at a fine restaurant with a gourmet meal accompanied by the best wines and strolling violins. You love to be treated like a King or Queen and never rushed!

You take your lovemaking seriously and want an appreciative audience. If your lover makes fun of any physical faults or cracks jokes at the wrong time, they've had it! You could, however, be persuaded to pose for a few photos in revealing positions (à la the *Playboy* centerfold) wearing luxurious lingerie or your birthday suit if you're particularly photogenic. You love to play fantasy roles, as long as you're the *star*. (The female Venus in Leo loves to receive exquisite X-rated undies, the better to watch her mate's temperature rise as she performs an X-pert striptease.)

Your lover should make love to you totally, stimulating all areas at once! A slight raking of the fingernails up your spine (but don't leave marks, please) can trigger a roar of passion from you. This placement will also signal approval with a rosy skin flush (watch for it!).

Though you enjoy all forms of lovemaking, you usually rule out gadgets and fetishes (no competition allowed!). Instead, your lover should massage you with costly scented oils. (Then watch the male Venus in Leo flex his muscles.)

VENUS IN VIRGO

You are an enigma. You're never satisfied with the status quo. Everything could be just a little bit better. Your lover must live up to pretty high standards for you to be satisfied even temporarily, never completely.

You'll go for the superior and unattainable every time, and should watch a tendency toward masochism because of this. You may even fall for persons who treat you badly because they *seem* superior.

You're a perfectionist who must have every detail perfect before you can relax and let yourself go. The sheets must be immaculate, the air fresh, the setting elegant and tasteful. And your lover must be freshly bathed. Then you'll perform beautifully and passionately, making all your lover's fantasies come true (as well as your own).

You'll often keep your eyes closed during sex while you fantasize about your imaginary "perfect" lover. Sometimes that lover will be just the opposite of your bed partner . . . "wild" instead of conservative, an uninhibited partner of a different class or of an exotic race. Often you chose partners for their ability to help you in some way — to build a working partnership with you (work comes FIRST).

You cultivate contrasts between the "clean" and "dirty" (you look for dirt so you can clean it up). The forbidden and the shocking, the sacred and the profane hold great fascination for you. You are also intrigued by sickness and health (maybe your ideal lover is someone in the medical or health profession). Healing your love could also be part of your fantasy. Long mutual bubble baths could give you lots of good clean fun.

The lower part of your body from the waist down is your erogenous zone. You can go to "the moon on gossamer wings" if your partner finds the key to your sexual turn-on here. Try reading the *Kama Sutra* aloud to each other and then practice what it preaches.

VENUS IN LIBRA

You are a lover who must be pampered and spoiled. Everything must look esthetically "right" before you can be aroused. Your ideal is the traditional classic beauty of ancient Greece or Rome. Perfectly balanced. You see and admire beauty in everything, both men and women (and could love *both* depending upon your Sun, Moon, or Venus placements).

You love compliments and are very susceptible to flattery. You look to see your pleasing reflection in your partner's eyes (and in every mirror you pass!).

Partnership is a must for you. You cannot be alone. You like to do everything together with your loved one, in an atmosphere surrounded by beauty. Your back is your erogenous zone, and you love back rubs with wonderfully scented creams, done rhythmically with your partner astride you. You'll respond to bites and tickles with the tongue from your neck all the way down your back. You also respond to the rear entry sexually — the "Persian" way of making love.

Lovemaking begins mentally with you, then proceeds, if the ambience is in total harmony, to the physical. You love a well-perfumed body and sheets, champagne, good music, and good food before and after. Ugliness or vulgarity is an instant turn-off.

You're quite sentimental and love to give and receive gifts. Lovers should remember all occasions — birthdays, Valentine's Day, the day you first met — well, you get the idea.

A strong lover is a must. One who takes over and directs you. No heavy decisions for you to make. You dream of a life of luxury and opulence where you and your lover can spoil each other beautifully.

VENUS IN SCORPIO

There's high drama in the boudoir when Venus in Scorpio is the star, the producer and the director all at the same time. (You may also be the set designer and stuntman!) Mind you, this is an intense mystery drama, not a musical comedy, and you will use it to showcase your formidable sexual techniques. (You prefer your partner to be a featured player but will settle for a co-star). The act of love is performed more for drama than for sentiment. Although Venus is considered passive, there's nothing passive about this placement. Your genital area responds instantly to the slightest sexual overture.

You like to un-wrap your lover, both physically and psychologically, then probe his (or her) depths, penetrating deeply. (You always leave a sting!) Mystery intrigues you and you love to clothe yourself for your lover in black or white. (Purity is a very sexy thing to you . . . as is the extreme opposite.)

You'd love your partner to adorn your body, perhaps with strategically knotted silken ropes, so you could then break free! Sex is just another expression of the master/slave relationship: Venus in Scorpio *must* be the master. To you love is a sacred rite or black magic. Your batteries always seem charged. If you are betrayed, you may seek revenge. In any case, you will never forgive or forget.

VENUS IN SAGITTARIUS

You're always on the move, flirting all the way. To you, love is a musical comedy with a touch of slapstick — light and gay! The serious you is philosophical and likes to tell your partner graphically just what he or she can do to please you. (You'll also let partners know what doesn't please you!) Just so it won't get too heavy in the romance department, you'll make an off-handed quip that's good for a giggle or a belly laugh. One thing's for sure, you're not boring. With you, love has its ups and downs, but it never gets you down for long.

You love the fast track in love, and enjoy sexual experiments in settings that suggest movement — in a stable, on a plane, or on a fast boat to China — but your favorite sexual playground is the great outdoors. Anything that moves engages your brain, and males with Venus in Sag prefer those moving objects to be long, shapely legs encased in sheer black stockings.

You like foreign or offbeat lovers with an ethnic twist. But, much as you like to explore sex, you are really more interested in friendship, the exchange of ideas and romantic adventures. You'll philosophize at length (how you love to fill those listening ears!) and enjoy playing teacher to your lovers, introducing them to new amorous concepts and discussing them in bed.

Your erogenous zones are your hips and thighs. Kisses on the inner thigh or the running of the tongue lightly from the knee up excites you. So does a massage with warm scented oil. Your partner should use circular motions on the hips, vertical strokes on the inner thigh continuing up toward the heart. The light touch of fingernails over your hips will send erotic sensations shooting up your spine. Your lover may never get to finish the massage!

You love a challenge and like to perform with your lover as you would in a horse show (sometimes with a riding crop), jumping over all taboo fences, spurred on by your audience's applause. (The audience may include a few barks from your canine friends who sleep near your bed!)

When you do fall in love, you don't like to feel as if you are signing a treaty. There should always be an escape clause for you perennial bachelors and bachelorettes!

VENUS IN CAPRICORN

You're an organized lover who likes to plan ahead. You hate being taken by surprise. Your love nest will be simple, though elegant, and well organized for your rendezvous (animal skins, like zebra or leopard, tossed on the bed or floor bring out the beast in you). You often live out fantasties with a lover from a different socioeconomic background, though your ideal is someone who presents a conservative image in public but just the opposite in the bedroom. You're turned on by X-rated words (in the boudoir only) and the deeds that accompany them.

You *use* your lovers for both pleasure and profit. Nothing is ever wasted. You'll use the nectar of love as a potion or a Love Facial . . . however it is offered. You like to earn your pleasure by working hard for your partner's appreciation and love your romantic sessions to be lengthy. (Maybe that's why you are often attracted to a much younger partner with great sexual stamina). You, however, only *improve* with age.

Your lusty side is aroused by stolen kisses in secret places (behind the knees, your erogenous zone, around the navel and ascending up the spine). You like to begin lovemaking on your knees, too, then slowly and sensuously work your way up the "ladder" to success.

VENUS IN AQUARIUS

Your passion is in the mind and it takes a long time to warm up your extremities. You tend to get cold feet, both literally and figuratively, when it comes to romance (and anything else involving the emotions). A good mental build-up (an avant-garde play or controversial film shared with your partner) could get your juices flowing.

You want lovemaking to be spur-of-the-moment sexual dynamite. Your calves and ankles are your erogenous zones and any position that contacts these areas will stimulate desire. (Try making love standing up in a swimming pool where your weightless limbs can easily entwine those of your lover).

You love the surprise encounter where someone might catch you in the act. It should be unpredictable, spontaneous, *sudden* (perhaps when your best friend might desire to make the relationship nonplatonic).

You're also excited by someone who makes love a transcendental experience, literally out of this world, who will jolt you out of your "take it or leave it" attitude. The preliminaries to sex can be more important than the experience itself. Men with this placement will take the "sexual scientist" approach, experimenting with all the positions in the *Kama Sutra*. Women tend to idealize love (it's a Mozart symphony, a Puccini opera). You could be helped along by some exciting electronic devices and perhaps a friend or two or three.

VENUS IN PISCES

You love a combination of strength and weakness in your lovers . . . this gives you a chance to respect them but still take care of them. A sob story, a tragicomedy, a bittersweet twist will tug at your heart (and purse) strings every time. You can love an ugly duckling (with talent) and probably house one or more strays (animals and people).

In love, you enjoy giving vent to your dramatic flair, displaying your many different emotional facets with a wide variety of erotic foreplay. You love a slow, subtle tease, a lover who writes you poetry or who inspires you to dress up or to un-dress to suit the occasion.

You love to have your feet massaged and your toes and Achilles' heel tickled. You'd love to make love in or under water and can be found skinny-dipping, taking midnight jacuzzis, or experimenting with a pulsating shower massage.

You need to be needed and like to help your lovers overcome any problems (you are the sex therapists of the zodiac), but you always get emotionally involved and love to hear those words of undying affection.

You could be a bit self-sacrificing (watching your lover's pleasure is sometimes more important to you than experiencing your own), and perhaps masochistic, if you have a demanding lover. You receive pleasure by giving it . . . but be sure your lover wants to please you, too!

You want everything in love: romance, moonlight, roses, poetry, home, contentment, security, and fidelity. But you respond too easily, both mentally and physically, to romantic overtures, and may not always be faithful. You're partial to clandestine affairs and secret meetings, to experienced, highly-sexed partners, and to subtle romantic treatment that is first class all the way.

HOW TO FIND THE PLACEMENT OF YOUR VENUS

The placement of your Venus is determined by the year, month, and day you were born. Venus will be located in a zodiac sign close to that of your Sun, since it never moves more than *two* signs (about 48 degrees) from the Sun in either direction. (If you have a Virgo Sun, for instance, your Venus would either be in Cancer, Leo, Virgo, Libra, or Scorpio.)

Look up your Venus placement and that of your love partner in the following tables under the year, month, and day of your birthdays. Then read the descriptions for those placements and compare.

SYMBOLS

The Love Planets		*Signs of the Zodiac*					
Sun	☉	Aries	♈	Leo	♌	Sagittarius	♐
Moon	☽	Taurus	♉	Virgo	♍	Capricorn	♑
Venus	♀	Gemini	♊	Libra	♎	Aquarius	♒
Mars	♂	Cancer	♋	Scorpio	♏	Pisces	♓

("R" and "D" notations signify Retrograde and Direct.)

January

	1st	3rd	5th	7th	9th	11th	13th	15th	17th	19th	21st	23rd	25th	27th	29th	31st
1900	06♒	08	11	13	16	18	21	23	26	28	01♓	03	06	08	11	13♓
1901	10♐	13	15	18	20	23	25	28	00♑	03	05	08	10	13	15	18♑
1902	23♑	24	26	27	28	29	00♒	01	02	02	03	03	03	03R	03	02♓
1903	17♑	19	22	24	27	29	02♒	04	07	09	12	14	17	19	22	24♒
1904	25♏	27	29	02♐	04	06	09	11	13	16	18	21	23	25	28	00♑
1905	22♒	24	26	29	01♓	03	06	08	10	13	15	17	19	22	24	26♓
1906	29♐	01♑	04	06	09	11	14	16	19	21	24	26	29	01♒	04	06♒
1907	01♐	02	03	04	05	07	08	10	11	13	14	16	18	19	21	23♐
1908	05♒	08	10	13	15	18	20	23	25	28	00♓	02	05	07	10	12♓
1909	11♐	13	16	18	21	23	26	28	01♑	03	06	08	11	13	16	18♑
1910	22♒	24	25	26	27	28	29	29	00♓	00	00	00R	00	00	00	29♒
1911	17♑	20	23	25	28	00♒	03	05	08	10	13	15	18	20	23	25♒
1912	25♏	27	00♐	02	04	07	09	12	14	16	19	21	24	26	28	01♑
1913	22♒	25	27	29	02♓	04	06	08	11	13	15	18	20	22	24	26♓
1914	29♐	02♑	04	07	09	12	14	17	19	22	24	27	29	02♒	04	07♒
1915	00♐	01	02	03	05	06	07	09	11	12	14	16	17	19	21	23♐
1916	06♒	08	11	13	16	18	21	23	26	28	01♓	03	06	08	10	13♓
1917	12♐	14	16	19	21	24	26	29	01♑	04	06	09	11	14	16	19♑
1918	21♒	23	24	25	26	26	27	27	28	28R	28	28	28	27	26	26♒
1919	18♑	21	23	26	28	01♒	03	06	08	11	13	16	18	21	23	26♒
1920	26♏	28	00♐	03	05	07	10	12	14	17	19	22	24	26	29	01♑
1921	23♒	25	27	00♓	02	04	07	09	11	13	16	18	20	22	24	27♓
1922	00♑	02	05	07	10	12	15	18	20	23	25	28	00♒	03	05	08♒
1923	29♏	00♐	01	02	04	05	07	08	10	12	14	15	17	19	21	23♏
1924	07♒	09	12	14	16	19	21	24	26	29	01♓	04	06	09	11	14♓
1925	12♐	15	17	20	22	25	27	00♑	02	05	07	10	12	15	17	20♑
1926	20♒	22	22	23	24	25	25	25	26R	26	25	25	25	24	23	22♒
1927	19♑	21	24	26	29	01♒	04	06	09	11	14	16	19	21	24	26♒
1928	26♏	28	01♐	03	05	08	10	13	15	17	20	22	25	27	29	02♑
1929	23♒	25	28	00♓	02	05	07	09	11	14	16	18	20	22	25	27♓
1930	01♑	03	06	08	11	13	16	18	21	23	26	28	01♒	03	06	08♒
1931	28♏	29	00♐	02	03	05	06	08	10	11	13	15	17	19	21	23♐
1932	07♒	10	12	15	17	20	22	24	27	29	02♓	04	07	09	12	14♓
1933	13♐	15	18	20	23	25	28	00♑	03	05	08	10	13	15	18	20♑
1934	19♒	20	21	22	22	23	23	23R	23	23	23	22	21	20	19	18♒
1935	20♑	22	25	27	01♒	02	05	07	10	12	15	17	20	22	25	27♒
1936	26♏	29	01♐	04	06	08	11	13	16	18	20	23	25	28	00♑	02♑
1937	24♒	26	28	00♓	03	05	07	10	12	14	16	18	21	23	25	27♓
1938	01♑	04	06	09	11	14	16	19	21	24	26	29	01♒	04	06	09♒
1939	27♏	28	00♐	01	03	04	06	08	09	11	13	15	17	19	21	23♐
1940	08♒	10	13	15	18	20	23	25	28	00♓	02	05	07	10	12	15♓
1941	13♐	16	18	21	23	26	28	01♑	03	06	08	11	13	16	18	21♑
1942	18♒	19	19	20	20	21	21R	21	20	20	19	19	18	17	16	14♒
1943	20♑	23	25	28	00♒	03	05	08	10	13	15	18	20	23	25	28♒
1944	27♏	29	02♐	04	06	09	11	14	16	18	21	23	26	28	01♑	03♑
1945	24♒	26	29	01♓	03	05	08	10	12	14	17	19	21	23	25	27♓
1946	02♑	04	07	09	12	15	17	20	22	25	27	00♒	02	06	07	10♒
1947	26♏	27	29	01♐	02	04	06	07	09	11	13	15	17	19	21	23♐
1948	08♒	11	13	16	18	21	23	26	28	01♓	03	06	08	10	13	15♒
1949	14♐	17	19	22	24	27	29	02♑	04	07	09	12	14	17	19	22♑
1950	16♒	17	18	18	18R	18	18	18	17	17	16	15	14	13	12	11♒
1951	21♑	23	26	28	01♒	03	06	08	11	13	16	18	21	23	26	28♒
1952	27♏	00♐	02	05	07	09	12	14	17	19	21	24	26	29	01♑	04♑
1953	24♒	27	29	01♓	04	06	08	10	12	15	17	19	21	23	25	27♓
1954	03♑	05	08	10	13	15	18	20	23	25	28	00♒	03	05	08	10♒
1955	25♏	27	28	00♐	02	04	05	07	09	11	13	15	17	19	21	23♐
1956	09♒	12	14	16	19	21	24	26	29	01♓	04	05	09	11	13	16♓
1957	15♐	17	20	17	18	19	20	21	23	24	25	26	27	29	00♑	01♑
1958	15♒	15	16	16R	16	16	15	15	14	13	12	11	10	09	08	07♒
1959	22♑	24	27	29	02♒	04	07	09	12	14	17	19	22	24	27	29♒
1960	28♏	00♐	03	05	07	10	12	15	17	20	22	24	27	29	02♑	04♑
1961	25♒	27	29	02♓	04	06	08	10	13	15	17	19	21	23	25	27♓
1962	03♑	06	08	11	13	16	18	21	23	26	28	01♒	03	06	08	11♒
1963	25♏	26	28	00♐	02	03	05	07	09	11	13	15	17	19	21	23♐
1964	10♒	12	15	17	20	22	24	27	29	02♓	04	07	09	12	14	16♓
1965	15♐	18	20	23	25	28	00♑	03	05	08	10	13	15	18	20	23♑
1966	13♒	13	13R	13	13	13	12	12	11	10	09	08	06	05	04	03♒
1967	22♑	25	27	00♒	02	05	07	10	12	15	17	20	22	25	27	00♓
1968	28♏	01♐	03	06	08	10	13	15	18	20	23	25	27	00♑	02	05♑
1969	25♒	27	00♓	02	04	06	09	11	13	15	17	19	21	23	25	27♓
1970	04♑	06	09	12	14	17	19	22	24	27	29	02♒	04	07	09	12♒
1971	24♏	26	28	29	01♐	03	05	07	09	11	13	15	17	19	21	23♐
1972	10♒	13	15	18	20	23	25	28	00♓	02	05	07	10	12	15	17♓
1973	16♐	19	21	24	26	29	01♑	04	06	09	11	14	16	19	21	24♑
1974	11♒	11R	11	11	10	10	09	08	07	06	05	04	02	01	00	29♑
1975	23♑	25	28	00♒	03	05	08	10	13	15	18	20	23	25	28	00♓
1976	29♏	01♐	04	06	09	11	13	16	18	21	23	26	28	00♑	03	05♑
1977	26♒	28	00♓	02	04	07	09	11	13	15	17	19	21	23	25	27♓
1978	05♑	07	10	12	15	17	20	22	25	27	00♒	02	05	07	10	12♒
1979	24♏	26	27	29	01♐	03	05	07	09	11	13	15	17	19	21	24♐
1980	11♒	13	16	18	21	23	26	28	01♓	03	05	08	10	13	15	18♓
1981	17♐	19	22	24	27	29	02♑	04	07	09	12	14	17	19	22	24♑
1982	08♒	08	08	08	07	06	05	04	03	02	01	00	28♑	27	26	25♑
1983	24♑ R	26	29	01♒	04	06	09	11	14	16	19	21	24	26	29	01♓
1984	29♏	02♐	04	07	09	11	14	16	19	21	24	26	29	01♑	03	06♑
1985	26♒	28	00♓	03	05	07	09	11	13	15	17	19	21	23	25	27♓
1986	05♑	08	10	13	15	18	20	23	25	28	00♒	03	05	08	11	13♒
1987	24♏	25	27	29	01♐	03	05	06	09	11	13	15	17	20	22	24♐
1988	12♒	14	16	19	21	24	26	29	01♓	04	06	08	11	13	16	18♓
1989	17♐	20	22	25	27	00♑	02	05	07	10	12	15	17	20	22	25♑

February

	1st	3rd	5th	7th	9th	11th	13th	15th	17th	19th	21st	23rd	25th	27th	29th
1900	14♓	17	19	22	24	26	29	01♈	04	06	08	11	13	16♈	
1901	19♑	21	24	16	29	01♒	04	06	09	11	14	16	19	21♒	
1902	02♓ R	01	00	29♒	28	27	26	25	24	22	21	20	19	19♒	
1903	26♒	28	01♓	03	06	08	11	13	16	18	21	23	26	28♓	
1904	01♑	04	06	09	11	14	16	18	21	23	26	28	01♒	03	05♒
1905	27♓	29	01♈	04	06	08	10	12	14	16	18	20	21	23♈	
1906	08♒	10	13	15	18	20	23	25	28	00♓	03	05	08	10♓	
1907	24♐	26	28	00♑	02	04	06	08	10	12	14	16	19	21♑	
1908	14♓	16	28	21	23	26	28	01♈	03	05	08	10	13	15	17♈
1909	19♑	22	24	27	29	02♒	04	07	09	12	14	17	19	22♒	
1910	29♒ R	28	27	26	25	23	22	21	20	19	18	17	16	15♒	
1911	26♒	29	01♓	04	06	09	11	14	16	19	21	24	26	29♓	
1912	02♑	04	07	09	12	14	17	19	21	24	16	29	01♒	04	06♒
1913	27♓	00♈	02	04	06	08	10	12	14	16	18	20	21	23♈	
1914	08♒	11	13	16	18	21	23	26	28	01♓	03	06	08	22♓	
1915	24♐	26	28	00♑	02	04	06	08	10	12	15	17	19	21♑	
1916	14♓	17	19	21	24	26	29	01♈	04	06	08	11	13	16	18♈
1917	20♑	23	25	28	00♒	03	05	08	10	13	15	18	20	23♒	
1918	25♒ R	24	23	22	21	29	18	17	16	15	14	13	13	13♒	
1919	27♒	00♓	02	05	07	10	12	15	17	19	22	24	27	29♓	
1920	03♑	05	07	10	12	15	17	20	22	24	27	29	02♒	04	07♒
1921	28♓	00♈	02	04	06	08	10	12	14	16	18	19	21	23♈	
1922	09♒	11	14	16	19	21	24	26	29	01♓	04	06	09	11♓	
1923	24♐	26	28	00♑	02	04	06	08	10	13	15	17	19	21♑	
1924	15♓	17	20	22	24	27	29	02♈	04	07	09	11	14	16	18♈
1925	21♑	23	26	28	01♒	03	06	08	11	13	16	18	21	23♒	
1926	22♒ R	20	19	18	17	16	14	13	12	12	11	10	10	10♒ D	
1927	28♒	00♓	03	05	08	10	13	15	18	20	23	25	28	00♈	
1928	03♑	06	08	10	13	15	18	20	23	25	27	00♒	02	05	07♒
1929	28♓	00♈	02	04	06	08	10	12	14	16	17	19	21	23♈	
1930	10♒	12	15	17	20	22	25	27	00♓	02	05	07	10	12♓	
1931	24♐	26	28	00♑	02	04	06	09	11	13	15	17	19	22♑	
1932	15♓	18	20	23	25	27	00♈	02	05	07	09	12	14	17	19♈
1933	21♑	24	26	29	01♒	04	06	09	11	14	16	19	21	24♒	
1934	18♒ R	17	15	14	13	12	11	10	09	08	08	08	07D	07♒	
1935	28♒	01♓	03	06	08	11	13	16	18	21	23	26	28	01♈	
1936	04♑	06	09	11	13	16	18	21	23	26	28	01♒	03	05	08♒
1937	28♓	00♈	02	04	06	08	10	12	14	16	17	19	21	22♈	
1938	10♒	13	15	18	20	23	25	28	00♓	03	05	08	10	13♓	
1939	24♐	26	28	00♑	02	04	07	09	11	13	15	18	20	22♑	
1940	16♓	18	21	23	26	28	00♈	03	05	08	10	12	15	17	19♈
1941	22♑	25	27	00♒	02	05	07	10	12	15	17	20	22	25♒	
1942	14♒ R	13	11	10	09	08	07	06	06	05	05D	05	05	05♒	
1943	29♒	02♓	04	07	09	12	14	16	19	21	24	26	29	01♈	
1944	04♑	07	09	12	14	16	19	21	24	26	29	01♒	04	06	08♒
1945	28♓	00♈	02	04	06	08	10	12	14	15	17	19	20	22♈	
1946	11♒	13	16	18	21	23	26	28	01♓	03	06	08	11	13♓	
1947	24♐	26	28	00♑	02	05	07	09	11	13	16	18	20	22♑	
1948	16♓	19	21	24	26	29	01♈	03	06	08	11	13	15	18	20♈
1949	23♑	25	28	00♒	03	05	08	10	13	15	18	20	23	25♒	
1950	10♒ R	09	07	06	05	05	04	03	03	03D	03	03	03	03♒	
1951	00♓	02	05	07	10	12	15	17	20	22	25	27	00♈	02♈	
1952	05♑	07	10	12	15	17	19	22	24	27	29	02♒	04	07	09♒
1953	28♓	00♈	02	04	06	08	10	12	13	15	17	18	20	21♈	
1954	12♒	14	17	19	22	24	27	29	02♓	04	07	09	12	14♓	
1955	24♐	26	28	01♑	03	05	07	09	12	14	16	18	21	23♑	
1956	17♓	19	22	24	27	29	02♈	04	06	09	11	13	16	18	20♈
1957	23♑	26	28	01♒	03	06	08	11	13	16	18	21	23	26♒	
1958	06♒ R	05	04	03	02	01	01	00	00D	00	00	01	01	02♒	
1959	00♓	03	05	08	10	13	15	18	20	23	25	28	00♈	03♈	
1960	05♑	08	10	13	15	18	20	23	25	27	00♒	02	05	07	10♒
1961	28♓	00♈	02	04	06	08	10	11	13	15	16	18	19	21♈	
1962	12♒	15	17	20	22	25	27	00♓	02	05	07	10	12	15♓	
1963	24♐	26	29	01♑	03	05	07	10	12	14	16	19	21	23♑	
1964	18♓	20	22	25	27	00♈	02	04	07	09	12	14	16	19	21♈
1965	24♑	27	29	02♒	04	07	09	12	14	17	19	22	24	27♒	
1966	02♒ R	01	00	29♑	29	28	28	28D	28	28	28	29	29	00♒	
1967	01♓	04	06	08	11	13	16	18	21	23	26	28	01♈	03♈	
1968	06♑	08	11	13	16	18	21	23	26	28	00♒	03	05	10♒	
1969	28♓	00♈	02	04	06	08	09	11	13	14	16	17	18	20♈	
1970	13♒	15	18	20	23	25	28	01♓	03	06	08	11	13	16♓	
1971	24♐	27	29	01♑	03	05	08	10	12	14	17	19	21	24♑	
1972	18♓	21	23	25	28	00♈	03	05	07	10	12	14	17	19	21♈
1973	25♑	27	00♒	02	05	07	10	12	15	17	20	22	25	27♒	
1974	28♑ R	27	27	26	26	25	25D	25	26	26	26	27	28	29♑	
1975	02♓	04	07	09	12	14	17	19	22	24	27	29	01♈	04♈	
1976	07♑	09	11	14	16	19	21	24	26	29	01♒	04	06	08	11♒
1977	28♓	00♈	02	04	06	07	09	11	12	14	15	16	18	19♈	
1978	14♒	16	19	21	24	26	29	01♓	04	06	09	11	14	16♓	
1979	25♐	27	29	01♑	04	06	08	10	13	15	17	19	22	24♑	
1980	19♓	21	24	26	28	01♈	03	05	08	10	13	15	17	19	22♈
1981	25♑	28	00♒	03	05	08	10	13	15	18	20	23	25	28♒	
1982	25♑ R	24	24	23	23D	23	23	23	24	24	25	26	27	28♑	
1983	02♓	05	07	10	12	15	17	20	22	25	27	00♈	02	05♈	
1984	07♑	10	12	14	17	19	22	24	27	29	02♒	04	07	09	12♒
1985	28♓	00♈	02	04	05	07	09	10	12	13	14	16	17	18♈	
1986	14♒	17	19	22	24	27	29	02♓	04	07	09	12	14	17♓	
1987	25♐	27	29	02♑	04	06	08	11	13	15	18	20	22	24♑	
1988	19♓	22	24	26	29	01♈	04	06	08	11	13	15	18	20	22♈
1989	26♑	29	01♒	04	06	09	11	14	16	19	21	24	26	29♒	

March

	1st	3rd	5th	7th	9th	11th	13th	15th	17th	19th	21st	23rd	25th	27th	29th	31st
1900	18♈	20	23	25	27	00♉	02	04	07	09	11	14	16	18	20	23♉
1901	24♒	26	29	01♓	04	06	09	11	14	16	19	21	24	26	29	01♈
1902	18♒R	17	17	17D	17	17	18	18	19	19	20	21	22	23	25	26♒
1903	01♈	03	06	08	10	13	15	18	20	13	25	28	00♉	03	05	07♉
1904	07♒	09	12	14	16	19	21	24	26	29	01♓	04	06	08	11	13♓
1905	25♈	27	29	00♉	02	03	05	06	07	08	10	11	12	12	13	13♉
1906	13♓	15	18	20	23	25	28	00♈	03	05	08	10	12	15	17	20♈
1907	23♑	25	27	00♒	02	04	06	09	11	13	16	18	20	22	25	27♒
1908	19♈	21	23	26	28	00♉	03	05	07	10	12	14	16	19	21	23♉
1909	24♒	27	29	02♓	04	07	09	12	14	17	19	22	24	27	29	02♈
1910	15♒R	15	15D	15	15	15	16	16	17	18	19	20	21	23	24	25♒
1911	01♈	04	06	09	11	14	16	19	21	23	26	28	01♉	03	06	08♉
1912	07♒	10	12	16	17	20	22	24	27	29	02♓	04	07	09	12	14♓
1913	25♈	27	28	00♉	01	03	04	05	06	08	09	09	10	11	11	12♉
1914	13♓	16	18	21	23	26	28	01♈	03	06	08	11	13	16	18	21♈
1915	23♑	26	28	00♒	02	05	07	09	11	14	16	18	21	23	25	28♒
1916	19♈	21	24	26	28	01♉	03	05	08	10	12	15	17	19	21	23♉
1917	25♒	28	00♓	03	05	08	10	13	15	17	20	22	25	27	00♈	02♈
1918	12♒R	12D	12	13	13	14	14	15	16	17	18	19	21	22	23	25♒
1919	02♓	04	07	09	12	14	17	19	22	24	27	29	01♈	04	06	09♈
1920	08♒	10	13	15	18	20	23	25	27	00♓	02	05	07	10	12	15♓
1921	25♈	26	28	29	01♉	02	03	04	06	06	07	08	09	09	10	10♉
1922	14♓	16	19	21	24	26	29	01♈	04	06	09	11	14	16	19	21♈
1923	24♑	26	28	00♒	03	05	07	10	12	14	16	19	21	23	25	28♒
1924	20♈	22	24	27	29	02♉	07	06	08	10	13	15	17	19	22	24♉
1925	26♒	28	01♓	03	06	08	11	13	16	18	21	23	26	28	01♈	03♈
1926	10♒	10	10	11	11	12	13	14	15	16	17	18	20	21	23	24♒
1927	03♈	05	07	10	12	15	17	20	22	25	27	00♉	02	04	07	09♉
1928	08♒	11	13	16	18	21	23	26	28	01♓	03	05	08	10	13	15♓
1929	24♈	26	27	29	00♉	01	02	03	04	05	06	07	07	07	08R	08♉
1930	15♓	17	20	22	25	27	00♈	02	05	07	10	12	14	17	19	22♈
1931	24♑	26	28	01♒	03	05	08	10	12	15	17	19	22	24	26	29♒
1932	20♈	22	25	27	29	02♉	04	06	09	11	13	15	18	20	22	24♉
1933	26♒	29	01♓	04	06	09	11	14	16	19	21	24	26	29	01♈	04♈
1934	08♒	08	08	09	10	11	12	13	14	15	16	18	19	21	22	24♒
1935	03♈	06	08	11	13	16	18	20	23	25	28	00♉	03	05	07	10♉
1936	09♒	12	14	16	19	21	24	26	29	01♓	04	06	09	11	13	16♓
1937	24♈	25	27	28	29	00♉	01	02	03	04	04	05	05	05R	05	05♉
1938	15♓	18	20	23	25	28	00♈	03	05	08	10	13	15	18	20	23♈
1939	24♑	27	29	01♒	03	06	08	10	13	15	17	20	22	24	27	29♒
1940	21♈	23	25	28	00♉	02	04	07	09	11	13	16	18	20	22	24♉
1941	27♒	00♓	02	05	07	10	12	15	17	20	22	24	27	29	02♈	04♈
1942	06♒	06	07	08	08	09	11	12	13	14	16	17	19	20	22	24♒
1943	04♈	06	09	11	14	16	19	21	23	26	28	01♉	03	06	08	11♉
1944	10♒	12	15	17	20	22	24	27	29	02♓	04	07	09	12	14	17♓
1945	23♈	25	26	27	28	29	00♉	01	02	02	03	03	03R	03	03	02♉
1946	16♓	18	21	23	26	28	01♈	03	06	08	11	13	16	18	21	23♈
1947	25♑	27	29	02♒	04	06	09	11	13	15	18	20	23	25	27	00♓
1948	21♈	23	26	28	00♉	03	05	07	09	12	14	16	18	20	23	25♉
1949	28♒	00♓	03	05	08	10	13	15	18	20	23	25	28	00♈	03	05♈
1950	04♒	05	05	06	07	08	10	11	12	14	15	17	18	20	22	23♒
1951	04♈	07	09	12	14	17	19	22	24	27	29	01♉	04	06	09	11♉
1952	10♒	13	15	18	20	23	25	28	00♓	02	05	07	10	12	15	17♓
1953	23♈	24	25	26	27	28	29	00♉	00	01	01	01R	01	01	00	00♉
1954	17♓	19	22	24	27	29	02♈	04	07	09	12	14	17	19	21	24♈
1955	25♑	27	00♒	02	04	07	09	11	14	16	18	21	23	25	28	00♓
1956	22♈	24	26	28	01♉	03	05	08	10	12	14	16	19	21	23	25♉
1957	28♒	01♓	03	06	08	11	13	16	18	21	23	26	28	01♈	03	06♈
1958	02♒	03	04	05	06	07	09	10	12	13	15	16	18	20	21	23♒
1959	05♈	08	10	13	15	17	20	22	25	27	00♉	02	04	07	09	12♉
1960	11♒	13	16	18	21	23	26	28	01♓	03	06	08	11	13	15	18♓
1961	22♈	23	24	25	26	27	27	28	28	29	29R	29	28	28	27	26♈
1962	17♓	20	22	25	27	00♈	02	05	07	10	12	15	17	20	22	25♈
1963	25♑	28	00♒	02	05	07	09	12	14	16	19	21	24	26	28	01♓
1964	22♈	24	27	29	01♉	03	06	08	10	12	15	17	19	21	23	25♉
1965	29♒	02♓	04	07	09	12	14	17	19	22	24	27	29	01♈	04	06♈
1966	01♒	02	03	04	05	07	08	10	11	13	14	16	18	19	21	23♒
1967	06♈	08	11	13	16	18	20	23	25	28	00♉	03	05	07	10	12♉
1968	12♒	14	16	19	21	24	26	29	01♓	04	06	09	11	14	16	J9♓
1969	21♈	22	23	24	25	25	26	26	26	26R	26	26	25	25	24	23♈
1970	18♓	21	23	26	28	00♈	03	05	08	10	13	15	18	20	23	25♈
1971	26♑	28	01♒	03	05	08	10	12	15	17	19	22	24	26	29	01♓
1972	22♈	25	27	29	02♉	04	06	08	11	13	15	17	19	21	23	25♉
1973	00♓	02	05	07	10	12	15	17	20	22	25	27	00♈	02	05	07♈
1974	00♒	01	02	03	05	06	07	09	11	12	14	16	17	19	21	23♒
1975	06♈	09	11	14	16	19	21	24	26	28	01♉	03	06	08	11	13♉
1976	12♒	15	17	20	22	25	27	29	02♓	04	07	09	12	14	17	19♓
1977	20♈	21	22	22	23	24	24	24R	24	24	24	23	22	22	21	20♈
1978	19♓	21	24	26	29	01♈	04	06	09	11	14	16	19	21	23	26♈
1979	26♑	29	01♒	03	06	08	10	13	15	17	20	22	25	27	29	02♓
1980	23♈	25	27	00♉	02	04	05	09	11	13	15	17	19	22	24	26♉
1981	00♓	03	05	08	10	13	15	18	20	23	25	28	00♈	03	05	08♈
1982	29♑	00♒	01	02	04	05	07	09	10	12	14	16	17	19	21	23♒
1983	07♈	09	12	14	17	19	22	24	27	29	01♉	04	06	09	11	13♉
1984	13♒	15	18	20	23	25	28	00♓	03	05	07	10	12	15	17	20♓
1985	19♈	20	20	21	21	22	22R	22	22	21	21	20	19	18	17	16♈
1986	19♓	22	24	27	29	02♈	04	07	09	12	14	17	19	22	24	27♈
1987	27♑	29	01♒	04	06	09	11	13	16	18	20	23	25	28	00♓	02♓
1988	23♈	26	28	00♉	02	05	07	09	11	13	15	18	20	22	24	26♉
1989	01♓	04	06	09	11	14	16	19	21	24	26	29	01♈	04	06	08♈

April

	1st	3rd	5th	7th	9th	11th	13th	15th	17th	19th	21st	23rd	25th	27th	29th
1900	24♉	26	28	00♊	03	05	07	09	11	13	15	17	19	21	23♊
1901	02♈	05	07	10	12	15	17	20	22	25	27	00♉	02	04	07♉
1902	27♒	28	00♓	01	03	04	06	08	10	12	13	15	17	19	21♓
1903	09♉	11	14	16	18	21	23	25	28	00♊	03	05	08	10	12♊
1904	15♓	17	20	22	24	27	29	02♈	04	07	09	12	14	16	19♈
1905	14♉	14	14R	14	14	14	13	13	12	11	10	09	07	06	05♉
1906	21♈	24	26	29	01♉	04	06	08	11	13	16	18	21	23	26♉
1907	28♒	01♓	03	05	08	10	12	15	17	19	22	24	27	29	01♈
1908	24♉	26	29	01♊	03	05	07	09	11	13	15	17	19	21	23♊
1909	03♈	05	08	10	13	15	18	20	23	25	28	00♉	03	05	08♉
1910	26♒	28	29	01♓	02	04	06	08	10	11	13	15	17	19	21♓
1911	09♉	12	14	17	19	21	24	26	29	01♊	03	06	08	10	13♊
1912	15♓	18	20	23	25	28	00♈	02	05	07	10	12	15	17	20♈
1913	12♉	12R	12	12	11	11	10	09	09	07	06	05	04	03	01♉
1914	22♈	24	27	29	02♉	04	07	09	12	14	17	19	21	24	26♉
1915	29♒	01♓	03	06	08	11	13	15	18	20	22	25	27	29	02♈
1916	25♉	27	29	01♊	03	05	07	09	12	14	16	18	20	21	23♊
1917	04♈	06	09	11	14	16	19	21	23	26	28	01♉	03	06	08♉
1918	26♒	27	29	00♓	02	04	06	08	10	11	13	15	17	19	21♓
1919	10♉	12	15	17	20	22	24	27	29	02♊	04	06	09	11	13♊
1920	16♓	18	21	23	26	28	01♈	03	06	08	10	13	15	18	20♈
1921	10♉R	10	10	09	09	08	07	06	05	04	03	01	00	29♈	28♈
1922	23♈	25	27	00♉	02	05	07	10	12	15	17	20	22	25	27♉
1923	29♒	02♓	04	06	09	11	13	16	18	21	23	25	28	00♈	02♈
1924	25♉	27	29	01♊	03	06	08	10	12	14	16	18	20	21	23♊
1925	04♈	07	09	12	14	17	19	22	24	27	29	02♉	04	06	09♉
1926	25♒	27	29	00♓	02	04	06	08	09	11	13	15	17	19	21♓
1927	11♉	13	15	18	20	23	25	27	00♊	02	04	07	09	12	24♊
1928	17♓	19	21	24	26	29	01♈	04	06	09	11	14	16	18	21♈
1929	07♉R	07	07	06	06	05	04	03	01	00	29♈	28	26	25	24♈
1930	23♈	26	28	01♉	03	06	08	10	13	15	18	20	23	25	28♉
1931	00♓	02	04	07	09	12	14	16	19	21	23	26	28	01♈	03♈
1932	25♉	27	29	02♊	04	06	08	10	12	14	16	18	20	21	23♊
1933	05♈	07	10	12	15	17	20	22	25	27	00♉	02	05	07	10♉
1934	25♒	27	28	00♓	02	04	06	08	10	11	13	16	18	20	22♓
1935	11♉	14	16	18	21	23	26	28	00♊	03	05	07	10	12	15♊
1936	17♓	20	22	25	27	29	02♈	04	07	09	12	14	17	19	22♈
1937	05♉R	05	04	03	02	01	00	29♈	28	27	25	24	23	22	21♈
1938	24♈	26	29	01♉	04	06	09	11	14	16	19	21	23	26	28♉
1939	00♓	03	05	07	10	12	14	17	19	22	24	26	29	01♈	04♈
1940	26♉	28	00♊	02	04	06	08	10	12	14	16	18	20	21	23♊
1941	06♈	08	11	13	16	18	21	23	25	28	00♉	03	05	08	10♉
1942	25♒	26	28	00♓	02	04	06	08	10	12	14	16	18	20	22♓
1943	12♉	14	17	19	21	24	26	28	01♊	03	06	08	10	13	15♊
1944	18♓	20	23	25	28	00♈	03	05	07	10	12	15	17	20	22♈
1945	02♉R	02	01	00	29♈	28	27	25	24	23	22	21	20	19	18♈
1946	25♈	27	28	02♉	04	07	09	12	14	17	19	22	24	27	29♉
1947	01♓	03	06	08	10	13	15	17	20	22	25	27	29	02♈	04♈
1948	26♉	28	00♊	02	04	06	08	10	12	14	16	18	19	21	23♊
1949	06♈	09	11	14	16	19	21	24	26	29	01♉	04	06	09	11♉
1950	24♒	26	28	00♓	02	04	06	08	10	12	14	16	18	20	22♓
1951	12♉	15	17	20	22	24	27	29	01♊	04	06	09	11	13	26♊
1952	18♓	21	23	26	28	01♈	03	06	08	11	13	16	18	20	23♈
1953	29♈R	28	28	26	25	24	23	22	20	19	18	17	16	16	15♈
1954	25♈	28	00♉	03	05	08	10	12	15	17	20	22	25	29	00♊
1955	01♓	04	06	08	11	13	16	18	20	23	25	28	00♈	02	05♈
1956	26♉	28	00♊	02	04	06	08	10	12	14	16	18	19	21	23♊
1957	07♈	10	12	14	17	19	22	24	27	29	02♉	04	07	09	12♉
1958	24♒	26	28	00♓	02	04	06	08	10	12	14	16	18	20	22♓
1959	13♉	15	18	20	23	25	27	00♊	02	04	07	09	11	14	16♊
1960	19♓	22	24	27	29	01♈	04	06	09	11	14	16	19	21	24♈
1961	26♈R	25	24	23	22	20	19	18	17	16	15	14	13	13	23♈
1962	26♈	28	01♉	03	06	08	11	13	16	18	20	23	25	28	00♊
1963	02♓	04	07	09	11	14	16	19	21	23	26	28	01♈	03	05♈
1964	26♉	28	00♊	02	04	06	08	10	12	14	16	17	19	21	22♊
1965	08♈	10	13	15	18	20	23	25	28	00♉	02	05	07	10	12♉
1966	24♒	26	28	00♓	02	04	06	08	10	12	14	16	18	21	23♓
1967	14♉	16	18	21	23	25	28	00♊	03	05	07	10	12	14	17♊
1968	20♓	22	25	27	00♈	02	05	07	09	12	14	17	19	22	24♈
1969	23♈R	22	20	19	18	17	15	14	13	12	12	11	10	10	10♈D
1970	27♈	29	01♉	04	06	09	11	14	16	19	21	24	26	28	01♊
1971	02♓	05	07	10	12	14	17	19	22	24	26	29	01♈	04	06♈
1972	27♉	29	01♊	03	05	06	08	10	12	14	16	17	19	20	22♊
1973	08♈	11	13	16	18	21	23	26	28	01♉	03	06	08	11	13♉
1974	24♒	26	28	00♓	02	04	06	08	10	12	14	17	19	21	23♓
1975	14♉	17	19	21	24	26	28	01♊	03	05	08	10	12	15	17♊
1976	20♓	23	25	28	00♈	03	05	08	10	13	15	18	20	22	25♈
1977	19♈R	18	17	15	14	13	12	11	10	09	09	08	08	08D	08♈
1978	27♈	00♉	02	05	07	10	12	14	17	19	22	24	27	29	02♊
1979	03♓	05	08	10	12	15	17	20	22	24	27	29	02♈	04	07♈
1980	27♉	29	01♊	03	05	06	08	10	12	14	15	17	19	20	22♊
1981	09♈	12	14	16	19	21	24	26	29	01♉	04	06	09	11	14♉
1982	24♒	26	28	00♓	02	04	06	08	10	13	15	17	19	21	23♓
1983	15♉	17	19	22	24	27	29	01♊	04	06	08	11	13	15	18♊
1984	21♓	24	26	28	01♈	03	06	08	11	13	16	18	21	23	26♈
1985	15♈R	14	13	12	10	09	08	08	07	06	06	06	06D	06	06♈
1986	28♈	00♉	03	05	08	10	13	15	18	20	22	25	27	00♊	02♊
1987	03♓	06	08	11	13	15	18	20	23	25	27	00♈	02	05	07♈
1988	27♉	29	01♊	03	05	06	08	10	12	13	15	17	18	20	21♊
1989	10♈	12	15	17	20	22	25	27	00♉	02	05	07	09	12	14♉

May

	1st	3rd	5th	7th	9th	11th	13th	15th	17th	19th	21st	23rd	25th	27th	29th	31st
1900	25♊	27	29	01♋	03	04	06	08	09	11	12	14	15	16	17	19♋
1901	09♉	12	14	17	19	22	24	27	29	02♊	04	07	09	11	14	16♊
1902	23♓	25	27	29	01♈	03	05	08	10	12	14	16	18	21	23	25♈
1903	15♊	17	19	22	24	26	29	01♋	03	06	08	10	13	15	17	19♋
1904	21♈	24	26	29	01♉	04	06	09	11	13	15	18	21	23	26	28♉
1905	04♉R	03	01	01	00	29♈	28	28	28D	28	28	28	29	29	00♉	00♉
1906	28♉	01♊	03	05	08	10	13	15	18	20	23	25	27	00♋	02	05♋
1907	04♈	06	08	11	13	16	18	20	23	25	28	00♉	02	05	07	10♉
1908	25♊	27	29	01♋	02	04	06	07	09	10	12	13	14	16	17	18♋
1909	10♉	13	15	17	20	22	25	27	00♊	02	05	07	10	12	15	17♊
1910	23♓	25	27	29	01♈	04	06	08	10	12	14	17	19	21	23	25♈
1911	15♊	18	20	22	25	27	29	02♋	04	06	08	11	13	15	18	20♋
1912	22♈	25	27	29	02♉	04	07	09	12	14	17	19	20	24	26	29♉
1913	00♉R	29♈	28	27	27	26	26	26D	26	26	26	26	27	28	28	29♈
1914	29♉	01♊	04	06	09	11	13	16	18	21	23	26	28	00♋	03	05♋
1915	04♈	07	09	11	14	16	19	21	23	26	28	01♉	03	05	08	10♉
1916	25♊	27	29	00♋	02	04	05	07	08	10	11	12	14	15	16	17♋
1917	11♉	13	16	18	21	23	26	28	00♊	03	05	08	10	13	15	18♊
1918	23♓	25	28	00♈	02	04	06	08	10	13	15	17	19	21	24	26♈
1919	16♊	18	20	23	25	27	00♋	02	04	07	09	11	13	16	18	20♋
1920	23♈	25	28	00♉	03	05	07	10	12	15	17	20	22	25	27	30♉
1921	27♈R	26	25	24	24	24	23D	23	24	24	24	25	26	26	27	28♈
1922	29♉	02♊	04	07	09	12	14	17	19	21	24	26	29	01♋	03	06♋
1923	05♈	07	10	12	14	17	19	22	24	26	29	01♉	04	06	08	11♉
1924	25♊	27	29	00♋	02	03	05	06	08	09	10	12	13	14	15	15♋
1925	11♉	14	16	19	21	24	26	29	01♊	04	06	09	11	13	16	18♊
1926	24♓	26	28	00♈	02	04	06	09	11	13	15	17	20	22	24	26♈
1927	16♊	19	21	23	26	28	00♋	03	05	07	09	12	14	16	18	21♋
1928	23♈	26	28	01♉	03	06	08	11	13	15	18	20	23	25	28	00♊
1929	23♈R	23	22	22	21	21D	21	21	22	22	23	23	24	25	26	27♈
1930	00♊	03	05	07	10	12	15	17	20	22	24	27	29	02♋	04	07♋
1931	05♈	08	10	13	15	17	20	22	25	27	29	02♉	04	07	09	11♉
1932	25♊	27	28	00♋	02	03	05	06	07	08	10	11	12	12	13	14♋
1933	12♉	15	17	20	22	24	27	29	02♊	04	07	09	12	14	17	19♊
1934	24♓	26	28	00♈	02	05	07	09	11	13	16	18	20	22	24	27♈
1935	17♊	19	22	24	26	28	01♋	03	05	08	10	12	14	17	19	21♋
1936	24♈	26	29	01♉	04	06	09	11	14	16	19	21	23	26	28	01♊
1937	20♈R	20	19	19	19D	19	19	20	20	21	21	22	23	24	25	27♈
1938	01♊	03	06	08	11	13	15	18	20	24	25	27	00♋	02	05	07♋
1939	06♈	08	11	13	16	18	20	23	25	28	00♉	02	05	07	10	12♉
1940	25♊	26	28	00♋	01	03	04	05	07	08	09	10	10	11	12	12♋
1941	13♉	15	18	20	13	25	28	00♊	02	05	07	10	12	15	17	20♊
1942	24♓	26	28	00♈	03	05	07	09	11	14	16	18	20	23	25	27♈
1943	17♊	20	22	24	27	29	01♋	04	06	08	10	13	15	17	19	21♋
1944	25♈	27	00♉	02	05	07	09	12	14	17	19	22	24	27	29	02♊
1945	17♈R	17	17	17D	17	17	17	18	19	19	20	21	22	23	25	26♈
1946	01♊	04	06	09	11	14	16	18	21	23	26	28	01♋	03	05	08♋
1947	07♈	09	11	14	16	19	21	23	26	28	01♉	03	05	08	10	13♉
1948	25♊	26	28	29	01♋	02	03	05	06	07	08	08	09	10	10	10♋
1949	13♉	16	18	21	23	26	28	01♊	03	06	08	11	13	15	18	20♊
1950	24♓	26	29	01♈	03	05	07	10	12	14	16	19	21	23	25	28♈
1951	18♊	20	23	25	27	29	02♋	04	06	08	11	13	15	17	20	22♋
1952	25♈	28	00♉	03	05	08	10	13	15	17	20	22	25	27	00♊	02♊
1953	15♈R	15	14D	15	15	15	16	16	17	18	19	20	21	23	24	25♈
1954	02♊	04	07	09	12	14	17	19	22	24	26	29	01♋	04	06	08♋
1955	07♈	10	12	14	17	19	22	24	26	29	01♉	04	06	08	11	13♉
1956	24♊	26	27	29	00♋	01	03	04	05	06	06	07	08	08	08	09♋R
1957	14♉	17	19	22	24	26	29	01♊	04	06	09	11	14	16	19	21♊
1958	25♓	27	29	01♈	03	06	08	10	12	15	17	19	21	24	26	28♓
1959	18♊	21	23	25	28	00♋	02	04	07	09	11	13	16	18	20	22♋
1960	26♈	28	01♉	03	06	08	11	13	16	18	21	23	26	28	00♊	03♊
1961	12♈R	12D	12	13	13	14	14	15	16	17	18	19	21	22	23	25♈
1962	03♊	05	08	10	12	15	17	20	22	25	27	29	02♋	04	07	09♋
1963	08♈	10	13	15	17	20	22	25	27	29	02♉	04	07	09	12	14♉
1964	24♊	25	27	28	29	01♋	02	03	04	04	05	06	06	06	06R	06♋
1965	15♉	17	20	22	25	27	00♊	02	05	07	09	12	14	17	19	22♊
1966	25♓	27	29	02♈	04	06	08	10	13	15	17	19	22	24	26	29♈
1967	19♊	21	24	26	28	00♋	03	05	07	09	12	14	16	18	20	22♋
1968	27♈	29	02♉	04	07	09	11	14	16	19	21	24	26	29	01♊	04♊
1969	10♈	10	11	11	12	12	13	14	15	16	17	19	20	21	23	25♈
1970	03♊	06	08	11	13	16	18	20	23	25	28	00♋	02	05	07	10♋
1971	08♈	11	13	16	18	20	23	25	18	00♉	03	05	07	10	12	15♉
1972	23♊	25	26	27	29	00♋	01	02	02	03	04	04	04	04R	04	04♋
1973	16♉	18	20	23	25	28	00♊	03	05	08	10	13	15	18	20	22♊
1974	25♓	27	00♈	02	04	06	09	11	13	15	18	20	22	25	27	29♈
1975	19♊	22	24	26	29	01♋	03	05	08	10	12	14	16	18	21	23♋
1976	27♈	00♉	02	05	07	10	12	15	17	19	22	24	27	29	02♊	04♊
1977	08♈	08	09	09	10	11	12	13	14	15	17	18	20	21	23	24♈
1978	04♊	06	09	11	14	16	19	21	23	26	28	01♋	03	05	08	10♋
1979	09♈	11	14	16	19	21	23	26	28	01♉	03	06	08	10	13	15♉
1980	23♊	24	25	27	28	29	00♋	00	01	01	02	02R	02	02	02	01♋
1981	16♉	19	21	24	26	28	01♊	03	06	08	11	13	16	18	21	23♊
1982	26♓	28	00♈	02	05	07	09	11	14	16	18	20	23	25	27	00♉
1983	20♊	22	24	27	29	01♋	03	06	08	10	12	14	17	19	21	23♋
1984	28♈	00♉	03	05	08	10	13	15	18	20	23	25	28	00♊	02	05♊
1985	06♈	07	07	08	09	10	11	12	13	15	16	18	19	21	22	24♈
1986	05♊	07	09	12	14	17	19	22	24	26	29	01♋	04	06	08	11♋
1987	10♈	12	14	17	19	22	24	26	29	01♉	04	06	09	11	13	16♉
1988	22♊	24	25	26	27	28	28	29	29	00♋	00R	00	00	00	29♊	29♊
1989	17♉	19	22	24	27	29	02♊	04	07	09	11	14	16	19	21	24♊

June

	1st	3rd	5th	7th	9th	11th	13th	15th	17th	19th	21st	23rd	25th	27th	29th
1900	19♋	20	21	22	22	23	23	23	24R	23	23	23	22	22	21♋
1901	18♊	20	22	25	27	00♋	02	05	07	10	12	15	17	19	22♋
1902	26♈	28	01♉	03	05	07	10	12	14	17	19	21	23	26	28♉
1903	20♋	23	25	27	29	02♌	04	06	08	10	12	14	17	19	21♌
1904	29♉	02♊	04	07	09	12	14	17	19	21	24	26	29	01♋	04♋
1905	01♉	02	03	04	05	06	08	09	11	12	14	15	17	19	21♉
1906	06♋	08	11	13	15	18	20	23	25	27	00♌	02	05	07	09♌
1907	11♉	13	16	18	20	23	25	28	00♊	03	05	07	10	12	15♊
1908	18♋	19	20	20	21	21	21R	21	21	21	21	20	19	18	17♋
1909	18♊	21	23	26	28	00♋	03	05	08	10	13	15	18	20	23♋
1910	27♈	29	01♉	03	06	08	10	12	15	17	19	22	24	26	29♉
1911	21♋	23	25	28	00♌	02	04	06	08	11	13	15	17	19	21♌
1912	00♊	03	05	07	10	12	15	17	20	22	25	27	29	02♋	04♋
1913	00♉	01	02	03	05	06	07	09	10	12	14	15	17	19	21♉
1914	06♋	09	11	14	16	19	21	23	26	28	00♌	03	05	08	10♌
1915	11♉	14	16	19	21	23	26	28	01♊	03	06	08	10	13	15♊
1916	17♋	18	18	19	19	19R	19	19	19	18	18	17	16	15	14♋
1917	19♊	21	24	26	29	01♋	04	06	09	11	13	16	18	21	23♋
1918	27♈	29	02♉	04	05	08	11	13	15	18	20	22	24	27	29♉
1919	21♋	24	26	28	00♌	02	04	07	09	11	13	15	17	19	21♌
1920	01♊	03	06	08	11	13	15	18	20	23	25	28	00♋	03	05♋
1921	29♈	00♉	01	03	04	05	07	08	10	12	13	15	17	19	21♉
1922	07♋	10	12	14	17	19	22	24	26	29	01♌	03	06	08	11♌
1923	12♉	14	17	19	22	24	26	29	01♊	04	06	09	11	13	16♊
1924	16♋	16	17	17	17R	17	17	17	16	15	15	14	13	12	10♋
1925	20♊	22	24	27	29	02♋	04	07	09	12	14	17	19	21	24♋
1926	27♈	00♉	02	04	07	09	11	13	16	18	20	23	25	27♊	00♊
1927	22♋	24	26	28	00♌	03	05	07	09	11	13	15	17	19	21♌
1928	01♊	04	06	09	11	14	16	19	21	23	26	28	01♋	03	06♋
1929	28♈	29	01♉	02	03	05	07	08	10	12	13	15	17	19	21♉
1930	08♋	10	13	15	17	20	22	25	27	29	02♌	04	06	09	11♌
1931	13♉	15	17	20	22	25	27	00♊	02	04	07	09	12	14	17♊
1932	14♋	15	15	15R	15	15	14	14	13	12	11	10	09	08	07♋
1933	20♊	23	25	28	00♋	03	05	07	10	12	15	17	20	22	25♋
1934	28♈	00♉	02	05	07	09	12	14	16	19	21	23	26	28	00♊
1935	22♋	24	26	29	01♌	03	05	07	09	11	13	15	17	19	21♌
1936	02♊	05	07	09	12	14	17	19	22	24	27	29	02♋	04	06♋
1937	27♈	29	00♉	01	03	05	06	08	10	11	13	15	17	19	21♉
1938	08♋	11	13	16	18	20	23	25	27	00♌	02	05	07	09	12♌
1939	13♉	16	18	21	23	25	28	00♊	03	05	07	10	12	15	17♊
1940	12♋	13	13R	13	13	12	12	11	10	09	08	07	06	05	03♋
1941	21♊	23	26	28	01♋	03	06	08	11	13	15	18	20	23	25♋
1942	28♈	01♉	03	05	08	10	12	14	17	19	21	24	26	28	01♊
1943	22♋	25	27	29	01♌	03	05	07	09	11	13	15	17	19	21♌
1944	03♊	05	08	10	13	15	17	20	22	25	27	00♋	02	05	07♋
1945	27♈	28	00♉	01	03	04	06	08	09	11	13	15	17	19	21♉
1946	09♋	11	14	16	19	21	23	26	28	00♌	03	05	08	10	12♌
1947	14♉	16	19	21	24	26	28	01♊	03	06	08	11	13	15	18♊
1948	11♋	11R	11	10	10	09	09	08	07	06	05	03	02	01	00♋
1949	22♊	24	27	29	01♋	04	06	09	11	14	16	19	21	23	26♋
1950	29♈	01♉	03	06	08	10	13	15	17	20	22	24	27	29	01♊
1951	23♋	25	27	29	01♌	03	06	08	10	12	14	16	18	19	21♌
1952	03♊	06	08	11	13	16	18	21	23	26	28	00♋	03	05	08♋
1953	26♈	28	29	01♉	02	04	06	08	09	11	13	15	17	19	21♉
1954	10♋	12	14	17	19	22	24	26	29	01♌	03	06	08	10	13♌
1955	15♉	17	19	22	24	27	29	01♊	04	06	09	11	14	16	19♊
1956	09♋R	08	08	08	07	06	06	05	03	02	01	00	29♊	27	26♊
1957	22♊	25	27	00♋	02	05	07	09	12	14	17	19	22	24	27♋
1958	29♈	02♉	04	06	09	11	13	15	18	20	23	25	27	00♊	02♊
1959	23♋	25	27	00♌	02	04	06	08	10	12	14	16	18	19	21♌
1960	04♊	07	09	11	14	16	19	21	24	26	29	01♋	04	06	09♋
1961	26♈	27	29	01♉	02	04	06	08	09	11	13	15	17	19	21♉
1962	10♋	13	15	17	20	22	25	27	29	02♌	04	06	09	11	13♌
1963	15♉	18	20	22	25	27	00♊	02	05	07	09	12	14	17	19♊
1964	06♋R	06	06	05	04	03	02	01	00	29♊	27	26	25	24	23♊
1965	23♊	25	28	00♋	03	05	08	10	13	15	17	20	22	25	27♋
1966	00♉	02	04	07	09	11	14	16	18	21	23	25	28	00♊	02♊
1967	24♋	26	28	00♌	02	04	06	08	10	12	14	16	18	19	21♌
1968	05♊	07	10	12	15	17	20	22	24	27	29	02♋	04	07	09♋
1969	25♈	27	29	00♉	02	04	06	08	09	11	13	15	17	19	21♉
1970	11♋	13	16	18	20	23	25	27	00♌	02	05	07	09	12	14♌
1971	16♉	18	21	23	26	28	00♊	03	05	08	10	13	15	17	20♊
1972	04♋R	03	03	02	01	00	29♊	28	26	25	24	23	22	21	20♊
1973	24♊	26	29	01♋	03	06	08	11	13	16	18	21	23	25	28♋
1974	00♉	03	05	07	10	12	14	17	19	21	24	26	28	01♊	03♊
1975	24♋	26	28	00♌	02	04	06	08	10	12	14	16	18	19	21♌
1976	05♊	08	10	13	15	18	20	23	25	28	00♋	02	05	07	10♋
1977	25♈	27	28	00♉	02	04	06	08	09	11	13	15	17	19	22♉
1978	11♋	14	16	19	21	23	26	28	00♌	03	05	07	10	12	14♌
1979	16♉	19	21	24	26	29	01♊	03	06	08	11	13	16	18	21♊
1980	01♋R	00	00	29♊	28	26	25	24	23	22	20	19	18	18	17♊
1981	24♊	27	29	02♋	04	07	09	11	14	16	19	21	24	26	28♋
1982	01♉	03	05	08	10	12	15	17	19	22	24	27	29	01♊	04♊
1983	24♋	26	28	00♌	02	04	06	08	10	12	14	16	17	19	21♌
1984	06♊	09	11	14	16	18	21	23	26	28	01♋	03	06	08	11♋
1985	25♈	27	28	00♉	02	04	06	08	10	12	14	16	18	20	22♉
1986	12♋	14	17	19	21	24	26	29	01♌	03	06	08	10	13	15♌
1987	17♉	20	22	24	27	29	02♊	04	07	09	11	14	16	19	21♊
1988	28♊R	27	26	25	24	23	22	20	19	18	17	16	15	15	14♊
1989	25♊	27	00♋	02	05	07	10	12	15	17	19	22	24	27	29♋

July

	1st	3rd	5th	7th	9th	11th	13th	15th	17th	19th	21st	23rd	25th	27th	29th	31st
1900	20♋R	19	17	16	15	14	13	11	10	09	09	08	08	07	07D	07♋
1901	24♋	27	29	02♌	04	07	09	11	14	16	19	21	24	26	29	01♍
1902	00♊	03	05	07	10	12	14	17	19	21	24	26	29	01♋	03	06♋
1903	23♌	25	27	29	01♍	03	04	06	08	10	12	13	15	17	18	20♍
1904	06♋	09	11	14	16	18	21	23	26	28	01♌	03	06	08	11	13♌
1905	22♉	24	26	28	00♊	02	04	06	08	10	12	14	16	18	20	23♊
1906	12♌	14	17	19	21	24	26	28	01♍	03	05	08	10	12	15	17♍
1907	17♊	19	22	24	27	29	02♋	04	06	09	11	14	16	19	21	24♋
1908	16♋R	15	14	13	11	10	09	08	07	06	06	05	05	05D	05	05♋
1909	25♋	27	00♌	02	05	07	10	12	15	17	19	22	24	27	29	02♍
1910	01♊	03	06	08	10	13	15	17	20	22	24	27	29	02♋	04	06♋
1911	23♌	25	27	29	01♍	03	04	06	08	10	11	13	15	16	18	19♍
1912	07♋	09	12	14	17	19	22	24	27	29	01♌	04	06	09	11	14♌
1913	22♉	24	26	28	00♊	02	04	06	08	10	12	14	17	19	21	23♊
1914	12♌	15	17	19	22	24	26	29	01♍	03	06	08	10	13	15	17♍
1915	18♊	20	23	25	27	00♋	02	05	07	10	12	14	17	19	22	24♋
1916	13♋R	12	10	09	08	07	06	05	04	04	03	03	03D	03	03	03♋
1917	26♋	28	01♌	03	05	08	10	13	15	18	20	23	25	27	00♍	02♍
1918	01♊	04	06	08	11	13	16	18	20	23	25	27	00♋	02	05	07♋
1919	23♌	25	27	29	01♍	02	04	06	08	09	11	13	14	16	17	18♍
1920	08♋	10	12	15	17	20	22	25	27	00♌	02	05	07	10	12	14♌
1921	22♉	24	26	28	00♊	02	04	06	08	10	13	15	17	19	21	23♊
1922	13♌	15	18	20	22	25	27	29	02♍	04	06	09	11	13	15	18♍
1923	18♊	21	23	26	28	00♋	03	05	08	10	13	15	18	20	23	25♋
1924	09♋R	08	07	06	04	03	03	02	01	01	01	01D	01	01	01	02♋
1925	26♋	29	01♌	04	06	09	11	13	16	18	21	23	26	28	00♍	03♍
1926	02♊	04	07	09	11	14	16	18	21	23	26	28	00♋	03	05	08♋
1927	23♌	25	27	29	01♍	02	04	06	08	09	11	12	14	15	16	18♍
1928	08♋	11	13	16	18	21	23	25	28	00♌	03	05	08	10	13	15♌
1929	23♉	24	26	28	00♊	02	05	07	09	11	13	15	17	19	22	24♊
1930	13♌	16	18	21	23	25	28	00♍	02	04	07	09	11	14	16	18♍
1931	19♊	21	24	26	29	01♋	04	06	08	11	13	16	18	21	23	26♋
1932	06♋R	04	03	02	01	00	00	29♊	29	28D	28	29	29	29	00♋	00♋
1933	27♋	29	02♌	04	07	09	12	14	17	19	21	24	26	19	01♍	04♍
1934	03♊	05	07	10	12	14	17	19	21	24	26	29	01♋	03	06	08♋
1935	23♌	25	27	29	01♍	02	04	06	07	09	10	12	13	14	16	17♍
1936	09♋	11	14	16	19	21	24	26	29	01♌	04	06	08	11	13	16♌
1937	28♉	25	27	29	01♊	03	05	07	09	11	13	15	18	20	22	24♊
1938	14♌	16	19	21	23	26	28	00♍	03	05	07	10	12	14	16	19♍
1939	20♊	22	25	27	29	02♋	04	07	09	12	14	17	19	21	24	26♋
1940	02♋R	01	00	29♊	28	27	27	27	26D	26	26	27	27	28	28	29♊
1941	28♋	00♌	03	05	07	10	12	15	17	20	22	24	27	29	02♍	04♍
1942	03♊	05	08	10	13	15	17	20	22	24	27	29	02♋	04	06	09♋
1943	23♌	25	27	29	00♍	02	04	05	07	08	10	11	12	14	15	16♍
1944	10♋	12	15	17	19	22	24	27	29	02♌	04	07	09	12	14	17♌
1945	23♉	25	27	29	01♊	03	05	07	09	11	14	16	18	20	22	25♊
1946	15♌	17	19	22	24	26	29	01♍	03	05	08	10	12	15	17	19♍
1947	20♊	23	25	28	00♋	02	05	07	10	12	15	17	20	22	25	27♋
1948	29♊R	28	27	26	25	25	24	24	24D	24	25	25	26	26	27	28♊
1949	28♋	01♌	03	06	08	11	13	15	18	20	23	25	28	00♍	02	05♍
1950	04♊	06	08	11	13	16	18	20	23	25	27	00♋	02	05	07	09♋
1951	23♌	25	27	28	00♍	02	03	05	06	08	09	10	12	13	14	15♍
1952	10♋	13	15	18	20	23	25	27	00♌	02	05	07	10	12	15	17♌
1953	23♉	25	27	29	01♊	03	05	07	10	12	14	16	18	21	23	25♊
1954	15♌	17	20	22	24	27	29	01♍	04	06	08	11	13	15	17	20♍
1955	21♊	23	26	28	01♋	03	06	08	11	13	15	18	20	23	25	28♋
1956	25♊R	24	24	23	22	22	22D	22	22	23	23	24	24	25	26	27♊
1957	29♋	01♌	04	06	09	11	14	16	18	21	23	26	28	01♍	03	05♍
1958	04♊	07	09	11	14	16	18	21	23	26	28	00♋	03	05	08	10♋
1959	23♌	25	27	28	00♍	01	03	04	06	07	08	10	11	12	13	13♍
1960	11♋	13	16	18	21	23	26	28	01♌	03	06	08	10	13	15	18♌
1961	23♉	25	27	29	01♊	04	06	08	10	12	14	17	19	21	23	25♊
1962	16♌	18	20	23	25	27	00♍	02	04	06	09	11	13	15	18	20♍
1963	22♊	24	27	29	01♋	04	06	09	11	14	16	19	21	23	26	28♋
1964	22♊R	21	21	20	20	20	20D	20	20	21	21	22	23	24	25	26♊
1965	00♌	02	04	07	09	12	14	17	19	21	24	26	29	01♍	04	06♍
1966	05♊	07	10	12	14	17	19	21	24	26	29	01♋	03	06	08	11♋
1967	23♌	25	26	28	00♍	01	03	04	05	07	08	09	10	11	11	12♍
1968	12♋	14	17	19	21	24	26	29	01♌	04	06	09	11	14	16	19♌
1969	23♉	25	27	00♊	02	04	06	08	10	13	15	17	19	21	24	26♊
1970	16♌	19	21	23	25	28	00♍	02	05	07	09	11	14	16	18	20♍
1971	22♊	25	27	00♋	02	05	07	09	12	14	17	19	22	24	27	29♋
1972	19♊R	18	18	18	18D	18	18	18	19	19	20	21	22	23	24	25♊
1973	00♌	03	05	08	10	12	15	17	20	22	25	27	29	02♍	04	07♍
1974	05♊	08	10	13	15	17	20	22	24	27	29	02♋	04	07	09	11♋
1975	23♌	24	26	28	29	01♍	02	03	05	06	07	08	09	09	10	11♍
1976	12♋	15	17	20	22	25	27	00♌	02	04	07	09	12	14	17	19♌
1977	24♉	26	28	00♊	02	04	06	09	11	13	15	17	20	22	24	26♊
1978	17♌	19	21	24	26	28	01♍	03	05	07	10	12	14	16	18	21♍
1979	23♊	25	28	00♋	03	05	08	10	13	15	17	20	22	25	27	00♌
1980	16♊R	16	16D	16	16	16	16	17	17	18	19	20	21	22	23	25♊
1981	01♌	03	06	08	11	13	15	18	20	23	25	28	00♍	02	05	07♍
1982	06♊	08	11	13	16	18	20	23	25	27	00♋	02	05	07	10	12♋
1983	23♌	24	26	27	29	00♍	01	03	04	05	06	07	07	08	08	09♍
1984	13♋	15	18	20	23	25	28	00♌	03	05	08	10	13	15	17	20♌
1985	24♉	26	28	00♊	02	05	07	09	11	13	16	18	20	22	25	27♊
1986	17♌	20	22	24	26	29	01♍	03	06	08	10	12	14	17	19	21♍
1987	24♊	26	28	01♋	03	06	08	11	13	16	18	21	23	25	28	00♌
1988	14♊R	13D	13	14	14	14	15	15	16	17	18	19	20	21	23	24♊
1989	02♌	04	06	09	11	14	16	19	21	23	26	28	01♍	03	05	08♍

August

	1st	3rd	5th	7th	9th	11th	13th	15th	17th	19th	21st	23rd	25th	27th	29th	31st
1900	07♋	07	08	08	09	10	10	11	12	14	15	16	17	19	20	22♋
1901	02♍	05	07	09	12	14	17	19	22	24	26	29	01♎	04	06	09♎
1902	07♋	09	12	14	17	19	21	24	26	29	01♌	03	06	08	11	13♌
1903	20♍	22	23	24	25	27	28	28	29	00♎	00	01	01	01R	01	01♎
1904	14♌	17	19	22	24	27	29	02♍	04	07	09	12	14	16	19	21♍
1905	24♊	26	28	00♋	02	05	07	09	11	14	16	18	20	23	25	27♋
1906	18♍	20	23	25	27	29	02♎	04	06	08	11	13	15	17	19	21♎
1907	25♋	27	00♌	02	05	07	10	12	15	17	19	22	24	27	29	02♍
1908	05♋	06	06	07	07	08	09	10	12	13	14	16	17	18	20	22♋
1909	03♍	05	08	10	13	15	17	20	22	25	27	29	02♎	04	07	09♎
1910	08♋	10	12	15	17	20	22	24	27	29	02♌	04	07	09	11	14♌
1911	20♍	21	22	23	24	25	26	27	28	28	29	29	29R	29	29	28♍
1912	15♌	17	20	22	25	27	00♍	02	05	07	10	12	15	17	20	22♍
1913	24♊	26	28	01♋	03	05	07	10	12	14	16	19	21	23	26	28♋
1914	18♍	21	23	25	28	00♎	02	04	06	09	11	13	15	17	20	22♎
1915	26♋	28	00♌	03	05	08	10	13	15	18	20	23	25	28	00♍	03♍
1916	04♋	04	05	05	06	07	08	10	11	12	14	15	17	18	20	21♋
1917	03♍	06	08	11	13	16	18	20	23	25	28	00♎	03	05	07	10♎
1918	08♋	11	13	15	18	20	23	25	27	00♌	02	05	07	10	12	14♌
1919	19♍	20	21	22	23	24	25	26	26	26	27R	27	27	26	26	25♍
1920	16♌	18	21	23	26	28	01♍	03	05	08	10	13	15	18	20	23♍
1921	24♊	27	29	01♋	03	06	08	10	12	15	17	19	21	24	26	28♋
1922	19♍	21	23	26	28	00♎	02	05	07	09	11	13	16	18	20	22♎
1923	26♋	29	01♌	04	06	09	11	13	16	18	21	23	26	28	01♍	03♍
1924	02♋	03	03	04	05	06	08	09	10	12	13	15	16	18	20	21♋
1925	04♍	07	09	11	14	16	19	21	23	26	28	01♎	03	06	08	10♎
1926	09♋	11	14	16	18	21	23	26	28	00♌	03	06	08	10	13	15♌
1927	18♍	19	20	21	22	23	23	24	24	24	25R	24	24	24	23	22♍
1928	16♌	19	21	24	26	29	01♍	04	06	09	11	14	16	18	21	23♍
1929	25♊	27	29	01♋	04	06	08	10	13	15	17	20	22	24	27	29♋
1930	19♍	22	24	26	28	01♎	03	05	07	09	12	14	16	18	20	22♎
1931	27♋	29	02♌	04	07	09	12	14	17	19	22	24	26	29	01♍	04♍
1932	01♋	01	02	03	05	06	07	08	10	11	13	14	16	18	19	21♋
1933	05♍	07	10	12	14	17	19	22	24	26	29	01♎	04	06	08	11♎
1934	09♋	12	14	17	19	21	24	26	29	01♌	04	06	08	11	13	16♌
1935	17♍	18	19	20	21	21	22	22	22R	22	22	22	21	21	20	19♍
1936	17♌	20	22	24	27	29	02♍	04	07	09	12	14	17	19	22	24♍
1937	25♊	27	00♋	02	04	06	09	11	13	16	18	20	22	25	27	00♌
1938	20♍	22	24	27	29	01♎	03	05	08	10	12	14	16	18	20	22♎
1939	28♋	00♌	02	05	07	10	12	15	17	20	22	25	27	00♍	02	05♍
1940	29♊	00♋	01	03	04	05	06	08	09	11	12	14	16	18	19	21♋
1941	05♍	08	10	13	15	17	20	22	25	27	29	02♎	04	07	09	11♎
1942	10♋	12	15	17	20	22	24	27	29	02♌	04	07	09	12	14	16♌
1943	16♍	17	18	19	19	20	20	20R	20	20	20	19	18	18	17	16♍
1944	18♌	20	23	26	28	00♍	03	05	07	10	12	15	17	20	22	25♍
1945	26♊	28	00♋	02	05	07	09	11	14	16	18	21	23	25	28	00♌
1946	20♍	22	25	27	29	01♎	04	06	08	10	12	14	16	18	20	23♎
1947	28♋	01♌	03	06	08	11	13	15	18	20	23	25	28	00♍	03	05♍
1948	28♊	29	01♋	02	03	04	06	07	09	11	12	14	16	17	19	21♋
1949	06♍	08	11	13	16	18	20	23	25	28	00♎	02	05	07	10	12♎
1950	11♋	13	15	18	20	23	25	28	00♌	02	05	07	01	12	15	17♌
1951	15♍	16	17	17	17	18	18R	18	18	17	17	16	15	14	13	12♍
1952	18♌	21	23	26	28	01♍	03	06	08	11	13	16	18	20	23	25♍
1953	26♊	28	01♋	03	05	07	10	12	14	17	19	21	24	26	28	01♌
1954	21♍	23	25	27	29	02♎	04	06	08	10	12	14	17	19	21	23♎
1955	29♋	01♌	04	06	09	11	14	16	19	21	24	26	29	01♍	03	06♍
1956	27♊	29	00♋	01	03	04	06	07	09	10	12	14	16	17	19	21♋
1957	07♍	09	11	14	16	19	21	23	26	28	01♎	03	05	08	10	13♎
1958	11♋	14	16	19	21	23	26	28	01♌	03	06	08	10	13	15	19♌
1959	14♍	14	15	15	16R	16	16	15	15	14	14	13	12	11	10	08♍
1960	19♌	22	24	26	29	01♍	04	06	09	11	14	16	19	21	24	26♍
1961	27♊	29	01♋	03	06	08	10	12	15	17	19	22	24	26	29	01♌
1962	21♍	23	25	28	00♎	02	04	06	08	10	13	15	17	19	21	23♎
1963	00♌	02	05	07	09	12	14	17	19	22	24	27	29	02♍	04	07♍
1964	27♊	28	29	01♋	02	04	05	07	08	10	12	14	16	17	19	21♋
1965	07♍	10	12	14	17	19	22	24	26	29	01♎	04	06	08	11	13♎
1966	12♋	14	17	19	22	24	26	29	01♌	04	06	09	11	14	16	18♌
1967	12♍	13	13	13R	13	13	13	13	12	11	10	09	08	07	06	05♍
1968	20♌	22	25	27	00♍	02	05	07	09	12	14	17	19	22	24	27♍
1969	27♊	29	02♋	04	06	08	11	13	15	18	20	22	25	27	29	02♌
1970	21♍	24	26	28	00♎	02	04	07	09	10	12	14	16	18	20	23♎
1971	00♌	03	05	08	10	13	15	18	20	22	25	27	00♍	02	05	07♍
1972	26♊	27	29	00♋	02	03	05	07	08	10	12	14	16	18	19	21♋
1973	08♍	10	13	15	17	20	22	25	27	29	02♎	04	07	09	11	14♎
1974	13♋	15	17	20	22	25	27	00♌	02	04	07	09	12	14	17	19♌
1975	11♍	11	11R	11	11	11	10	10	09	08	07	06	05	03	02	01♍
1976	20♌	23	25	28	00♍	03	05	08	10	13	15	18	20	22	25	27♍
1977	27♊	00♋	02	04	07	09	11	14	16	18	21	23	25	28	00♌	02♌
1978	22♍	24	26	28	00♎	03	05	07	09	11	13	15	17	19	21	23♎
1979	01♌	03	06	08	11	13	16	18	21	23	26	28	01♍	03	06	08♍
1980	25♊	27	28	00♋	01	03	05	06	08	10	12	14	16	18	20	22♋
1981	08♍	11	13	16	18	20	23	25	28	00♎	02	05	07	10	12	14♎
1982	13♋	16	18	20	23	25	28	00♌	03	05	07	10	12	15	17	20♌
1983	09♍	09R	09	09	08	08	07	07	06	05	03	02	01	00	29♌	27♌
1984	21♌	24	26	28	01♍	03	06	08	11	13	16	18	21	23	26	28♍
1985	28♊	00♋	03	05	07	09	12	14	16	19	21	23	26	28	01♌	03♌
1986	22♍	24	26	29	01♎	03	05	07	09	11	13	15	17	19	21	23♎
1987	01♌	04	07	09	11	14	16	19	21	24	26	29	01♍	04	06	09♍
1988	25♊	26	28	00♋	01	03	05	06	08	10	12	14	16	18	20	22♋
1989	09♍	11	14	16	19	21	23	26	28	01♎	03	05	08	10	12	15♎

September

	1st	3rd	5th	7th	9th	11th	13th	15th	17th	19th	21st	23rd	25th	27th	29th
1900	23♋	24	26	28	00♌	01	03	05	07	09	11	13	15	17	19♌
1901	10♎	12	15	17	19	22	24	27	29	01♏	04	06	08	11	13♏
1902	14♌	17	19	22	24	27	29	02♍	04	07	09	11	14	16	19♍
1903	01♎R	00	00	29♍	28	27	26	25	24	23	21	20	19	18	17♍
1904	23♍	25	28	00♎	03	05	07	10	12	15	17	20	22	25	27♎
1905	29♋	01♌	03	06	08	10	13	15	17	20	22	24	27	29	02♍
1906	22♎	24	26	28	00♏	02	04	06	08	10	12	14	16	18	20♏
1907	03♍	06	08	11	13	16	18	20	23	25	28	00♎	03	05	08♎
1908	23♋	24	26	28	00♌	01	03	05	07	09	11	13	15	17	20♌
1909	10♎	13	15	18	20	22	25	27	29	02♏	04	07	09	11	14♏
1910	15♌	18	20	22	25	27	00♍	02	05	07	10	12	15	17	20♍
1911	28♍R	28	27	26	25	24	24	21	20	19	18	17	16	15	14♍
1912	23♍	26	28	01♎	03	06	08	11	13	16	18	20	23	25	28♎
1913	29♋	01♌	04	06	08	11	13	16	18	20	23	25	27	00♍	02♍
1914	23♎	25	27	29	01♏	03	05	07	09	11	13	15	17	19	20♏
1915	04♍	06	09	11	14	16	19	21	24	26	29	01♎	04	06	09♎
1916	22♋	24	26	28	00♌	01	03	05	07	09	11	13	16	18	20♌
1917	11♎	13	16	18	21	23	25	28	00♏	02	05	07	10	12	14♏
1918	16♌	18	21	23	26	28	00♍	03	05	08	10	13	15	18	20♍
1919	25♍R	24	23	22	21	20	19	18	16	15	14	13	12	12	11♍
1920	24♍	26	29	01♎	04	06	09	11	14	16	19	21	24	26	28♎
1921	00♌	02	04	07	09	11	14	16	18	21	23	26	28	01♍	03♍
1922	23♎	25	27	29	01♏	03	05	07	09	11	13	15	17	18	20♏
1923	04♍	07	09	12	14	17	19	22	24	27	29	02♎	04	07	09♎
1924	22♋	24	26	28	00♌	02	03	05	08	10	12	14	16	18	20♌
1925	12♎	14	16	19	21	24	26	28	01♏	03	05	08	10	12	15♏
1926	16♌	19	21	24	26	29	01♍	04	06	09	11	13	16	18	21♍
1927	22♍R	21	20	19	18	16	15	14	13	12	11	10	09	09	09♍
1928	25♍	27	00♎	02	04	07	09	12	14	17	19	22	24	27	29♎
1929	00♌	02	05	07	10	12	14	17	19	21	24	26	29	01♍	04♍
1930	23♎	25	27	29	01♏	03	05	07	09	11	13	15	16	18	20♏
1931	05♍	08	10	13	15	18	20	23	25	28	00♎	03	05	07	10♎
1932	22♋	24	26	28	00♌	02	04	06	08	10	12	14	16	18	20♌
1933	12♎	14	17	19	22	24	26	29	01♏	04	06	08	11	13	15♏
1934	17♌	19	22	24	27	29	02♍	04	07	09	12	14	17	19	22♍
1935	19♍R	17	16	15	14	13	11	10	09	08	08	07	07	06	06♍D
1936	25♍	28	00♎	03	05	08	10	13	15	17	20	22	25	27	00♏
1937	01♌	03	05	08	10	13	15	17	20	22	24	27	29	02♍	04♍
1938	23♎	25	27	29	01♏	03	05	07	09	11	13	14	16	18	19♏
1939	06♍	08	11	13	16	18	21	23	26	28	01♎	03	06	08	11♎
1940	22♋	24	26	28	00♌	02	04	06	08	10	12	14	16	19	21♌
1941	13♎	15	17	20	22	25	27	29	02♏	04	06	09	11	13	16♏
1942	18♌	20	23	25	28	00♍	02	05	07	10	12	15	17	20	22♍
1943	15♍R	14	13	11	10	09	08	07	06	05	05	04	04	04D	04♍
1944	26♍	28	01♎	03	06	08	11	13	16	18	21	23	26	28	00♏
1945	01♌	04	06	08	11	13	15	18	20	23	25	27	00♍	02	05♍
1946	24♎	26	28	00♏	01	03	05	07	09	11	12	14	16	17	19♏
1947	07♍	09	11	14	16	19	21	24	26	29	01♎	04	06	09	11♎
1948	22♋	24	26	28	00♌	02	04	06	08	10	12	15	17	19	21♌
1949	13♎	16	18	20	23	25	27	00♏	02	05	07	09	12	14	16♏
1950	18♌	21	23	26	28	01♍	03	06	08	11	13	16	18	20	23♍
1951	11♍R	10	09	08	07	05	05	04	03	02	02	02	02D	02	02♍
1952	27♍	29	02♎	04	06	09	11	14	16	19	21	24	26	29	01♏
1953	02♌	04	07	09	11	14	16	18	21	23	26	28	01♍	03	05♍
1954	24♎	26	28	00♏	01	03	05	07	09	10	12	14	15	17	18♏
1955	07♍	10	12	15	17	20	22	25	27	00♎	02	05	07	10	12♎
1956	22♋	24	26	28	00♌	02	04	06	08	11	13	15	17	19	21♌
1957	14♎	16	19	21	23	26	28	00♏	03	05	07	10	12	14	17♏
1958	19♌	21	24	26	29	01♍	04	06	09	11	14	16	19	21	24♍
1959	08♍R	07	05	04	03	02	01	01	00	00	29♌D	29	29	00♍	00♍
1960	27♍	00♎	02	05	07	10	12	15	17	19	22	24	27	29	02♏
1961	02♌	05	07	09	12	14	17	19	21	24	26	29	01♍	04	06♍
1962	24♎	26	28	00♏	01	03	05	07	08	10	12	13	15	16	18♏
1963	08♍	10	13	15	18	20	23	25	28	00♎	03	05	08	10	13♎
1964	22♋	24	26	28	00♌	02	04	07	09	11	13	15	17	20	22♌
1965	14♎	17	19	21	24	26	29	01♏	03	06	08	11	13	15	17♏
1966	20♌	22	25	27	00♍	02	04	07	09	12	14	17	19	22	24♍
1967	04♍R	03	02	01	00	29♌	28	28	27	27D	27	27	28	28	29♌
1968	28♍	00♎	03	05	08	10	13	15	18	20	23	25	27	00♏	02♏
1969	03♌	05	08	10	12	15	17	20	22	24	27	29	02♍	04	07♍
1970	24♎	26	28	29	01♏	03	05	07	08	10	11	13	14	16	17♏
1971	09♍	11	14	16	19	21	23	26	28	01♎	03	06	08	11	13♎
1972	22♋	24	26	29	01♌	03	05	07	09	11	13	16	18	20	22♌
1973	15♎	17	20	22	24	27	29	01♏	04	06	08	11	13	15	18♏
1974	20♌	23	25	28	00♍	03	05	08	10	13	15	18	20	23	25♍
1975	00♍R	29♌	28	27	27	26	25	25	25D	25	25	25	26	26	27♌
1976	29♍	01♎	04	06	08	11	13	16	18	21	23	26	28	01♏	03♏
1977	04♌	06	08	11	13	15	18	20	23	25	28	00♍	02	05	07♍
1978	24♎	26	27	29	01♏	03	05	06	08	09	11	12	14	15	16♏
1979	09♍	12	14	17	19	22	24	27	29	02♎	04	07	09	12	14♎
1980	23♋	25	27	29	02♌	03	05	07	09	12	14	16	18	20	23♌
1981	15♎	18	20	23	25	27	00♏	02	04	07	09	11	14	16	18♏
1982	21♌	23	26	28	01♍	03	06	08	11	13	16	18	21	23	26♍
1983	27♌R	26	25	24	24	23	23	23D	23	23	23	24	24	25	26♌
1984	29♍	02♎	04	07	09	12	14	16	19	21	24	26	29	01♏	04♏
1985	04♌	06	09	11	14	16	18	21	23	26	28	01♍	03	05	08♍
1986	24♎	26	27	29	01♏	03	04	06	07	09	10	12	13	14	15♏
1987	10♍	12	15	17	20	22	25	27	00♎	02	05	07	10	12	15♎
1988	23♋	25	27	29	01♌	03	05	08	10	12	14	16	19	21	23♌
1989	16♎	18	21	23	25	28	00♏	02	05	07	09	12	14	16	19♏

October

	1st	3rd	5th	7th	9th	11th	13th	15th	17th	19th	21st	23rd	25th	27th	29th	31st
1900	21♌	23	26	28	00♍	02	04	07	09	11	13	16	18	20	23	25♍
1901	16♏	18	20	23	25	27	00♐	02	04	07	09	11	14	16	18	21♐
1902	21♍	24	26	29	01♎	04	06	09	11	14	16	19	21	24	26	29♎
1903	17♍R	16	16	15	15D	15	15	16	16	17	18	19	20	21	22	23♍
1904	00♏	02	05	07	01	12	14	17	19	22	24	27	29	02♐	04	07♐
1905	04♍	07	09	11	14	16	19	21	24	26	29	01♎	03	06	08	11♎
1906	22♏	24	26	28	29	01♐	02	04	05	06	08	09	10	11	12	13♐
1907	10♎	13	15	18	20	23	25	28	00♏	03	06	08	10	13	15	18♏
1908	22♌	24	26	28	00♍	03	05	07	09	12	14	16	18	21	23	25♍
1909	16♏	18	21	23	26	28	00♐	03	05	07	10	12	14	16	19	21♐
1910	22♍	25	27	00♎	02	05	07	10	12	15	17	20	22	25	27	00♏
1911	14♍R	13	13	13D	13	13	14	14	15	16	17	18	19	20	21	22♍
1912	00♏	03	05	08	10	13	15	18	20	22	25	27	00♐	02	05	07♐
1913	05♍	07	10	12	14	17	19	22	24	27	29	02♎	04	07	09	12♎
1914	22♏	24	26	27	29	00♐	02	03	04	06	07	08	09	10	10	11♐
1915	11♎	14	16	19	21	24	26	29	01♏	04	06	09	11	14	16	19♏
1916	22♌	24	26	28	01♍	03	05	07	10	12	14	17	19	21	24	26♍
1917	17♏	19	21	24	26	28	01♐	03	05	08	10	12	15	17	19	21♐
1918	23♍	25	28	00♎	03	05	08	10	13	15	18	20	23	25	28	00♏
1919	11♍R	11D	11	11	11	11	12	13	13	14	15	17	18	19	20	22♍
1920	01♏	03	06	08	11	13	16	18	21	23	26	28	00♐	03	05	08♐
1921	05♍	08	10	13	15	18	21	22	25	27	00♎	02	05	07	10	12♎
1922	22♏	23	25	27	28	00♐	01	02	03	05	06	06	07	08	09	09♐
1923	12♎	14	17	19	22	24	27	29	02♏	04	07	09	12	14	17	19♏
1924	22♌	24	27	29	01♍	03	06	08	10	12	15	17	19	22	24	26♍
1925	17♏	19	22	24	26	29	01♐	03	06	08	10	13	15	17	19	22♐
1926	23♍	26	28	01♎	03	06	08	11	13	16	18	21	23	26	28	01♏
1927	08♍R	08D	09	09	09	10	11	11	12	13	14	16	17	18	20	21♍
1928	02♏	04	07	09	11	14	16	19	21	24	26	29	01♐	04	06	08♐
1929	06♍	08	11	13	16	18	21	23	26	28	00♎	03	05	08	10	13♎
1930	21♏	23	25	26	27	29	00♐	01	02	03	04	05	06	06	07	07♐
1931	12♎	15	17	20	22	25	27	00♏	02	05	07	10	12	15	18	20♏
1932	23♌	25	27	29	01♍	04	06	08	11	13	15	18	20	22	25	27♍
1933	18♏	20	22	25	27	29	02♐	04	06	09	11	13	15	18	20	22♐
1934	24♍	27	29	02♎	04	07	09	12	14	17	19	22	24	27	29	02♏
1935	06♍	06	07	07	08	08	09	10	11	12	14	15	16	18	19	21♍
1936	02♏	05	07	10	12	15	17	19	22	24	27	29	02♐	04	07	09♐
1937	07♍	09	11	14	16	19	21	24	26	29	01♎	04	06	09	11	14♎
1938	21♏	23	24	25	27	28	29	00♐	01	02	03	03	04	04	04R	04♐
1939	13♎	16	18	21	23	26	28	01♏	03	06	08	11	13	16	18	21♏
1940	23♌	25	27	00♍	02	04	06	09	11	13	16	18	20	23	25	27♍
1941	18♏	20	23	25	27	00♐	02	04	07	09	11	13	16	18	20	22♐
1942	25♍	27	00♎	02	05	07	10	12	15	17	20	22	25	27	00♏	02♏
1943	04♍	04	05	06	06	07	08	09	10	12	13	14	16	17	19	21♍
1944	03♏	05	08	10	13	15	18	20	23	25	27	00♐	02	05	07	10♐
1945	07♍	10	12	15	17	19	22	24	27	29	02♎	04	07	09	12	14♎
1946	20♏	22	23	25	26	27	28	29	00♐	00	01	01	02	02	02R	02♐
1947	14♎	16	19	21	24	26	29	01♏	04	06	09	11	14	16	19	21♏
1948	23♌	26	28	00♍	02	05	07	09	12	14	16	19	21	23	26	28♍
1949	19♏	21	23	26	28	00♐	02	05	07	09	12	14	16	18	21	23♐
1950	25♍	28	00♎	03	05	08	10	13	15	18	20	23	25	28	00♏	03♏
1951	02♍	03	03	04	05	06	07	08	10	11	12	14	15	17	19	20♍
1952	04♏	06	08	11	13	16	18	21	23	26	28	00♐	03	05	08	10♐
1953	08♍	10	13	15	18	20	23	25	27	00♎	02	05	07	10	12	15♎
1954	20♏	21	22	24	25	26	27	27	28	29	29	29	00♐R	00	29♏	29♏
1955	15♎	17	20	22	24	27	29	02♏	04	07	09	12	14	17	19	22♏
1956	24♌	26	28	00♍	03	05	07	10	12	14	17	19	21	24	26	29♍
1957	19♏	21	24	26	28	01♐	03	05	07	10	12	14	16	19	21	23♐
1958	26♍	29	01♎	04	06	09	11	14	16	19	21	24	26	29	01♏	04♏
1959	01♍	01	02	03	04	05	06	08	09	10	12	13	15	17	18	20♍
1960	04♏	07	09	12	14	16	19	21	24	26	29	01♐	04	06	08	11♐
1961	08♍	11	13	16	18	21	23	26	28	01♎	03	06	08	11	13	16♎
1962	19♏	20	22	23	24	24	25	26	26	27	27	27R	27	27	26	26♏
1963	15♎	18	20	23	25	28	00♏	03	05	08	10	13	15	18	20	23♏
1964	24♌	26	29	01♍	03	06	08	10	12	15	17	20	22	24	27	29♍
1965	20♏	22	24	26	29	01♐	03	06	08	10	12	14	17	19	21	23♐
1966	27♍	29	02♎	04	07	09	12	14	17	19	22	24	27	29	02♏	04♏
1967	29♌	00♍	01	02	03	04	06	07	08	10	11	13	15	17	18	20♍
1968	05♏	07	10	12	15	17	19	22	24	27	29	02♐	04	07	09	11♐
1969	09♍	12	14	16	19	21	24	26	29	01♎	04	06	09	11	14	16♎
1970	18♏	19	20	21	22	23	24	24	24	25	25R	25	24	24	23	23♏
1971	16♎	18	21	23	26	28	01♏	03	06	08	11	13	16	18	21	23♏
1972	25♌	27	29	01♍	04	06	08	11	13	15	18	20	22	25	27	00♎
1973	20♏	22	25	27	29	01♐	04	06	08	10	13	15	17	19	21	24♐
1974	28♍	00♎	03	05	08	10	13	15	18	20	23	25	28	00♏	03	05♏
1975	28♌	29	00♍	01	02	04	05	06	08	10	11	13	15	16	18	20♍
1976	05♏	08	10	13	15	18	20	23	25	27	00♐	02	05	07	10	12♐
1977	10♍	12	15	17	20	22	24	27	29	02♎	04	07	09	12	14	17♎
1978	17♏	18	19	20	21	21	22	22	22	22R	22	22	21	21	20	19♏
1979	17♎	19	22	24	27	29	01♏	04	06	09	11	14	16	19	21	24♏
1980	25♌	27	00♍	02	04	06	09	11	14	16	18	21	23	25	28	00♎
1981	20♏	23	25	27	00♐	02	04	06	08	11	13	15	17	19	22	24♐
1982	28♍	01♎	03	06	08	11	13	16	18	21	23	26	28	01♏	03	06♏
1983	27♌	28	29	00♍	02	03	04	06	08	09	11	13	14	16	18	20♍
1984	06♏	08	11	13	16	18	21	23	26	28	00♐	03	05	08	10	13♐
1985	10♍	13	15	18	20	23	25	28	00♎	03	05	08	10	12	15	17♎
1986	16♏	17	18	19	19	19	20	20R	20	20	19	19	18	17	16	15♏
1987	17♎	20	22	25	27	00♏	02	05	07	10	12	15	17	20	22	25♏
1988	25♌	28	00♍	02	05	07	09	12	14	16	19	21	24	26	28	01♎
1989	21♏	23	25	28	00♐	02	04	07	09	11	13	15	17	20	22	24♐

November

	1st	3rd	5th	7th	9th	11th	13th	15th	17th	19th	21st	23rd	25th	27th	29th
1900	26♍	28	01♎	03	06	08	10	13	15	17	20	22	25	27	00♏
1901	22♐	24	26	29	01♑	03	05	08	10	12	14	16	18	21	23♑
1902	00♏	03	05	08	10	13	15	18	20	23	25	28	00♐	03	05♐
1903	24♍	25	27	28	00♎	01	03	05	07	09	10	12	14	16	18♎
1904	08♐	10	13	15	18	20	23	25	27	00♑	02	05	07	10	12♑
1905	12♎	15	17	20	22	25	27	00♏	02	05	07	10	12	15	17♏
1906	13♐	13	14	14	14R	14	14	14	13	12	12	11	10	09	07♐
1907	19♏	22	24	27	29	02♐	04	07	09	12	14	17	19	22	24♐
1908	27♍	29	01♎	04	06	08	11	13	16	18	20	23	25	28	00♏
1909	22♐	24	27	29	01♑	03	06	08	10	12	14	17	19	21	23♑
1910	01♏	03	06	08	11	13	16	18	21	23	26	28	01♐	03	06♐
1911	23♍	25	26	28	29	01♎	03	05	07	09	10	12	14	16	18♎
1912	08♐	11	13	16	18	21	23	26	28	00♑	03	05	08	10	13♑
1913	13♎	15	18	20	23	25	28	00♏	03	05	08	10	13	15	18♏
1914	11♐	11	12	12R	12	11	11	11	10	09	08	07	06	05	03♐
1915	20♏	22	25	27	00♐	02	05	07	10	12	15	17	20	22	25♐
1916	27♍	29	02♎	04	07	09	11	14	16	19	21	23	26	28	01♏
1917	23♐	25	27	29	02♑	04	06	08	10	12	15	17	19	21	23♑
1918	02♏	04	07	09	12	14	17	19	22	24	27	29	02♐	04	07♐
1919	23♍	24	26	27	29	01♎	03	05	07	08	10	12	14	17	19♎
1920	09♐	12	14	16	19	21	24	26	29	01♑	03	06	08	11	13♑
1921	13♎	16	18	21	23	26	28	01♏	03	06	08	11	13	16	18♏
1922	09♐	09R	09	09	09	09	08	07	06	05	04	02	01	00	29♏
1923	20♏	23	25	28	00♐	03	05	08	10	13	15	18	20	23	25♐
1924	28♍	00♎	02	05	07	10	12	14	17	19	22	24	26	29	01♏
1925	23♐	25	27	00♑	02	04	06	08	10	13	15	17	19	21	23♑
1926	02♏	05	07	10	12	15	17	20	22	25	27	00♐	02	05	07♐
1927	22♍	24	26	27	29	01♎	03	05	07	08	10	13	15	17	19♎
1928	10♐	12	15	17	19	22	24	27	29	02♑	04	06	09	11	14♑
1929	14♎	17	19	22	24	27	29	02♏	04	07	09	12	14	17	19♏
1930	07♐ R	07	07	06	06	05	05	04	03	01	00	29♏	28	27	26♏
1931	21♏	24	26	29	01♐	04	06	09	11	14	16	19	21	24	26♐
1932	28♍	00♎	03	05	08	10	12	15	17	20	22	25	27	00♏	02♏
1933	23♐	25	28	00♑	02	04	06	09	11	13	15	17	19	21	23♑
1934	03♏	05	08	10	13	15	18	20	23	25	28	01♐	03	06	08♐
1935	22♍	24	25	27	29	01♎	03	05	07	09	11	13	15	17	19♎
1936	10♐	13	15	18	20	22	25	27	00♑	02	05	07	09	12	14♑
1937	15♎	17	20	22	25	27	00♏	02	05	07	10	12	15	17	20♏
1938	04♐ R	04	04	03	03	02	01	00	29♏	28	26	25	24	23	22♏
1939	22♏	24	27	29	02♐	04	07	09	12	14	17	19	22	24	27♐
1940	19♍	01♎	03	06	08	11	13	15	18	20	23	25	28	00♏	03♏
1941	24♐	26	28	00♑	02	04	07	09	11	13	15	17	29	21	23♑
1942	04♏	06	09	11	14	16	19	21	24	26	29	01♐	04	06	09♐
1943	22♍	23	25	27	29	01♎	03	05	07	09	11	13	15	17	19♎
1944	11♐	13	16	18	21	23	25	28	00♑	03	05	08	10	12	15♑
1945	15♎	18	20	23	25	28	00♏	03	05	08	10	13	15	18	20♏
1946	02♐ R	01	01	00	29♏	28	27	26	25	24	22	21	20	19	18♏
1947	23♏	25	27	00♐	02	05	07	10	12	15	17	20	22	25	27♐
1948	29♍	02♎	04	06	09	11	14	16	18	21	23	26	28	01♏	03♏
1949	24♐	26	28	00♑	03	05	07	09	11	13	15	17	19	21	23♑
1950	04♏	07	09	12	14	17	19	22	24	27	29	02♐	04	07	09♐
1951	21♍	23	25	27	29	01♎	03	05	07	09	11	13	15	17	19♎
1952	11♐	14	16	19	21	24	26	28	01♑	03	06	08	11	13	15♑
1953	16♎	19	21	24	26	29	01♏	04	06	09	11	14	16	19	21♏
1954	29♏R	28	27	27	26	24	23	22	21	20	19	18	17	16	15♏
1955	23♏	26	28	01♐	03	06	08	11	13	15	18	21	23	26	28♐
1956	00♎	02	05	07	09	12	14	17	19	21	24	26	29	01♏	04♏
1957	24♐	26	28	01♑	03	05	07	09	11	13	15	17	19	21	23♑
1958	05♏	07	10	12	15	17	20	22	25	28	00♐	03	05	08	10♐
1959	21♍	23	25	27	29	01♎	03	05	07	09	11	13	15	18	20♎
1960	12♐	14	17	19	22	24	27	29	01♑	04	06	09	11	14	16♑
1961	17♎	19	22	24	27	29	02♏	04	07	09	12	14	17	19	22♏
1962	26♏R	25	24	23	22	21	19	18	17	16	15	14	13	13	12♏
1963	24♏	25	29	01♐	04	06	09	11	14	16	19	21	24	26	29♐
1964	00♎	03	05	07	10	12	15	17	20	22	25	27	29	02♏	04♏
1965	24♐	27	29	01♑	03	05	07	09	11	13	15	17	19	21	23♑
1966	06♏	08	11	13	16	18	21	23	26	28	01♐	03	06	08	11♐
1967	21♍	23	25	27	29	01♎	03	05	07	09	11	13	16	18	20♎
1968	13♐	15	18	20	22	25	27	00♑	02	04	07	09	12	14	16♑
1969	17♎	20	22	25	27	00♏	02	05	07	10	12	15	17	20	22♏
1970	22♏R	21	20	19	18	17	15	14	13	12	11	11	10	10	09♏
1971	25♏	27	29	02♐	04	07	09	12	14	17	19	22	24	27	29♐
1972	01♎	03	06	08	10	13	15	18	20	23	25	28	00♏	03	05♏
1973	25♐	27	29	01♑	03	05	07	09	11	13	15	17	19	20	22♑
1974	06♏	09	11	14	16	19	21	24	26	29	01♐	04	06	09	11♐
1975	21♍	23	25	27	29	01♎	03	05	07	09	12	14	16	18	20♎
1976	13♐	16	18	21	23	25	28	00♑	03	05	07	10	12	15	17♑
1977	18♎	21	23	26	28	01♏	03	06	08	11	13	16	18	21	23♏
1978	19♏R	18	16	15	14	13	12	11	10	09	08	07	07	07	07♏D
1979	25♏	28	00♐	03	05	08	10	13	15	18	20	23	25	28	00♑
1980	01♎	04	06	09	11	14	16	18	21	23	26	28	01♏	03	06♏
1981	25♐	27	29	01♑	03	05	07	09	11	13	15	17	18	20	22♑
1982	07♏	09	12	14	17	20	22	25	27	00♐	02	05	07	10	12♐
1983	21♍	23	25	27	29	01♎	03	05	07	10	12	14	16	18	21♎
1984	14♐	16	19	21	23	26	28	01♑	03	06	08	10	13	15	17♑
1985	19♎	21	24	26	29	01♏	04	06	09	11	14	16	19	21	24♏
1986	15♏R	14	12	11	10	09	08	07	06	05	05	05	04D	04	05♏
1987	26♏	28	01♐	03	06	08	11	13	16	18	21	23	26	28	01♑
1988	02♎	04	07	09	12	14	17	19	21	24	26	29	01♏	04	06♏
1989	25♐	27	29	01♑	03	05	07	09	11	13	15	16	18	20	21♑

December

	1st	3rd	5th	7th	9th	11th	13th	15th	17th	19th	21st	23rd	25th	27th	29th	31st
1900	02♏	04	07	09	12	14	17	19	22	24	27	29	02♐	04	07	09♐
1901	25♑	27	29	01♒	03	05	07	09	11	12	14	16	18	19	21	22♒
1902	08♐	10	13	15	18	20	23	25	28	00♑	03	05	08	11	13	16♑
1903	20≏	22	25	27	29	01♏	03	05	08	10	12	14	17	19	21	24♏
1904	15♑	17	19	22	24	27	29	01♒	04	06	09	11	13	16	18	21♒
1905	20♏	21	25	27	00♐	02	05	07	10	12	15	17	20	22	25	27♐
1906	06♐R	05	04	03	02	01	00	00	29♏	29D	29	29	29	00♐	00	01♐
1907	27♐	29	02♑	04	07	09	12	14	17	19	22	24	27	29	02♒	04♒
1908	03♏	05	08	10	12	15	17	20	22	25	27	00♐	02	05	07	10♐
1909	25♑	27	29	01♒	03	05	07	09	10	12	14	16	17	19	20	22♒
1910	09♐	11	14	16	19	21	24	26	29	01♑	04	06	09	11	14	16♑
1911	21≏	23	25	27	29	01♏	03	06	08	10	12	15	17	19	22	24♏
1912	15♑	18	20	22	25	27	00♒	02	04	07	09	12	14	16	19	21♒
1913	20♏	23	25	28	00♐	03	05	08	10	13	15	18	20	23	25	28♐
1914	02♐R	01	00	29♏	28	28	27	27	27	26D	27	27	27	28	29	00♐
1915	27♐	00♑	02	05	07	10	12	15	17	20	22	25	27	00♒	02	05♒
1916	03♏	06	08	11	13	16	18	20	23	25	28	00♐	03	05	08	10♐
1917	25♑	27	29	01♒	03	05	07	08	10	12	13	15	17	18	19	21♒
1918	09♐	12	14	17	19	22	24	27	29	02♑	04	07	09	12	14	17♑
1919	21≏	23	25	27	29	02♏	04	06	08	11	13	15	17	20	22	24♏
1920	16♑	18	20	23	25	28	00♒	03	05	07	10	12	14	17	19	22♒
1921	21♏	23	26	28	01♐	03	06	09	11	14	16	19	21	24	26	29♐
1922	28♏R	27	26	26	25	24	24	24D	24	24	25	25	26	26	27	28♏
1923	28♐	00♑	03	05	08	10	13	15	18	20	23	25	28	00♒	03	05♒
1924	04♏	06	09	11	14	16	19	21	24	26	28	01♐	03	06	08	11♐
1925	25♑	27	29	01♒	03	05	06	08	10	11	13	15	16	17	19	20♒
1926	10♐	12	15	17	20	22	25	27	00♑	03	05	08	10	13	15	18♑
1927	21≏	23	25	27	00♏	02	04	06	09	11	13	15	18	20	22	25♏
1928	16♑	19	21	23	26	28	01♒	03	05	08	10	13	15	17	20	22♒
1929	22♏	24	27	29	02♐	04	07	09	12	14	17	19	22	24	27	29♐
1930	25♏R	24	23	22	22	22	22D	22	22	22	23	23	24	25	26	27♏
1931	29♐	01♑	04	06	09	11	14	16	19	21	24	26	28	01♒	03	06♒
1932	04♏	07	09	12	14	17	19	22	24	27	29	02♐	04	07	09	12♐
1933	25♑	27	29	01♒	02	04	06	08	09	11	12	14	15	16	18	19♒
1934	11♐	13	16	18	21	23	26	28	01♑	03	06	08	11	13	16	18♑
1935	21≏	23	26	28	00♏	02	04	07	09	11	14	16	18	21	23	25♏
1936	17♑	19	22	24	26	29	01♒	04	06	08	11	13	15	18	20	22♒
1937	22♏	25	27	00♐	02	05	07	10	12	15	17	20	22	25	27	00♑
1938	21♏R	20	20	19	19D	19	19	19	20	20	21	22	23	24	25	26♏
1939	29♐	02♑	04	07	09	12	14	17	19	22	24	27	29	02♒	04	07♒
1940	05♏	07	10	12	15	17	20	22	25	27	00♐	02	05	07	10	12♐
1941	25♑	27	29	00♒	02	04	06	07	09	10	12	13	14	15	17	18♒
1942	11♐	14	16	19	21	24	26	29	01♑	04	06	09	11	14	16	19♑
1943	21≏	24	26	28	00♏	03	05	07	09	12	14	16	19	21	23	26♏
1944	17♑	20	22	24	27	29	02♒	04	06	09	11	13	16	18	21	23♒
1945	23♏	25	28	00♐	03	06	08	11	13	16	18	21	23	26	28	01♑
1946	18♏R	17	17	17	17D	17	17	17	18	19	20	21	22	23	24	25♏
1947	00♑	02	05	07	10	12	15	17	20	22	25	27	00♒	02	05	07♒
1948	06♏	08	11	13	15	18	20	23	25	28	00♐	03	05	08	10	13♐
1949	25♑	27	28	00♒	02	04	05	07	08	10	11	12	13	14	15	16♒
1950	12♐	14	17	19	22	24	27	00♑	02	05	07	10	12	15	17	20♑
1951	22≏	24	26	28	01♏	03	05	07	10	12	14	17	19	21	24	26♏
1952	18♑	20	23	25	27	00♒	02	05	07	09	12	14	16	19	21	23♒
1953	24♏	26	29	01♐	04	06	09	11	14	16	19	21	24	26	29	01♑
1954	15♏R	14	14D	14	14	15	15	16	16	17	18	19	21	22	23	25♏
1955	01♑	03	06	08	11	13	15	18	20	23	25	28	00♒	03	05	08♒
1956	06♏	09	11	14	16	19	21	24	26	29	01♐	03	06	08	11	13♐
1957	25♑	26	28	00♒	01	03	05	06	07	09	10	11	12	13	14	15♒
1958	13♐	15	18	20	23	25	28	00♑	03	05	08	11	13	15	18	20♑
1959	22≏	24	26	29	01♏	03	06	08	10	13	15	17	20	22	24	27♏
1960	18♑	21	23	26	28	00♒	03	05	07	10	12	14	17	19	21	24♒
1961	24♏	27	29	02♐	04	07	09	12	14	17	19	22	24	27	00♑	02♑
1962	12♏R	12	12D	12	12	13	13	14	15	16	17	18	21	21	22	24♏
1963	01♑	04	06	09	11	14	16	19	21	24	26	29	01♒	03	06	08♒
1964	04♏	09	12	14	17	19	22	24	27	29	02♐	04	07	09	12	14♐
1965	24♑	26	28	29	01♒	02	04	05	07	08	09	10	11	12	12	13♒
1966	13♐	16	18	21	23	26	28	01♑	03	06	08	11	13	16	18	21♑
1967	22≏	25	27	29	01♏	04	06	08	11	13	15	18	20	22	25	27♏
1968	19♑	21	24	26	28	01♒	03	05	08	10	12	15	17	19	22	24♒
1969	25♏	27	00♐	03	05	08	10	13	15	18	20	23	25	28	00♑	03♑
1970	09♏D	09	10	10	11	11	12	13	14	15	16	18	19	20	22	23♏
1971	02♑	04	07	09	12	14	17	19	22	24	27	29	02♒	04	07	09♒
1972	07♏	10	12	15	17	20	22	25	27	00♐	02	05	07	10	12	15♐
1973	24♑	26	27	29	00♒	02	03	04	06	07	08	08	09	10	10	11♒
1974	14♐	16	19	22	24	27	29	02♑	04	07	09	12	14	17	19	22♑
1975	23≏	25	27	29	02♏	04	06	09	11	13	16	18	21	23	25	28♏
1976	19♑	22	24	27	29	01♒	04	06	08	11	13	15	18	20	22	24♒
1977	26♏	28	01♐	03	06	08	11	13	16	18	21	23	26	28	01♑	03♑
1978	07♏	07	08	08	09	10	11	12	13	14	15	17	18	20	21	23♏
1979	02♑	05	07	10	12	15	17	20	22	25	27	00♒	02	05	07	10♒
1980	08♏	11	13	16	18	20	23	25	28	00♐	03	05	08	10	13	15♐
1981	24♑	25	27	28	00♒	01	02	03	04	05	06	07	07	08	08	08♒R
1982	15♐	17	20	22	25	27	00♑	02	05	07	10	12	15	17	20	22♑
1983	23≏	25	28	00♏	02	05	07	09	12	14	16	19	21	23	26	28♏
1984	20♑	22	25	27	29	02♒	04	06	09	11	13	16	18	20	22	25♒
1985	26♏	29	01♐	04	06	09	11	14	16	19	21	24	27	29	02♑	04♑
1986	05♏	05	06	07	07	08	10	11	12	13	15	16	18	19	21	23♏
1987	03♑	06	08	11	13	16	18	21	23	25	28	00♒	03	05	08	10♒
1988	09♏	11	14	16	19	21	24	26	29	01♐	04	06	09	11	14	16♐
1989	23♑	25	26	27	29	00♒	01	02	03	04	05	05	06	06	06R	06♒

15
DOING IT!

THE LOVE PLANET MARS

Mars is what you want to DO to people. This planet stands for action, energy, and desire in your horoscope. Its force is directed toward a goal (like the arrow of its symbol) and can be vented through sex or anger. (Mars was named for the Roman God of War and rules your sex drive and your muscles.)

By knowing where Mars is in your chart, you can learn how best to channel your energies and take advantage of your creative forces. Mars pinpoints how you like to make love and what you like to DO to your partner. It indicates your sexual technique and whether or not you want to control the situation or *be* controlled.

To find out how Mars operates in your Lovescope, check how it influences the Love planets (Venus, Sun, and Moon) in your chart and that of your loved one. You'll find the locations of Venus and the Moon in the ephemeris at the end of their respective chapters. Then fill out the Lovescope chart at the end of this book. After reading the Sun, Moon, and Venus chapters, you should have a good idea of how those planets are working in your love life. (To simplify: the Sun is *who you are*, your fundamental personality and character; the Moon shows your *emotional* feelings and sexual preferences; Venus shows *how* you *react* and *what* you react to; and Mars is the mischief or merry-maker that shows how you *act*.)

When Mars in your horoscope affects *any* of the Love planets in the horoscope of your partner, it will activate them, for better or for worse. In comparing your charts, you can find out what you have in common, where you are harmonious, and where the troublesome spots may be, so that you can identify and work them out for a more fulfilling and loving relationship.

MARS (active) ASPECTING THE SUN (active):

Both Mars and the Sun are active planets. When someone's Mars aspects (activates) your Sun, it will either reinforce and support you or stymie and frustrate you.

MARS (active) ASPECTING THE MOON (passive):

Active Mars affects the emotional nature of the passive Moon. This aspect shows what your strongest feelings are, indicates how you handle your temper and sex drive. A difficult Mars aspect with your partner can wound the sensitive Moon person's feelings. Here, too, is where jealousy, anger, and emotional frustrations show up. Emotional feelings are the key here: how that Mars force can be used positively to support and reinforce the feelings of the Moon person. The Moon person in turn must learn how to deal emotionally with the energy of Mars.

MARS (active) ASPECTING MARS (active):

Here is where action meets action. Are your goals compatible? Will you work together or at cross purposes? Are you lazy or energetic? Do your energies complement each other? These are some of the questions that your Mars/Mars aspects can answer.

MARS (active) ASPECTING VENUS (passive):

This is the best indicator of sexual compatibility. If your lover's Mars favorably aspects (or is in the same sign as) your Venus, they desire you, pursue you, burn for you! Here is where "chemistry" or physical attraction comes in. Sometimes the "so-called" unfavorable aspects (for example, Mars in Leo in one chart and Venus in Scorpio in another) can make for an even *stronger* physical attraction than a "so-called" harmonious aspect such as Mars in Leo and Venus in Sagittarius! *Challenge* is always sexy. Opposites attract and fascinate.

MARS IN ARIES

Mars in Aries is the Big I . . . Impulsive, Impatient, and Inventive. (You're so impatient that your partner may not have time to get undressed!) Love is a challenge to you and a little combat first makes later happenings all the sweeter.

Since Aries rules the head and face, these areas figure strongly in your sexual technique. You love to use your lower lip, your tongue, your breath, and even your eyelashes to maximum erotic effect. Men with this placement often cultivate luxuriant (not bristly) moustaches or beards, and use them artfully in making love.

Here, Mars is a bit self-centered in bed. Once you're satisfied, you may not pay much attention to your partner's needs. Your favorite position is always on top (in control) one way or another. Oral sex is one of your specialties. So is the Love Facial.

Lady Yvonne Mendl, the lovely second wife of the late Sir Charles Mendl, attributed her radiant complexion to this particular "formula," which I call the "Love Facial." Its secret ingredient is a man's semen released at the height of physical love.

This is the most beautifying, natural facial of all — as many celebrated ladies with legendary complexions have known for centuries — because of the life-giving properties in it (vitamins and minerals, too!). Let it dry completely (don't rush!) and rinse off with lukewarm water. Then see for yourself how it tightens the pores, improves circulation and gives your complexion a radiant glow.

The late Jacqueline Susann, with whom I shared this secret, included it in her book *Once Is Not Enough*. That title applies to this treatment as well. Many ladies make it a beauty ritual and enlist the aid of her love partner at least once or twice a week.

If your partner is not in the mood for love or some of your newest experiments, you can become disagreeable and use force. (Work off your disappointments and temper by peddling on an exercise bike you've stashed in the closet.)

MARS IN TAURUS

You're earthy and lusty in bed, with great staying power. You love to explore all the senses and sensations during a lovemaking session: you want to see, smell, hear, taste, and touch your partner . . . and you're an expert at giving pleasure in all these areas.

Since Taurus rules the throat (Mars in Taurus women are the "deep throats" of the zodiac), both sexes are the best at oral sex and should develop their techniques in this area. Passionate kisses in all variations from deep soul-kissing to love bites are your forte. You love to explore your lovers orally and will charge like a Bull if they block off any erotic territory to you!

You like a long, well-organized lovemaking session and hate interruptions . . . you can keep going for hours! Time must be allowed to explore all areas, with no distractions or rushing.

You're a very vocal lover and enjoy voicing your feelings with operatic passion. (Be sure to soundproof your rooms or you may be interrupted by neighbors or even the police!) With you, practice makes perfect and you'll spend all the time necessary to assure an equally vocal reaction from your partner. Your favorite position: charging from behind in a lovely pastoral setting!

MARS IN GEMINI

This is a mental Mars that is intrigued with variety. You want constant change and are never quite content with the way things are. You can play a dual role sexually with one side of your nature participating, the other side viewing the events.

You are very articulate and like to communicate on all levels. Gemini rules the hands, so your hands are especially effective and sensitive. (You give *great* massages, literally taking your partner in the palm of your hands.) You like to play with sexual gadgets, things you can turn on with your touch.

You must have two of everything (often two "special friends") and you're great at doing two things at once. You're apt to watch erotic movies while making love or give a massage while pleasuring your lover in other ways. You also like to explore new ideas with your lover, experimenting on all parts of the anatomy.

Those of you with this placement love a constant change of scenery and will experiment on the floor, sofa, coffee table, kitchen chair . . . well, you get the idea! (Men sometimes go to "professionals" to explore their more erotic ideas.) You love the telephone and specialize in long, loving late night phone calls. Your sense of timing is terrific for comedy as well as drama. (Women have been known to "fake it" beautifully, for dramatic effect.)

MARS IN CANCER

You do your best work at night . . . especially under the light of the full moon. Your sexual action stems from a nurturing instinct. You love to take care of your lovers in every way. You'll bring them breakfast in bed and help them feather the nest. You'll even provide a roof over their head if they need it.

Your erogenous zone is the breasts. Women with this placement are often dissatisfied with theirs and sometimes have surgery to enlarge or reduce them. The man with this placement will fantasize about breasts and choose a very well-endowed playmate, devoting most of love's foreplay to the breasts, either playing with the nipples or tickling them with his tongue.

This placement is very possessive. You want to know all your love's deepest secrets and will use all sorts of techniques to ferret out information while revealing little of your own innermost thoughts.

The sight and sound of the sea inspires and increases your passion . . . that's why you love to make love in or near water (including the bathtub or swimming pool). A moonlit beach is your very favorite setting; listening to rain on the roof is another sweet inspiration. You reach the highest peaks of passion on the days before, during, and immediately after a full moon.

Mars in Cancer people prefer to make love in familiar, comfortable surroundings. (You're not ones for motel "quickies.") You'll take your time, using splendid oral techniques, paying lots of attention to the breasts. You are traditional, tender lovers and will make up in care and consideration what you may lack in variety.

MARS IN LEO

All of love's a stage for Mars in Leo people. You play to your audience and will double your efforts for more applause. Since you aim to please and must win the heart of your partner as well as his or her body, you have been known to make undying promises during the sexual act which you may later regret. In any case, you'll always try to give your audience what they want, be it laughter or tears.

Your approach is physical and direct. You must be The Best (and love to hear it confirmed by your partner). You have great endurance and style. The male of this placement likes to sweep his loved one off her feet and into bed.

You're very thoughtful and generous. You go first class all the way, building up the sexual experience with flowers, theater, wining and dining, and special gifts. Afterward, you need a lot of sleep to rebuild your energy for the next act!

You prefer the traditional manner of lovemaking (concentrating on maximum pleasure, not pain) and *not* group sex (no others should dominate the stage). The Mars in Leo people take great pride in their body. They like to show it off and observe it in the mirror while making love. The male will prance in silken robes before pouncing. The female might perform a graceful striptease, removing provocative lingerie, before joining her partner in bed, where she'll be a fiercely responsive partner. Both sexes love performing on a fur rug or bed throw. Their favorite positions give them a full view of the love act in strategically placed mirrors, and they will take turns getting and giving applause to build the drama of the occasion.

MARS IN VIRGO

You may be Sterling or Stella Trueheart on the surface, but, Oh, those fantasies! Your standards are very high, so you may have trouble finding a lover who satisfies them all. You're really looking for someone you've dreamed up or read about who may not actually exist. But you do enjoy dreaming and fantasizing about them. You may even imagine a centerfold sweetie, with a great mind, from a "good" family. (Many men with this placement have a stack of dog-eared, favorite X-rated magazines.) The buildup of fantasy in your *mind* is what counts. (An erotic phone call can set it aflame!)

You like to reform your lovers or teach them something that can improve their lives: how to quit smoking, lose twenty pounds, develop their bodies in exercise classes, and prolong their health with vitamin supplements, so that one day they'll turn into your dream lovers. You're basically conservative in your approach to love and may take a literary tack, such as reading a love poem like *Toi et Moi* by Paul Géraldy or Chinese love poems to your partner first.

You love to make love in the morning, when you're relaxed and rested. Having read *The Joy of Sex* twice, you'll perfect a technique that pleases your partners so they'll want *you* more than you want *them*. You may go to extremes, choosing a far-out lover that you will then try to make over. Either way, you're more interested in technique than feeling. Sex for you is pure white ideals or naughty black fantasies. (Gifts of erotic lingerie could be your favorite gifts to give or get.) Your erogenous zones are the navel area and below.

MARS IN LIBRA

This zodiac lover goes for Beauty every time . . . and knows what to do with it. You want sex to be a beautiful experience. You must be *inspired*. Then and only then can you reach the heights of self-expression.

You prefer to come on slowly, artistically. You approach lovemaking like a dance: poetry in motion. You will do *everything* to create harmony. Even so, you sometimes seem superficial, since you can be thrown off course by the slightest flaw. You make love when *you're* in the mood, otherwise, forget it! If the magic works, the experience is unforgettable.

Mars in Libra loves to flirt and have a mental affair first. You can be a trifle narcissistic, too engrossed in yourself and your performance. And, if your partner is not esthetically pleasing undressed, that can turn you off quickly. (Try turning off the lights, first!)

This placement (though it loves partnership and doing everything in tandem) really only demands beauty of your lover. You often fall for flatterers, hate to be alone, and like a live-in lover who shows much appreciation. You also look for comfort, ambience, and a partner who is decisive and slightly aggressive, one who can play both active and passive parts.

This is usually not an active Mars placement. You like to do everything lying down and prefer that your partner do the work. If inspired, you can be quite creative . . . but you're not a self-starter unless everything is "perfect."

Unfortunately, your erogenous zone, the lower back, is also a very vulnerable area. But the more you exercise to strengthen this area, the more you will bring to your "sexual athletics."

MARS IN SCORPIO

Mars in Scorpios have a plan for YOU, if they decide that you're for *them*. They'll use any technique to sway you. They are very perceptive, and use this power to play on your weak spots until they get you where they want you (usually horizontal). They have no restrictions as to race, or sex.

You Mars in Scorpios like to be in control, call the shots in bed. Your energy is overpowering; you'll push sex to the limits. You love strategy and games, but not an easy conquest. With this strong Mars position, a heated argument first will challenge and excite you.

You never forget an injury or a kindness and don't like to compromise on anything. You'll give your lover more than he or she bargained for in bed, where your endurance can be indefatigable. You love all kinds of fantasy (including S & M). Wetness appeals to you, too. (You'll swamp your lover.) You're open to all sorts of exotic variations (with no holds barred).

Sometimes you can get too involved with electronic gadgets. You prefer a mysterious, erotic atmosphere in which to perform and must possess your partners totally, with no distractions. You'll stop at nothing to give your partners an experience they'll never forget.

MARS IN SAGITTARIUS

A sexual adventurer and romantic wanderer, you have to be fancy free. (Unfortunately, you'll leave lots of broken hearts on the path behind you!) Lovemaking is a sport to you and it's the chase that counts. (You'll need a large bedroom to accommodate this.) Love is a game and you enjoy zeroing in on your target.

Like the Centaur, you're half human, half beast in bed. You'll travel a lot and enjoy many romantic expeditions on your trips. In fact, out of town romances are the most exciting to you. "Love on the Run" is often your *modus operandi*.

Your thighs are your erogenous zones. Maybe that's why you enjoy riding horseback so much! You also like to "ride" your lover, and even a subtle touch on the inner thigh can get you galloping.

You don't usually take sex seriously and are famous for one-line quips in bed, meant to tickle as well as titillate. Your laugh is pure joy when your partner answers in kind. (You'll always leave them laughing with some famous last words!) You love animals — dogs and horses in particular — though your partners, finding themselves in bed with Fido, could feel you're carrying this a bit too *fur*!

You're really an idealist in search of an ideal lover. But you respond to the unconventional and daring. You have great stamina and energy, and like to get to the point, fast!

MARS IN CAPRICORN

Money and power excite you and you'll often use the bedroom to further other ambitions. You'll work with great sexual discipline at becoming a superlative lover, bringing everything into play, constantly improving your technique to make your partner reach the greatest heights of ecstasy. Fortunately for your partner, you'll improve with age! Both sexes enjoy dominating the scene and setting the rhythm for the proceedings.

You often choose older lovers (for power) or younger ones (for play) . . . Daddy's Girls or Mama's Boys. Not the impulsive type, you like to plan your sexual encounters in advance (the better to control the situation); then you enjoy watching everything fall into place.

You often use sex to unwind after a hard day's work. You have great stamina and will enjoy making love regardless of your age (you'll be the sexiest Senior Citizen around!). You have a dutiful feeling about sex: you feel responsible for your lucky lovers' enjoyment and will do anything to bring out the best . . . or the beast . . . in them!

MARS IN AQUARIUS

You're a wishful thinker, spontaneous and unpredictable. You'd like love to come in a flash of lightning out of the blue. This doesn't always happen. You have to be turned on mentally before you get other ideas.

You often confuse love and friendship, turning friends into lovers and vice versa. Since you're not bound by convention and consider the world one big family, this could get you into trouble. (Do, please, stay away from your best friend's mate!) When this happens, you never understand why your friendly gesture is not approved!

You love to be highly inventive during foreplay and may get so involved you forget the main event. You like to experiment with electrical gadgets and may fall more in "love" with the gadget than with your partner.

This Mars is sexually dynamic, open to any new ideas. Love is a playground and you seldom play the same game twice. You also like everyone to participate . . . *ménage à trois* and mutual-massage sessions (starting with your feet, which are usually cold) are quite common with this placement. You may decide to collect oriental erotica and live out those *Kama Sutra* variations.

In any case, you follow your own special star, play by your own set of rules and ethics. Your loyalty follows these principles, and you'll try to "reform" your partner according to them. (You may need some reforming yourself, once in a while.)

MARS IN PISCES

You have great theatrical talent, especially when it comes to playing on another's sympathies. You look for lovers who will take care of you . . . and intuitively know how to take care of *them* in return!

You'll psych out their needs and use your considerable erotic talents to turn them on! You'll play any role from shy and passive to "anything goes"! Rain on the roof, waterfalls, showers, beach houses, waterbeds, and jacuzzis are special love inspirations. You'll use pulsating jets of water during the act of love the way others use vibrators. And the weightlessness of water can help you try many new positions.

You'll appeal to your partner's emotions with a sob story or a poetic fantasy (you're one of the poets of the zodiac). There's always a touch of the bittersweet tragicomedy here.

For more theatrics, you'll be inspired by erotic movies (while you duplicate the same action off the screen with your partner). And, chances are, you'll have a collection of lotions and potions nearby (scented beautifully) to rub on your partner's feet and body.

Beautiful feet turn you on and, if you're a man, you'll love to see your partner with beautifully pedicured toes in sexy sandals. If a woman, you'll have a fabulous collection of shoes. (Sore feet and uncomfortable shoes can upset you totally; so can a partner with ugly feet.) You love to dance (and roller-skate) and will often seduce your partner while dancing.

HOW TO FIND THE PLACEMENT OF YOUR MARS

Mars rules your energy and sex drive — your love-power! To find the placement of your Mars and that of your partner, look up your birthday and year in the following ephemeri tables. Mars will usually stay a month and a half to two months in each sign. Now read the description of your Mars and that of your lover. Then compare for compatibility.

SYMBOLS

The Love Planets		*Signs of the Zodiac*			
Sun	☉	Aries	♈	Libra	♎
Moon	☽	Taurus	♉	Scorpio	♏
Venus	♀	Gemini	♊	Sagittarius	♐
Mars	♂	Cancer	♋	Capricorn	♑
		Leo	♌	Aquarius	♒
		Virgo	♍	Pisces	♓

("R" and "D" notations signify Retrograde and Direct.)

January

	1st	3rd	5th	7th	9th	11th	13th	15th	17th	19th	21st	23rd	25th	27th	29th	31st
1900	13♑	15	16	18	20	21	23	24	26	27	29	00♒	02	04	05	07♒
1901	11♍	11	12	12	12	12	12	12R	12	12	12	11	11	11	10	10♍ R
1902	29♑	00♒	02	03	05	07	08	10	11	13	14	16	18	19	21	22♒
1903	05♎	05	06	07	08	08	09	10	10	11	11	12	12	13	13	14♎
1904	15♒	16	18	20	21	23	24	26	27	29	01♓	02	04	05	07	08♓
1905	23♎	24	25	26	27	28	29	00♏	01	02	03	04	05	06	07	08♏
1906	03♓	04	06	07	09	11	12	14	15	17	18	20	21	23	24	26♓
1907	08♏	10	11	12	13	14	16	17	18	19	20	22	23	24	25	26♏
1908	22♓	24	25	27	28	29	01♈	02	04	05	06	08	09	11	12	13♈
1909	23♏	25	26	27	29	00♐	01	03	04	05	07	08	09	11	12	13♐
1910	17♈	18	19	21	22	23	24	25	26	27	28	29	01♉	02	03	04♉
1911	08♐	09	10	12	13	15	16	17	19	20	22	23	25	26	27	29♐
1912	24♉	24	24	24	24	25	25	25	26	26	27	27	28	28	29	00♊
1913	22♐	24	25	27	28	00♑	01	03	04	06	07	09	10	12	13	15♑
1914	16♋R	15	14	14	13	12	11	11	10	09	09	08	08	07	07	06♋R
1915	07♑	08	10	12	13	15	16	18	19	21	22	24	25	27	29	00♒
1916	29♌ R	29	29	29	29	29	28	28	28	27	27	26	26	25	24	23♌ R
1917	23♑	24	26	28	29	01♒	02	04	05	07	09	10	12	13	15	16♒
1918	27♍	27	28	28	29	29	00♎	00	01	01	01	02	02	02	02	02♎
1919	09♒	10	12	13	15	17	18	20	21	23	24	26	28	29	01♓	02♓
1920	16♎	17	18	19	20	21	22	23	23	24	25	26	27	28	28	29♎
1921	26♒	28	29	01♓	02	04	05	07	09	10	12	13	15	16	18	19♓
1922	03♏	04	05	06	07	08	10	11	12	13	14	15	16	17	19	20♏
1923	15♓	16	17	19	20	22	23	25	26	28	29	01♈	02	04	05	06♈
1924	17♏	19	20	21	23	24	25	26	28	29	00♐	02	03	04	05	07♐
1925	07♈	08	10	11	12	13	15	16	17	18	20	21	22	23	25	26♈
1926	02♐	04	05	06	08	09	11	12	13	15	16	17	19	20	22	23♐
1927	08♉	08	09	09	10	11	12	12	13	14	15	15	16	17	18	19♉
1928	16♐	18	19	21	22	24	25	27	28	29	01♑	02	04	05	07	08♑
1929	25♊ R	24	24	23	23	22	22	22	21	21	21	21	21	20D	21	21♊
1930	01♑	03	04	06	07	09	10	12	14	15	17	18	20	21	23	24♑
1931	15♌ R	15	14	14	13	13	12	11	11	10	09	08	08	07	06	05♌ R
1932	16♑	18	19	21	22	24	26	27	29	00♒	02	03	05	07	08	10♒
1933	18♍	18	18	19	19	19	19	20	20	20	20	20R	20	20	19	19♍ R
1934	03♒	04	06	07	09	10	12	14	15	17	18	20	21	23	25	26♒
1935	09♎	10	11	12	13	13	14	15	16	16	17	18	18	19	20	20♎
1936	19♒	20	22	24	25	27	28	00♓	01	03	05	06	08	09	11	12♓
1937	27♎	28	29	00♏	01	02	03	04	05	07	08	09	10	11	12	13♏
1938	07♓	09	10	12	13	15	16	18	19	21	22	24	25	27	28	00♈
1939	12♏	13	14	16	17	18	19	21	22	23	24	26	27	28	29	00♐
1940	27♓	29	00♈	02	03	04	06	07	08	10	11	12	14	15	17	18♈
1941	27♏	28	00♐	01	02	04	05	06	08	09	10	12	13	15	16	17♐
1942	24♈	25	26	27	28	29	00♉	01	02	03	04	05	06	07	08	09♉
1943	11♐	12	14	15	17	18	20	21	22	24	25	27	28	00♑	01	03♑
1944	05♊ R	05	05	04	04	04D	04	05	05	05	05	05	06	06	06	07♊
1945	26♐	27	29	00♑	02	03	05	06	08	09	11	12	14	15	17	18♑
1946	28♋R	27	26	26	25	24	23	22	22	21	20	19	19	18	17	17♋R
1947	11♑	12	14	15	17	18	20	21	23	24	26	28	29	01♒	02	04♒
1948	07♍	07	07	07	07R	07	07	07	07	06	06	06	05	05	04	04♍ R
1949	27♑	28	00♒	01	03	04	06	08	09	11	12	14	15	17	19	20♒
1950	02♎	02	03	04	04	05	06	06	07	07	08	08	09	09	09	10♎
1951	13♒	14	16	17	19	20	22	24	25	27	28	00♓	01	03	05	06♓
1952	20♎	21	22	23	24	25	26	27	28	29	00♏	01	02	03	04	04♏
1953	00♓	02	03	05	07	08	10	11	13	14	16	17	19	20	22	23♓
1954	06♏	08	09	10	11	12	14	15	16	17	18	19	21	22	23	24♏
1955	19♓	21	22	24	25	27	28	29	01♈	02	04	05	07	08	09	11♈
1956	21♏	22	24	25	26	27	29	00♐	01	03	04	05	07	08	09	11♐
1957	13♈	14	15	17	18	19	20	21	23	24	25	26	27	29	00♉	01♉
1958	06♐	07	08	10	11	13	14	15	17	18	20	21	23	24	25	27♐
1959	17♉	17	18	18	18	19	19	20	20	21	22	22	23	24	24	25♉
1960	20♐	21	23	24	26	27	29	00♑	02	03	05	06	08	09	11	12♑
1961	08♋R	07	06	05	05	04	03	03	02	02	01	01	00	00	00	00♋R
1962	05♑	07	08	10	11	13	14	16	17	19	20	22	23	25	26	28♑
1963	24♌ R	24	24	23	23	23	22	22	21	21	20	19	19	18	17	16♌ R
1964	20♑	22	23	25	26	28	29	01♒	02	04	06	07	09	10	12	13♒
1965	23♍	24	24	25	25	26	26	26	27	27	27	27	27	28	28R	28♍ R
1966	06♒	08	10	11	13	14	16	17	19	21	22	24	25	27	28	00♓
1967	14♎	15	15	16	17	18	19	20	21	21	22	23	24	24	25	26♎
1968	23♒	25	26	28	29	01♓	02	04	05	07	09	10	12	13	15	16♓
1969	01♏	02	03	04	05	06	07	09	10	11	12	13	14	15	16	17♏
1970	12♓	13	15	16	18	19	21	22	24	25	27	28	00♈	01	03	04♈
1971	16♏	17	18	19	21	22	23	24	26	27	28	29	01♐	02	03	05♐
1972	03♈	04	05	07	08	09	11	12	13	15	16	17	19	20	21	23♈
1973	00♐	02	03	05	06	07	09	10	11	13	14	15	17	18	20	21♐
1974	02♉	03	04	04	05	06	07	08	09	09	10	11	12	13	14	15♉
1975	14♐	16	17	19	20	22	23	25	26	27	29	00♑	02	03	05	06♑
1976	17♊ R	16	16	16	15	15	15	14	14	14	14D	14	14	14	15	15♊
1977	29♐	01♑	02	04	05	07	09	10	12	13	15	16	18	19	21	22♑
1978	09♌ R	08	07	07	06	05	05	04	03	02	02	01	00	29♋	28	28♋R
1979	14♑	16	17	19	20	22	23	27	27	28	00♒	01	03	04	06	08♒
1980	13♍	14	14	14	15	15	15	15	15R	15	15	15	14	14	14	13♍ R
1981	00♒	02	03	05	07	08	10	11	13	15	16	18	19	21	22	24♒
1982	07♎	07	08	09	10	10	11	12	12	13	14	14	15	15	16	16♎
1983	17♒	18	20	21	23	24	26	28	29	01♓	02	04	05	07	08	10♓
1984	24♎	26	26	27	28	29	00♏	01	02	03	04	05	06	07	08	09♏
1985	05♓	06	08	09	11	12	14	15	17	18	20	21	23	24	26	27♓
1986	10♏	11	13	14	15	16	17	19	20	21	22	23	25	26	27	28♏
1987	24♓	26	27	28	00♈	01	03	04	05	07	08	10	11	12	14	15♈
1988	24♏	26	27	28	00♐	01	02	04	05	06	08	09	10	12	13	14♐
1989	20♈	21	22	23	24	25	26	27	28	29	00♉	02	03	04	05	06♉

February

	1st	3rd	5th	7th	9th	11th	13th	15th	17th	19th	21st	23rd	25th	27th	29th
1900	08♒	09	11	12	14	15	17	19	20	22	23	25	26	28♒	
1901	10♍R	09	09	08	07	07	06	05	05	04	03	02	01	01♍	
1902	23♒	25	26	28	00♓	01	03	04	06	07	09	11	12	14♓	
1903	14♎	14	15	15	15	15	16	16	16R	16	16	16	16	15♎	
1904	09♓	11	12	14	15	17	19	20	22	23	25	26	28	29	01♈
1905	08♏	09	10	11	12	12	13	14	15	16	16	17	18	18♏	
1906	26♓	28	00♈	01	03	04	06	07	09	10	11	13	14	16♈	
1907	27♏	28	29	00♐	02	03	04	05	06	07	08	10	11	12♐	
1908	14♈	16	17	18	20	21	22	24	25	27	28	29	01♉	02	04♉
1909	14♐	15	17	18	19	21	22	23	25	26	27	29	00♑	01♑	
1910	05♉	06	07	08	09	11	12	13	14	15	17	18	19	20♉	
1911	00♑	01	02	04	05	07	08	10	11	13	14	16	17	18♑	
1912	00♊	01	01	02	03	03	04	05	06	07	08	08	09	10	11♊
1913	16♑	17	19	20	22	23	25	26	28	29	01♒	02	04	05♒	
1914	06♋R	06	06	05	05	05D	05	05	05	05	06	06	06	06♋	
1915	01♒	02	04	06	07	09	10	12	13	15	17	18	20	21♒	
1916	23♌R	22	22	21	20	19	18	18	17	16	15	15	14	13	13♌
1917	17♒	19	20	22	24	25	27	28	00♓	01	03	05	06	08♓	
1918	03♎	03R	03	03	02	02	02	02	01	01	01	00	00	29♍	
1919	03♓	05	06	08	09	11	13	14	16	17	19	20	22	23♓	
1920	00♏	00	01	02	02	03	04	04	05	05	06	06	07	07	07♏
1921	20♓	22	23	25	26	28	29	01♈	02	04	05	07	08	10♈	
1922	20♏	21	22	23	24	26	27	28	29	00♐	01	02	03	04♐	
1923	07♈	09	10	12	13	14	16	17	19	20	22	23	25	26♈	
1924	07♐	09	10	11	12	14	15	16	18	19	20	21	23	24	25♐
1925	27♈	28	29	01♉	02	03	04	06	07	08	10	11	12	13♉	
1926	24♐	25	27	28	29	01♑	02	04	05	06	08	09	11	12♑	
1927	19♉	20	21	22	23	24	25	26	27	28	29	00♊	01	02♊	
1928	09♑	11	12	14	15	17	18	20	21	23	24	26	27	29♑	00♒
1929	21♊	21	21	21	21	22	22	22	23	23	24	24	25	26♊	
1930	25♑	27	28	00♒	01	03	04	06	07	09	11	12	14	15♒	
1931	05♌R	04	03	02	02	01	01	00	29♋	29	28	28	28	28♋	
1932	10♒	12	14	15	17	18	20	22	23	25	26	28	29	01♓	03♓
1933	19♍R	19	18	18	17	17	16	16	15	14	14	13	12	11♍	
1934	27♒	29	00♓	02	03	05	06	08	10	11	13	14	16	17♓	
1935	20♎	21	21	22	22	23	23	23	23	24	24	24	24	24♎	
1936	13♓	15	16	18	19	21	22	24	26	27	29	00♈	02	03	05♈
1937	13♏	14	15	16	17	18	19	20	20	21	22	23	24	25♏	
1938	01♈	02	04	05	07	08	10	11	12	14	15	17	18	20♈	
1939	01♐	02	04	05	06	07	08	10	11	12	13	14	15	17♐	
1940	19♈	20	21	23	24	25	27	28	29	01♉	02	04	05	06	08♉
1941	18♐	19	21	22	23	25	26	27	29	00♑	02	03	04	05♑	
1942	10♉	11	12	13	14	15	17	18	19	20	21	22	23	25♉	
1943	03♑	05	06	08	09	11	12	14	15	16	18	19	21	22♑	
1944	07♊	08	08	09	09	10	11	11	12	13	13	14	15	16	16♊
1945	19♑	21	22	24	25	27	28	00♒	02	03	05	06	08	09♒	
1946	16♋R	16	15	15	15	14	14	14	14	14	14	14D	14	14♋	
1947	05♒	06	07	08	11	12	14	16	17	19	20	22	23	25♒	
1948	04♍R	03	02	02	01	00	29♌	28	28	27	26	25	25	24	23♌
1949	21♒	23	24	26	27	29	01♓	02	04	05	07	08	10	12♓	
1950	10♎	10	10	10	10	11R	11	11	10	10	10	10	10	09♎	
1951	07♓	09	10	12	13	15	16	18	19	21	23	24	26	27♓	
1952	05♏	06	06	07	08	09	09	10	11	12	12	13	13	14	14♏
1953	24♓	26	27	29	00♈	02	03	05	06	08	09	11	12	14♈	
1954	25♏	26	27	28	29	00♐	01	02	03	05	06	07	08	09♐	
1955	12♈	13	14	16	17	19	20	21	23	24	26	27	29	00♉	
1956	11♐	13	14	15	16	18	19	20	22	23	24	26	27	28	00♑
1957	02♉	03	04	05	06	08	09	10	11	13	14	15	16	18♉	
1958	28♐	29	00♑	02	03	05	06	08	09	10	12	13	15	16♑	
1959	26♉	26	27	28	29	00♊	01	01	02	03	04	05	06	07♊	
1960	13♑	14	16	17	19	20	22	23	24	26	28	29	01♒	02	04♒
1961	00♋R	00	00♊	00	00♋D	00	00	00	00	00	01	01	02	02♋	
1962	29♑	00♒	02	03	05	07	08	10	11	13	14	16	17	19♒	
1963	16♌R	15	14	13	13	12	11	10	10	09	08	08	07	07♌	
1964	14♒	16	17	19	21	22	24	25	27	28	00♓	02	03	05	06♓
1965	27♍R	27	27	27	27	26	26	26	25	25	24	24	23	22♍	
1966	01♓	02	04	06	07	08	10	12	13	15	17	18	20	21♓	
1967	26♎	27	27	28	29	29	00♏	00	01	01	01	02	02	02♏	
1968	17♓	19	20	22	23	25	26	28	29	01♈	02	04	06	07	09♈
1969	18♏	19	20	21	22	23	24	25	26	27	28	28	29	00♐	
1970	05♈	06	07	09	11	12	14	15	16	18	19	21	22	24♈	
1971	05♐	06	08	09	10	11	13	14	15	16	18	19	29	21♐	
1972	23♈	25	26	27	28	00♉	01	02	04	05	06	08	09	10	12♉
1973	22♐	23	24	26	27	29	00♑	01	03	04	06	07	08	10♑	
1974	16♉	17	18	19	20	21	22	23	24	25	26	27	28	29♉	
1975	07♑	08	10	11	13	14	16	17	19	20	22	23	25	26♑	
1976	15♊	15	16	16	16	17	17	18	18	19	19	20	21	21	22♊
1977	23♑	25	26	28	29	01♒	02	04	05	07	08	10	12	13♒	
1978	27♋R	27	26	25	25	24	24	23	23	23	22	22	22	22♋	
1979	08♒	10	11	13	15	16	18	19	21	23	24	26	27	29♒	
1980	13♍R	13	12	12	11	11	10	09	08	08	07	06	05	05	04♍
1981	25♒	26	28	00♓	01	03	04	06	07	09	11	12	14	15♓	
1982	16♎	17	17	18	18	18	18	18	19	19R	19	19	19	18♎	
1983	11♓	12	14	16	17	19	20	22	23	25	26	28	29	01♈	
1984	10♏	11	12	12	13	14	15	16	17	17	18	19	20	20	21♏
1985	28♓	00♈	01	03	04	06	07	09	10	12	13	15	16	18♈	
1986	29♏	00♐	01	02	03	05	06	07	08	09	10	12	13	14♐	
1987	16♈	17	19	20	21	23	24	26	27	28	00♉	01	03	04♉	
1988	15♐	16	18	19	20	22	23	25	26	27	29	00♑	01	03	04♑
1989	07♉	08	09	10	11	13	14	15	16	17	18	20	21	22♉	

March

	1st	3rd	5th	7th	9th	11th	13th	15th	17th	19th	21st	23rd	25th	27th	29th	31st
1900	00♓	01	03	04	06	07	09	11	12	14	15	17	18	20	22	23♓
1901	00♍R	29♌	28	28	27	26	26	25	25	24	24	24	23	23	23	23♌
1902	15♓	17	18	20	22	23	25	26	28	29	01♈	02	04	06	07	09♈
1903	15♎R	15	14	14	14	13	13	12	11	11	10	09	09	08	07	06♎
1904	02♈	03	05	06	08	09	11	12	14	15	17	18	20	21	23	24♈
1905	19♏	20	20	21	21	22	22	23	23	23	24	24	24	24	24	25♏
1906	17♈	19	20	22	23	25	26	28	29	01♉	02	03	05	06	08	09♉
1907	13♐	14	15	16	17	18	19	21	22	23	24	25	26	27	28	29♐
1908	04♉	06	07	08	10	11	12	14	15	17	18	19	21	22	23	25♉
1909	03♑	04	05	07	08	10	11	12	14	15	16	18	19	20	22	23♑
1910	21♉	23	24	25	26	27	29	00♊	01	02	04	05	06	07	09	10♊
1911	20♑	21	23	24	26	27	29	00♒	02	03	05	06	08	09	11	12♒
1912	12♊	12	13	14	15	16	17	18	19	20	21	22	23	24	26	27♊
1913	07♒	08	10	12	13	15	16	18	19	21	22	24	25	27	29	00♓
1914	07♋	07	07	08	08	09	09	10	11	11	12	12	13	14	15	15♋
1915	23♒	24	26	28	29	01♓	02	04	05	07	09	10	12	13	15	16♓
1916	13♌R	12	12	11	11	11	10	10	10	10	10D	10	10	10	10	10♌
1917	09♓	11	12	14	16	17	19	20	22	23	25	27	28	00♈	01	03♈
1918	29♍R	28	27	27	26	25	24	23	23	22	21	20	20	19	18	18♍
1919	25♓	27	28	00♈	01	03	04	06	07	09	10	12	14	15	17	18♈
1920	07♏	08	08	08	08	09	09	09R	09	09	08	08	08	08	07	07♏
1921	11♈	13	14	16	17	19	20	22	23	25	26	28	29	01♉	02	04♉
1922	05♐	06	06	07	08	09	10	11	12	13	13	14	15	16	17	17♐
1923	27♈	29	00♉	02	03	04	06	07	09	10	11	13	14	16	17	18♉
1924	26♐	27	28	00♑	01	02	03	05	06	07	08	10	11	12	13	15♑
1925	15♉	16	17	19	20	21	22	24	25	26	28	29	00♊	01	03	04♊
1926	14♑	15	16	18	19	21	22	24	25	26	28	29	01♒	02	04	05♒
1927	03♊	04	05	06	07	09	10	11	12	13	14	15	16	17	19	20♊
1928	01♒	02	04	05	07	08	10	11	13	15	16	18	19	21	22	24♒
1929	26♊	27	27	28	29	00♋	00	01	02	03	03	04	05	06	07	08♋
1930	17♒	18	20	21	23	25	26	28	29	01♓	02	04	06	07	09	10♓
1931	27♋R	27	27	27D	27	27	27	27	27	28	28	28	28	29	29	00♌
1932	03♓	05	07	08	10	11	13	14	16	18	19	21	22	24	25	27♓
1933	11♍R	10	09	08	08	07	06	05	05	04	04	03	02	02	02	01♍
1934	19♓	21	22	24	25	27	28	00♈	02	03	05	06	08	09	11	12♈
1935	24♎R	24	24	24	24	23	23	23	22	22	21	21	20	19	19	18♎
1936	06♈	07	09	10	12	13	15	16	18	19	21	22	24	25	27	28♈
1937	25♏	26	27	27	28	29	29	00♐	01	01	02	02	03	03	03	04♐
1938	21♈	23	24	26	27	29	00♉	01	03	04	06	07	09	10	11	13♉
1939	18♐	19	20	21	23	24	25	26	27	28	29	00♑	02	03	04	05♑
1940	08♉	10	11	12	14	15	16	18	19	20	22	23	24	26	27	28♉
1941	07♑	08	10	11	13	14	15	17	18	19	21	22	24	25	26	28♑
1942	26♉	27	28	29	00♊	02	03	04	05	06	08	09	10	11	12	14♊
1943	24♑	25	27	28	00♒	01	03	04	06	07	09	10	12	13	15	16♒
1944	17♊	18	19	19	20	21	22	23	24	25	26	27	28	29	00♋	01♋
1945	11♒	12	14	15	17	19	20	22	23	25	26	28	29	01♓	03	04♓
1946	14♋	14	14	15	15	15	16	16	17	17	18	19	19	19	20	21♋
1947	27♒	28	00♓	01	03	04	06	08	09	11	12	14	15	17	19	20♓
1948	23♌R	22	21	21	20	20	19	19	19	18	18	18	18	18	18	18♌
1949	13♓	15	16	18	19	21	23	24	26	27	29	00♈	02	03	05	07♈
1950	09♎R	08	08	07	07	06	05	05	04	03	02	02	01	00	29♍	29♍
1951	29♓	00♈	02	03	05	07	08	10	11	13	14	16	17	19	20	22♈
1952	15♏	15	16	16	16	17	17	17	18	18	18	18	18R	18	18	18♏
1953	15♈	17	18	20	21	23	24	26	27	29	00♉	01	02	04	06	07♉
1954	10♐	11	12	13	14	15	16	17	18	19	20	21	22	23	24	24♐
1955	01♉	03	04	05	07	08	10	11	12	14	15	17	18	19	21	22♉
1956	00♑	02	03	04	06	07	08	09	11	12	13	15	16	17	19	20♑
1957	19♉	20	21	23	24	25	26	28	29	00♊	01	03	04	05	06	08♊
1958	18♑	19	21	22	23	25	26	28	29	01♒	02	04	05	07	08	10♒
1959	08♊	09	10	11	12	13	14	15	16	17	18	19	20	22	23	24♊
1960	05♒	06	08	09	11	12	14	15	17	19	20	22	23	25	26	28♒
1961	02♋	03	03	04	05	05	06	06	07	08	09	09	10	11	12	13♋
1962	21♒	22	24	25	27	28	00♓	02	03	05	06	08	09	11	13	14♓
1963	06♌R	06	06	05	05	05	05	05	05D	05	05	05	05	05	06	06♌
1964	07♓	09	10	12	13	15	17	18	20	21	23	24	26	28	29	01♈
1965	22♍R	21	20	19	18	18	17	16	15	15	14	13	13	12	11	11♍
1966	23♓	24	26	28	29	01♈	02	04	05	07	08	10	11	13	14	16♈
1967	02♏	03	03	03R	03	03	03	02	02	02	02	01	01	01	00	00♏
1968	09♈	11	12	14	15	17	18	20	21	23	24	26	27	29	00♉	02♉
1969	01♐	02	03	04	05	05	06	07	08	08	09	10	10	11	12	12♐
1970	25♈	27	28	29	01♉	02	04	05	07	08	09	11	12	14	15	16♉
1971	23♐	24	25	26	27	29	00♑	01	02	03	05	06	07	08	09	11♑
1972	12♉	14	15	16	18	19	20	22	23	24	25	27	28	29	01♊	02♉
1973	11♑	13	14	15	17	18	20	21	23	24	25	27	28	00♒	01	02♒
1974	00♊	01	03	04	05	06	07	08	09	11	12	13	14	15	16	18♊
1975	28♑	29	01♒	02	04	05	07	08	10	11	13	14	16	17	19	21♒
1976	22♊	23	24	25	26	26	27	28	29	00♋	01	01	02	03	04	05♋
1977	15♒	16	18	19	21	22	24	26	27	29	00♓	02	03	05	06	08♓
1978	22♋R	22D	22	22	22	22	22	23	23	23	24	24	25	25	26	26♋
1979	00♓	02	04	05	07	08	10	11	13	15	16	18	19	21	22	24♓
1980	03♍R	03	02	01	00	00	29♌	29	28	28	27	27	26	26	26	26♌
1981	17♓	18	20	22	23	25	26	28	29	01♈	03	04	06	07	09	10♈
1982	18♎R	18	18	17	17	17	16	16	15	14	14	13	12	12	11	10♎
1983	03♈	04	06	07	09	10	12	13	15	16	18	19	21	22	24	25♈
1984	21♏	22	23	23	24	24	25	25	26	26	26	27	27	27	28	28♏
1985	19♈	21	22	24	25	26	28	29	01♉	02	04	05	07	08	09	11♉
1986	15♐	16	17	18	19	20	22	23	24	25	26	27	28	29	00♑	01♑
1987	05♉	07	08	09	11	12	13	15	16	18	19	20	22	23	24	26♉
1988	05♑	06	07	09	10	11	12	13	15	17	18	19	21	22	24	25♑
1989	23♉	24	26	27	28	29	01♊	02	03	04	05	07	08	09	10	12♊

April

	1st	3rd	5th	7th	9th	11th	13th	15th	17th	19th	21st	23rd	25th	27th	29th
1900	24♓	25	27	29	00♈	02	03	05	06	08	09	11	13	14	16♈
1901	23♌ R	23D	23	23	23	23	23	23	24	24	24	25	25	25	26♌
1902	09♈	11	12	14	16	17	19	20	22	23	25	26	28	29	01♉
1903	06♎ R	05	04	04	03	02	02	01	00	00	29♍	29	28	28	28♍ R
1904	25♈	27	28	00♉	01	03	04	06	07	09	10	11	13	14	16♉
1905	25♏	25R	25	25	24	24	24	24	23	23	23	22	22	21	20♏
1906	10♉	11	13	14	16	17	19	20	21	23	24	26	27	28	00♊
1907	29♐	00♑	01	02	03	04	05	06	06	07	08	09	10	10	11♑
1908	25♉	27	28	29	01♊	02	03	05	06	07	09	10	11	13	14♊
1909	24♑	25	26	28	29	00♒	02	03	04	06	07	08	10	11	12♒
1910	10♊	12	13	14	15	17	18	19	20	22	23	24	25	26	28♊
1911	13♒	14	16	17	19	20	22	23	26	26	28	29	01♓	02	04♓
1912	27♊	28	29	00♋	01	03	04	05	06	07	08	09	10	11	13♋
1913	01♓	02	04	06	07	09	10	12	13	15	16	18	19	21	23♓
1914	16♋	17	17	18	19	20	21	22	23	23	24	25	26	27	28♋
1915	17♓	19	20	22	23	25	27	28	00♈	01	03	04	06	07	09♈
1916	10♌	11	11	11	12	12	13	13	14	14	15	15	16	17	17♌
1917	04♈	05	07	08	10	11	13	14	16	17	19	20	22	24	25♈
1918	17♍ R	17	16	16	15	15	14	14	14	14	13	13	13	13D	13♍
1919	19♈	20	22	23	25	26	28	29	01♉	02	04	05	07	08	10♉
1920	07♏ R	06	06	05	05	04	03	03	02	01	01	00	29♎	28	28♎ R
1921	04♉	06	07	09	10	12	13	15	16	17	19	20	22	23	25♉
1922	18♐	18	19	20	20	21	21	22	22	23	23	23	24	24	24♐
1923	19♉	20	22	23	25	26	27	29	00♊	01	03	04	06	07	08♊
1924	15♑	16	18	19	20	21	23	24	25	26	27	29	00♒	01	02♒
1925	05♊	06	07	08	10	11	12	14	15	16	17	19	20	21	23♊
1926	06♒	07	09	10	12	13	15	16	17	19	20	22	23	25	26♒
1927	20♊	21	23	24	25	26	27	28	29	01♋	02	03	04	05	07♋
1928	24♒	26	28	29	01♓	02	04	05	07	08	10	11	13	14	16♓
1929	08♋	09	10	11	12	13	14	15	16	17	18	19	20	21	22♋
1930	11♓	13	14	16	17	19	20	22	24	25	27	28	00♈	01	03♈
1931	00♌	00	01	02	02	03	03	04	05	05	06	07	08	08	09♌
1932	28♓	29	01♈	02	04	05	07	09	10	12	13	15	16	18	19♈
1933	01♍ R	01	01	01	00	00	00D	00	01	01	01	01	01	02	02♍
1934	13♈	15	16	18	19	21	22	24	25	27	28	00♉	01	03	04♉
1935	18♎ R	17	16	15	15	14	13	12	12	11	10	10	09	08	08♎ R
1936	29♈	00♉	02	03	05	06	08	09	11	12	13	15	16	18	19♉
1937	04♐	04	04	05	05	05	05	05R	05	05	05	05	04	04	04♐ R
1938	14♉	15	16	18	19	21	22	23	25	26	28	29	00♊	02	03♊
1939	05♑	06	08	09	10	11	12	13	14	15	16	17	18	19	19♑
1940	29♉	00♊	02	03	04	06	07	08	10	11	12	13	15	16	17♊
1941	28♑	00♒	01	03	04	05	07	08	10	11	12	14	15	16	18♒
1942	14♊	15	17	18	19	20	21	23	24	25	26	28	29	00♋	01♋
1943	17♒	19	20	22	23	25	26	28	29	01♓	02	04	05	07	08♓
1944	01♋	02	03	04	05	06	08	09	10	11	12	13	14	15	16♋
1945	05♓	06	08	10	11	13	14	16	17	19	20	22	23	25	27♓
1946	21♋	22	22	23	24	25	25	26	27	28	29	00♌	00	01	02♌
1947	21♓	23	24	26	27	29	00♈	02	03	05	07	08	10	11	13♈
1948	18♌	18	18	18	18	19	19	19	20	20	20	21	21	22	22♌
1949	07♈	09	10	12	13	15	17	18	20	21	23	24	26	27	29♈
1950	28♍ R	27	27	26	25	25	24	24	23	23	23	22	22	22	22♍ R
1951	22♈	24	25	27	28	00♉	01	03	04	06	07	09	10	12	13♉
1952	18♏ R	18	17	17	17	16	16	15	15	14	14	13	13	13	11♏ R
1953	08♉	09	11	12	14	15	17	18	19	21	22	24	25	27	28♉
1954	25♐	26	27	27	28	29	00♑	00	01	02	02	03	04	04	05♑
1955	23♉	24	25	27	28	00♊	01	02	04	05	06	08	09	10	12♊
1956	21♑	22	23	24	26	27	28	00♒	01	02	03	05	06	07	08♒
1957	08♊	10	11	12	13	15	16	17	18	20	21	22	23	25	26♊
1958	10♒	12	13	14	16	18	19	21	22	24	25	26	28	29	01♓
1959	24♊	25	26	28	29	00♋	01	02	03	04	05	07	08	09	10♋
1960	29♒	00♓	02	03	05	06	08	09	11	12	14	15	17	19	20♓
1961	13♋	14	15	16	16	17	18	19	20	21	22	23	24	25	26♋
1962	15♓	17	18	20	21	23	24	26	27	29	01♈	02	04	05	07♈
1963	06♌	07	07	07	08	08	09	09	10	11	11	12	13	13	14♌
1964	01♈	03	05	06	08	09	11	12	14	15	17	18	20	21	23♈
1965	11♍ R	10	10	09	09	09	09	08	08	08	08D	08	08	09	09♍
1966	17♈	18	20	21	23	24	26	27	29	00♉	02	03	05	06	08♉
1967	29♎ R	29	28	27	27	26	25	25	24	23	22	21	21	20	19♎ R
1968	02♉	04	05	07	08	10	11	13	14	16	17	18	20	21	23♉
1969	12♐	13	13	14	14	15	15	15	16	16	16	16	16	16	16♐ R
1970	17♉	19	20	21	23	24	26	27	28	00♊	01	02	04	05	07♊
1971	11♑	12	14	15	16	17	18	19	20	22	23	24	25	26	27♑
1972	03♊	04	05	07	08	09	10	12	13	14	16	17	18	20	21♊
1973	03♒	05	06	07	09	10	12	13	15	16	17	19	20	22	23♒
1974	18♊	19	20	22	23	24	25	26	28	29	00♋	01	02	03	05♋
1975	21♒	23	24	26	27	29	00♓	02	03	05	07	08	10	11	13♓
1976	06♋	07	08	09	10	11	12	13	14	15	16	17	18	19	20♋
1977	09♓	10	12	13	15	17	18	20	21	23	24	26	27	29	01♈
1978	26♋	27	28	28	29	00♌	00	01	02	03	03	04	05	06	07♌
1979	25♓	26	28	29	01♈	03	04	06	07	09	10	12	13	15	16♈
1980	26♌ R	25	25	25D	25	26	26	26	26	26	27	27	27	28	28♌
1981	11♈	13	14	16	17	19	20	22	23	25	26	28	29	01♉	02♉
1982	10♎ R	09	08	07	07	06	05	04	04	03	03	02	02	01	01♎ R
1983	26♈	28	29	01♉	02	04	05	06	08	09	11	12	14	15	17♉
1984	28♏	28	28	28R	28	28	28	27	27	27	26	26	25	25	24♏ R
1985	12♉	13	14	16	17	19	20	22	23	24	26	27	29	00♊	01♊
1986	01♑	02	03	04	05	06	07	08	09	10	11	11	12	13	14♑
1987	26♉	28	29	00♊	02	03	04	06	07	08	10	11	12	14	15♊
1988	26♑	27	28	00♒	01	02	04	05	06	08	09	10	12	13	14♒
1989	12♊	13	15	16	17	18	20	21	22	23	24	26	27	28	29♊

May

	1st	3rd	5th	7th	9th	11th	13th	15th	17th	19th	21st	23rd	25th	27th	29th	31st
1900	17♈	19	20	22	23	25	26	28	29	01♉	02	04	05	07	08	10♉
1901	26♌	27	28	28	29	29	00♍	01	02	02	03	04	05	05	06	07♍
1902	02♉	04	05	07	08	10	11	13	14	15	17	18	20	21	23	24♉
1903	27♍R	27	27	27	27D	27	27	27	27	27	28	28	28	29	29	00♎
1904	17♉	19	20	22	23	24	26	27	29	00♊	02	03	04	06	07	09♊
1905	20♏R	19	18	18	17	16	16	15	14	13	13	12	11	11	10	10♏
1906	01♊	02	04	05	07	08	09	11	12	13	15	16	18	19	20	22♊
1907	12♑	12	13	14	14	15	15	16	16	17	17	17	18	18	18	18♑
1908	15♊	17	18	19	21	22	23	25	26	27	28	00♋	01	02	07	05♋
1909	13♒	15	16	17	19	20	21	23	24	25	26	28	29	00♓	01	03♓
1910	29♊	00♋	01	03	04	05	06	08	09	10	11	13	14	15	16	18♋
1911	05♓	07	08	10	11	13	14	16	17	19	20	22	23	24	26	27♓
1912	14♋	15	16	17	18	19	21	22	23	24	25	26	28	29	00♌	01♌
1913	24♓	26	27	29	00♈	02	03	05	06	08	09	11	12	14	15	17♈
1914	29♋	00♌	01	02	03	04	05	06	07	08	09	10	11	13	14	15♌
1915	10♈	12	13	15	17	18	20	21	23	24	26	27	29	00♉	02	03♉
1916	18♌	19	19	20	21	22	23	23	24	25	26	27	28	29	00♍	01♍
1917	27♈	28	00♉	01	03	04	06	07	09	10	11	13	14	16	17	19♉
1918	14♍	14	14	14	14	15	15	15	16	16	17	17	18	19	19	20♍
1919	11♉	13	14	16	17	18	20	21	23	24	26	27	29	00♊	01	03♊
1920	27♎R	26	25	25	24	24	23	23	22	22	22	21	21	21	21	21♎D
1921	26♉	27	29	00♊	02	03	04	06	07	09	10	11	13	14	15	17♊
1922	24♐	25	25	25R	25	25	25	25	24	24	24	23	23	23	22	22♐
1923	10♊	11	12	14	15	16	18	19	20	22	23	24	26	27	28	00♋
1924	03♒	04	05	07	08	09	10	11	12	13	14	15	16	17	18	19♒
1925	24♊	25	26	28	29	00♋	01	03	04	05	07	08	09	10	12	13♋
1926	28♒	29	00♓	02	03	05	06	08	09	10	12	13	15	16	18	19♓
1927	08♋	09	10	11	12	14	15	16	17	18	20	21	22	23	24	26♋
1928	17♓	19	20	22	24	25	27	28	00♈	01	03	04	06	07	09	10♈
1929	23♋	24	25	26	27	28	29	01♌	02	03	04	05	06	07	08	09♌
1930	04♈	06	07	09	10	12	14	15	17	18	20	21	23	24	26	27♈
1931	10♌	11	12	13	13	14	15	16	17	18	19	20	21	22	23	24♌
1932	21♈	22	24	25	27	28	00♉	01	03	04	06	07	09	10	12	13♉
1933	02♍	03	03	04	04	05	05	06	07	07	08	09	09	10	11	12♍
1934	06♉	07	09	10	12	13	15	16	17	19	20	22	23	25	26	28♉
1935	07♎R	07	07	06	06	06	06	06	06	06D	06	06	06	06	06	07♎
1936	21♉	22	24	25	26	28	29	01♊	02	03	05	06	08	09	10	12♊
1937	03♐R	03	02	02	01	01	00	29♏	29	28	27	27	26	26	26	24♏
1938	04♊	06	07	09	10	11	13	14	15	17	18	19	21	22	23	25♊
1939	20♑	21	22	23	24	25	25	26	27	28	28	29	30	00♒	01	01♒
1940	19♊	20	21	23	24	25	27	28	29	00♋	02	03	04	06	07	08♋
1941	19♒	21	22	23	25	26	26	29	00♓	01	03	04	05	07	08	09♓
1942	02♋	04	05	06	07	08	10	11	12	13	15	16	17	18	20	21♋
1943	10♓	11	13	14	16	17	19	20	22	23	25	26	28	29	01♈	02♈
1944	23♋	24	25	26	28	29	00♌	01	02	04	05	06	07	09	10	11♌
1945	28♓	00♈	01	03	04	05	07	09	10	12	13	15	16	18	19	21♈
1946	03♌	04	05	06	07	08	09	10	11	12	13	14	15	16	17	18♌
1947	14♈	16	17	19	20	22	23	25	26	28	29	01♉	02	04	05	07♉
1948	23♌	24	24	25	26	26	27	28	29	00♍	00	01	02	03	04	05♍
1949	00♉	02	03	05	06	08	09	11	12	14	15	16	18	19	21	22♉
1950	22♍R	22	22D	22	22	22	22	22	23	23	23	24	24	25	25	26♍
1951	15♉	16	18	19	20	22	23	25	26	28	29	00♊	02	03	05	06♊
1952	10♏R	09	09	08	07	07	06	05	05	04	03	03	02	02	02	01♏
1953	29♉	01♊	02	04	05	06	08	09	10	12	13	15	16	17	19	20♊
1954	05♑	06	06	06	07	07	07	08	08	08	08	08	08	08	08	08♑
1955	13♊	14	16	17	18	20	21	22	24	25	26	28	29	00♋	01	03♋
1956	10♒	11	12	13	15	16	17	18	19	21	22	23	24	25	26	28♒
1957	27♊	28	00♋	01	02	03	05	06	07	09	10	11	12	14	15	16♋
1958	02♓	04	05	07	08	10	11	13	14	16	17	18	20	21	23	24♓
1959	11♋	12	14	15	16	17	18	19	21	22	23	24	25	26	28	29♋
1960	22♓	23	25	26	28	29	01♈	02	04	05	07	08	10	11	13	14♈
1961	27♋	28	29	00♌	01	02	03	04	05	06	07	09	10	11	12	13♌
1962	08♈	10	11	13	14	16	17	19	20	22	24	25	27	28	00♉	01♉
1963	15♌	15	16	17	18	19	20	20	21	22	23	24	25	26	27	28♌
1964	25♈	26	28	29	01♉	02	04	05	07	08	10	11	12	14	15	17♉
1965	09♍	09	10	10	10	11	11	12	12	13	13	14	15	15	16	17♍
1966	09♉	11	12	14	15	17	18	20	21	22	24	25	27	28	00♊	01♊
1967	19♎R	18	18	17	17	16	16	15	15	15	15	15	15	14D	15	15♎
1968	24♉	26	27	28	00♊	01	03	04	05	07	08	10	11	12	14	15♊
1969	16♐R	16	16	16	15	15	15	14	14	13	13	12	12	11	10	10♐
1970	08♊	09	11	12	13	15	16	17	19	20	21	23	24	25	27	28♊
1971	28♑	29	00♒	01	02	03	04	05	06	07	08	09	10	11	11	12♒
1972	22♊	23	25	26	27	29	00♋	01	02	04	05	06	07	09	10	11♋
1973	24♒	26	27	29	00♓	02	03	04	06	07	09	10	11	13	14	15♓
1974	06♋	07	08	09	11	12	13	14	16	17	18	19	20	22	23	24♋
1975	14♓	16	17	19	20	22	23	25	26	28	29	01♈	02	04	05	07♈
1976	21♋	22	23	24	25	26	28	29	00♌	01	02	03	04	05	07	08♌
1977	02♈	04	05	07	08	10	11	13	14	16	17	19	20	22	23	25♈
1978	07♌	08	09	10	11	12	13	14	15	16	17	18	19	20	21	22♌
1979	18♈	20	21	23	24	26	27	29	00♉	02	03	05	06	08	09	11♉
1980	29♌	29	00♍	00	01	02	02	03	04	04	05	06	07	07	08	09♍
1981	04♉	05	07	08	10	11	13	14	16	17	19	20	21	23	24	26♉
1982	01♎R	00	00	00	00	00D	00	00	00	00	00	01	01	01	02	02♎
1983	18♉	20	21	22	24	25	27	28	00♊	01	02	04	05	07	08	09♊
1984	24♏R	23	23	22	21	20	20	19	18	18	17	16	16	15	14	14♏
1985	03♊	04	05	07	08	10	11	12	14	15	16	18	19	20	22	23♊
1986	15♑	15	16	17	17	18	19	19	20	20	21	21	21	22	22	22♑
1987	16♊	18	19	20	22	23	24	26	27	28	29	01♋	02	03	05	06♋
1988	16♒	17	18	20	21	22	23	25	26	27	29	00♓	01	02	04	05♓
1989	01♋	02	03	04	06	07	08	09	11	12	13	14	15	17	18	19♋

June

	1st	3rd	5th	7th	9th	11th	13th	15th	17th	19th	21st	23rd	25th	27th	29th
1900	10♉	12	13	15	16	18	19	21	22	24	25	26	28	29	01♊
1901	08♍	09	09	10	11	12	13	14	15	16	17	18	19	20	21♍
1902	25♉	26	28	29	01♊	02	03	05	06	08	09	10	12	13	15♊
1903	00♎	00	01	01	02	03	03	04	05	05	06	07	08	09	10♎
1904	09♊	11	12	13	15	16	18	19	20	22	23	24	26	27	28♊
1905	10♏R	09	09	09	08	08	08	08	08D	08	08	08	08	08	09♏
1906	22♊	24	25	26	28	29	00♋	02	03	04	06	07	08	10	11♋
1907	18♑	18	18R	18	18	18	18	18	18	17	17	16	16	16	15♑
1908	06♋	07	08	10	11	12	13	15	16	17	19	20	21	22	24♋
1909	03♓	04	06	07	08	09	10	12	13	14	15	16	17	18	19♓
1910	18♋	19	21	22	23	24	26	27	28	29	01♌	02	03	04	06♌
1911	28♓	00♈	01	02	04	05	07	08	10	11	13	14	15	17	18♈
1912	02♌	03	04	05	06	08	09	10	11	12	14	15	16	17	18♌
1913	18♈	19	21	22	24	25	27	28	29	01♉	02	04	05	07	08♉
1914	15♌	16	17	19	20	21	22	23	24	25	27	28	29	00♍	01♍
1915	04♉	05	07	08	10	11	13	14	16	17	19	20	21	23	24♉
1916	01♍	02	03	04	05	06	07	08	09	10	11	12	13	14	16♍
1917	20♉	21	22	24	25	27	28	00♊	01	02	04	05	07	08	09♊
1918	20♍	21	22	22	23	24	25	26	26	27	28	29	00♎	01	02♎
1919	03♊	05	06	08	09	10	12	13	15	16	17	19	20	22	23♊
1920	21♎	21	21	21	21	21	22	22	22	23	23	24	24	25	25♎
1921	17♊	19	20	22	23	24	26	27	28	00♋	01	02	04	05	06♋
1922	21♐R	21	20	20	19	18	18	17	16	16	15	14	14	13	13♐
1923	00♋	02	03	04	05	07	08	09	11	12	13	15	16	17	19♋
1924	20♒	21	22	23	23	24	25	26	27	27	28	29	00♓	00	01♓
1925	13♋	15	16	17	19	20	21	22	24	25	26	27	29	00♌	01♌
1926	20♓	21	23	24	25	27	28	29	01♈	02	04	05	06	08	09♈
1927	26♋	27	29	00♌	01	02	03	05	06	07	08	10	11	12	13♌
1928	11♈	12	14	15	17	18	20	21	23	24	26	27	29	00♉	01♉
1929	10♌	11	12	13	15	16	17	18	19	20	22	23	24	25	26♌
1930	28♈	29	01♉	02	04	05	07	08	10	11	13	14	16	17	18♉
1931	24♌	26	27	28	29	00♍	01	02	03	04	05	06	07	08	10♍
1932	14♉	15	17	18	20	21	23	24	26	27	29	00♊	01	03	04♊
1933	12♍	13	14	15	16	17	17	18	19	20	21	22	23	24	25♍
1934	28♉	00♊	01	03	04	05	07	08	10	11	12	14	15	17	18♊
1935	07♎	07	08	08	08	09	09	10	11	11	12	13	13	14	15♎
1936	13♊	14	15	17	18	19	21	22	23	25	26	28	29	00♋	02♋
1937	24♏R	23	22	22	21	21	20	20	20	20	19	19	19	19D	19♏
1938	25♊	27	28	29	01♋	02	03	05	06	07	09	10	11	13	14♋
1939	01♒	02	02	03	03	03	04	04	04	04	04	04	04	04	04♒
1940	09♋	10	11	13	14	15	16	18	19	20	22	23	24	25	27♋
1941	10♓	11	13	14	15	17	18	19	20	22	23	24	25	26	28♓
1942	21♋	23	24	25	26	28	29	00♌	01	02	04	05	06	07	09♌
1943	03♈	04	06	07	09	10	12	13	15	16	18	19	20	22	23♈
1944	05♌	06	07	08	10	11	12	13	14	15	17	18	19	20	22♌
1945	22♈	23	25	26	28	29	01♉	02	04	05	07	08	09	11	12♉
1946	19♌	20	21	22	23	24	25	27	28	29	00♍	01	02	03	04♍
1947	08♉	09	11	12	14	15	16	18	19	21	22	24	25	27	28♉
1948	05♍	06	07	08	09	10	11	12	13	14	15	16	17	18	19♍
1949	23♉	24	26	27	29	00♊	02	03	04	06	07	09	10	12	12♊
1950	26♍	27	27	28	28	29	00♎	01	01	02	03	04	05	06	07♎
1951	07♊	08	10	11	12	14	15	17	18	19	21	22	23	25	26♊
1952	01♏R	01	01	01	01D	01	01	01	01	01	01	02	02	02	03♏
1953	21♊	22	23	25	26	27	29	00♋	01	03	04	05	07	08	09♋
1954	08♑R	07	07	07	06	06	05	05	04	04	03	03	02	01	01♑
1965	17♍	18	19	19	20	21	22	23	24	25	26	27	28	28	29♍
1966	02♊	03	05	06	07	09	10	12	13	14	16	17	18	20	21♊
1967	15♎	15	15	15	16	16	16	17	17	18	18	19	20	20	21♎
1968	16♊	17	19	20	21	23	24	25	27	28	29	01♋	02	03	05♋
1969	09♐R	09	08	07	07	06	05	05	04	04	03	03	02	02	02♐
1970	29♊	00♋	01	03	04	05	07	08	09	11	12	13	14	16	17♋
1971	13♒	13	14	15	16	16	17	17	18	19	19	19	20	20	21♒
1972	12♋	13	14	16	17	18	20	21	22	23	25	26	27	28	00♌
1973	16♓	18	19	20	22	23	24	26	27	28	00♈	01	02	03	05♈
1974	25♋	26	27	28	29	01♌	02	03	04	06	07	08	09	11	12♌
1965	17♍	18	19	19	20	21	22	23	24	25	26	27	28	28	29
1966	02♊	03	05	06	07	09	10	12	13	14	16	17	18	20	21
1967	15♎	15	15	15	16	16	16	17	17	18	18	19	20	20	21♎
1968	16♊	17	19	20	21	23	24	25	27	28	29	01♋	02	03	05
1969	09♐R	09	08	07	07	06	05	05	04	04	03	03	02	02	02♐
1970	29♊	00♋	01	03	04	05	07	08	09	11	12	13	14	16	17
1971	13♒	13	14	15	16	16	17	17	18	19	19	19	20	20	21♒
1972	12♋	13	14	16	17	18	20	21	22	23	25	26	27	28	00♌
1973	16♓	18	19	20	22	23	24	26	27	28	00♈	01	02	03	05♈
1974	25♋	26	27	28	29	01♌	02	03	04	06	07	08	09	11	12♌
1975	07♈	09	10	12	13	15	16	18	19	21	22	24	25	27	28♈
1976	08♌	09	11	12	13	14	15	16	18	19	20	21	22	24	25♌
1977	26♈	27	29	00♉	02	03	05	06	08	09	10	12	13	15	16♉
1978	22♌	24	25	26	27	28	29	00♍	01	02	03	04	06	07	08♍
1979	11♉	13	14	16	17	19	20	22	23	24	26	27	29	00♊	02♊
1980	10♍	10	11	12	13	14	15	16	17	18	19	20	21	22	23♍
1981	26♉	28	29	01♊	02	04	05	06	08	09	11	12	13	15	16♊
1982	02♎	03	03	04	04	05	06	06	07	08	08	09	10	11	12♎
1983	10♊	12	13	14	16	17	18	20	21	23	24	25	27	28	29♊
1984	14♏R	13	13	12	12	12	12	11	11	11D	11	11	11	12	12♏
1985	24♊	25	27	28	29	01♋	02	03	05	06	07	09	10	11	12♋
1986	22♑	22	23	23R	23	23	23	22	22	22	22	21	21	21	20♑
1987	07♋	08	09	10	12	13	14	16	17	18	19	21	22	23	25♋
1988	06♓	07	08	09	11	12	13	14	15	16	18	19	20	21	22♓
1989	20♋	21	22	24	25	26	27	29	00♌	01	01	03	05	06	07♌

July

	1st	3rd	5th	7th	9th	11th	13th	15th	17th	19th	21st	23rd	25th	27th	29th	31st
1900	02♊	03	05	06	08	09	10	12	13	15	16	17	19	20	21	23♊
1901	22♍	24	25	26	27	28	29	00♎	01	02	04	05	06	07	08	10♎
1902	16♊	17	19	20	22	23	24	26	27	28	00♋	01	02	04	05	06♋
1903	10♎	11	12	13	14	15	16	17	18	19	20	21	22	23	25	26♎
1904	00♋	01	02	04	05	06	08	09	10	12	13	14	16	17	18	20♋
1905	09♏	09	10	10	11	11	12	13	13	14	15	15	16	17	18	19♌
1906	12♋	14	15	16	17	19	20	21	23	24	25	27	28	29	00♌	02♑
1907	15♑ R	14	13	13	12	12	11	10	10	09	09	08	08	08	07	07♑
1908	25♋	26	27	29	00♌	01	03	04	05	06	08	09	10	12	13	14♌
1909	20♓	21	22	23	24	25	26	27	28	29	29	00♈	01	02	02	03♈
1910	07♌	08	09	11	12	13	14	16	17	18	19	21	22	23	24	25♌
1911	20♈	21	22	24	25	26	28	29	00♉	02	03	04	06	07	08	09♉
1912	20♌	21	22	23	25	26	27	28	29	01♍	02	03	04	06	07	08♍
1913	10♉	11	13	14	15	17	18	20	21	22	24	25	26	28	29	01♊
1914	02♍	03	05	06	07	08	09	11	12	13	14	15	17	18	19	20♍
1915	26♉	27	29	00♊	01	03	04	05	07	08	10	11	13	14	15	17♊
1916	17♍	18	19	20	21	22	24	25	26	27	28	29	01♎	02	03	04♎
1917	11♊	12	14	15	16	18	19	21	22	23	25	26	27	29	00♋	01♋
1918	03♎	04	05	06	07	08	09	10	11	12	13	15	16	17	18	19♎
1919	24♊	26	27	28	00♋	01	02	04	05	06	08	09	10	12	13	14♋
1920	26♎	27	27	28	29	00♏	00	01	02	03	04	05	06	07	08	09♏
1921	08♋	09	10	12	13	14	16	17	18	19	21	22	23	25	26	27♋
1922	12♐ R	12	12	11	11	11	11	11D	11	11	11	11	11	11	12	12♐
1923	20♋	21	22	24	25	26	28	29	00♌	01	03	04	05	07	08	09♌
1924	01♓	02	02	03	03	04	04	04	04	05	05	05R	05	05	05	05♓
1925	02♌	04	05	06	07	09	10	11	13	14	15	16	18	19	20	21♌
1926	10♈	12	13	14	15	17	18	19	20	22	23	24	25	26	28	29♈
1927	14♌	16	17	18	19	21	22	23	24	26	27	28	29	01♍	02	03♍
1928	03♉	04	06	07	08	10	11	13	14	15	17	18	20	21	22	24♉
1929	27♌	29	00♍	01	02	03	05	06	07	08	10	11	12	13	14	16♍
1930	20♉	21	23	24	26	27	28	00♊	01	03	04	05	07	08	10	11♊
1931	11♍	12	13	14	15	17	18	19	20	21	22	24	25	26	27	28♍
1932	06♊	07	08	10	11	13	14	15	17	18	19	21	22	24	25	27♊
1933	26♍	27	28	00♎	01	02	03	04	05	06	07	09	10	11	12	13♎
1934	19♊	21	22	23	25	26	28	29	00♋	02	03	04	06	07	08	10♋
1935	16♎	17	17	18	19	20	21	22	23	24	25	26	27	28	29	00♏
1936	03♋	04	06	07	08	10	11	12	14	15	16	18	19	20	21	23♋
1937	19♏	19	19	20	20	20	21	21	22	22	23	23	24	24	25	26♏
1938	15♋	17	18	19	20	22	23	24	26	27	28	00♌	01	02	03	05♌
1939	04♒ R	04	03	03	03	02	02	01	01	00	00	29♑	29	28	28	27♑
1940	28♋	29	01♌	02	03	04	06	07	08	09	11	12	13	14	16	17♌
1941	29♓	00♈	01	02	03	04	06	07	08	09	10	11	12	13	13	14♈
1942	10♌	11	12	14	15	16	17	19	20	21	22	24	25	26	27	29♌
1943	25♈	26	27	29	00♉	02	03	04	06	07	08	10	11	12	14	15♉
1944	23♌	24	25	26	28	29	00♍	01	02	04	05	06	07	09	10	11♍
1945	14♉	15	17	18	19	21	22	24	25	26	28	29	01♊	02	03	05♊
1946	06♍	07	08	09	10	11	13	14	15	16	17	19	20	21	22	24♍
1947	29♉	01♊	02	04	05	06	08	09	11	12	13	15	18	18	19	20♊
1948	20♍	21	23	24	25	26	27	28	29	01♎	02	03	04	05	06	08♎
1949	14♊	16	17	18	20	21	23	24	25	27	28	29	01♋	02	03	05♋
1950	08♎	08	09	10	11	12	13	14	16	17	18	19	20	21	22	23♎
1951	27♊	29	00♋	02	03	04	06	07	08	10	11	12	14	15	16	17♋
1952	03♏	04	04	05	06	06	07	08	08	09	10	11	12	13	14	14♏
1953	11♋	12	13	15	16	17	19	20	21	22	24	25	26	28	29♋	00♌
1954	00♑ R	00♐	29	28	28	27	27	27	26	26	26	25	25	25	25D	25♐
1955	23♋	24	25	27	28	29	01♌	02	03	04	06	07	08	09	11	12♌
1956	13♓	14	15	16	17	17	18	19	19	20	20	21	21	22	22	22♓
1957	05♌	07	08	09	10	12	13	14	15	17	18	19	21	22	23	24♌
1958	16♈	17	19	20	22	23	24	25	27	28	29	01♉	02	03	04	06♉
1959	18♌	19	20	21	22	24	25	26	27	29	00♍	01	02	04	05	06♍
1960	07♉	09	10	11	13	14	16	17	19	20	21	23	24	25	27	28♉
1961	01♍	02	03	04	05	07	08	09	10	11	13	14	15	16	18	19♍
1962	24♉	25	27	28	29	01♊	02	04	05	06	08	09	11	12	13	15♊
1963	14♍	15	17	18	19	20	21	22	23	25	26	27	28	29	01♎	02♎
1964	09♊	10	12	13	15	16	17	19	20	22	23	24	26	27	28	00♋
1965	00♎	02	03	04	05	06	07	08	09	10	11	12	13	15	16	17♎
1966	23♊	24	25	27	28	29♋	01	02	03	05	06	07	09	10	11	13♋
1967	22♎	22	23	24	25	25	26	27	28	29	00♏	01	02	03	04	05♏
1968	06♋	07	09	10	11	13	14	15	17	18	19	21	22	23	25	26♋
1969	02♐ R	01	01	01D	01	01	01	02	02	02	02	03	03	04	04	05♐
1970	18♋	20	21	22	24	25	26	27	29	00♌	01	03	04	05	06	08♌
1971	21♒	21	21	21	21	21	21R	21	21	21	21	21	20	20	20	19♒
1972	01♌	02	04	05	06	07	09	10	11	12	14	15	16	17	19	20♌
1973	06♈	07	09	10	11	12	13	15	16	17	18	19	20	21	22	23♈
1974	13♌	14	15	17	18	19	20	22	23	24	25	27	28	29	00♍	02♍
1975	29♈	01♉	02	04	05	06	08	09	11	12	13	15	16	17	19	20♉
1976	26♌	27	28	00♍	01	02	03	04	06	07	08	09	11	12	13	14♍
1977	18♉	19	21	22	23	25	26	28	29	00♊	02	03	05	06	07	09♊
1978	09♍	10	11	12	14	15	16	17	18	20	21	22	23	24	26	27♍
1979	03♊	04	06	07	09	10	11	13	14	16	17	18	20	21	22	24♊
1980	24♍	25	26	27	29	00♎	01	02	03	04	05	06	08	09	10	11♎
1981	18♊	19	20	22	23	25	26	27	29	00♋	01	03	04	05	07	08♋
1982	12♎	13	14	15	16	17	18	19	20	21	22	23	24	25	26	28♎
1983	01♋	02	03	05	06	07	09	10	11	13	14	15	17	18	19	21♋
1984	12♏	12	13	13	14	14	15	15	16	16	17	18	19	19	20	21♏
1985	14♋	15	16	18	19	20	22	23	24	26	27	28	29	01♌	02	03♌
1986	20♑ R	19	19	18	18	17	16	16	15	15	14	14	13	13	12	12♑
1987	26♋	27	28	00♌	01	02	04	05	06	07	09	10	11	12	14	15♌
1988	23♓	24	25	26	27	28	29	00♈	01	02	03	03	04	05	06	06♈
1989	08♌	10	11	12	13	15	16	17	18	20	21	22	23	25	26	27♌

August

	1st	3rd	5th	7th	9th	11th	13th	15th	17th	19th	21st	23rd	25th	27th	29th	31st
1900	23♊	25	26	27	29	00♋	02	03	04	05	07	08	09	11	12	13♋
1901	10♎	11	13	14	15	16	18	19	20	21	23	24	25	26	28	29♎
1902	04♋	08	10	11	12	14	15	16	18	19	20	21	23	24	25	27♋
1903	26♎	27	29	00♏	01	02	03	04	06	07	08	09	11	12	13	14♏
1904	20♋	22	23	24	26	27	28	29	01♌	02	03	05	06	07	08	10♌
1905	19♏	20	21	22	23	24	25	26	27	28	29	00♐	01	02	04	05♐
1906	02♌	04	05	06	07	09	10	11	13	14	15	16	18	19	20	22♌
1907	07♑ R	07	07	07	06D	07	07	07	07	07	07	08	08	09	09	10♑
1908	15♌	16	17	19	20	21	22	24	25	26	27	29	00♍	01	03	04♍
1909	03♈	04	04	05	05	05	06	06	06	06	06	06R	06	06	06	06♈
1910	26♌	28	29	00♍	01	03	04	05	06	08	09	10	12	13	14	15♍
1911	10♉	11	12	14	15	16	17	18	19	21	22	23	24	25	26	27♉
1912	09♍	10	11	13	14	15	16	18	19	20	21	23	24	25	26	28♍
1913	01♊	03	04	05	07	08	09	10	12	13	14	15	17	18	19	20♊
1914	21♍	22	23	25	26	27	29	00♌	01	02	04	05	06	07	09	10♌
1915	17♊	19	20	21	23	24	25	27	28	29	01♋	02	03	04	06	07♋
1916	05♎	06	07	08	10	11	12	13	15	16	17	19	20	21	22	24♎
1917	02♋	03	05	06	07	09	10	11	13	14	15	17	18	19	20	22♋
1918	20♎	21	22	23	24	26	27	28	29	01♏	02	03	04	06	07	08♏
1919	15♋	16	18	19	20	22	23	24	25	27	28	29	01♌	02	03	04♌
1920	09♏	10	11	12	14	15	16	17	18	19	20	22	23	24	25	26♏
1921	28♋	29	01♌	02	03	04	06	07	08	10	11	12	13	15	16	17♌
1922	12♐	13	13	14	14	15	15	16	17	17	18	19	20	21	22	23♐
1923	10♌	11	12	14	15	16	17	19	20	21	22	24	25	26	28	29♌
1924	04♓ R	04	04	04	03	03	02	02	02	01	00	00	29♒	29	28	28♒
1925	22♌	23	25	26	27	28	00♍	01	02	03	05	06	07	08	10	11♍
1926	29♈	00♉	01	03	04	05	06	07	08	08	09	10	11	12	13	13♉
1927	04♍	05	06	07	09	10	11	12	14	15	16	18	19	20	21	23♍
1928	24♉	26	27	28	29	01♊	02	03	04	06	07	08	09	10	12	13♊
1929	16♍	18	19	20	21	23	24	25	26	28	29	00♎	01	03	04	05♎
1930	12♊	13	14	16	17	18	20	21	22	23	25	26	27	29	00♋	01♋
1931	29♍	00♎	02	03	04	05	07	08	09	10	12	13	14	15	17	18♎
1932	27♊	28	00♋	01	02	04	05	06	08	09	10	11	13	14	15	17♋
1933	14♎	15	16	17	19	20	21	22	24	25	26	27	29	00♏	01	03♏
1934	10♋	12	13	14	16	17	18	19	21	22	23	25	26	27	29	00♌
1935	01♏	02	03	04	05	06	08	09	10	11	12	14	15	16	17	19♏
1936	23♋	25	26	27	29	00♌	01	02	04	05	06	08	09	10	11	13♌
1937	26♏	27	28	29	00♐	00	01	01	03	04	05	06	07	08	10	11♐
1938	05♌	07	08	09	10	12	13	14	16	17	18	19	21	22	23	25♌
1939	27♑ R	26	26	25	25	25	24	24	24	24	23	23	23D	23	24	24♑
1940	18♌	19	20	21	23	24	25	27	28	29	00♍	02	03	04	05	07♍
1941	15♈	16	16	17	18	18	19	20	20	21	21	22	22	22	23	23♈
1942	29♌	01♍	02	03	04	06	07	08	09	11	12	13	14	16	17	18♍
1943	16♉	17	18	19	21	22	23	24	25	27	28	29	00♊	01	02	03♊
1944	12♍	13	14	16	17	18	19	21	22	23	24	26	27	28	29	01♎
1945	05♊	07	08	09	11	12	13	15	16	17	19	20	21	22	24	25♊
1946	24♍	25	27	28	29	00♎	02	03	04	05	07	08	09	11	12	13♎
1947	21♊	22	24	25	26	28	29	00♋	02	03	04	05	07	08	09	11♋
1948	08♎	09	11	12	13	14	16	17	18	19	21	22	23	25	26	27♎
1949	05♋	07	08	09	11	12	13	15	18	17	19	20	21	22	24	25♋
1950	24♎	25	26	27	28	00♏	01	02	03	05	06	07	08	10	11	12♏
1951	18♋	19	21	22	32	25	26	27	29	00♌	01	02	04	05	06	08♌
1952	15♏	16	17	18	19	20	21	22	23	24	26	27	28	29	00♐	01♐
1953	01♌	02	04	05	06	07	09	10	11	12	14	15	16	18	19	20♌
1954	25♐	25	25	26	26	26	27	27	27	28	28	29	00♑	00	01	02♑
1955	13♌	14	15	17	18	19	20	22	23	24	25	27	28	29	01♍	02♍
1956	23♓	23	23	23	23	23R	23	23	23	23	22	22	22	21	21	21♓
1957	25♌	26	27	29	00♍	01	03	04	05	07	08	09	10	11	13	14♍
1958	06♉	07	08	10	11	12	13	14	15	16	17	18	19	20	21	22♉
1959	07♍	08	09	10	12	13	14	15	17	18	19	21	22	23	24	26♍
1960	29♉	00♊	01	03	04	05	07	08	09	10	12	13	14	15	17	18♊
1961	19♍	21	22	23	24	26	27	28	29	01♎	02	03	05	06	07	08♎
1962	15♊	17	18	19	21	22	23	25	26	27	29	00♋	01	02	04	05♋
1963	02♎	04	05	06	07	09	10	11	12	14	15	16	17	19	20	21♎
1964	00♋	02	03	04	06	07	08	10	11	12	14	15	16	17	19	20♋
1965	18♎	19	20	21	22	24	25	26	27	29	00♏	01	02	04	05	06♏
1966	13♋	15	16	17	19	20	21	23	24	25	27	28	29	00♌	02	03♌
1967	06♏	07	08	09	10	11	12	13	15	16	17	18	19	21	22	23♏
1968	26♋	28	29	00♌	01	03	04	06	07	08	09	11	12	13	14	16♌
1969	05♐	05	06	07	08	08	09	10	11	12	12	13	14	15	16	17♐
1970	08♌	10	11	13	13	15	16	17	19	20	21	22	24	25	26	27♌
1971	19♒ R	18	18	17	17	16	16	15	15	14	14	13	13	13	12	12♒
1972	21♌	22	23	24	26	27	28	29	01♍	02	03	05	06	07	08	10♍
1973	24♈	25	26	27	28	29	00♉	01	01	02	03	04	04	05	05	06♉
1974	02♍	04	05	06	07	09	10	11	12	14	15	16	17	19	20	21♍
1975	21♉	22	23	25	26	27	28	00♊	01	02	03	04	06	07	08	09♊
1976	15♍	16	17	19	20	21	22	24	25	26	27	29	00♎	01	03	04♎
1977	09♊	11	12	13	15	16	17	19	20	21	23	24	25	26	28	29♊
1978	27♍	29	00♎	01	02	04	05	06	07	09	10	11	13	14	15	16♎
1979	24♊	25	27	28	00♋	01	02	04	05	06	08	09	10	12	13	14♋
1980	12♎	13	14	15	17	18	19	21	22	23	24	25	27	28	29	01♏
1981	09♋	10	11	13	14	15	17	18	19	20	22	23	24	26	27	28♋
1982	28♎	29	00♏	02	03	04	05	06	07	09	10	11	12	14	15	16♏
1983	21♋	23	24	25	26	28	29	00♌	02	03	04	05	07	08	09	11♌
1984	21♏	22	23	24	25	26	27	28	29	00♐	01	02	03	05	06	07♐
1985	04♌	05	06	08	09	10	12	13	14	15	17	18	19	21	22	23♌
1986	12♑ R	12	11	11	11	11D	11	11	11	11	11	12	12	12	13	13♑
1987	16♌	17	18	19	21	22	23	25	26	27	28	00♍	02	02	03	05♍
1988	07♈	07	08	08	09	09	10	10	10	11	11	11	11R	11	11	11♈
1989	28♌	29	00♍	02	03	04	05	07	08	09	11	12	13	14	16	17♍

September

	1st	3rd	5th	7th	9th	11th	13th	15th	17th	19th	21st	23rd	25th	27th	29th
1900	14♋	15	16	17	19	20	21	22	24	25	26	27	28	00♌	01♌
1901	00♏	01	02	04	05	06	08	09	10	12	13	14	16	17	19♏
1902	27♋	28	00♌	01	02	04	05	06	07	09	10	11	12	13	15♌
1903	15♏	16	18	19	20	22	23	24	26	27	28	00♐	01	03	04♐
1904	10♌	12	13	14	15	17	18	19	20	22	23	24	25	27	28♌
1905	05♐	07	08	09	10	12	13	14	15	17	18	19	21	22	23♐
1906	22♌	23	25	26	27	29	00♍	01	02	04	05	06	07	09	10♍
1907	10♑	11	11	12	13	13	14	15	16	17	18	19	20	20	22♑
1908	04♍	06	07	08	10	11	12	13	15	16	17	18	20	21	22♍
1909	06♈R	05	05	05	04	04	03	03	02	02	01	01	00	29♓	29♓
1910	16♍	17	19	20	21	22	24	25	26	28	29	00♎	01	03	04♎
1911	27♉	28	29	00♊	01	02	03	03	04	05	06	06	07	07	08♊
1912	28♍	00♎	01	02	04	05	06	07	09	10	11	13	14	15	17♎
1913	21♊	22	23	25	26	27	28	29	00♋	01	02	03	04	06	07♋
1914	11♎	12	13	15	16	17	19	20	21	22	24	25	27	28	29♎
1915	08♋	09	10	11	13	14	15	16	17	19	20	21	22	23	25♋
1916	24♎	26	27	28	00♏	01	02	04	05	06	08	09	10	12	13♏
1917	22♋	24	25	26	27	29	00♌	01	02	04	05	06	07	08	10♌
1918	09♏	10	12	13	14	16	17	18	20	21	22	24	25	26	28♏
1919	05♌	06	08	09	10	11	13	14	15	16	18	19	20	21	23♌
1920	27♏	28	00♐	01	02	03	05	06	07	09	10	11	13	14	16♐
1921	18♌	19	20	22	23	24	25	27	28	29	00♍	02	03	04	05♍
1922	23♐	24	25	26	27	28	29	00♑	01	03	04	05	06	07	09♑
1923	29♌	01♍	02	03	05	06	07	08	10	11	12	13	15	16	17♍
1924	28♒R	27	27	26	26	26	25	25	25	25	25D	25	25	25	25♒
1925	12♍	13	14	15	17	18	19	21	22	23	24	26	27	28	00♎
1926	14♉	14	15	16	16	17	17	18	18	18	18	19	19	19	19♉R
1927	23♍	25	26	27	28	00♎	01	02	04	05	06	08	09	10	12♎
1928	13♊	15	16	17	18	19	20	21	22	23	24	25	26	27	28♊
1929	06♎	07	09	10	11	13	14	15	16	18	19	20	22	23	24♎
1930	02♋	03	04	05	07	08	09	10	11	13	14	15	16	17	18♋
1931	19♎	20	21	23	24	25	27	28	29	01♏	02	03	05	06	07♏
1932	17♋	18	20	21	22	23	25	26	27	28	00♌	01	02	03	04♌
1933	03♏	05	06	07	09	10	11	13	14	15	17	18	19	21	22♏
1934	00♌	02	03	04	05	07	08	09	11	12	13	14	15	17	18♌
1935	19♏	21	22	23	24	26	27	28	00♐	01	03	04	05	07	08♐
1936	13♌	15	16	17	18	20	21	22	23	25	26	27	28	00♍	01♍
1937	11♐	12	14	15	16	17	18	20	21	22	23	25	26	27	29♐
1938	25♌	26	28	29	00♍	02	03	04	05	07	08	09	10	12	13♍
1939	24♑	24	24	25	25	26	26	27	27	28	28	29	00♒	01	01♒
1940	07♍	09	10	11	12	14	15	16	18	19	20	21	23	24	25♍
1941	23♈	23	23	23R	23	23	23	23	22	22	22	21	21	20	20♈
1942	19♍	20	22	23	24	25	27	28	29	01♎	02	03	04	06	07♎
1943	04♊	05	06	07	08	09	10	11	12	12	13	14	15	16	16♊
1944	01♎	03	04	05	07	08	09	11	12	13	14	16	17	18	20♎
1945	25♊	27	28	29	00♋	01	03	04	05	06	07	08	09	10	11♋
1946	14♎	15	16	18	19	20	22	23	24	16	27	28	00♏	01	02♏
1947	11♋	12	14	15	16	17	19	20	21	22	24	25	26	27	28♋
1948	28♎	29	00♏	02	03	04	06	07	08	10	11	13	14	15	17♏
1949	26♋	27	28	29	01♌	02	03	04	06	07	08	09	11	12	13♌
1950	13♏	14	15	17	18	19	21	22	23	25	26	28	29♐	00	02♐
1951	08♌	09	11	12	13	15	16	17	18	20	21	22	23	25	26♌
1952	02♐	03	05	06	07	08	10	11	12	14	15	16	18	19	20♐
1953	21♌	22	23	25	26	27	28	00♍	01	02	03	05	06	07	08♍
1954	02♑	03	04	05	06	06	07	08	09	10	11	12	14	15	16♑
1955	02♍	04	05	06	08	09	10	11	13	14	15	16	18	19	20♍
1956	20♓R	20	19	19	18	18	17	17	16	16	15	15	14	14	14♓
1957	15♍	16	17	18	20	21	22	24	25	26	27	29	00♎	01	03♎
1958	22♉	23	24	25	26	26	27	28	28	29	29	00♊	00	01	01♊
1959	26♍	28	29	00♎	01	03	04	05	07	08	09	11	12	13	15♎
1960	18♊	19	21	22	23	24	25	26	27	28	29	00♋	01	02	03♋
1961	09♎	10	12	13	14	16	17	18	20	21	22	24	25	26	28♎
1962	06♋	07	08	09	11	12	13	14	15	17	18	19	20	21	22♋
1963	22♎	23	25	26	27	29	00♏	01	03	04	05	07	08	09	11♏
1964	21♋	22	23	24	26	27	28	29	01♌	02	03	04	05	07	08♌
1965	07♏	08	10	11	12	13	15	16	18	19	20	22	23	24	26♏
1966	04♌	05	06	07	09	10	11	12	14	15	16	17	19	20	21♌
1967	24♏	25	26	28	29	00♐	01	03	04	05	07	08	10	11	12♐
1968	16♌	18	19	20	21	23	24	25	27	28	29	00♍	02	03	04♍
1969	18♐	19	20	21	22	23	25	26	27	28	29	01♑	02	03	04♑
1970	28♌	29	01♍	02	03	04	06	07	08	10	11	12	13	15	16♍
1971	12♓R	12	12	11	11	11D	11	12	12	12	12	13	13	13	14♒
1972	10♍	12	13	14	15	17	18	19	21	22	23	24	26	27	28♍
1973	06♉	07	07	08	08	08	08	09	09	09	09R	09	09	08	08♉
1974	22♍	23	24	26	27	28	00♎	01	02	04	05	06	07	09	10♎
1975	10♊	11	12	13	14	15	16	17	18	19	20	21	22	23	23♊
1976	04♎	06	07	08	10	11	12	14	15	16	18	19	20	22	23♎
1977	00♋	01	02	03	04	06	07	08	09	10	11	13	14	15	16♋
1978	17♎	18	20	21	22	24	25	26	26	29	00♏	02	03	04	06♏
1979	15♋	16	17	19	20	21	22	24	25	26	27	28	00♌	01	02♌
1980	01♏	03	04	05	07	08	09	11	12	13	15	16	17	19	20♏
1981	29♋	00♌	01	03	04	05	06	08	09	10	11	13	14	15	16♌
1982	17♏	18	19	21	22	23	25	26	27	29	00♐	02	03	04	06♐
1983	11♌	13	14	15	16	18	19	20	21	23	24	25	26	28	29♌
1984	07♐	09	10	11	12	14	15	16	17	19	20	21	23	24	25♐
1985	24♌	25	26	28	29	00♍	01	03	04	05	06	08	09	10	11♍
1986	14♑	14	15	15	16	17	17	18	19	20	21	21	22	23	24♑
1987	05♍	07	08	09	10	12	13	14	16	17	18	19	21	22	23♍
1988	11♈R	11	10	10	10	09	09	08	08	07	07	06	06	05	04♈
1989	18♍	19	20	21	23	24	25	27	28	29	00♎	02	03	04	06♎

October

	1st	3rd	5th	7th	9th	11th	13th	15th	17th	19th	21st	23rd	25th	27th	29th	31st
1900	02♌	03	04	05	07	08	09	10	11	12	13	14	15	16	17	19♌
1901	20♏	21	23	24	28	27	26	00♐	01	03	04	06	07	09	10	11♐
1902	16♌	17	18	19	21	22	23	24	25	27	28	29	00♍	01	02	04♍
1903	05♐	07	08	10	11	12	14	15	17	18	20	21	23	24	26	27♐
1904	29♌	00♍	02	03	04	05	07	08	09	10	11	13	14	15	16	17♍
1905	25♐	26	27	29	00♑	02	03	04	06	07	09	10	12	13	15	16♑
1906	11♍	12	14	15	16	17	19	20	21	22	24	25	26	28	29	00♎
1907	23♑	24	25	26	27	28	29	00♒	02	03	04	05	06	08	09	10♒
1908	24♍	25	26	27	29	00♎	01	03	04	05	06	08	09	10	12	13♎
1909	28♓R	28	27	27	27	26	26	26	25	25	25	25D	25	25	25	25♓
1910	05♎	07	08	09	11	12	13	15	16	17	18	20	21	22	24	25♎
1911	08♊	09	09	10	10	10	10	10	10R	10	10	10	10	10	10	09♊
1912	18♎	19	21	22	23	25	26	27	29	00♏	01	03	04	06	07	08♏
1913	08♋	09	09	10	11	12	13	14	15	16	16	17	18	18	19	20♋
1914	01♏	02	03	05	06	07	09	10	12	13	14	16	17	19	20	21♏
1915	26♋	27	28	29	00♌	01	02	03	04	05	07	08	09	10	11	12♌
1916	15♏	16	17	19	20	22	23	24	26	27	29	00♐	02	03	04	06♐
1917	11♌	12	13	14	16	17	18	19	20	21	23	24	25	26	27	28♌
1918	29♏	01♐	02	04	05	06	08	09	11	12	14	15	17	18	19	21♐
1919	24♌	25	26	28	29	00♍	01	02	04	05	06	07	08	10	11	12♍
1920	17♐	18	20	21	23	24	25	27	28	00♑	01	03	04	06	07	09♑
1921	07♍	08	09	10	12	13	14	15	17	18	19	20	22	23	24	25♍
1922	10♑	11	12	14	15	16	17	19	20	21	23	24	26	27	28	00♒
1923	19♍	20	21	22	24	25	26	27	29	00♎	01	03	04	05	06	08♎
1924	25♒	26	26	26	27	27	28	28	29	29	00♓	01	01	02	02	03♓
1925	01♎	02	04	05	06	07	09	10	11	13	14	15	17	18	19	21♎
1926	19♉R	19	19	19	18	18	18	17	17	16	16	15	14	14	13	12♉
1927	13♎	14	15	17	18	19	21	22	23	25	26	27	29	00♏	02	03♏
1928	29♊	29	00♋	01	02	03	03	04	05	05	06	06	07	07	07	08♋
1929	26♎	27	28	00♏	01	03	04	05	07	08	09	11	12	14	15	16♏
1930	19♋	20	22	23	24	25	26	27	28	29	00♌	01	02	02	03	04♌
1931	09♏	10	12	13	14	16	17	18	20	21	23	24	26	27	28	00♐
1932	06♌	07	08	09	10	11	13	14	15	16	17	18	19	20	21	22♌
1933	24♏	25	26	28	29	01♐	02	03	05	05	08	09	11	12	14	15♐
1934	19♌	20	22	23	24	25	26	28	29	00♍	01	02	04	05	06	07♍
1935	09♐	11	12	14	15	17	18	19	21	22	24	25	27	28	00♑	01♑
1936	02♍	03	05	06	07	08	10	11	12	13	15	16	17	18	19	21♍
1937	00♑	01	03	04	05	07	08	10	11	12	14	15	17	18	19	21♑
1938	14♍	15	17	18	19	21	22	23	24	26	27	28	29	01♎	02	03♎
1939	02♒	03	04	05	06	07	08	09	10	11	12	13	14	15	16	18♒
1940	27♍	28	29	00♎	02	03	04	06	07	08	09	11	12	13	15	16♎
1941	19♈R	19	18	17	17	16	16	15	14	14	13	13	12	12	12	11♈
1942	08♎	10	11	12	14	15	16	18	19	20	22	23	24	26	27	28♎
1943	17♊	18	18	19	19	20	20	21	21	21	21	22	22	22R	22	22♊
1944	21♎	22	24	25	26	28	29	01♏	02	03	05	06	07	09	10	11♏
1945	12♋	13	14	15	16	17	18	19	20	21	22	23	24	24	25	26♋
1946	04♏	05	07	08	09	11	12	13	15	16	18	19	20	22	23	25♏
1947	29♋	01♌	02	03	04	05	06	07	08	10	11	12	13	14	16	16♌
1948	18♏	19	21	22	24	25	26	28	29	01♐	02	04	05	07	08	09♐
1949	14♌	15	17	18	19	20	21	23	24	25	26	27	28	29	01♍	02♍
1950	03♐	05	06	07	09	10	12	13	15	16	17	19	20	22	23	25♐
1951	27♌	28	00♍	01	02	03	04	06	07	08	09	10	12	13	14	15♍
1952	22♐	23	24	26	27	29	00♑	02	03	04	06	07	09	10	12	13♑
1953	10♍	11	12	14	15	16	17	19	20	21	22	24	25	26	27	29♍
1954	17♑	18	19	20	22	23	24	25	27	28	29	00♒	02	03	04	06♒
1955	22♍	23	24	25	27	28	29	00♎	02	03	04	06	07	08	09	11♎
1956	13♓R	13	13	13	13D	13	13	13	13	13	13	14	14	14	15	15♓
1957	04♎	05	07	08	09	10	12	13	14	16	17	18	20	21	22	24♎
1958	01♊	02	02	02	02R	02	02	02	02	01	01	01	00	00	00	29♉
1959	16♎	17	19	20	21	23	24	25	27	28	29	01♏	02	03	05	06♏
1960	04♋	05	06	07	08	09	10	10	11	12	13	13	14	14	15	15♋
1961	29♎	00♏	02	03	04	06	07	09	10	11	13	14	15	17	18	20♏
1962	23♋	25	26	27	28	29	00♌	01	02	03	04	05	06	07	08	09♌
1963	12♏	14	15	16	18	19	20	22	23	25	26	28	29	00♐	02	03♐
1964	09♌	10	11	13	14	15	16	17	18	20	21	22	23	24	25	26♌
1965	27♏	29	00♐	01	03	04	06	07	09	10	11	13	14	16	17	19♐
1966	22♌	24	25	26	27	28	00♍	01	02	03	04	06	07	08	09	10♍
1967	14♐	15	16	18	19	21	22	24	25	27	28	29	01♑	02	04	05♑
1968	05♍	07	08	09	10	12	13	14	15	16	18	19	20	21	23	24♍
1969	06♑	07	08	10	11	12	14	15	16	18	19	20	22	23	25	26♑
1970	17♍	18	20	21	22	24	25	26	27	29	00♎	01	02	04	05	06♎
1971	14♒	15	16	16	17	18	18	19	20	21	22	22	23	24	25	26♒
1972	00♎	01	02	03	05	06	07	09	10	11	12	14	15	16	18	19♎
1973	08♉R	08	07	07	06	06	05	04	04	03	02	02	01	00	00	29♈
1974	11♎	13	14	15	17	18	19	21	22	23	25	26	27	29	00♏	01♏
1975	24♊	25	26	26	27	28	28	29	29	00♋	00	01	01	01	02	02♋
1976	24♎	26	27	28	00♏	01	02	04	05	06	08	09	11	12	13	15♏
1977	17♋	18	19	20	21	22	23	24	25	26	27	28	29	00♌	00	01♌
1978	07♏	08	10	11	13	14	15	17	18	20	21	22	23	24	26	27♏
1979	03♌	04	05	07	08	09	10	11	12	13	14	16	17	18	19	20♌
1980	22♏	23	24	26	27	29	00♐	01	03	04	06	07	09	10	12	13♐
1981	18♌	19	20	21	22	24	25	26	27	28	29	01♍	02	03	04	05♍
1982	07♐	08	10	11	13	14	16	17	18	20	21	23	24	26	27	29♐
1983	00♍	01	03	04	05	06	08	09	10	11	12	14	15	16	17	19♍
1984	27♐	28	29	01♑	02	04	05	06	08	09	11	12	13	15	16	18♑
1985	13♍	14	15	17	18	19	20	22	23	24	25	27	28	29	00♎	02♎
1986	25♑	26	27	28	29	01♒	02	03	04	05	06	08	09	10	11	12♒
1987	25♍	26	27	28	00♎	01	02	03	05	06	07	09	10	11	13	14♎
1988	04♈R	03	03	02	02	01	01	01	00	00	00	00	29♓	29D	29	29♓
1989	07♎	08	10	11	12	13	15	16	17	19	20	21	23	24	25	27♎

November

	1st	3rd	5th	7th	9th	11th	13th	15th	17th	19th	21st	23rd	25th	27th	29th
1900	19♌	20	21	22	23	24	25	26	27	28	28	29	00♍	01	02♍
1901	12♐	14	15	17	18	20	21	23	24	26	27	29	00♑	02	03♑
1902	04♍	05	06	07	09	10	11	12	13	14	15	16	17	18	19♍
1903	28♐	29	01♑	02	04	05	07	08	10	11	13	14	16	18	19♑
1904	18♍	19	20	22	23	24	25	26	28	29	00♎	01	02	03	05♎
1905	17♑	18	20	21	23	24	26	27	29	00♒	02	03	05	06	08♒
1906	01♎	02	03	04	06	07	08	09	11	12	13	14	16	17	18♎
1907	11♒	12	13	15	16	17	19	20	21	23	24	25	27	28	29♒
1908	14♎	15	16	17	19	20	21	23	24	25	27	28	29	00♏	02♏
1909	25♓	26	26	26	27	27	27	28	28	29	00♈	00	01	02	02♈
1910	26♎	27	28	00♏	01	02	04	05	07	08	09	11	12	13	15♏
1911	09♊ R	09	08	08	07	06	06	05	04	04	03	02	01	01	00♊
1912	09♏	10	12	13	15	16	17	19	20	22	23	24	26	27	29♏
1913	20♋	21	21	22	22	22	23	23	23	24	24	24	24R	24	24♋
1914	22♏	23	25	26	28	29	01♐	02	04	05	06	08	09	11	12♐
1915	12♌	13	14	15	16	17	17	18	19	20	21	21	22	23	23♌
1916	07♐	08	10	11	13	14	15	17	18	20	21	23	24	26	27♉
1917	29♌	00♍	01	02	03	04	05	06	07	08	09	10	11	12	13♍
1918	22♐	23	25	26	28	29	01♑	02	04	05	07	08	10	11	13♑
1919	13♍	14	15	16	17	18	20	21	22	23	24	25	26	28	29♍
1920	09♑	11	12	14	15	17	18	20	21	23	24	26	28	29	01♒
1921	26♍	27	28	00♎	01	02	03	05	06	07	08	09	11	12	13♎
1922	00♒	02	03	05	06	07	09	10	12	13	15	16	17	19	20♒
1923	08♎	10	11	12	13	15	16	17	19	20	21	22	24	25	26♎
1924	04♓	05	06	07	08	08	09	10	11	12	13	15	16	17	18♓
1925	21♎	22	24	25	26	28	29	00♏	02	03	04	06	07	08	10♏
1926	12♉ R	11	11	10	09	08	08	07	07	06	06	05	05	05	04♉
1927	04♏	05	06	08	09	10	12	13	15	16	17	19	20	21	23♏
1928	08♋	08	08	09	09	09R	09	09	09	08	08	08	08	07	07♋
1929	17♏	18	20	21	23	24	26	27	28	00♐	01	03	04	06	07♐
1930	05♌	06	06	07	08	09	09	10	11	11	12	13	13	14	14♌
1931	01♐	02	03	05	06	08	09	11	12	14	15	17	18	20	21♐
1932	23♌	24	25	26	27	28	29	00♍	01	02	03	04	05	06	06♍
1933	16♐	17	19	20	22	23	25	26	28	29	01♑	02	04	05	07♑
1934	08♍	09	10	11	12	13	14	16	17	18	19	20	21	22	23♍
1935	02♑	03	05	06	08	09	11	12	14	16	17	19	20	22	23♑
1936	21♍	23	24	25	26	27	29	00♎	01	02	03	04	06	07	08♎
1937	22♑	23	25	26	27	29	00♒	02	03	05	06	08	09	11	12♒
1938	04♎	05	06	08	09	10	11	13	14	15	16	18	19	20	21♎
1939	18♒	19	20	22	23	24	25	27	28	29	00♓	02	03	04	05♓
1940	17♎	18	19	21	22	23	24	26	27	28	00♏	01	02	04	05♏
1941	11♈ R	11	11	11	11D	11	11	11	11	11	11	12	12	12	13♈
1942	29♎	01♏	02	03	04	06	07	08	10	11	12	14	15	17	18♏
1943	22♊ R	21	21	21	21	20	20	19	19	18	18	17	16	16	15♊
1944	12♏	14	15	16	18	19	21	22	23	25	26	28	29	00♐	02♐
1945	26♋	27	28	28	29	29	00♌	00	01	01	01	02	02	02	03♌
1946	25♏	27	28	00♐	01	03	04	05	07	08	10	11	13	14	16♐
1947	16♌	17	18	19	20	21	22	23	24	25	25	26	27	28	29♌
1948	10♐	12	13	15	16	18	19	21	22	24	25	27	28	00♑	01♑
1949	02♍	03	05	06	07	08	09	10	11	12	13	14	15	16	17♍
1950	26♐	27	29	00♑	02	03	05	06	08	09	11	12	14	15	17♑
1951	16♍	17	18	19	21	22	23	24	25	26	28	29	00♎	01	02♎
1952	14♑	15	17	18	20	21	23	24	26	27	29	00♒	02	03	05♒
1953	29♍	00♎	02	03	04	05	07	08	09	10	12	13	14	15	16♎
1954	06♒	08	09	10	12	13	15	16	17	19	20	22	23	24	26♒
1955	11♎	13	14	15	17	18	19	20	22	23	24	26	27	28	29♎
1956	16♓	16	17	17	18	19	19	20	21	22	22	23	24	25	26♓
1957	24♎	26	27	28	00♏	01	02	04	05	06	08	09	10	12	13♏
1958	29♉ R	28	27	27	26	25	25	24	23	22	22	21	20	20	19♉
1959	07♏	08	09	11	12	14	15	16	18	19	21	22	23	25	26♏
1960	16♋	16	17	17	17	18	18	18	18	18	18	18	18	18	18♋
1961	20♏	22	23	25	26	27	29	00♐	02	03	05	06	08	09	10♐
1962	09♌	10	11	12	13	14	15	15	16	17	18	18	19	19	20♌
1963	04♐	05	07	08	10	11	13	14	16	17	19	20	22	23	25♐
1964	27♌	28	29	00♍	01	02	03	04	05	06	07	08	09	10	11♍
1965	20♐	21	23	24	26	27	29	00♑	02	03	05	06	08	09	11♑
1966	11♍	12	13	14	16	17	18	19	20	21	22	23	25	26	27♍
1967	06♑	08	09	11	12	14	15	17	18	20	21	23	24	26	27♑
1968	24♍	26	27	28	29	01♎	02	03	04	05	07	08	09	10	11♎
1969	27♑	28	00♒	01	03	04	05	07	08	10	11	13	14	16	17♒
1970	07♎	08	09	11	12	13	14	16	17	18	20	21	22	23	25♎
1971	27♒	28	29	00♓	01	02	03	04	05	06	08	09	10	11	12♓
1972	20♎	21	22	24	25	26	28	29	00♏	02	03	04	06	07	08♏
1973	29♈ R	28	28	27	27	26	26	26	25	25	25	25	25	25D	25♈
1974	02♏	03	05	06	07	09	10	12	13	14	16	17	18	20	21♏
1975	02♋	02	02R	02	02	02	02	02	01	01	01	00	00	29♊	29♊
1976	15♏	17	18	20	21	22	24	25	27	28	00♐	01	02	04	05♐
1977	02♌	02	03	04	05	05	06	07	07	08	08	09	09	10	10♌
1978	29♏	00♐	02	03	05	06	07	09	10	12	13	15	16	18	19♐
1979	20♌	21	22	23	24	25	26	27	28	29	00♍	01	02	03	03♍
1980	14♐	15	17	18	20	21	23	24	26	27	29	00♑	02	03	05♑
1981	06♍	07	08	09	10	11	13	14	15	16	17	18	19	20	21♍
1982	00♑	01	03	04	06	07	09	10	12	13	15	16	18	19	21♑
1983	19♍	20	22	23	24	25	26	27	29	00♎	01	02	03	05	06♎
1984	19♑	20	22	23	24	26	27	29	00♒	02	03	05	06	08	09♒
1985	02♎	03	05	06	07	09	10	11	12	13	15	16	17	18	20♎
1986	13♒	14	16	17	18	19	21	22	23	25	26	27	29	00♓	01♓
1987	14♎	16	17	18	20	21	22	24	25	26	27	29	00♏	01	03♏
1988	29♓	00♈	00	00	00	01	01	01	02	02	03	03	04	05	05♈
1989	27♎	29	00♏	01	03	04	05	07	08	09	11	12	14	15	16♏

December

	1st	3rd	5th	7th	9th	11th	13th	15th	17th	19th	21st	23rd	25th	27th	29th	31st
1900	03♍	03	04	05	05	06	07	07	08	08	09	09	10	10	11	11♍
1901	05♑	06	08	09	11	12	14	15	17	19	20	22	23	25	26	28♑
1902	20♍	21	22	23	24	25	26	27	28	29	00♎	01	02	02	03	04♎
1903	20♑	22	24	25	27	28	00♒	02	03	05	06	08	09	11	12	14♒
1904	06♎	07	08	09	10	11	13	14	15	16	17	18	19	20	21	22♎
1905	09♒	11	12	14	15	17	18	20	21	23	24	26	28	29	01♓	02♓
1906	19♎	21	22	23	24	26	27	28	29	00♏	02	03	04	06	07	08♏
1907	01♓	02	04	05	06	08	09	10	12	13	15	16	17	19	20	22♓
1908	03♏	04	06	07	08	10	11	12	14	15	16	17	19	20	21	23♏
1909	03♈	04	05	05	06	07	08	09	10	11	12	13	14	15	16	17♈
1910	16♐	17	19	20	22	23	24	26	27	28	00♑	01	03	04	05	07♑
1911	29♉ R	29	28	27	27	26	26	25	25	25	24	24	24	24	24	24♉
1912	00♐	01	03	04	06	07	09	10	11	13	14	16	17	19	20	22♐
1913	24♋R	24	24	23	23	23	22	22	21	21	20	19	19	18	17	16♋
1914	14♐	15	17	18	20	21	23	24	26	27	29	00♑	02	03	05	06♑
1915	24♌	25	25	26	26	27	27	28	28	28	29	29	29	29	29	29♌ R
1916	29♐	00♑	02	04	05	07	08	10	11	13	14	16	17	19	20	22♑
1917	14♍	15	16	17	18	19	19	20	21	22	23	23	24	25	26	26♍
1918	14♑	16	18	19	21	22	24	25	27	28	00♒	02	03	05	06	08♒
1919	00♎	01	02	03	04	05	06	07	08	09	10	12	13	14	15	16♎
1920	02♒	04	05	07	08	10	11	13	15	16	18	19	21	22	24	25♒
1921	14♎	16	17	18	19	20	22	23	24	25	26	27	29	00♏	01	02♏
1922	22♒	23	25	26	28	29	01♓	02	04	05	06	08	09	11	12	14♓
1923	28♎	29	00♏	01	03	04	05	07	08	09	10	12	13	14	16	17♏
1924	19♓	20	21	22	23	25	26	27	28	29	00♈	02	03	04	05	07♈
1925	11♏	13	14	15	17	18	19	21	22	23	25	26	27	29	00♐	02♈
1926	04♉ R	04	04	04D	04	04	04	04	05	05	05	06	06	06	07	07♉
1927	24♏	26	27	28	00♐	01	03	04	06	07	08	10	11	13	14	16♐
1928	06♋R	06	05	04	04	03	02	02	01	00	29♊	28	28	27	26	25♊
1929	08♐	10	11	13	14	16	17	19	20	22	23	25	26	28	29	01♑
1930	14♌	15	15	15	16	16	16	16	16R	16	16	16	16	16	16	15♌
1931	23♐	24	26	27	29	00♑	02	03	05	06	08	09	11	12	14	15♑
1932	07♍	08	09	10	11	11	12	13	13	14	15	15	16	16	17	17♍
1933	08♑	10	11	13	15	16	18	19	21	22	24	25	27	29	00♒	02♒
1934	24♍	25	26	27	28	29	00♎	01	02	03	04	05	06	07	08	09♎
1935	25♑	26	28	29	01♒	02	04	06	07	09	10	12	13	15	17	18♒
1936	09♎	10	12	13	14	15	16	17	18	20	21	22	23	24	25	26♎
1937	14♒	15	17	18	20	21	23	24	26	27	29	00♓	02	03	05	07♓
1938	23♎	24	25	26	28	29	00♏	01	03	04	05	06	08	09	10	11♏
1939	07♓	08	09	11	12	13	15	16	17	19	20	21	23	24	25	27♓
1940	06♏	08	09	10	12	13	14	16	17	18	20	21	22	24	25	26♏
1941	13♈	14	14	15	15	16	17	17	18	19	20	20	21	22	23	24♈
1942	19♏	21	22	23	25	26	28	29	00♐	02	03	05	06	07	09	10♐
1943	14♊ R	13	13	12	11	10	10	09	08	08	07	07	06	06	05	05♊
1944	03♐	05	06	08	09	11	12	13	15	16	18	19	21	22	24	25♐
1945	03♌	03	03R	03	03	02	02	02	02	01	01	00	00	29♋	29	28♋
1946	17♐	19	20	22	23	25	26	28	29	01♑	02	04	05	07	08	10♑
1947	29♌	00♍	01	01	02	03	03	04	04	05	05	05	06	06	06	07♍
1948	03♑	04	06	07	09	10	12	13	15	16	18	20	21	23	24	26♑
1949	18♍	19	20	21	22	23	24	25	26	27	27	28	29	00♎	01	01♎
1950	18♑	20	21	23	25	26	28	29	01♒	02	04	05	07	09	10	12♒
1951	03♎	04	06	07	08	09	10	11	12	13	14	15	17	18	19	20♎
1952	07♒	08	10	11	13	14	16	17	19	20	22	23	25	27	28	00♓
1953	18♎	19	20	21	23	24	25	26	27	29	00♏	01	02	03	05	06♏
1954	27♒	29	00♓	01	03	04	06	07	09	10	11	13	14	16	17	19♓
1955	01♏	01	03	05	06	07	09	10	11	12	14	15	16	18	19	20♏
1956	27♓	28	29	00♈	01	02	03	04	05	06	07	08	09	10	11	13♈
1957	14♏	16	17	18	20	21	23	24	25	27	28	29	01♐	02	04	05♐
1958	19♉ R	18	18	17	17	17	16	16	16	16	16	16	16	16	17	17♉
1959	28♏	29	00♐	02	03	05	06	08	09	10	12	13	15	16	18	19♐
1960	17♋R	17	17	16	16	15	15	14	13	13	12	11	10	10	09	08♋
1961	12♐	13	15	16	18	19	21	22	24	25	27	28	00♑	01	03	04♑
1962	21♌	21	22	22	23	23	23	24	24	24	24	24	24	24R	24	24♌
1963	26♐	28	29	01♑	02	04	05	07	08	10	11	13	15	16	18	19♑
1964	12♍	13	14	14	15	16	17	18	18	19	20	21	21	22	22	23♍
1965	12♑	14	15	17	18	20	22	23	25	26	28	29	01♒	02	04	06♒
1966	28♍	29	00♎	01	02	03	04	05	06	07	08	09	10	11	12	13♎
1967	29♑	00♒	02	03	05	07	08	10	11	13	14	16	17	19	21	22♒
1968	13♎	14	15	16	17	19	20	21	22	23	24	26	27	28	29	00♏
1969	19♒	20	22	23	25	26	28	29	01♓	02	04	05	07	08	10	11♓
1970	26♎	27	28	00♏	01	02	04	05	06	07	09	10	11	12	14	15♏
1971	13♓	15	16	17	18	20	21	22	23	25	26	27	28	00♈	01	02♈
1972	10♏	11	12	14	15	16	18	19	20	22	23	24	26	27	28	00♐
1973	25♈	25	25	26	26	26	27	27	28	28	29	29	00♉	00	01	02♉
1974	23♏	24	25	27	28	00♐	01	02	04	05	07	08	09	11	12	14♐
1975	28♊ R	27	27	26	25	24	23	23	22	21	20	20	19	18	18	17♊
1976	07♐	08	10	11	13	14	15	17	18	20	21	23	24	26	27	29♐
1977	10♌	10	11	11	11	11	11R	11	11	11	11	10	10	10	09	09♌
1978	21♐	22	24	25	27	28	00♑	01	03	04	06	07	09	10	12	13♑
1979	04♍	05	06	07	07	08	09	09	10	10	11	12	12	12	13	13♍
1980	06♑	08	09	11	12	14	16	17	19	20	22	23	25	26	28	00♒
1981	22♍	23	24	25	26	27	28	29	00♎	01	02	03	04	04	05	06♎
1982	22♑	24	25	27	29	00♒	02	03	05	06	08	09	11	13	14	16♒
1983	07♎	08	09	10	11	13	14	15	16	17	18	19	20	21	23	24♎
1984	11♒	13	14	16	17	19	20	22	23	25	26	28	29	01♓	02	04♓
1985	21♎	22	23	25	26	27	28	00♏	01	02	03	05	06	07	08	09♏
1986	03♓	04	06	07	08	10	11	12	14	15	17	18	19	21	22	24♓
1987	04♏	05	07	08	09	11	12	13	15	16	17	18	20	21	22	24♏
1988	06♈	07	07	08	09	10	11	12	12	13	14	15	16	17	18	19♈
1989	18♏	19	20	22	23	25	26	27	29	00♐	01	03	04	06	07	08♐

16

HOW TO CAST YOUR LOVESCOPE

It's surprising how many "incompatible" signs are attracted to each other and wind up together, sometimes in very fulfilling relationships. The saying "opposites attract" is very true and those signs that *square** each other are sometimes mysteriously drawn together. (Astrological signs that are at a 90 -degree angle to each other in a horoscope are said to be in a "square" or angular relationship. Signs that are 180 degrees apart are in "opposition" to each other.)

THESE SIGNS "SQUARE" EACH OTHER

ARIES squares CANCER, CAPRICORN
TAURUS squares LEO, AQUARIUS
GEMINI squares VIRGO, PISCES
CANCER squares LIBRA, ARIES
LEO squares SCORPIO, TAURUS
VIRGO squares SAGITTARIUS, GEMINI
LIBRA squares CANCER, CAPRICORN
SCORPIO squares AQUARIUS, LEO
SAGITTARIUS squares PISCES, VIRGO
CAPRICORN squares ARIES, LIBRA
AQUARIUS squares TAURUS, SCORPIO
PISCES squares GEMINI, SAGITTARIUS

THESE SIGNS ARE IN OPPOSITION:

ARIES - LIBRA
TAURUS - SCORPIO
GEMINI - SAGITTARIUS
CANCER - CAPRICORN
LEO - AQUARIUS
VIRGO - PISCES

*Most love affairs occur between Squaring signs. Most marriages occur between Opposing signs. Most friendships occur between Compatible signs.

HOW TO CAST YOUR LOVESCOPE

Here's an easy and fun way to forecast your love relationship(s) and pinpoint where the Sun, Clouds and Sun/Clouds fall.

- Begin by setting up a Lovescope chart, like the one on the following page, for you and your lover. (You may want to use tracing paper and copy over the one in the book, so that you can make several charts for other important relationships in your life.)
- Write your *Sun* sign in the blank space on top as well as that of your partner directly across from it. (If it's a cusp birthday, turn to the chapter relating to the Sun sign and check the dates for accuracy.)
- Now look up the placement of your Moon, Mars and Venus at the time of your birth as well as those of your mate in the ephemeris tables following each chapter, and record them similarly in each blank space. (Check the sample chart.)
- Next, fill in the *Outlook* boxes in the *center* of each line, comparing your Sun with your partner's, your Moon, your Mars, etc., as well as the other boxes comparing the aspects of the Sun, Moon, Mars and Venus between you. To do this, you will need to know how many astrological signs apart are the planets of you and your partner. You can find this out quite easily by using tracing paper again and by copying the two Lovescope Wheels shown on the following page — one for your partner's planets and one for yours. Each Lovescope Wheel has four concentric circles (representing the Sun, Moon, Mars and Venus) divided into twelve segments (representing the twelve signs of the zodiac.) Complete your Lovescope Wheel first. Put the symbol for your Sun (☉) in the appropriate section of the outer circle. (See sample Wheel.) Then, starting with your sign, write in the numbers from 0 to 11 clockwise around the large circle. Do the same for your Moon (☽) in the next circle, Mars (♂) in the smaller circle and Venus (♀) in the center circle.

Now the *fun* begins.

Fill in your partner's Wheel in the same manner (using a different color ink to make location easier). Start with the Sun numbering from 0 to 11 clockwise around the Wheel. Next, the Moon, Mars and, finally, Venus. Place your Lovescope Wheel over that of your partner's. The numbers in each segment will tell you how many signs apart they are. The chart below will tell you how to interpret these numbers in each planetary pairing, so you can fill in the rest of the outlook boxes on your Lovescope chart with a Sun, Clouds or Sun/Clouds.

0,2,4,8, or 10 astrological signs apart on the Lovescope Wheel:
An easy aspect. You'll shine together.

3,6, or 9 astrological signs apart on the Lovescope Wheel:
A difficult aspect—the stormy side of love. Lots of clashes, but sexy chemistry. You'll have to work hard to communicate on all levels.

1,5,7, or 11 astrological signs apart on the Lovescope Wheel:
A neutral aspect or indifference.

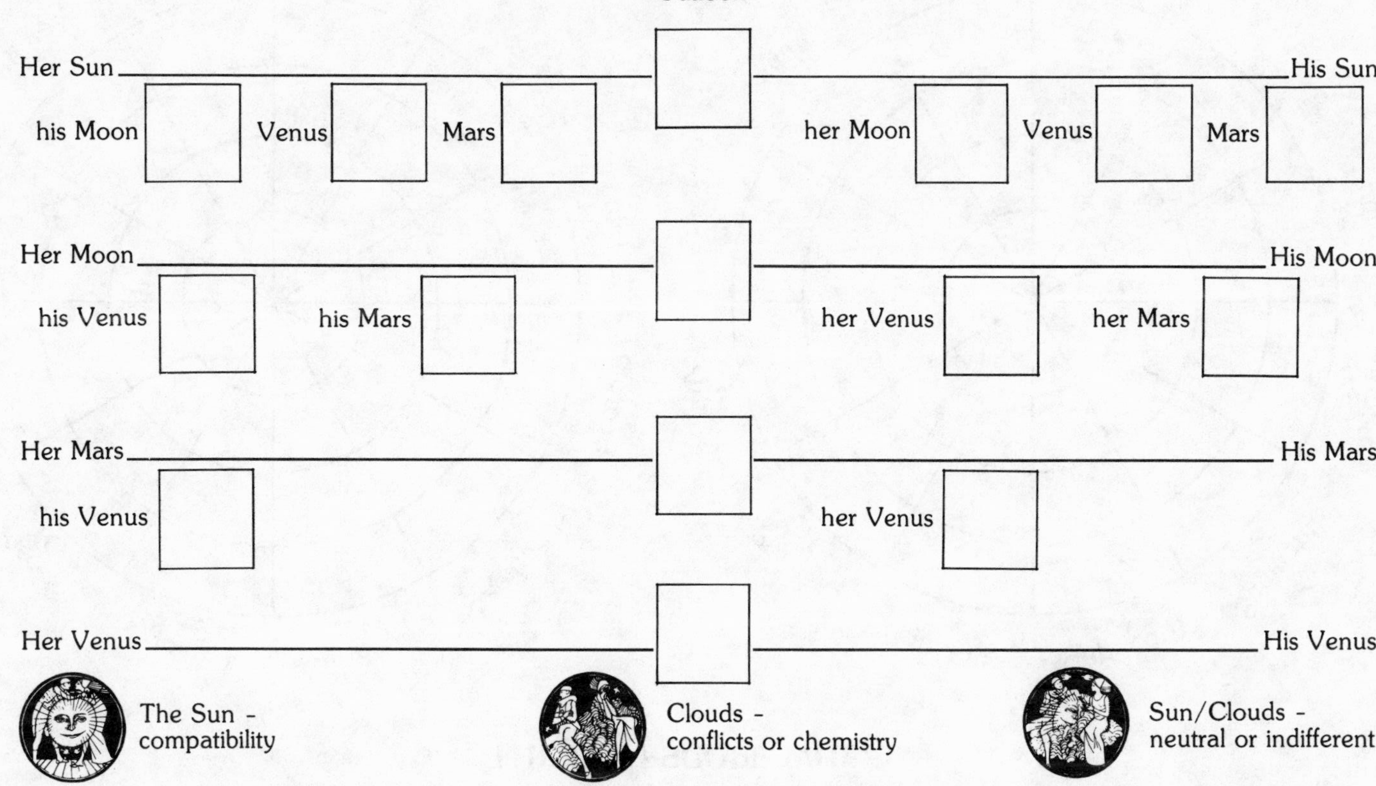
THE LOVESCOPE CHART
Outlook
Her Sun
His Sun
his Moon
Venus
Mars
her Moon
Venus
Mars
Her Moon
His Moon
his Venus
his Mars
her Venus
her Mars
Her Mars
His Mars
his Venus
her Venus
Her Venus
His Venus
The Sun - compatibility
Clouds - conflicts or chemistry
Sun/Clouds - neutral or indifferent

THE LOVESCOPE WHEEL

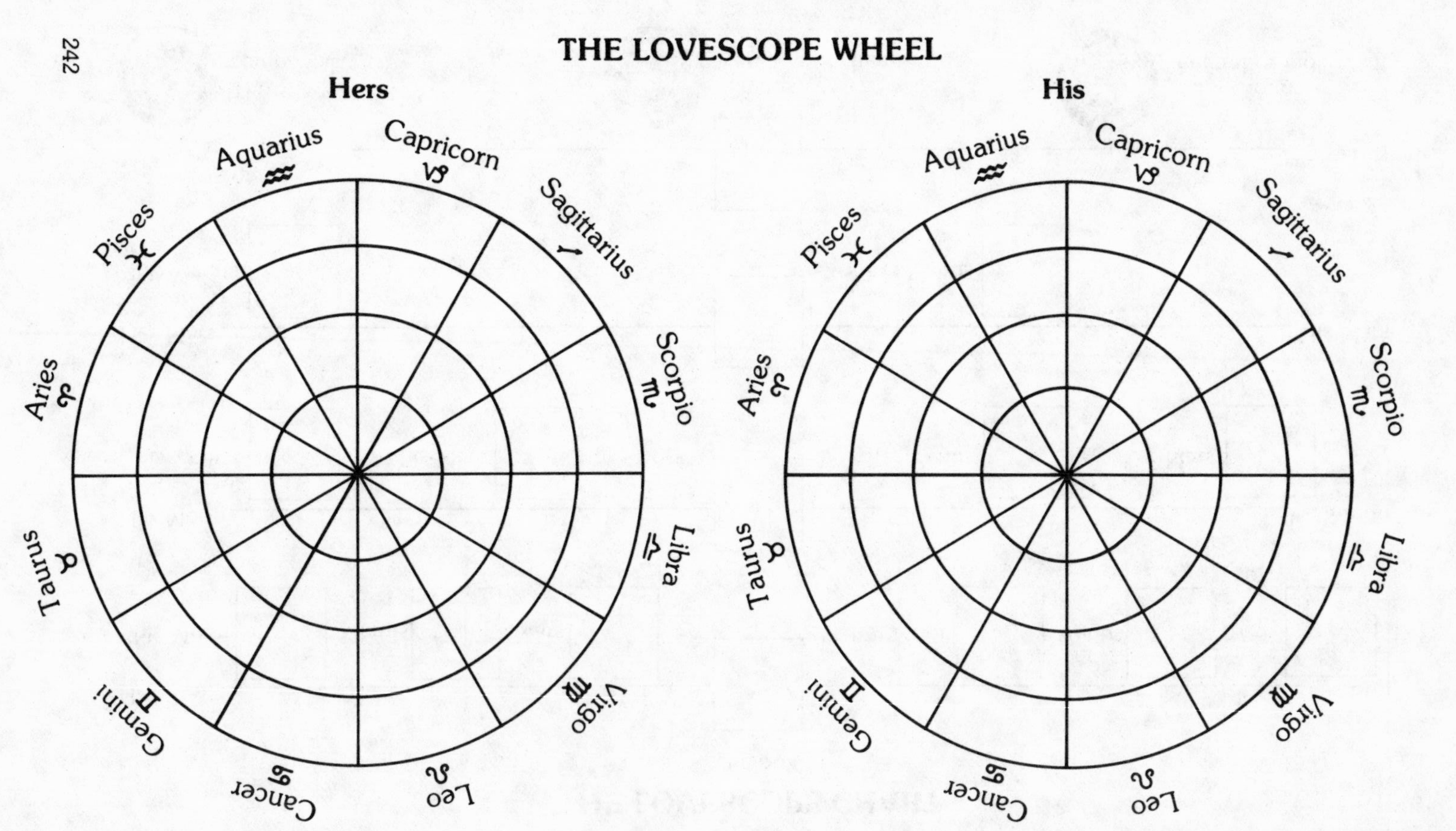

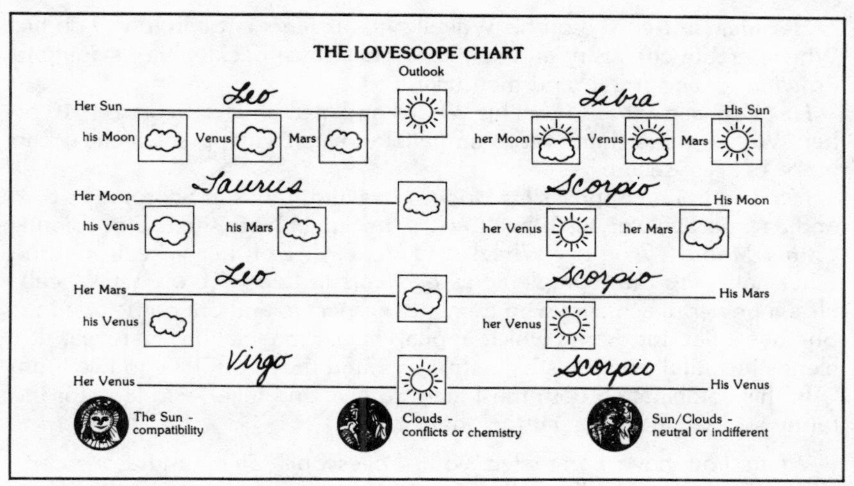

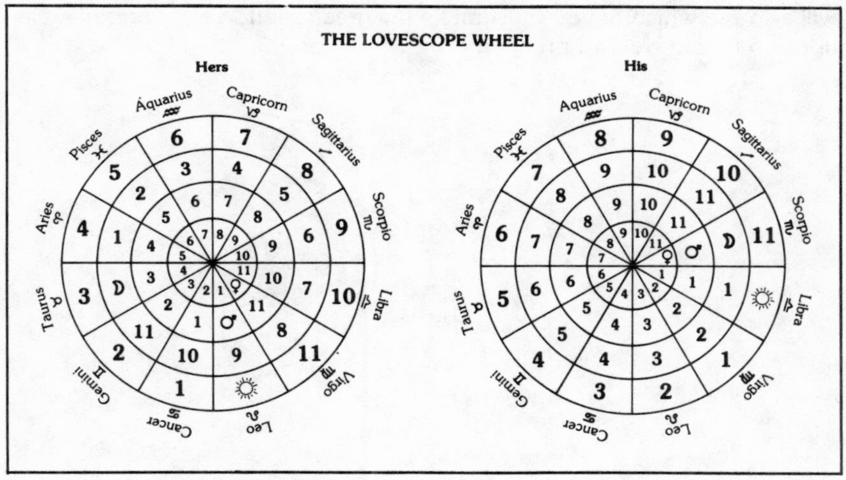

Upon examining this sample chart, one can see at a glance that *she* has most of the clouds on her side; therefore, she must make more compromises for this romance to last. On the positive side, *his Sun* in Libra (#10 on her Wheel) and *her Sun* in Leo (#2 on his Wheel) are extremely complementary. They'll be very social together and very supportive of each other.

Her Moon in Taurus and *his Moon* in Scorpio are exactly opposite each other (#6 on both Wheels) making for lots of chemistry and attraction between them (conflicts too). His Scorpio Moon will want to control at all times, and Taurus is stubborn! Here's where a good sense of humor can come in handy.

Her Mars in Leo (#3 on his Wheel) and *his Mars* in Scorpio (#9 on her Wheel) create chemistry and conflicts. They must decide *who* is going to do *what* to *whom* . . . and then take turns.

Her Venus in Virgo (#2 on his Wheel) and *his Venus* in Scorpio (#10 on her Wheel) make them very compatible lovers. His possessiveness can make her feel secure.

Her Sun in Leo opposes *his Moon, Mars* and *Venus* in Scorpio (#'s 3,3, and 3 respectively on his Wheel), while *his Sun* in Libra sheds Sun/Clouds on *her Moon* (#7 on her Wheel) and *Venus* (#1 on her Wheel). On the other hand, *his Sun* complements *her Mars* in Leo (#10 on her Wheel). He's a powerful achiever who demands respect in and out of the boudoir. She has a flair for drama which appeals to his imagination. Her solar flair blends beautifully with his high style . . . and they both love to live it up!

In this combination both must learn to give and take — to look for the funny side when things get too "heavy."

When you have completed your *Lovescope Chart* and *Lovescope Wheel,* you will instantly see where you and your partner are apt to have differences — which areas are compatible and which ones need work. You will also see which of you must make the greatest effort for your love relationship to survive and prosper.

17 APPENDIX

SEXUAL ASTROLOGY — FINER TUNING

(Character and motivation at a glance)

Wants to *do* it!	**ARIES** The self-appointed hero. The front-runner who gets credit for being a pioneer, an inventive, brave and courageous leader. (Fascinated by guns, firearms, explosives, matches — would love to light a fire under the world and you!)
Wants to *possess* it!	**TAURUS** The reliable money-maker; belongs in a responsible financial position because he or she can assess the economic situation with accuracy. Lucky in real estate and minerals. Loves to collect beautiful objects.
Wants to *communicate* with it!	**GEMINI** Generally a communicator (the written and spoken word) — a writer, speaker, teacher, theatrical designer or leader in the art world.
Wants to *take care* of it!	**CANCER** Knows the needs of people and has both the desire and ability to meet them. Good in business and nurturing a business relationship.
Wants to *be* it!	**LEO** The dramatic lover, who either portrays love in the theater or acts it out in real life (or both). The beneficient ruler or Lady Bountiful.

Wants to *analyze* (organize) it!

VIRGO
Supervises the world with supreme executive ability and keeps everything in working order. The VIP executive, the household manager who likes to give orders and knows how things should be done to the last detail.

Wants to *cooperate* with it!

LIBRA
The beauty-conscious partnership sign: charming, lovely, well-dressed, surrounded by elegance and an atmosphere preferably devoid of ugly sounds or distressing notes. Must have peace and calm at all costs.

Wants to *control* it!

SCORPIO
An indomitable force that drives him or her to carry out all endeavors to perfection.

Wants to *record* it!

SAGITTARIUS
A brilliant mind, a traveler who knows the world, a bon vivant, the lawyer or scholar who is knowledgeable about world affairs. (Sports-minded — the hunter, the Don Juan, the chase in a fast-paced world.)

Wants to *use* it!

CAPRICORN
A character of integrity and breeding . . . The president of a large corporation and a status-seeking social climber.

Wants to *share it* with mankind.

AQUARIUS
Belongs in the Hall of Fame. The humanitarian of the zodiac; cool, detached, great friend of mankind. Impersonal. Women gossip — small audiences; men write or speak — large audiences.

Wants to *commune* (empathize) with it.

PISCES
Compassionate, makes sacrifices, shares misfortunes with others — creative, enticing, esthetic (Lorelei enticing sailors to their ruin). Nonjudgmental.